P9-AFV-839

Fundamentals of Speech Synthesis and Speech Recognition

Fundamentals of Speech Synthesis and Speech Recognition

Basic Concepts, State of the Art and Future Challenges

Edited by

Eric Keller
University of Lausanne, Switzerland

JOHN WILEY & SONS
Chichester • New York • Brisbane • Toronto • Singapore

Copyright © 1994 by John Wiley & Sons Ltd,
Baffins Lane, Chichester,
West Sussex PO19 1UD, England
National Chichester (0243) 779777
International (+44) 243 779777

Reprinted April 1995

All rights reserved.

No part of this book may be reproduced by any means,
or transmitted, or translated into a machine language
without the written permission of the publisher.

Designations used by companies to distinguish their products
are often claimed as trademarks. In all instances where
John Wiley & Sons Ltd. is aware of a claim, the product
names appear in initial capital or all capital letters. Readers,
however, should contact the appropriate companies for more
complete information regarding trademarks and registration.

Other Wiley Editorial Offices

John Wiley & Sons, Inc., 605 Third Avenue,
New York, NY 10158-0012, USA

Jacaranda Wiley Ltd, 33 Park Road, Milton,
Queensland 4064, Australia

John Wiley & Sons (Canada) Ltd, 22 Worcester Road,
Rexdale, Ontario M9W 1L1, Canada

John Wiley & Sons (SEA) Pte Ltd, 37 Jalan Pemimpin #05-04,
Block B, Union Industrial Building, Singapore 2057

Library of Congress Cataloguing-in-Publication Data

Fundamentals of speech synthesis and speech recognition : basic
    concepts, state of the art and future challenges / edited by Eric
    Keller.
        p.   cm.
    Includes bibliographical references and index.
    ISBN 0 471 94449 1
    1. Speech synthesis.   2. Automatic speech recognition.
    I. Keller, Eric.
    TK7882.S65F86   1994
    006.4'54–dc20   94-18020
                                                   CIP

British Library Cataloguing in Publication Data

A catalogue record for this book is available from the British Library

ISBN 0 471 94449 1

Produced from camera-ready copy supplied by the editor using Word.
Printed and bound in Great Britain by Bookcraft (Bath) Ltd.

Contents

**8 Stochastic Models and Artificial Neural Networks for Automatic Speech
   Recognition   149**
   K. Torkkola

SECTION 3   CHALLENGES   171
E. Keller and J. Caelen

9 The Prediction of Vowel Systems: Perceptual Contrast and Stability   185
   L.-J. Boë, J.-L. Schwartz and N. Vallée

10 Articulatory Models in Speech Synthesis   215
   B. Gabioud

**11 Dynamic Modelling and Control of Speech Articulators:
    Application to Vowel Reduction   231**
   P. Perrier and D. J. Ostry

16 Multimodal Human-Computer Interface   339
J. Caelen

Preface

After years of unfulfilled promises, speech has finally arrived on the personal computer. We can finally ask the computer in so many words to do something — and more often than not, it will follow our instructions. And after years of affecting a Mickey Mouse voice, computers can now finally speak with something resembling a human voice.

There were some excellent reasons why it took so long. Speech is an exceedingly complex human activity, and it took a great deal of scientific exploration, experimentation, development, as well as considerable computational power to deal successfully with speech. Moreover, the challenge hasn't been fully met yet. Change the way you pronounce your commands ever so subtly, and the computer won't understand what it understood a minute ago. Or put even good computer speech and human speech side by side, and most listeners will still show a clear preference for human speech.

As a result, the race is on to improve computer speech interfaces, a race that has recently been joined by some of the world's major computer firms. It can be expected that over the next ten years, major efforts will be launched to create competing products, and to improve on existing software. Moreover, the world is a multilingual place, and at least the synthesis side of computer speech will have a distinctly international flavour. The recognition side may initially be handled in language-independent fashion, but in the long run, even in this area, "one size may not fit all". Increasingly, the aim will be to create and understand natural, error-free and truly human-like speech. Efforts will thus have to be made to deal appropriately not only with those aspects of speech that are similar from one language to the next, but also with those that determine their differences.

An additional major challenge will be to produce and recognise so-called "connected speech". Moving from simple, one- or two-word commands chosen from a small vocabulary, to complete sentences, i.e., to connected speech, involving tens of thousands of different words, is not simply a matter of multiplying existing techniques or of increasing computing power. To attain truly satisfactory performance, entirely new types of knowledge about speech and language will likely have to be incorporated into speech algorithms.

So all signs point to increasing world-wide efforts to create speech-based computer interfaces during the next decade and beyond. Attempts will be made to bring to the personal computer logic and programs that have so far required mainframe resources. A whole new generation of computer scientists will thus wonder "what speech is all about", and how to bring it to the computer in new and better ways. This was the main motivation for creating this book. The student new to computer speech has few places to turn to acquire the basic notions of this field. The (excellent) books that do exist are generally too technical, or tend to require too much prior knowledge and familiarity with terminology from adjoining fields, such as signal processing, linguistics, or phonetic science. This volume was carefully written and edited to be as clear as possible, to be incrementally structured, and to provide explanations of terminology that is not necessarily familiar to computer scientists.

There is another apparent lack in the current literature, somewhat more elusive in nature. Technical volumes on speech synthesis and speech recognition tend to concentrate on the "tried and true" methods, as they have been developed over the last two decades. Few pose the question of the challenges of tomorrow, that is, issues such as how computer speech can be made to sound more natural and more human-like, how to deal with the problem of speaker-to-speaker variation, or how to develop techniques to distinguish input speech from background noise or from other, irrelevant voices in the environment. And yet, those are exactly the issues that will confront young scientists entering the field in a few years' time. Many will be asked not to re-invent the wheel and create yet another speech I/O system, but rather, to develop techniques that will advance the field in general. Consequently, a major section of this book was devoted to the question of how humans seem to solve these problems — explorations that should provide a rich source of ideas of how such problems could be solved by machines.

To sum up, the present volume was designed to accomplish three overall objectives, each of which is associated with a major section of the book. A few introductory chapters about the nature of speech and speech signals are given at the beginning of the book (the *"Background"* section). These are designed to bring the well-motivated computer scientist "up to speed", and to facilitate an understanding of those adjoining areas that are least likely to be taught in computer science courses. These chapters not only present some of the well-known aspects of speech, such as articulation and its basic relationship with the acoustic signal, but they also point out some of the less evident aspects that speech devices must deal with, such as intonation, timing and pausing.

The second objective is to provide a quick overview of existing methods in speech synthesis and speech recognition. These chapters have been collected in the *State of the Art* section of the volume. Because of the great volatility of the field, the emphasis was placed on fundamental principles of operation, rather than on the presentation of commercially available systems. Three chapters deal with synthesis and two with recognition. Further general information on recognition is found in the introduction to Section 3.

The third objective is to present a number of areas that represent challenges for future development in computer speech devices. These articles are presented in the *Challenges* section of the book. How can computer speech be made more human-like? Is a close modelling of human articulatory behaviour the answer? What improvements can arise from a study of the detailed timing structure of speech? And what about the infamous variability of human speech? Have we simply not yet discovered the least variable parameters of speech, or do we need large-scale combinatorial logic to eliminate alternative interpretations? What techniques are required to synthesise or to recognise connected speech? And what about the identification of speech in "difficult" circumstances? How does the human ear perform this task? Can we learn something from human processing that can be translated into successful algorithms?

Clearly, it is impossible to cover *all* questions of this sort. However, a sufficient sampling of future challenges has been collected here to stimulate the desire to dig deeper, to know more, to experiment, and to implement. The authors of this volume have made a conscientious effort to write clearly, and to cover the major concepts of their fields. It is hoped that readers will find much of interest here to advance their understanding of speech synthesis and speech recognition. Readers new to the field are strongly encouraged to study the introductions to each of the sections. Particularly the introduction to the *Challenges* section is useful for a good understanding of the relevance of these more technical chapters of the volume.

A great many thanks are due to the authors contributing to this volume. It is not an easy task — nor necessarily a very prestigious one — to write readily accessible chapters in a clear, even a didactic style. This is of course especially true of the many authors whose native language is not English. But after an initial discussion, everyone agreed that the need was real, and that the effort was worthwhile. The papers all arrived in time, and publication of the volume became possible with a minimum of delay. Also, the financial aid of the 3e Cycle Suisse-Romand is acknowledged which permitted the organisation of an unforgettable conference in the Swiss Alps, where many of these articles were presented in their initial form.

Lausanne, March 1994 *Eric Keller*

SECTION
1

BACKGROUND

SECTION 1: BACKGROUND

E. Keller and Jean Caelen
Introduction to Section 1: Background

E. Keller
Fundamentals of Phonetic Science

S. Werner
Prosodic Aspects of Speech

B. Zellner
Pauses and the Temporal Structure of Speech

Introduction to Section 1: Background

Eric Keller[1] and *Jean Caelen*[2]

[1] Université de Lausanne, LAUSANNE, Switzerland
[2] Institut de la Communication Parlée, GRENOBLE, France

The essential representation of speech on the computer is the *acoustic signal* (Figure 1). During speech input, acoustic waveforms or impulses are captured by a microphone, and are translated into long strings of numbers, i.e., *acoustic signals*, before they are interpreted by speech recognition algorithms[1]. During speech output, the final, synthetic form is nearly always an analogous acoustic signal, which now traverses the inverse path between numeric form and the acoustic waveform issuing from a loudspeaker or earphones. The I/O processes mediating between the acoustic waveform and the corresponding signal are handled in fairly standard fashion, and are thus not of interest here. The crucial relationship that a computer has to deal with in speech synthesis and speech recognition is the higher-level relationship between the acoustic signal and a chain of language symbols.

The first few chapters of this book explain the main characteristics of this relationship. In the first chapter by Keller, the emphasis is on the basic nature of the link between a given *speech sound* (a "phoneme" or a

---

[1] Please note the use of the term "speech recognition", instead of the popular term "voice recognition", throughout this volume. The difference is semantically relevant. The recognition of the voice of a particular speaker, as suggested by the term "voice recognition", is used in applications that determine access to information or to locales on the basis of the identification of voice characteristics of a speaker. As Chapter 7 by Gérard Chollet indicates, "voice recognition" or "speaker recognition" is a special area of investigation, quite separate in its aims, objectives and working principles from the area of speech recognition proper.

"speech segment"), its articulatory realisation and its acoustic waveform. This chapter illustrates therefore the *segmental aspect* of speech and provides an explanation of the basic concepts of speech analysis.

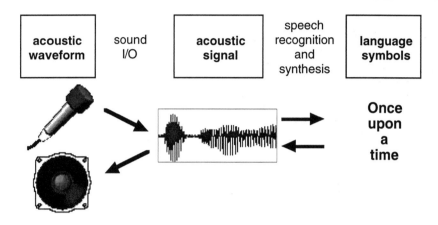

Figure 1. The position of speech recognition and speech synthesis in the relationship between sound input/output (I/O), acoustic signals and language symbols.

In the chapter by Werner and Keller, relationships involving longer-term parameters, known as *"supra-segmental"* or *"prosodic"* parameters, are explained. Common supra-segmental parameters are intonation, rhythm and phrasal timing. Prosodic parameters are used to distinguish between statements ("declarative sentences"), questions ("interrogative sentences"), and commands ("imperative sentences"). They are also employed to clarify the sentence structure and to indicate emphasis.

The third chapter by Zellner addresses a related set of concepts in the organisation of speech, temporal structure and pausing. The importance of this area arises from the very nature of the link between the acoustic signal and the various elements of the language chain. Much as in music, the key element of successful synthesis is the correctly-timed orchestration of all components. Synthesised speech with bad timing is just as difficult to understand as speech made up of the wrong speech sounds. If computer speech is to sound anything like human speech, if it is to be comfortable and pleasant to listen to, it will therefore have to implement pauses very much as human speakers do. Consequently a sophisticated understanding of speech timing is required for the implemention of satisfactory synthesis models.

Even speech recognition — which so far has ignored timing and pausing issues — may benefit from this type of knowledge. Zellner indicates that speech employs pauses to structure the various chunks of meaning in a message. Pauses may ultimately be just as important as segmental information for deriving meaning from connected speech.

Fundamentals of Phonetic Science

1

Eric Keller

Laboratoire d'analyse informatique de la parole (LAIP)
Université de Lausanne, CH-1015 LAUSANNE, Switzerland

The chapter presents basic information about the human production of speech sounds and their manifestations in the speech signal. At the laryngeal level, the vocal cords provide the acoustic vibrations required for voiced and vowel sounds. At the supra-laryngeal level, resonance, plosion and frication in the various speech cavities furnishes distinctive sound quality for the various speech sounds. The relations between production and acoustic representation are examined in some detail for different types of speech sounds (vowels, fricatives, plosives). Finally, a short review of spectral analysis techniques is given.

The purpose of this initial chapter is to prepare the uninitiated reader for the subsequent chapters of this volume by providing a succinct review of how speech sounds are produced and how they appear in the acoustic waveform. A number of major principles will be presented, and the application of each of these principles to its related acoustic manifestation will be illustrated. The present chapter deals with segmental, and the next chapter with suprasegmental aspects of speech.

The Communication Process: Transmission Despite a Noisy Line

Speech is largely used for the purpose of *communication*, i.e., for the transmission of information from person to person. A communication succeeds, if information considered to be important by both speaker and hearer is understood essentially as intended. Speech need not be perfect

— i.e., need not be exactly reproducible — neither in terms of its production, nor in terms of its perception. It suffices that certain crucial *distinctions* be transmitted correctly. For example, the answer to the question "Did you get the sandwich for me?" can be "yes", "uh-huh", "sure" or any number of other "yes-or-no" responses. For the communication to succeed, all the questioner needs to know is whether the sense of the answer is yes or no.

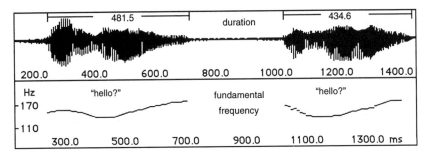

Figure 1. The acoustic signal of the word "hello", produced twice by the same speaker. Above, signal; below, voice fundamental frequency. It can be seen that duration and fundamental frequency (among other parameters) vary considerably from the first to the second production of the word.

As a consequence, the speech signal is generally quite "noisy", that is, one representation of a given signal can be — and usually will be — quite different from the next. Also, the signal is not necessarily well-defined with respect to background noise. For example, the top illustration of Figure 1 shows the signal of the word "hello", pronounced twice in a row by the same speaker. The bottom panel shows the fundamental frequency for the signal. The two signals differ with respect to all three aspects shown here: overall duration, amplitude development, and fundamental frequency. They probably differ also with respect to a number of other physical parameters that are not shown here.

Not all parameters vary to the same degree. For example, the data shown in figure 2 illustrate that durations of word-final syllables and their adjoining pauses are less variable than the fundamental frequency patterns measured in the same word-final syllables. Still, some variation is inevitable, even in the most regular of speech parameters (for more on variability in speech, see Lisker, 1985; Stevens, 1989).

This variation is not simply a matter of "sloppy speech habits". Even when trained speakers attempt to produce the same utterance repeatedly under laboratory conditions, neural and physiological factors render an exact reproduction impossible. The same is true, of course, when different speakers repeat the same utterance. Patterns also diverge as a result of dialectal and social differences, and as a consequence of age and personal characteristics. In other words, two utterances not only *needn't* be carbon copies of each other, they simply *can't*.

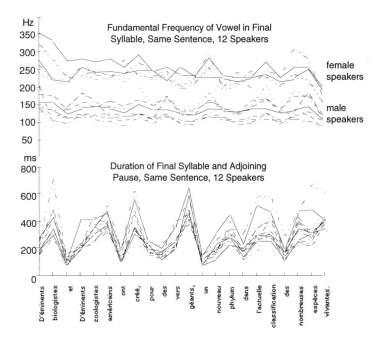

Figure 2. Variability in the frequency and durational domains. The fundamental frequency (Fo) of the final vowel (top panel) varies more than the duration of the corresponding final syllable + pause segment (bottom panel). Fo varies considerably, not only from males to females, but also from speaker to speaker. Measurements performed by Caelen-Haumont, 1991. The sentence translates as "Eminent American biologists and zoologists have created a new phylum for giant worms in the current classification of the numerous living species".

The consequences of this "imperfection" are different for synthesis and recognition. If human speech is never produced in exactly the same way, synthesised speech need not conform 100% to a specific speech model either, though it might help if variations occurring in synthesis resemble those of human speech. Speech recognition devices, on the other hand, must be particularly sophisticated, since they must pick out relevant, but highly variable information from a mass of irrelevant noise. It is an essential tenet of this book that both synthesis and recognition are likely to benefit from closer approximations to human communicative principles. Of particular interest are principles that govern the way that human communicative material or channels can be deficient, or variable, without failing in their central purpose of transmitting information.

Communication Despite Intra- and Inter-Speaker Variability

What are the origins of this variability? To go back to the question "Did you get the sandwich for me?", how does the listener know that the answer is part of the "yes"-class, not part of the "no-" or the "didn't-understand/hear-your-question" class? The answer is rather complex and involves picking out the target signal from background noise and competing speech signals, distinguishing certain sound patterns from other, similar sound patterns, matching the input to the right pre-stored words, and making a host of grammatical and semantic judgements in accordance with learned linguistic patterns[1]. But an excellent place to start the discussion is at the "speech-sound", or the "phonetic", level.

It was said above that transmission depends less on a narrowly defined set of physical parameters, than on a *distinctive* set of parameters. That is, physical parameters need not have specific values, but they must be part of *mutually exclusive envelopes of permissible values*. At the acoustic level, this means that two different speech sounds must belong to distinctive clusters. Example: the vowel /æ/ in "pat" differs only slightly from the vowel /ɛ/ in "pet", but most instances of /æ/ form a cluster distinctive from the cluster formed by the various instances of /ɛ/[2].

The clusters' shapes — and their deformations — are largely determined by the mechanics and the acoustics of the human speech tract. Two speech sounds generally belong to the same cluster, if their production and the resulting acoustic representation are similar[3]. To

---

1 For more details on some of these issues, see chapters 14 and 15 of this volume.

2 Throughout this text, three types of transcription are used: Sound symbols ("phonemes") between slashes (e.g. /e/, /s/), "allophones" or "phones" between brackets (e.g. the "back" [ɑ] and the "front" [a], or [r] and [R]), and letters ("graphemes") between quotation marks (e.g. "e", "s", etc). Phonemes, allophones and phones have to do with acoustic sounds, while graphemes are letters as they appear on the written page. More specifically, phonemes are *distinctive* sounds, "allophones" are *non-distinctive* sounds, and "phones" are acoustically coherent *portions* of sounds. Distinctiveness is established by the minimal-pair test: Two sounds are distinctive if they distinguish two words of a language. E.g. in English, /t/ and /d/ are distinctive, since they distinguish, among others, the words "tin" and "din". However, the "back" [ɑ] and the "front" [a] are non-distinctive, since they only distinguish two dialectal variants of the English /a/-sound. The two types of /a/ are thus called "allophones of the phoneme /a/". *Phones* refer to segments of speech sounds that show a certain internal coherence. Diphthongs like /aj/ in "like" or /aw/ in "house", for example, can be seen as being made up of two phones each, [a] and [i], or [a] and [u].

3 Though sometimes only the acoustic representation is similar, as the rolled [r] and the fricated [R] of French, which belong to the same distinctive *acoustic* envelope, but are *produced* in two entirely different ways.

explain how, we shall now turn to a capsule summary of speech articulation, and its relationship to the associated acoustic waveforms.

A Capsule Summary of Speech Articulation

The Various Ports

Figure 3 provides the overall view of the speech production process. To illustrate the sounds produced in the speech tract, we shall refer to the sounds of English. This will do for an introductory discussion, but it is understood that the production of the sounds of other languages can be quite different from that which is sketched here. Although various languages employ the speech apparatus in essentially similar fashion, some sounds of non-English languages (like clicks and trills, for example) involve uses of the apparatus which are not described here.

The speech production process is initiated by a release of air from the lungs into the vocal tract. At the larynx, the air is either simply *passed through*, or it is *set into vibration* by a rapid, repeated closing action of the vocal cords (see figure 4). In the first case, the resulting sounds become "unvoiced" (typically consonants, like /s/, /t/, or /f/), in the second case, they become "voiced" (vowels or "voiced consonants", such as /m/, /z/, or /g/). The difference between the two types of sounds is quite evident in the resulting acoustic signal (Figure 5).

Above the larynx, there are four major areas ("ports" or "valves") where constrictions in the vocal tract can occur. Each of these areas is associated with a typical set of sounds that owe a major component of their acoustic characteristics to the location of the port.

The *velar port* controls access to the nasal cavity. When it is open, air can escape via this cavity to produce the "nasal consonants" (e.g. /m/ and /n/) and the "nasal vowels" (as in French "franc", "cinq", or in pre-nasal vowels, such as [ũ] in "noon"). When the velar port is closed, air is forced to escape via the oral cavity, giving rise to all remaining sounds.

The next port is the *linguo-palatal port* (Figure 3). It is closed during the production of /k/, /g/ and /ŋ/ "ng". The tongue is a bit removed from the palate, and the port is somewhat opened for the production of /u/ and /o/ vowels, but it is entirely open for the back /a/ (the sound phoneticians write as "closed a" [ɑ], the vowel in the midwestern American pronunciation of "car"). This series of vowels ranging from /u/ to /a/ via /o/ is known as the *back vowel* series.

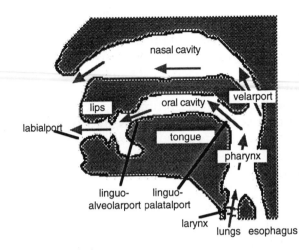

Figure 3. The human vocal tract and the basic speech production process. The air flow generated by the lungs propagates through the larynx, the pharynx and the upper vocal tract. *Oral sounds* (most vowels and consonants) are produced by modifications of the oral cavity. *Nasal sounds* (nasal consonants like /n/ and /m/, and nasal vowels) are produced with air passing through the velar port and the nasal cavity.

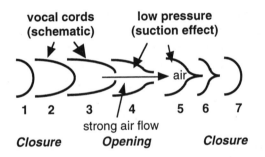

Figure 4. The schematised action of the vocal cords in voiced sounds. During closure, vocal cords force an air pressure build-up. During the opening phase, air escapes rapidly, setting up a suction effect, which leads to a tight closure of the vocal cords.

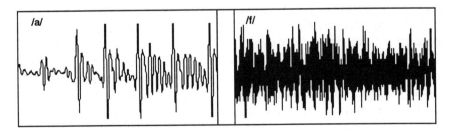

Figure 5. Voiced sounds (left) are easily recognised by their regular fundamental waveform which is absent in unvoiced sounds (right).

The *front vowels* are associated with the next port, the *linguo-alveolar port* (in some languages, the *linguo-dental port*). English vowels distinguished primarily by lingual opening at this location are /i/, /e/, /æ/, and front /a/ (the "open a" [a], the sound that corresponds to a Bostonian or Southern English pronunciation of the vowel in "car"). The linguo-alveolar port is also the location associated with the production of a great number of consonant sounds, such as the so-called *stops* (or *plosives*) /t/ and /d/, the fricatives /s/, /z/, /ʃ/ ("sh"), and /ʒ/ (the sound in "measure").

The *labial port*, finally, is centrally concerned in sounds like /p/, /b/, /f/ and /v/, where the lip opening is a major contributor to their production.

The acoustic function of these ports is to subdivide the vocal tract into various inter-connecting *resonating chambers*. Given the dimensions and wall characteristics of these chambers, acousticians can calculate reasonable approximations of the frequencies and amplitudes of the resonances that are generated in these chambers, and which are superimposed on the fundamental frequency vibration imparted by the vocal cords. In the spectrogram, these resonances are visible as resonance bands, or "formants" (see Figure 6, for example).

It can be appreciated that, given a strong theory on how cavity sizes relate to resonance frequencies, the approximate configuration of the vocal tract can be reconstructed (Fant, 1960, and successors; see also Stevens, 1989). In this way, likely distinctive speech sounds can be deduced from the speech signal, at least in those cases where articulations were clearly executed and ample acoustic energy was available.

The Different Speech Production Modes

In addition to the influence of port location, a second major acoustic component derives from the sounds' various *modes of production*. These modes determine the commonly-used classification of speech sounds into vowels, diphthongs, semi-vowels, stops, fricatives, etc.

Vowels and *diphthongs* are sounds that are produced with vibrating vocal chords and a minimum of obstruction in the upper vocal tract[4]. While both types of sounds are produced with a vocal tract that changes over time, changes are relatively small for vowels which are perceived as single sounds, while such changes are fairly extensive in the case of diphthongs, which are perceived as two vowels in sequence. In the

---

[4] For a detailed description of vowel in articulatory and acoustic space, please see the chapter by Boë, Schwartz and Vallée in this volume.

acoustic signal, vowels and diphthongs usually show stronger amplitude than consonants, and when viewed in detail, they show a characteristic fundamental frequency pattern (Figure 5, left panel). Detailed studies of *nasal vowels* in languages such as French have documented the frequent presence of supplementary nasal resonance bands arising in the nasal cavity (not shown, O'Shaughnessy, 1982).

Semi-vowels or *semi-consonants* (like /w/ and /j/) also show strong changes over time (that is why they are sometimes called "glides"). They either lead into vowels (e.g. /wæn/ "wan" or /jæk/ "yak"), or they terminate vowels (as in /paw/ "pow", /paj/ "pie", where they are part of diphthongs). These sounds are best thought of as transitions. The [j] or [w] phases of such transitions are produced with narrower port constrictions than the adjoining vocalic phases. Acoustically, the transition between the two phases is primarily reflected in the resonance patterns seen in spectrographic representations[5]. For example, the transition is prominently reflected in the time course of formants 1 and 2 (Figure 6).

Fricatives are sounds produced with a close approximation between two articulators, that is, with strong occlusions of the port in question. As a result, air turbulences are created that are seen as high-frequency noise in the signal (Figure 5, right panel).

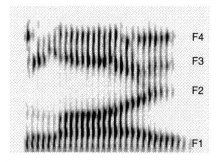

Figure 6. Spectrogram of the diphthong /aj/ in English. Four formants can easily be identified. The transition from [a] to [j] is associated with an increase in the gap between formants 1 and 2 (F1 and F2).

Stops or *plosives* are complex sounds that are made up of two distinct initial phases, followed by a transition phase (Figure 7). Initially, while the port is closed, the signal shows silence. At the opening of the port, there is usually a fairly sharp release of the air pressure that has built up in the oral tract during the closure phase. This gives rise to a so-called "burst"

---

[5] A spectrogram (or "sonogram") represents the three physical dimensions of speech sounds in the x, y and z axes. The x axis shows time, the y axis shows frequency, and the z axis (typically captured as levels of darkness) shows the amplitude or energy level.

and to a short period of frication. In the last stage, the frication merges into the characteristics of the succeeding sound (often a vowel).

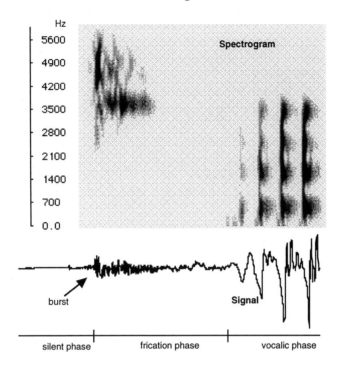

Figure 7. Spectrogram (top) and signal (bottom) of the three phases of the English stop /t/ in the word "test". The silent phase corresponds to the period where the tongue rests against the palate. The frication phase begins with an identifiable burst, as the tongue separates from the palate and an airstream begins rushing through the opening. The vocalic phase corresponds to the onset of vocal fold activity, which imparts a strong cyclic variation to the acoustic waveform.

Nasal consonants involve a complete, sustained occlusion of the oral vocal tract, with the air escaping through the nasal cavity. Acoustically, these sounds can be identified by prominent vocal chord vibrations, a lessened amplitude with respect to that of adjoining vowels, and a reduced presence of higher formants (Figure 8).

The /l/-sounds or *liquids* are produced with a partial and central occlusion of the linguo-alveolar port, whereby air is allowed to escape to either or both sides of the tongue. Acoustically, these sounds are similar to nasal consonants.

Aspirated consonants (such as /h/) arise through general frication in the vocal tract, with a strong component originating at the *glottis*, or at the laryngeal passage. Acoustically, such consonants appear as relatively weak frication noise showing formant components associated with the surrounding vowels.

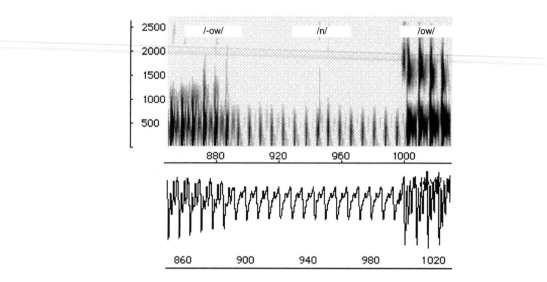

Figure 8. Spectrogram and signal of the nasal consonant /n/ between the two vowels /o/ of "no-*no*".

Speech as an Integrated String of Speech Sounds

It is of great importance to understand that unlike written text, and despite any perceptual impression, speech is *not a simple, linear sequence of events in time.* Rather, speech is an *integrated* string of speech sounds.

This integration has often been characterised as a simple "fading" from one set of characteristics to the next set of characteristics, occurring at the transition between two speech sounds (one form of this "fading" is known as "feature spreading"). Unfortunately, things are not quite as simple. Some speech sounds (such as vowels) have much greater acoustic impact ("salience") than do other sounds (such as aspirated or nasal consonants). For some other sounds, such as stops, fairly complicated transition patterns exist. Furthermore, transition patterns are not the same inside and between words, nor even inside and between syllables. Speech synthesis devices ignore these complexities at their own peril: devices that do not integrate a relatively sophisticated transitional logic are condemned to sound quite unnatural, and may even produce unusual clicking noises at sound transitions. On the other hand, a great deal of naturalness in synthetic speech can be gained by a good reproduction of human transition patterns.

Again, it is illustrative to examine the speech production process and its reflection in the acoustic waveform. Let us take the case of stops preceding vowels. For example, the sounds /k/ and /t/ are articulated quite differently in front of a /u/ (as in "'coon" or "too") than in front of /i/ (as in "keen" or "tea"). Consequently, the acoustic transition for /ku/ is rather different from that for /ki/, and the acoustic transition for /tu/ is different from that for /ti/.

Initially, this is surprising since to the human ear, the two k's are quite similar to each other, as are the two t's. However, in terms of the parameters that a computer examines, all four sounds are so different from each other that a simple pattern recogniser would be unlikely to assign the two types of /t/ to a single group. More likely, a straightforward classifying algorithm would group the /t/ and the /k/ in front of the /u/ into one group, and the /t/ and the /k/ in the context of the /i/ into another. To understand why, let us turn to how these sounds are produced in the human vocal tract (figures 9 and 10).

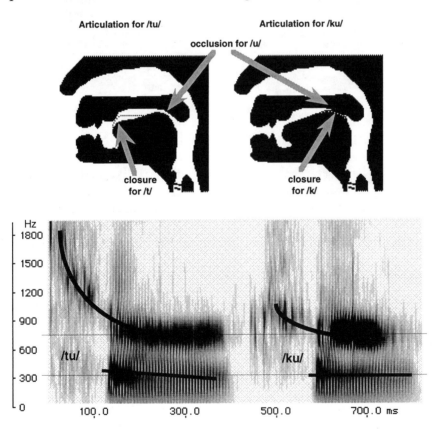

Figure 9. The articulation points for /tu/ and /ku/ and typical spectrograms associated with the two syllables when spoken in isolation. Acoustically /tu/ and /ku/ are quite similar.

As illustrated in Figures 9 and 10, the production of /u/ requires a strong narrowing of the linguo-pharyngeal port, and the production of /i/ requires a similar narrowing of the linguo-alveolar port.

Articulatorily, these are the dominant phenomena, since the tongue has to remain in those positions for the entire duration of the vowel in question. By contrast, the preceding stop closure is of short duration, it is a simple flap. Consequently, the location of the flap adjusts to that of the vocalic occlusion. In the case of /k/, the closure occurs in the rear when it precedes /u/, and it is more anterior when it precedes /i/. Similarly, the closure for /t/ is produced in more posterior position when it precedes an /u/, and it generally occurs more anterior when it precedes /i/.

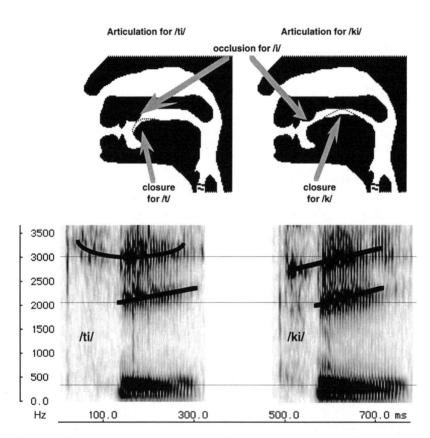

Figure 10. The articulation points for /ti/ and /ki/ and typical spectrograms associated with the two syllables when spoken in isolation. Again, /ti/ and /ki/ are quite similar, and collectively are quite dissimilar from /tu/ and /ku/.

The acoustic effects of these adjustments can be examined in the accompanying spectrograms. The formants that are discernible in the stops preceding /u/ can be seen to "meld into" /u/ while those of the stops preceding /i/ merge with the formants of /i/. The difference between /t/ and /k/ are minor. In fact, a case can be made for the hypothesis that the human ear is more strongly guided by vocalic than by consonantal differences when distinguishing the two stop consonants[6]. In this view, the main differential information is encoded, not in the stop itself (it is acoustically weak and largely silent anyway), but in the stop-vowel transition and in the adjoining vowel. That is where the ear apparently focuses when it makes its identification of the stop consonant (Fowler, 1979; Pompino-Marschall *et al.*, 1987), and that is where major physical differences can be found.

While the case of the stops is an illustrative extreme, the same principle also applies to a somewhat lesser extent to other sounds. Nasal and fricative consonants, for example, are best modelled in their vocalic context, whereby the type and form of contextual influence depends largely on the consonant's position within the syllable[7].

Speech Signal Analysis Techniques

Most discussion of speech presupposes some knowledge of speech signal analysis techniques. While a detailed review is well beyond the scope of this volume, it may serve to provide a general overview of these techniques, and to refer the reader to some excellent contemporary surveys of this field (e.g. Cooke *et al.*, 1993; Rosen and Howell, 1991).

The basic process of signal analysis is as illustrated in Figure 11. The analysis proceeds by a series of transformations, each of which prepares the signal in some way to highlight specific, speech-related features. Before performing a given transformation, the signal may have to be adequately prepared, e.g. it may have to be filtered or subsampled. Analyses are typically performed either in the temporal or the frequency domain.

Temporal domain: Features in the temporal domain are either evident in the raw signal, or they become (more) evident by deriving a secondary signal that has particular properties. The major time-domain parameters of interest are duration and amplitude. Durations of pauses, syllables, segments, etc., are typically measured directly in the raw signal, or are calculated on the basis of an amplitude envelope (see "RMS", Figure 11). The amplitude is obtained by averaging signal values over a moving time window. Values are squared, so that positive and negative values contribute equally to the amplitude, the mean is taken, and optionally, the square root is extracted. The final value plotted over time provides the amplitude curve.

---

[6] This point of view is not universally shared.

[7] For a more detailed characterization of the principles governing these interactions, please refer to John Local's chapter in Section 3 of this volume.

Frequency domain: Features in the frequency domain are identified by spectral analysis. There are a number of techniques that calculate the spectrum from a signal, such as FFT, LPC, Wigner-Ville and cone kernel techniques. Of these, the FFT (Fast Fourier Transform) is the most common. It provides a measure of the frequencies found in a given segment of a signal by decomposing it into its sine components. Another set of particularly useful techniques are the cone kernels (Loughlin *et al.*, 1993). These analyses enhance and isolate the peaked formations in the spectrogram, and thus help identify formants in speech sounds like /a/, where they are too closely spaced for a reliable distinction on the basis of FFT analysis (Figure 12).

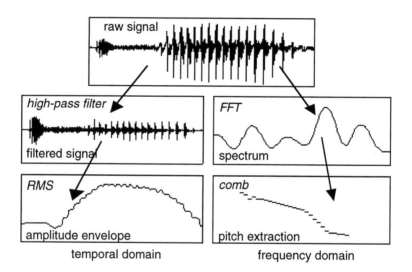

Figure 11. The basic design of speech signal analysis. Work proceeds from the raw signal (top) to a primary decoding level (middle), and/or to secondary and tertiary decoding levels (bottom). These decoding techniques can transform the time-domain primary signal either into a secondary signal, which is displayed in the time domain (left) or in the frequency domain (left). The analysis techniques used for this illustration are named in italics.

The next step in spectral analysis are tertiary signals extracted from spectral information. A typical example are *pitch extractors*, techniques that derive the fundamental frequency from a series of spectra (Hermes, 1993; Hess, 1983). Other common tertiary techniques are the *cepstrum* (a spectrum taken of a spectrum) and the *LPC* ("Linear Predictive Coding", which is often calculated by taking a spectrum taken of an autocorrelation). These algorithms help in removing a person's individual speech characteristics from the signal, and thus facilitate the identification of fundamental frequency and formants.

Detectors: A special class of analysis techniques is the detector class. These are algorithms designed to identify one particular aspect of speech in the on-going signal. For example, a simple short-term count of how many times the signal crosses the baseline every 10 ms provides a good first estimate of the location of fricative consonants[8] (*cf.* Figure 5). It is possible to write detectors for a number of aspects of speech, such as the silence-speech distinction, the presence of voicing, or the vowel-consonant distinction (Styger *et al.*, in press). Furthermore, artificial neural networks can be programmed to perform such detector functions on selected features of speech (see also article by Torkkola, this volume).

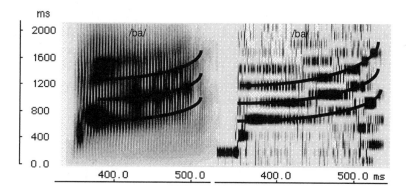

Figure 12. An FFT-based wide-band spectrogram for /ba/ (left) and a wide-band cone kernel spectrogram of the same syllable (right). Cone kernel techniques help isolate formant and fundamental frequency information in cases where resonance bands are closely spaced together.

Finally, *auditory models* take a particularly prominent place in this context[9]. When the speech signal is transformed very much in the way it is modified by the human ear, it becomes easier to separate from background noise. This has major implications for automatic speech recognition. For example, Hunt and Lefèbvre (1989) examined the performance of a recognition system which was given various transformations of a noisy raw signal as input. Transformations that incorporated concepts derived from auditory processing were much more resistent to noise than the standard "cepstrum"-type of signal transform. Depending on which measure was used, the authors' own model performed anywhere from 10 to 100 times better than the standard model. Their model works with a spectral representation based on linear discriminant analysis, a representation that had evolved from work on

---

[8] Simple zero-crossing counts do well with unvoiced fricatives, but tend to fail with strongly voiced fricatives whose signals often deviate substantially from the zero line. More reliable algorithms detect high-frequency components in the signal, no matter whether they cross the zero line or not.

[9] See the article by Summerfield and Culling, in Section 3 of this volume.

auditory modelling. As can be seen, knowledge about the human auditory capacity can go some distance in charting future directions in speech engineering.

Altogether, the field of speech analysis techniques has been very lively over the past 20 years. New techniques do a much better job at pinpointing speech-related features. Also, how the signal is interpreted has much to do with how it is viewed. In the future, we may view the speech signal in somewhat different ways than we do now, which no doubt will colour our understanding of how machines might better use and reproduce speech signal information. As techniques are developed to improve the identification of specific aspects of speech, recognition devices can be directed to either listen for, or to disregard, selected components of the speech signal. By the same token, synthesis techniques can be custom-tailored to employ such information in order to enhance speech in particular fashion.

Conclusion

Speech communication is based on the principle of distinction. At the speech sound level, classes of distinctive sounds are generally formed on the basis of articulatory organising principles. This is of particularly great importance with respect to stop consonants whose acoustic characteristics are directly related to articulatory execution. These concepts can be exploited for improving the naturalness of speech synthesis devices. Automatic speech recognition may also profit from these concepts by refining techniques of preparing the speech signal for higher-level analyses. A number of new speech analysis techniques go some distance in augmenting recognition capacities in continuous and noisy speech by identifying speech-related parameters against the usual background of irrelevant information.

References

Caelen-Haumont, G. (1991). *Stratégies des locuteurs et consignes de lecture d'un texte: Analyse des interactions entre modèles syntaxiques, sémantiques, pragmatique et paramètres prosodiques*, Thèse d'Etat, Aix-en-Provence.

Fant, G. (1960). *Acoustic theory of speech production*. The Hague: Mouton.

Fowler, C.A. (1979). Perceptual centers. *Speech Production and Perception: Perception & Psychophysics, 25*, 375-388.

Hermes, D.J. (1993). Pitch Analysis. In M. Cooke , S. Beet, & M. Crawford (Eds.), *Visual representations of speech signals* (pp. 3-25). Chichester: John Wiley & Sons.

Hess, W. (1983). *Pitch determination of speech signals (algorithms and devices)*. Springer-Verlag.

Hunt, M.J., & Lefèbvre, C. (1989). A comparison of several acoustic representations for speech recognition with degraded and undegraded speech. *Proceedings IEEE International Conference on Acoustics, Speech and Signal Processing, ICASSP-89*, Glasgow, Scotland, 262-265.

Lisker, L. (1985). The pursuit of invariance in speech signals. *Journal of the Acoustical Society of America*, 77, 1199-1202.

Loughlin, P.J., Atlas, L.E., & Pitton, J.W. (1993). Advanced time-frequency representations for speech processing. In M. Cooke, S. Beet, & M. Crawford (Eds.), *Visual representations of speech signals* (pp. 27-53). Chichester: John Wiley & Sons.

O'Shaughnessy, D.A. (1982). A study of French spectral patterns for synthesis. *Journal of Phonetics*, 10, 377-399.

Pompino-Marschall, B., Tillmann, H.G., & Kühnert, B. (1987). P-centers and the perception of "momentary tempo". *Proceedings of the 11th ICPhS. Vol. 4* (pp.94-97). Tallinn.

Stevens K.N. (1989). On the quantal nature of speech. *Journal of Phonetics*, 17, 3-45.

Styger, T., Gabioud, B., and Keller, E. (in press). Méthodes informatiques pour l'analyse de paramètres primaires en parole pathologique. In J.-P. Goudailler (Ed.), *Les faits intonatifs dans l'acquisition et la pathologie du langage*. CALAP, no. 11.

Introductions and Reviews

Cooke, M., Beet, S. & Crawford, M., (Eds). (1993). *Visual representations of speech signals.* Chichester: John Wiley & Sons.

Hardcastle, W.J. & Marchal, A., (Eds). (1990). *Speech production and speech modeling.* Dordrecht: Kluwer Academic Publishers.

Ladefoged, P. (1975). *A course in phonetics.* New York: Harcourt Brace Jovanovich.

MacNeilage, P.F., Studdert-Kennedy, M.G., and Lindblom, B. (1985). Planning and production of speech: An overview. *Journal of the American Speech and Hearing Association*, 15, 15-21.

MacNeilage, P.F., (Ed.). (1983). *The production of speech.* Berlin: Springer Verlag.

Rosen, S. & Howell, P. (1991). *Signals and systems for speech and hearing.* London: Academic Press.

Tohkura, Y., Vatikiotis-Bateson, E., & Sagisaka, Y., (Eds.). (1992). *Speech perception, production and linguistic structures.* Amsterdam: IOS Press.

Prosodic Aspects of Speech

2

Stefan Werner[1] and *Eric Keller*[2]

[1] Linguistics and Phonetics, Joensuu University, FIN-80101 JOENSUU, Finland and Laboratoire d'analyse informatique de la parole (LAIP) Université de Lausanne, CH-1015 LAUSANNE, Switzerland
[2] Laboratoire d'analyse informatique de la parole (LAIP) Université de Lausanne, CH-1015 LAUSANNE, Switzerland

This chapter contains a general introduction to the concepts of prosody, described primarily from a phenomenological point of view. Definitions of prosody are discussed, descriptions of its articulatory, acoustic and perceptual manifestations are provided, and the status of prosody within the larger domains of linguistics and phonetics is examined. Also included is a short overview of recent prosodic research in speech synthesis and recognition.

According to the classic definition, prosody has to do with speech features whose domain is not a single phonetic segment, but larger units of more than one segment, possibly whole sentences or even longer utterances. Consequently, prosodic phenomena are often called *supra-segmentals* (cf. the title of a classical study on prosody, Lehiste 1970). They appear to be used to structure the speech flow and are perceived as stress or accentuation, or as other modifications of intonation, rhythm and loudness.

Four principal manifestation levels of prosodic phenomena can be distinguished. Although there is considerable divergence between authors with respect to the use of terminology in prosody (see below), a first differentiation of prosodic phenomena according to these four manifestation levels is probably useful.

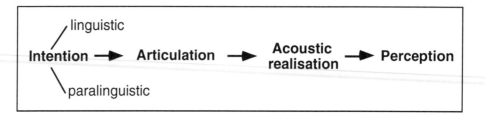

Figure 1: Stages of oral communication

The Linguistic Intention Level

In any language with oral expression, the speaker can be assumed to employ prosodic coding, as other elements of speech, with a certain *intention*. This intention can influence both linguistic and paralinguistic expression. By *linguistic expression* is meant any oral expression using language signs. *Paralinguistic phenomena* include non-verbal vocalisations like onomatopoeia and certain interjection-like expressions as well as speaking styles that make an utterance sound, e.g. angry, urgent or ironic.

Prosody clearly plays a major role in both types of phenomenon[1]. However, since the present volume is concerned with the more formal forms of speech used in automatic speech processing, this text will concentrate exclusively on the manifestations and the semiotic structure of the *linguistic* use of prosody. In this context, it is important to establish the exact *physical nature* of prosodic phenomena, as well as the use of prosodic phenomena for communicating linguistic *distinctions*. Examples of linguistic distinctions that tend to be communicated by prosodic means are the question-statement distinction, or the semantic emphasis of an element with respect to previously enunciated material. Systematic knowledge of how these phenomena are used in human speech can be expected to play a significant role in improving the naturalness of synthetic speech. Such knowledge may also some day contribute to the improved performance of speech recognition systems.

From the linguistic point of view, prosody is generally thought of as relating different linguistic elements to each other, above all by accentuating certain elements of a text, by marking boundaries and by

---

[1] Interestingly, evidence from speech pathology shows that linguistic and paralinguistic prosody seem to be processed in different hemispheres of the brain; see e.g., Fromkin, 1987. At the same time, this is not the only right-left hemisphere difference affecting prosody, since right-hemispheric anterior lesions have been reported to produce a monotonous and unemphatic, but otherwise unaffected speech — thus interfering selectively with stress and fundamental frequency and leaving other aspects (e.g. timing) unaffected.

defining transitions between words, phrases or sentences. Linguistically, differentiated prosodic phenomena are usually categorised as relating either to *tone, intonation,* or *stress (accent)*. These terms and their use will be described below in more detail.

The Articulatory Manifestation Level

At the articulatory level, prosodic phenomena are physically manifested as a series of modifications of articulatory movement which can be observed with sophisticated machinery (magnetography, ultrasound, X-ray etc.). Since prosodic phenomena are fundamentally to be understood as a distinctive layer of phenomena superimposed on the normal articulatory speech train, prosodic phenomena do not result in separate, identifiable articulations. Rather, they are manifested as systematic modifications of assumed underlying "neutral" articulatory behaviours.

So for example, the stressed syllable /ej/ in "átony" /'ejtəni/ does not involve an articulatory movement distinctive of a more neutral, destressed articulation of the same syllable in "atónic" /ej'tɒnɨk/. Rather, articulatory movements for the production of the stressed diphthong /ej/ would *tend* to be larger, longer in duration and more distinctive from other diphthongal movements than articulations of the unstressed variant. Pertinent physical observations of prosodic manifestations thus typically include variations in the *amplitude of articulatory movements*, variations in *air pressure*, or specific patterns of *electric impulses* in nerves leading to the articulatory musculature, especially those innervating the larynx.

The Acoustic Realisation Level

Muscle activity in the respiration system and along the vocal tract leads to the emission of sound waves. This acoustic realisation of prosodic phenomena can be observed and quantified using acoustic signal analysis. The main acoustic parameters bearing on prosody are *fundamental frequency, intensity* and *duration* (see chapter 1, this volume). Stressed syllables, for example, tend to be higher in fundamental frequency, of greater amplitude and longer in duration than comparable unstressed syllables[2].

---

[2] It is clearly understood that these are tendencies, not rules. For example, it is often found that stressed syllables are characterized by only one or two of the classic three parameters (fundamental frequency, amplitude, duration), and that sometimes, a stressed syllable can actually be lower on any of these parameters than its unstressed variant.

The Perceptual Level

Finally, speech sound waves usually enter the ear of a hearer who derives linguistic and paralinguistic information from prosodic phenomena via perceptual processing. At this point, psycholinguistic tests can provide evidence of hearer reactions to prosodic phenomena. This sort of test can verify the salience of different prosodic markers in speech, as well as the acoustic differentiations necessary to provoke minimal perceptual distinctions between different speaker intentions. At the level of perception, it is common to classify prosodic phenomena in terms of the hearer's subjective experience, such as *pauses, length, pitch/melody* and *loudness* .

Prosodic Phenomena in Detail

The acoustic domain, intermediary between the speaker's production and the hearer's perception, traditionally constitutes the main area of automatic speech processing for synthesis and recognition. The reproduction of acoustic signals uses generally available technology, the recording of acoustic manifestations of speech is inexpensive and non-invasive, and acoustic signals are easily evaluated by means of well-established techniques. By contrast, articulatory and perceptual analyses remain much more labour-intensive and often involve the use of complex, expensive and sometimes invasive technology. In the following description of prosodic phenomena, priority is thus given to relating linguistic distinctions to acoustic aspects of prosody.

Stressing or "Accentuation"

A given syllable can be pronounced with more or less perceived loudness, as in the examples "átony" *vs.* "atónic" given above. This phenomenon is generally called "stress" in English and is often called "accent" with respect to other languages. According to their different domains, three types of stress can be distinguished:
— word stress
— phrasal stress
— sentence stress

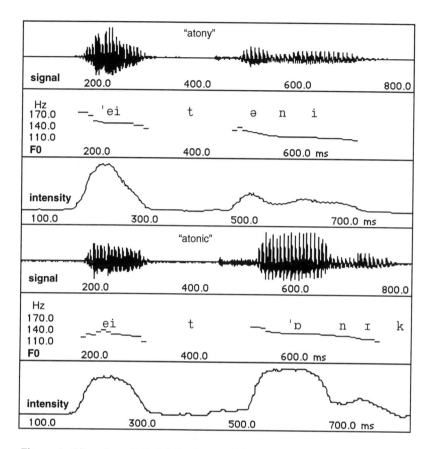

Figure 2. "átony" *vs.* "atónic", fundamental frequency and amplitude envelope analysis. The stressed syllable /ej/ shows a higher average F_0 and a greater amplitude than its unstressed variant.

Several rules concerning the distribution of stress and their systematic relations are widely agreed upon among linguists:

1. Although the *domain* of a stress may include whole words, phrases and sentences, it is always a single syllable that actually bears the stress.

2. In the procedure to identify the stressed syllable in a word, phrase or sentence that contains several stressed syllables, the main stress is identified before all other stresses.

3. Phrasal stress and sentence stress generally coincide with word stress. The different levels of stress supersede and reinforce each other. For example, in the sentence

The manifestátion of stress is different from its signíficance.

there are two main (primary) phrasal stresses, one on "manifestation", and the other on "significance". Each of these two words have their own, relatively complex stressing pattern[3]. It is found that the same word stress pattern is maintained when the phrasal stress is changed. For example, in the two sentences

> The <u>manifestátion</u> of its signíficance is not too <u>évident</u>.
> The manifestátion of its <u>signíficance</u> is not too <u>évident</u>.

only one of the two words carries primary phrasal stress and the other carries a reduced phrasal stress. (Exactly which word carries which stress evidently depends on the semantic intention). Despite the reduction of phrasal stress, each word maintains its "essential" lexical stress pattern.

The acoustic realisation of stress generally makes use of at least two, and often all three acoustic parameters of prosody (fundamental frequency, intensity and duration). Figure 2 illustrates these differences with respect to the syllable /ej/ in "átony" *vs.* "atónic". It can be seen that the stressed syllable /ej/ shows a higher average F_0 and a greater amplitude than its unstressed variant.

Intonation

The second important prosodic phenomenon is what is perceived as speech melody. This is generally called "intonation". Speakers of most Indo-European languages can communicate sentence mode, such as the declarative *vs.* the interrogative mode, by means of variations of the melody with which the sentence is conveyed. For example, the two sentences

> He did it!
> He did it?

are generally distinguished by a difference in intonation patterns, where the first sentence carries a falling and the second carries a rising intonation pattern (Figure 3).

Also, intonation can serve to communicate paralinguistic comments on the contents of an utterance. For example, in the following utterances

> Speaker 1: That's a good solution.
> Speaker 2: [doubtful] That's a good solution?

the intonational pattern expresses a complementary intonational layer of doubt which is not captured by the segmental information alone.

---

[3] In a system where stress levels are indicated by numbers preceding each syllable, the patterns would be something like ^{2}man-^{3}i-^{4}fest-^{1}a-^{3}tion and ^{4}sig-^{1}ni-^{3}fi-^{2}cance.

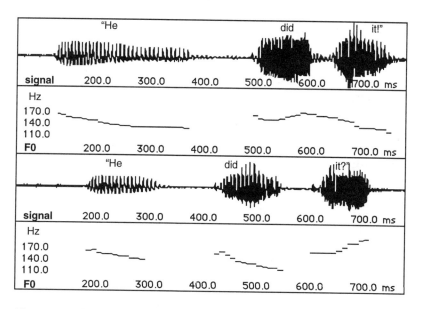

Figure 3. Fundamental frequency traces for the exclamatory and the interrogative forms of the sentence "He did it". In tune with the perceptual impression, F_0 falls during the final word of the exclamatory form and rises for the interrogative form of the sentence.

In its acoustic manifestation, intonation is primarily related to fundamental frequency (F_0). So for example, the utterance-final rises and falls of perceived intonation in "he did it!" *vs.* "he did it?" is well captured by the F_0 inflections shown in Figure 3.

In the context of speech synthesis, an interesting question concerns the interaction between variations in F_0 induced by stress and those induced by intonation. A simple hypothesis would suggest that the two effects are cumulative. So for example, in the two sentences

The manifestátion of stress is different from its <u>significance</u>.
Is the manifestátion of stress different from its <u>significance</u>?

the frequency difference between the unstressed and the stressed /i/s in "significance" of the declarative sentence should simply cumulate with the frequency rise in the intonational contour of the interrogative sentence.

However, actual frequency measurement shows that the story is quite a bit more complex. For Figure 4, the word "significance" was recorded in the declarative and interrogative contexts given above. Sound reproduction showed a fully acceptable American pronunciation of the two sentences.

The frequency measurements were in complete disagreement with the hypothesis. First, the frequency difference between unstressed and

stressed /i/ of the declarative "significance" was the inverse of what had
been expected, since the first unstressed /i/ had a slightly higher average
mid-vowel frequency (126 Hz) than the stressed /i/ (120 Hz). Second, the
interrogative form showed the same tendency, just more so (140 Hz for
the unstressed, 114 Hz for the stressed /i/). It turns out in this example
that interrogative intonation is not only characterised by a rising
intonation, but also by a greater 'dip' in the fundamental frequency prior
to the word-final rise in intonation. This 'dip' is often found in multi-
syllabic words with non-initial stress.

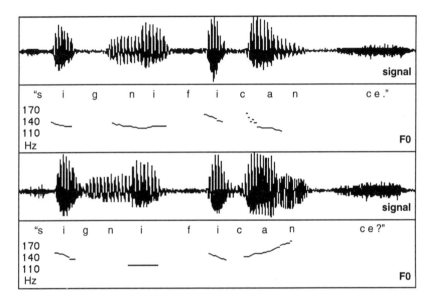

Figure 4. The word "significance" at the end of a declarative (above) and interrogative
(below) sentence. The stressed /i/ shows a lower average F_0 in the interrogative than in
the declarative context. The example shows that under certain circumstances such as
pre-sentence-final 'F_0-dip', stress can be characterised by particularly low F_0.

The consequences of such intricate F_0 interactions are manifold.
First of all, intonation is not at all simple to predict. The research of the
last thirty years has shown that F_0 structure is highly complex and shows
great inter- and intra-speaker variability. It is subject to variations due to
the number of syllables, placement of main and secondary stress,
placement within the sentence and interactions with intonational
variables. To top it off, the analyst can bank on few procedural certainties:
it is often unclear which speech segments should be measured (should
one include or exclude nasal and voiced fricative segments?), and which
are "accepted" or even "acceptable" categorisations of intonational
primitives.

Second, intonation as used in most speech synthesis is still quite
rudimentary. Few systems implement intonational modulations that go

much beyond the obligatory question-final F_0 rises. Fewer still implement believable word-level modulations. There is still much to be done to formalise resistant algorithms that predict intonational modulations with any degree of believability.

Rhythm, Speech Rate and Other Durational Effects

A third prosodic phenomenon relates to variations in speed of speech production. This gives rise to different perceptual impressions, depending on the length of the stretch of speech that is modified.

If an entire utterance or discourse is spoken either at a fast, comfortable or slow speed, this corresponds to a modification of *rhythm* or *speech rate*.

If time variations are of local nature, the durational effects are likely related to *stressing (accentuation)*. Local slowing, resulting in an increase in the duration of an entire word or at least some of its syllables, is representative of stressing. Even when pronounced without particular loudness, a slowed word tends to signal the particular importance of the content conveyed by the word. On the other hand, local acceleration signifies lessened semantic importance.

In the context of automatic speech processing, it is important to note that neither local nor global rate modifications are entirely linear. That is, it is not possible to produce entirely natural-sounding speech by simply accelerating or decelerating normal speech by a fixed rate. Speech rate modifications affect vocalic segments a great deal more than consonantal segments of speech, and within consonantal segments, VOTs of stop consonants and the duration of transitional portions of V-C or C-V boundaries are less variable than the durations of fricatives or nasals.

Tone

In tone languages (a well-known example is Mandarin Chinese), certain words are distinguished from others only by the direction and the contour of F_0 change. In these cases, melodic oppositions have phonemic value: word meaning is established by intonation. This distinctive use of a prosodic marker is exceptional, because generally, prosodic phenomena tend to modify words, phrases or sentences that have a meaning independently of their concrete prosodic realisation (Figure 5).

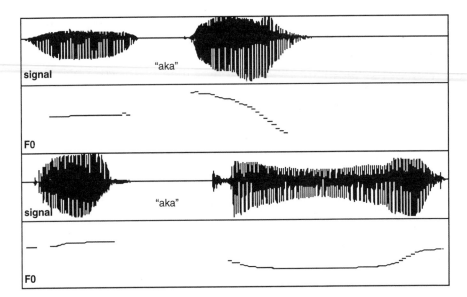

Figure 5. Two words with different significance from a tone language (Mandarin Chinese). The two words are distinguished solely by their intonational pattern.

Junctures

At transitions between words, there are often specific rules at work for stress placement and pausing, as well as for local modification of the segment structure.

A common finding is that pauses between words (if they do occur) tend to get longer as the phrase proceeds. The longest pauses are generally found between phrases (see Chapter 3, this volume). However, junctures are not always handled in the same manner. For instance, many languages suppress pauses between a word-final consonant and a word-initial vowel: French "il a" ->/ila/, not /il#a/, in accordance with the so-called "liaison rule". Such *liaisons* are obligatory in certain contexts (e.g. between a pronoun and the succeeding verb), but are prohibited in other contexts. For instance between two vowels enclosing a word boundary, the liaison is prohibited and a glottal stop is inserted: "des haricots" -> /deʔaʀiko/.

Microprosody

On a lower level, prosody is also influenced by segmental structure. It can be shown, at least for laboratory speech, that F_0 (and sometimes other prosodic parameters as well) are influenced by the surrounding sounds (e.g. voiced *vs.* voiceless consonant, stops *vs.* fricatives) and by the sound type (e.g. low *vs.* high vowel). For example, the initial F_0 of a vowel tends to be lower in post-plosive than in post-fricative position, and vowel duration are generally shorter in voiceless than in voiced contexts. These effects, however, are very difficult to trace in continuous speech, due to the more dominant manifestations of higher-level prosody.

Prosodic Universals and Language-Specific Differences

A common question in automatic speech processing concerns the universality of prosodic phenomena: Can a prosodic speech synthesis component for language x handle prosodic phenomena in language y? Indeed, many prosodic phenomena operate in a nearly indistinguishable manner in the various languages. Some of these probably have their roots in neurological and physiological aspects of human speech processing. Other phenomena, however, pattern quite differently from language to language (for a review of this question, see Hirst and Di Cristo, in press). Here is a short overview of the most common observations.

Physiologically-Based Universals: Declination and Range Reduction

Among the phenomena with apparent physiological roots, one may count "declination" and "range reduction". Within a breath-group, F_0 shows a general tendency for a decline, and at the beginning of each breath-group, the fundamental frequency starts again at a higher frequency (the "baseline reset") (Figure 6). Since this declination runs parallel with a gradual loss in subglottal pressure, it is quite likely that it is physiologically based. Indeed, declination lines have been documented for a large number of languages.

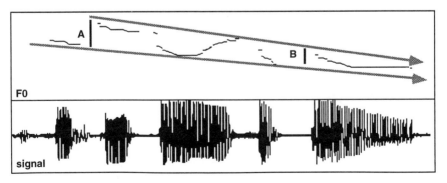

Figure 6. F_0 declination trend and reduction in F_0 range in the French sentence "certains pays se plaignent". The range at A is larger than the range at B, later on in the sentence.

Within a breath-group, the *variation* of the fundamental frequency
also decreases. Specifically, it is found that the upper limit of the F_0 range
decreases faster than the lower bound (which, in fact, often does not
decrease at all). It can be assumed that at the reduced subglottal pressures
found at the end of a breath group, the glottal tension necessary to
achieve high fundamental frequencies may be more difficult to obtain.

Other Generalised Observations

Some other observations of prosodic phenomena are generalised over a
large number of languages without apparent or evident connection with
physiological origins. Among these are *word grouping* , *syllabification* and
the *content word vs. function word opposition*.

Word grouping. In spontaneous speech, words can generally be observed
to be grouped according to prosodic principles (Figure 7). For example,
words connected (syntactically or otherwise) to a certain stress-bearing
word tend to show strong prosodic affinity. In French read speech, for
example, particularly long pauses, strong rises in F_0 and drops in
amplitude typically coincide at the end of phrase groups (Keller *et al.*,
1993). Such groups are variously called "tone groups", "stress groups",
"prosodic phrases" or "prosodic words". It remains that these tendencies
can be broken, because a speaker may choose to change the grouping
deliberately.

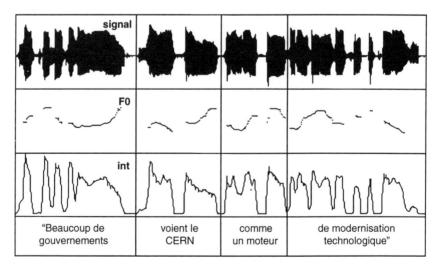

Figure 7. Word grouping in French. English word grouping is nearly indistinguishable.

Syllabification: Individual syllables are often clearly discernible from the acoustic signal (Figure 8). Most easily they are identified in a display of intensity over time where every major peak corresponds to one syllable. This phenomenon has been observed in every language analysed so far.

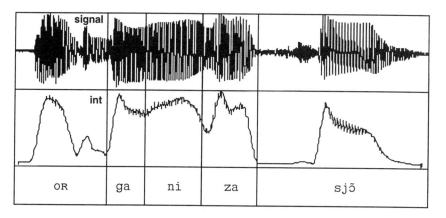

Figure 8. Syllable boundaries in the French word "organisation", as illustrated by features of the amplitude envelope (RMS) curve.

Content word vs. function word opposition: Content words, i.e. lexemes carrying an independent semantic meaning (like nouns, verbs, adjectives) are more likely to contain stressed syllables than function words, or, more generally speaking, grammatical lexemes and morphemes (like articles, conjunctions, suffixes, inflectional morphemes etc.). This dichotomy, however, is not categorical – exceptions occur and various morpheme classes can be ordered according to their gradual probability of receiving stress rather than according to a rigorous classification into one of two groups (Grosjean and Gee 1987).

Language-Specific Prosodic Differences

At the same time as there are many widespread prosodic phenomena, prosody structure is not the exactly same for every language. Differences that one should be on the lookout for in the context of automatic speech processing concern the exact manifestation of stress, the placement of stress and pauses, the communicative functions of intonation patterns, and the interaction between the parameters F_0, intensity and duration.

The Relevance of Prosody for Speech Synthesis and Speech Recognition

Prosody plays an important role in speech synthesis, both in terms of intelligibility and naturalness, which rely heavily on the assignment of correct prosodic structures. (The two concepts in fact seem to be positively correlated, cf. Carlson *et al.*, 1979). F_0, intensity and duration have to be modelled in accordance with information from segment structure, lexicon, syntax and semantics. Inversely, speech recognition needs to extract prosodic information in order to produce correct semantic and syntactic interpretations and successfully identify words. How, then, can one provide and retrieve prosodic knowledge for synthesis and recognition? What are the rules or constraints, and where can they be derived from?

These questions can only be answered by an examination of the way a particular language implements the essential features of prosody, which are *grouping* and *emphasis*. It has to be verified whether boundaries between groups of words are marked by temporal variation, by local modification of stress (e.g. so-called de-accentuation), by global intonation patterns or by a combination of all these — to name but one typical example. This knowledge, combined with rules covering universal prosodic features, then has to be translated into systems of control or measurement parameters.

An example of a comparatively simple set of control parameters for intonation contours in speech synthesis is the following list, taken from the description of a multi-language text-to-speech system (Olaszy, 1991[4]), with sample values for a male voice:

Table 1. Sample control parameters for F_0 control in speech synthesis (Olaszy 1991).

Parameter	min	max	unit
F_0 starting point	95	125	Hz
F_0 end point	95	125	Hz
degree of F_0 rise	5	25	%
degree of F_0 fall	5	25	%
steepness	0.25	2	Hz/ms
jump up	0	+30	Hz
jump down	0	-30	Hz
vowel lengthening	1.5	3	times

Prosodic parameters like these are influenced by a complex variety of factors. To illustrate this complexity, figure 9 provides an overview of

---

4 Many more interesting examples of models and parameters can be found in this and the other four volumes of the ICPhS XII proceedings.

linguistic and phonetic factors involved in determining syllable-level prosody.

Which of these factors are more relevant than others and how they translate into combined measures of F_O, intensity and duration, still remains largely to be explored. To complicate things even further, many influences have to be understood as two-way relationships; not only is prosody influenced by segment structure, but segmental features — like reduction and coarticulation — are often co-determined by prosodic features. In fact, this is probably more frequent than is traditionally acknowledged (cf. Fant, 1991).

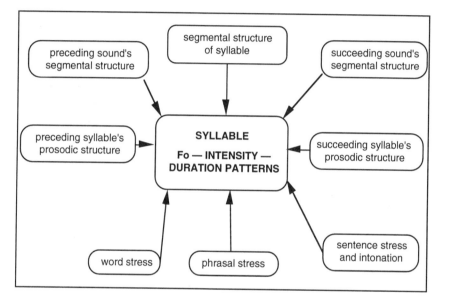

Figure 9. Linguistic and phonetic factors influencing syllable prosody.

Conclusion: Some Terminological Remarks and Relationships to Other Linguistic Domains

Prosodic phenomena are both wide-ranging and pervasive in speech. Consequently, speech synthesis without good prosodic component lacks a "certain human quality" and is quite tedious to listen to. Also, the speech signal is considerably modified by prosodic markers, and thus poses difficulties to speech recognition devices that are not programmed to look for phenomena extending over long stretches of speech. It is therefore imperative that practitioners of automatic speech processing become familiar with this domain.

This is more easily said than done. Writings in this field are full of terminological fuzziness, and work authored by persons with linguistic training is often totally esoteric to outsiders. We therefore end this chapter with a few remarks concerning terminology and links with various current forms of linguistic theory.

With respect to the terminology used in prosody, it must be admitted that there is still no such thing as a "standardised technical terminology" for prosody. To help in diffusing some of the confusion, here is an incomplete list of terms used in the literature with a particular diversity of meanings, terms that are particularly prone to misinterpretation.

In addition to the *syllable* (whose own definition is not universally agreed on), there are a number of other linguistic entities suggested as basic units of prosody: foot, stress foot, mora, tone group, intonational group, stress group, syntagm, rhythmic unit, prosodic word, prosodic phrase. In general, the most frequently used terms, like foot or tone group, are also the ones with the most problematic or even contradictory definitions. One way of injecting a greater degree of objectivity into these definitions is to base them on easily measurable criteria which are found in a large number of languages. For example, the "prosodic phrase" might usefully be defined by the presence of exceptionally long pauses, since in several languages, pauses of twice to four times the usual duration have been observed to occur at places that also corresponded to the end of a major syntactic structure. Generally speaking, a more empirically-oriented approach to these definitional problems would be all for the better.

Accent and stress both refer to basically the same phenomenon, i.e. emphasis or, more generally, prominence. But in the literature they are seldom used as synonyms. Very often, word-level prominence is referred to as word stress, whereas accentuation on the sentence level is called "sentence accent" in this framework[5]. Another distinction has to do with the actual physical realisation, e.g. pitch accent *vs.* stress (produced by means of duration and intensity).

Also the more detailed classification of sentence and phrasal accent (or stress) is not straightforward. There are no generally agreed-upon distinctions between focal, emphatic, contrastive, highlighting, etc., accents.

Tone: It is important not to confuse the tones of a tone language with intonational phenomena in non-tone languages that are sometimes also called "tones" (or tone levels or patterns).

Lines: In addition to the above-mentioned baseline and declination line, researchers also postulate a number of other abstract lines: top line, level line, reference line, grid line, focus line, and so on. Definitions can vary according to the theoretical framework and/or the experimental set-up employed.

---

[5]Again, prominent exceptions exist, see for example Gårding (1983).

With respect to other domains of linguistics, prosody is intricately connected with all other structural levels of language. The following are several examples of areas where phonetic research in prosody and linguistic theory interact.

– The correct identification of sentence stress is crucial for semantic and pragmatic analysis. On the other hand, information from semantics and pragmatics is needed for successful interpretation of sentence stress (e.g. emphasis *vs.* contrast).

– Prosodic identification of different phrase and sentence types as well as the marking of phrase boundaries and grouping of words interact with the syntactic organisation of the utterance. There have been many endeavours to predict prosodic phenomena either solely on the basis of syntactic structure or integrating additional information from lexicology and morphology. But more recently, evidence in apparent contradiction with syntactic structures has been taken into account in new theories of the structuring of speech (e.g. Gee and Grosjean, 1983; Beckman and Edwards, 1990).

– New approaches in phonological theory, auto-segmental (first conceived in Goldsmith, 1976) and metrical (both grid and tree versions first proposed in Liberman and Prince, 1977) phonology, owe much to inspiration from prosody: Classic segmental phonological analysis could not easily account for such phenomena as tone or stress distributions. Phonological frameworks and rule systems in turn motivate the investigation of specific prosodic facts whose relevance otherwise might still remain unobserved and/or facilitate the systematic aquisition and storage of prosodic data (like the Delta system, cf. Hertz, 1990).

References

Beckman, M.E., & Edwards, J. (1990). Lengthenings and shortenings and the nature of prosody. In J. Kingston, & M.E. Beckman (Eds.), *Between the Grammar and Physics of Speech (Papers in Laboratory Phonology I)* (pp. 152-178). Cambridge: Cambridge University Press.

Carlson, R., Granström, B., Klatt, D.H. (1979). Some notes on the perception of temporal patterns in speech. In B. Lindblom, & S. Öhman (Eds.), *Frontiers of speech communication research* (pp. 233-244). London: Academic Press.

Fant, G. (1991). What can basic research contribute to speech synthesis? *Journal of Phonetics, 19,* 75-90.

Fromkin, V.A. (1987). A note on the suprasegmental representation of prosody. In R. Shannon & L. Shockey (Eds.), *In Honor of Ilse Lehiste* (pp. 99-107). Foris: Dordrecht.

Gårding, E. (1983). A generative model of intonation. In A. Cutler, & D.R. Ladd (Eds.), *Prosody: Models and measurements* (pp. 11-25). Berlin: Springer.

Gee, J.P., & Grosjean, F. (1983). Performance structures: A psycholinguistic and linguistic appraisal. *Cognitive Psychology, 15,* 411-458.

Grosjean, F., & Gee, J.P. (1987). Prosodic structure and spoken word recognition. In U.H. Frauenfelder, & L.K. Tyler (Eds.), *Spoken word recognition* (pp. 135-155). Cambridge, MA: MIT Press.

Goldsmith, J. (1976). An overview of autosegmental phonology. *Linguistic Analysis, 2*, 23-68.

Hertz, S. (1990). The Delta programming language: An integrated aproach to nonlinear phonology, phonetics, and speech synthesis. In J. Kingston, & M.E. Beckman (Eds.), *Between the grammar and physics of speech (Papers in Laboratory Phonology I)* (pp. 215-257).

Hirst, D., & di Cristo, A. (in press). *Intonation systems: A survey of twenty languages.*

Keller, E., Zellner, B., Werner, S., and Blanchoud, N. (1993). The prediction of prosodic timing: Rules for final syllable lengthening in French. In D. House, & P. Touati (Eds.). *Proceedings of an ESCA workshop on Prosody (Working Papers 41).* (pp. 212-215) Lund: Dept. of Linguistics and Phonetics, Lund University.

Lehiste, I. (1970). *Suprasegmentals.* Cambridge, MA: MIT Press.

Liberman, M., & Prince, A. (1977). On stress and linguistic rhythm. *Linguistic Inquiry, 8*, 249-336.

Olaszy, G. (1991). A crosslinguistic description of intonation contours of a multilanguage text-to-speech system. In *Actes du XIIème Congrès International des Sciences Phonétiques. Vol. 4* (pp. 210-213). Aix-en-Provence: Université de Provence.

Further reading

Docherty, G., & Ladd, D.R., (Eds.). (1992). *Gesture, segment, prosody (Papers in Laboratory Phonology II).* Cambridge: Cambridge University Press.

Cutler, A., & Ladd, D.R., (Eds.). (1983). *Prosody: Models and measurements. (Springer Series in Language and Communication 14).* Berlin: Springer.

Halle, M., & Vergnaud, J.-R. (1987). *An essay on stress.* Cambridge, MA: MIT Press.

House, D., & Touati, P. (Eds.). (1993). *Proceedings of an ESCA workshop on prosody (Working Papers 41).* Lund: Dept. of Linguistics and Phonetics, Lund University.

t'Hart, J., Collier, R., & Cohen, A. (1990). *A perceptual study of intonation: An experimental-phonetic approach to speech melody (Cambridge studies in speech science and communication).* Cambridge: Cambridge University Press.

Pauses and the Temporal Structure of Speech   *3*

Brigitte Zellner

Laboratoire d'analyse informatique de la parole (LAIP)
Université de Lausanne, CH-1015 LAUSANNE, Switzerland

Natural-sounding speech synthesis requires close control over the temporal structure of the speech flow. This includes a full predictive scheme for the durational structure and in particuliar the prolongation of final syllables of lexemes as well as for the pausal structure in the utterance. In this chapter, a description of the temporal structure and the summary of the numerous factors that modify it are presented. In the second part, predictive schemes for the temporal structure of speech ("performance structures") are introduced, and their potential for characterising the overall prosodic structure of speech is demonstrated.

Text-to-speech synthesis requires the conversion of phonemic segments into audible speech events. To appear realistic to the human ear, artificial speech must contain natural-sounding vocal inflection, rhythm and stress placement. In other words, speech synthesis requires prosodic features. Temporal phenomena, such as pauses, syllable prolongations and overall timing structure, form an important part of these prosodic aspects of speech. Some such phenomena (like utterance-final syllable prolongations) have been implemented in speech synthesis devices for some time, while others (such as pauses and speech rhythm) are not yet in common use. A fully human-like implementation of these temporal aspects of speech can be expected to lead to important further improvements in speech synthesis by rendering it even more "fluent," more "human-like," and probably also quite a bit more intelligible.

Endowing speech synthesis with prosodic parameters means that intonation, stress, syllabic length and speech rate have to be generated on the basis of textual material. It is therefore important to consider how temporal phenomena occur in human speech, and how they relate to the textual material from which they are generated. At the level of the acoustic;signal, high-level temporal parameters are translated not only into corresponding low-level durational variations, but also into modifications of fundamental frequency and intensity. A second consideration thus concerns the relationship between the temporal phenomena postulated at the prosodic level and the precise acoustic implementation of these phenomena.

As will be seen later in the chapter, segment or syllable durations and pause phenomena are likely to be simply two sides of the same coin. We shall begin by describing pause phenomena, and in the second part of the chapter, we shall show how pause phenomena can be seen in terms of an integrated theory that relates temporal phenomena to a general, prosodic framework for speech.

Pauses

The Classification of Pauses

From a descriptive point of view, two classifications of pauses are in general use. The first one is a physical and linguistic classification, and the second one is a psychological and psycholinguistic classification.

The Physical and Linguistic Classification

In the traditional linguistic definition, normal speech flow is considered to be interrupted by a *physical pause* whenever a brief silence can be observed in the acoustic signal (i.e., a segment with no significant amplitude). Which exact duration of the silence is considered sufficient for the constitution of a physical pause depends on its linguistic context (for an overview, see in particular Dechert and Raupach, 1980):

— *Intra-segmental pauses* are those which are related to the occlusions of the vocal tract in normal speech production. Example: In the word "happy" (Figure 1), the pause component of the Voice Onset Time (VOT) for the consonant /p/ corresponds to a silence of 96 ms.

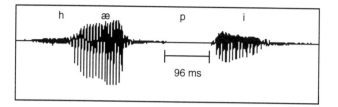

Figure 1. The acoustic signal of "happy" showing an intra–segmental pause.

— *Inter-lexical pauses* are those which may appear between two words. They constitute the first segmentation of speech, or the phrasing that is likely to facilitate the perceptual interpretation of the speech utterance. An example is the differentiation between "a Turkish (carpet salesman)" and "(a Turkish carpet) salesman" (Figure 2).

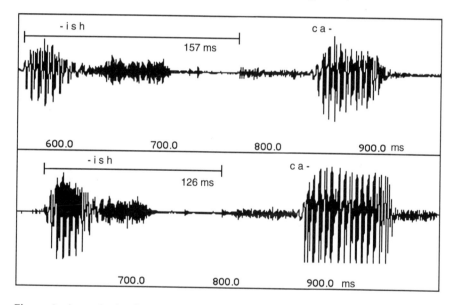

Figure 2:. Acoustic signals corresponding to the pronunciation of "a Turkish (carpet salesman)"(above) and "a (Turkish carpet) salesman" (below).

At the acoustic level, the differentiation of these two sentences is achieved both by variations of the melody (see also Chapter 2, this volume) and by variations of duration. In the first sentence, the duration of the combination of the final syllable duration of the word "Turkish" and the inter-lexical silence equals 157 ms, while in the second sentence, the same acoustic segment measures 126 ms.

It is important to note that what appears to the ear as a simple "pause phenomenon", actually translates at the signal level into a complex manipulation of duration and fundamental frequency that extends over both, the final syllable and the adjoining pause. The traditional linguistic and psycholinguistic notion of a unidimensional "pause phenomenon" has thus been amended by more recent research. It is nowadays recognised that these so-called "temporal" prosodic phenomena are actually inherently complex, multivariate and supersegmental, since they generally extend over a number of segments or syllables, and involve the interaction between a number of physical parameters.

A Psycholinguistic Classification

Even if the discussion is limited to strictly temporal phenomena, perceived pauses are not really the equivalent of physical pauses. This is due to a law of perception well known to physiologists: Whether in the visual, auditory, or in the tactile domain, the perceptual threshold is situated above the actual physical stimulus. Moreover, amplitude curves measured in detailed perceptual tests (e.g. responses to finely differentiated acoustic;stimuli) differ systematically from curves measured directly on the physical stimulus.

With respect to temporal phenomena, a number of psycho-acousticians have documented the importance of these aspects of perception for our understanding of speech processing (for an overview, see Zwicker and Feldkeller, 1981; Botte *et al.*, 1989). A correct perception of connected speech requires the ability to process about 15 to 30 distinctive sounds ("phonemes") per second. Variations in excess of about 20% of the duration of these sounds have been found to be perceptually relevant to the error-free perception of the speech flow.

Some pauses are more easily perceived than others, and generally, such pauses appear to support particular functions within the message, such as grammatical functions, semantic focus, hesitation, and so on. Also, pauses are more easily perceived if their duration is around 200 - 250 ms. That appears to be the standard auditory threshold for the perception of pauses (Goldman-Eisler, 1968; Grosjean and Deschamps, 1975). In languages where systematic pauses have been observed, two types can be distinguished, so-called "silent" and "filled" pauses:

— *Silent pauses* correspond to the perception of a silent portion in the speech signal. Such pauses may be produced in conjunction with an inspiration, swallowing, any laryngo-phonatory reflex, or a silent expiration.

— *Filled pauses* correspond to the perception of a voiced section in the speech signal. Most filled pauses in such languages as English and French are drawls, repetitions of utterances, words, syllables, sounds, and false starts (Grosjean and Deschamps, 1975; Bloodstein, 1981).

Generally, with normal speakers (speakers with no speech pathology), silent and filled pauses appear *between* words. Pauses of 200 ms and longer are seldom observed within a word.

The Origins of Pauses

Sites and durations of silent and filled pauses are subject to two types of constraints. First, they depend on physiological aspects of speech motor activity, and second, they reflect cognitive processes.

The Temporal Structure of Speech and its Constraints

Like any other human activity, speech production cannot be continuously exercised. Interruptions are necessary, since any specific motor activity runs in parallel and interacts with other types of motor activity. Since motor behaviour is generally acknowledged to be performed according to three successive stages (planning, execution, pausing), any interruption of one activity to admit another usually takes place during the pause segment.

Moreover, physiologically inevitable pauses regularly occur during the inspiration phase of respiration, since phonatory activity is intricately connected with respiratory activity. Finally, speech production may be considered to be a rhythmic activity, where word groups are produced at a particular rate. All these facts likely contribute to the production of regularly spaced pauses.

In addition, a number of other parameters can be shown to influence the occurrence of pauses:

Individual physiological constraints: Since speech motor activity is largely an individual activity, the occurrence of pauses depends to a considerable extent on the specific speaker. In general, weak respiration, low muscular tone, and slow articulatory rate is associated with a greater number of pauses than a rapid articulatory rate and good respiratory capacity.

Temporal constraints and the notion of a rhythmic span: Pauses;tend to occur between rhythmic groups. Dauer shows that the data from a comparative study of syllable-timed and stress-timed languages (e.g. French *vs.* English) support the hypothesis of universal features in rhythmic structure (Dauer, 1983). According to this hypothesis, speech planning is based on a psychological regulatory unit that allows for about two "acts" per second.

Evidence from timing in general motor behaviour tends to support the notion of some type of biological clock monitoring every rhythmic activity. The durations of some speech segments show two features that suggest the presence of an internal clocking mechanism: first, certain segments are quite regular, and second, the variations for some durations (e.g. the duration of the time between two CV transitions in French) show regular corrections — very much as if constant adjustments are made, so as to approximate certain idealised time frames. According to Barbosa and Bailly (1993), this internal clock is "a time-keeping function used for the synchronisation of impulses transmitted to the muscles". It programs the duration of rhythmic units, and clock regularity is maintained by means of pauses. In other words, the durations of pauses are constrained to a given number of clock units. Obviously, this notion of regularity is very attractive, particularly in the context of a rule-governed natural speech synthesis. However, Keller (1990) recalls that at the biological level, there exists no established link between a neural pulsation of central origin and speech timing. It may thus be safest to interpret the existing evidence as saying that some internal time regulation probably exists, but that its exact physiological mechanism is still unknown.

Dauer furnishes a somewhat similar argument. According to this author, regularity in stress-timed languages is manifested in the stress interval, where the mean interval ranges from 1.9 to 2.3 stresses per second. These stresses occur at much greater regularity than do syllables, where the mean inter-syllable interval ranges from 4.5 to 8 syllables per second. In Dauer's view, rhythmic grouping applies to all languages and interacts with their syllable structure, their rules of vowel reduction and accentuation. Based on such notions of durational regulation, it can be proposed that rhythmic grouping of speech favours the occurrence of pauses at certain intervals.

The Function of Perceived Inter-lexical Pauses (in Excess of 200 ms)

Beyond the largely physiological origins of the fairly regularly occurring pauses cited above, it is also possible to identify a number of cognitive origins for pauses. Although these latter pauses are less regular in occurrence, they do show patterning and could thus be used in generating natural-sounding synthetic speech.

Pauses as a reflection of cognitive activity: According to Goldman-Eisler (1968, 1972), a pause is the external reflection of some of the cognitive processes involved in speech production. In this sense, pauses provide additional time during which the final output can be planned and programmed. This hypothesis explains some common observations, such as when a speaker thinks a long time before providing a very quick, clear, and well-constructed reply. On the other hand, it can also be observed that sometimes, a speaker begins to reply at once, and then has to stop or retrace his steps to clarify his message. In this case, the hypothesis proposes that "speech has raced ahead of cognitive activity" and that the pause reflects the time needed for the cognitive planning process to catch up.

The Goldman-Eisler hypothesis further predicts commonly observed differences between spontaneous and read speech, in that spontaneous speech is much more conducive to pauses of cognitive origin than is read speech. In this sense, these are not simply nuisance variables. Since they probably reflect cognitive activity, they contribute to the hearer's understanding of how the speaker is structuring the utterance. And since pauses apparently participate in rendering human communication more intelligible, it can be postulated that some future, advanced automatic speech recognition mechanisms could conceivably benefit from this type of information to improve recognition performance.

Pauses acting as "beacons" for utterances: A number of psycholinguistic investigations have furnished some clear indications on how pauses are patterned. In a study on French, for example, Grosjean and Deschamps (1975) have shown that the more complex the communicative task, the greater the number of pauses (see Table 1). When describing cartoons, pauses are both longer and more frequent than when responding in an interview (Grosjean and Deschamps, 1975).

Table 1. Duration of pauses according to linguistic task.

	Mean duration of silent pauses:
Description of a cartoon:	1320 ms
Interview:	520 ms

Moreover, in both communicative situations, the duration of these pauses is quite impressive (1320 and 520 ms), particularly when considered in relation to the duration of a typical syllable (some 200-300 ms), or to that of a typical vowel (some 100-150 ms) (O'Shaughnessy, 1981). In other words, pauses "stick out like sore thumbs", and thus may occupy "beacon" positions in speech, serving to structure the entire utterance for both speaker and listener. By subdividing speech into smaller segments, pauses probably contribute a great deal to the improvement of speech comprehension.

In addition, there exists a relationship between the duration and frequency of pauses on the one hand, and the syntactic constituents hierarchy on the other. In a reading-aloud task, for example, there is a tendency for a pause to be longer, the more "profound" the syntactic boundary. Still, it will be seen below that temporal segmentation is not really equivalent to the syntactic structure of utterances.

Situational constraints: Finally, a consideration of the situational context is also important, because the temporal pressure on the speaker can favour or hinder his expressive capacities. (For example, it is difficult to furnish an important information very quickly in a noisy room.) The more difficult the communicative situation, the more pauses, hesitations, and stuttering events are likely to occur.

Speech production being a rhythmic activity as well as the reflection of the underlying cognitive processes, speakers thus produce pauses spontaneously. This and the links between temporal and syntactic structures lead us believe that perceived inter-lexical pauses should be predictable and open to algorithmic implementation in speech synthesis.

Pauses and the Notion of Verbal Fluency

The phenomena described here can be captured by the overall notion of *verbal fluency:* a speaker is *fluent* when he speaks easily, with smooth onsets and transitions, and at a relatively rapid clip (Pfauwadel, 1986). Conversely, a speaker is to some degree *dysfluent,* if he is hesitant, produces pauses at inappropriate places and makes speech errors. It is a well-documented fact of human communicative behaviour that speakers can range from extremely fluent to extremely dysfluent. Even without being affected by any manifest neurological impairment, some speakers are barely comprehensible because of excessive hesitations, pauses and speech errors.

From Extremely Dysfluent to Extremely Fluent

It is useful to think of speakers' fluency as if it were distributed on a Gaussian curve. Extremely dysfluent speakers would be located at the left of the curve, followed by various degrees of hesitant speakers, passing through the majority of speakers who are reasonably fluent, and ending at the right in a small group of extremely fluent speakers.

In spontaneous speech, it is not unusual to hear someone saying one word instead of another, or mixing up the syllables of a word. These are so-called *performance errors* or *normal dysfluencies.* In contrast with pauses which are quite regular, performance errors are unique. They are produced at specific moments, in particular situations, and they will not generally be produced again in other conditions. However, the irregular occurrence, as well as the frequent correction of this type of error leaves no doubt that the speaker really knew what he intended to say. In contrast to errors produced by children or foreign language learners, his "speech competence" is not in question.

The speech impairments at the left of the curve also include various degrees of stuttering. In these cases, the temporal structure of speech diverges from the expected pattern: the frequency, the durations and the sites of pauses are abnormal. When a *non-stuttering* speaker hesitates, his (silent/filled) pauses are generally located at syntactic or prosodic boundaries (Zellner-Bechel, 1992). A near-pathological or *pathological stutterer*, on the other hand, produces dysfluencies that are often located far from syntactic or prosodic boundaries (Starkweather, 1987). An abnormal segmentation tends to perturb the listener, sometimes quite strongly, while a normal segmentation is hardly ever perceived consciously. This permits the extrapolation that *abnormal pause insertion* can be as destructive to the perceptual decoding of an utterance, just as a normal use of pauses can be useful to its understanding.

Even highly fluent speakers vary the temporal structure of their speech. Miller *et al.* have shown that in spontaneous speech, a speaker can vary his rate considerably within the same utterance, whereby the more extensive rate variations are implemented by manipulations of number and duration of pauses (Miller *et al.*, 1984). Furthermore, rate variations are related to the use of variants of speech sounds, since at a fast speech rate, sounds (or "allophones") diverge more from "ideal" (non-reduced) phonetic variants of a given phoneme than at a slow speech rate (Lacheret-Dujour, 1991).

This characterisation of fluency in the speech flow poses a distinct challenge to speech synthesis and speech recognition. Neither technology currently exploits the occurrence of pauses and speech errors. In the future, it may well be of interest to generate patterned (normal) pauses in synthetic speech. The notion of "fluency" is directly interrelated with the prediction of quite a number of phonetic parameters, such as speech rate, pauses, errors and vowel reduction. If all these parameters are some day controlled in a coherent manner in speech synthesis, the artificial voice will probably convey an impression of greater ease and fluency of speech. Similarly, automatic speech recognition devices developed to deal with spontaneous speech will inevitably have to learn to deal with the phenomenon of pauses, speech errors and speech error repair some day.

To prepare the terrain, it may be useful to examine some details of the temporal structure of speech, as well as various predictive algorithms. This is what we turn to next.

The Durational Structure of Speech

We saw that speech rate constitutes an essential aspect of verbal fluency. Speech rate is determined not only by pauses, but also by the rate of articulation (Grosjean and Deschamps, 1975). Variations in the rate of articulation are induced by several factors, primarily by variations of the durational structure found in speech.

There is an extensive literature on this question, but we shall only refer to the well-known study of Klatt (1976), since his study was oriented towards the support of speech synthesis. In this study, the factors that had been found to influence the temporal structure in spoken English sentences were inventoried in the literature. Each factor was evaluated for its capacity to provide perceptual cues sufficient to make linguistic decisions. Seven factors were retained (and subsequently integrated in the statistical model of durational control used in MITalk):

1. Extralinguistic factors (e.g. speaker mood)
2. Discourse factors (position within a paragraph)
3. Semantic factors (emphasis and semantic novelty)
4. Syntactic factors (phrase structure lengthening)
5. Word factors (word-final lengthening)
6. Phonological/phonetic factors (inherent phonological duration, stress)
7. Physiological factors (inherent duration and incompressibility)

It can be seen that duration influences every level of speech production. However, it is useful to distinguish between two levels of durational control, extrinsic and intrinsic (Ferreira, 1993). Units of word length (lexemes, inflected words, fixed expressions, etc.) are said to have a set of *intrinsic* durations which are presumably stored in a mental lexicon. Each time they are used, the basic *distribution* of duration of its various segments will be roughly the same. As these units are integrated into larger entities (phrases, utterances), they get "stretched" and "squeezed" in accordance with the requirements of larger speech demands[1]. These larger demands correspond to an *extrinsic* level of durational control. There will be more or less expansion, depending on where the word occurs in the utterance, on whether the word is emphasised or not, and on what grammatical group the word belongs to.

Therefore, the first task in a text to speech system is to parse the sentential structure into "natural" word groups. Pauses tend to occur between such word groups. The correct prediction of sites and extent of silent and filled pauses is largely determined by the extent of prosodic units, the so-called *performance structures*.

A Parsing Tool: The Performance Structures

A performance structure is a psycholinguistic structure that captures the various degrees of cohesion between the words of an utterance. For

---

[1] It is to be noted that the "streching" and "squeezing" does not apply to all segments equally. Stop consonants, for example, are much less subject to temporal modification than other types of segments, such as vowels and fricative consonants (Fujimura, 1981).

example, in the preceding sentence, there is much greater cohesion between the words "the", "various" and "degrees" than between "structure" and the succeeding word "that". By "cohesion" is meant frequency of co-occurrence, semantico-syntactic relationships (such as determiner-noun or adjective-noun relationships), and syntactic relationship (like singular/plural agreement). There is now considerable evidence that speakers seem to organise their speech with reference to such an internal notion of cohesion between the various segments of an utterance. Essentially convergent performance structures have been demonstrated by several types of psycholinguistic experiments, such as memory tasks or intuitive parsing tasks performed by non-linguists, as well as by the measurement of pauses and syllable durations in speech. Since the empirical measurement of pauses and syllable durations are of the most direct relevance in the present context, we shall concentrate on this type of evidence.

Starting with Grosjean *et al.* (1979), a number of authors have shown that occurrence and lengths of pauses are strongly correlated with the degree of inter-lexical cohesion, that is, pauses tend to be long and frequent between words that show relatively little cohesion and they are much shorter and less frequent between words that are strongly interdependent. This grouping of words appears to be independent of respiratory constraints: The same structures are found in a reading aloud task of sentences produced with and without a respiratory break. Besides, whatever the experimental method, a similar sentence segmentation is obtained.

Table 2. Word grouping.

The verbal stream seen in the speech signal
speech flow / **pause** / speech flow / **pause** / speech flow / etc.
corresponds statistically, semantically and syntactically to
words with strong cohesion / **pause** / words with strong cohesion / **pause** /etc.
and corresponds psycholinguistically to
performance structure / **pause** / performance structure / **pause** / performance structure / etc.

To be able to use this notion in text-to-speech synthesis, reliable predictors must be identified. In this process, the main problem consists of identifying *automatically* where a performance structure begins and ends.

According to Grosjean (Grosjean and Dommergues, 1983; Monnin and Grosjean, 1993), performance structures have three main characteristics:

(1) *"Eurhythmy"*: the basic units tend to be of the same length.

(2) *Hierarchy:* the basic units are enclosed into larger units that are themselves incorporated into even larger units.

(3) *Symmetry:* performance structures tend to be balanced, and the major pause is located around the middle of the sentence.

A second problem concerns the internal organisation of this type of structure. To answer this question, it is necessary to clarify how the postulated psycholinguistic performance structures (and the subsumed temporal speech structures) relate to linguistically-based syntactic structures and/or to phonetically-based prosodic structures.

Are Performance Structures Based on Syntactic and/or on Prosodic Structures?

Performance Structures and Syntactic Structures

Given the extensive work performed on syntactic structures during the 1960s and 1970s, it was natural that performance structures were initially assimilated to syntactic structures. Since performance structures seem to be organised in terms of a cohesion between various words, this cohesion was seen as directly related to that expressed by syntactic structures, structures that are based on specific criteria for capturing grammatical inter-relations between lexical units (Martin, 1980).

For this reason, a number of initial studies were directed at generating performance structures from a syntactic analysis of the sentence (e.g. Grosjean, 1980a; Grosjean and Dommergues, 1983). It is recalled that syntactic structures are generally seen as upside-down trees, where the lower nodes (branching points) connect strongly related, typically proximal elements and higher nodes connect larger, less directly related groups of syntactic units. Within this type of structure, transitions between portions of the tree depending on different higher nodes were associated with longer silent pauses, according to the principle of "the more profound the transition, the longer the pause". However, obtained results were unsatisfactory, because syntactic and psycholinguistic structures were not found to be homomorphic (Grosjean and Dommergues, 1983). Mismatches between syntactically proposed structures and empirically derived performance structures were frequent.

This result was independent of the exact syntactic theory that was assumed.

More specifically, it was found that syntactic structures are insensitive to the length of their constituents, while the main performance units tend to be approximately equilibrated, in the sense that they contain about the same number of words, and that the lengths of their units are similar. If a sentence has, for example, a *short noun phrase* followed by a *long verb phrase*, the major syntactical boundary is situated between the two phrases. However according to the psycholinguistic evidence, the major "performance" break is located between the verb and the rest of the verb phrase. On the other hand, a *long noun phrase* and a *short verb phrase* are subdivided differently, so that the constituents end up being more or less balanced.

For example, when French speakers are asked to segment a sentence into intonational groups or units, they tend to balance out the number of syllables in each group (Grégoire, 1899; Grosjean and Dommergues, 1983; Monnin and Grosjean, 1993; Fónagy, 1992; Martin, 1992). The mean length of these units, in a reading aloud task of simple sentences, was estimated to be around 3.46 syllables with a standard deviation of 1.43 (Monnin and Grosjean, 1993).

The syntactic complexity analysis of a sentence is no doubt an important factor, but in itself, it has not turned out to be a sufficient predictor of performance structures. Lehiste (1972) examined the effects of morphological and syntactic boundaries on the temporal structure of spoken utterances. She concluded that temporal readjustment processes tend to ignore morpheme and word boundaries. The durational structure is, according to Lehiste, conditioned by the number of syllables, rather than by either the number of segments, or by the presence of boundaries. Moreover, Ferreira (1993), has shown by means of an elegant experiment that the temporal structure of a sentence is closely related to its prosodic structure. If a syntactic variation (number of syntactic boundaries following a key word) is introduced into the given textual material, temporal variables are not significantly affected. However, if a prosodic variation (a change of emphasis) is introduced, temporal variables such as final-word durations and pauses are notably affected. We may conclude that performance structures depend both on linguistic variables (such as syntactic boundaries), and on psycholinguistic variables (such as length or symmetry).

Performance Structure and Prosodic Units

If prosodic factors are related to, but not homomorphic with syntactic structure (for an overview, see Hirst *et al.*, in press), and if performance structures are related to, but are not veritably congruent with syntactic organisation, it remains to be seen if a closer relationship can be established between performance structures and prosodic units. In terms of our schema, that would give:

Table 3. Performance structures and prosodic units.

performance structure / **pause** / performance structure / **pause** / performance structure /etc.   as equivalent to   prosodic unit / **pause** / prosodic unit / **pause** / prosodic unit /etc.

There are some indications that this relationship holds. According to Hirst (in press), silent and filled pauses constitute the acoustic;marks that enclose the prosodic units (or as in the literature: "prosodic phrase", "prosodic structure", etc.). As the suprasegmental and audible tissue of speech, such prosodic units can be defined by the *relations* existing between prosodic parameters of speech (stress, intonation, duration, etc.). Some similar results appear to come out of our own algorithmic work (see below). In view of the apparent link with prosody, it may thus be useful to review at how humans appear to process prosodic structures.

How are Prosodic Structures Generated in the Human Mind?

The main question concerns the manner in which a performance structure – *i.e.*, the phrasing of the sentence – is constructed as an utterance is prepared for output. According to Bachenko and Fitzpatrick (1990), there exists a *neutral phrasing*, that is, a sentence-level phrasing pattern that is independent of discourse semantics. According to these authors, it is upon this neutral pattern that all the variants like focalisation, emphasis, etc., are grafted. They suggest that this discourse-neutral phrasing is built upon a knowledge of syntactic constituents, of string adjacency, and of phrase length.

In this way, recent phonological theories conceive of the sentence as a set of prosodic units that combine phonological and syntactic units. Each prosodic unit specifies rhythmic characteristics at the syllabic level as well as at the word-, the phrase-, and the sentence levels. For example from a prosodic point of view, the word is a set of feet, *i.e.*, a strong-to-weak syllable pattern. Such words are grouped into a *phonological phrase* (Selkirk, 1984). This phonological phrase is not necessarily isomorphic with the syntactic phrase. At the end, phonological phrases group into intonational phrases, which in turn combine to make an utterance.

The question is at which point during the process of speech production this neutral phonological phrase is encoded. Ferreira (1993) considers that the prosodic constituent structure is generated *without knowledge* of the segmental content, just as in Levelt's model of language production (for further details, see Levelt, 1989). According to this hypothesis, abstract timing intervals are assigned to various sentence locations early on in the speech planning process. Later, segmental factors are taken into account, but word and pause durations are in a trade-off relationship, so as to respect the total duration of the allocated interval. At the phonetic level, a long word takes up more space in the timing interval than a short word, but a greater word length also implies a shorter subsequent pause. That means that within an interval, word and pause lengths are inversely related. The size of a timing interval is determined by the number of prosodic constituents. The more prosodic constituent boundaries that end on a given word, the longer the timing interval for that word will be.

A general agreement concerning temporal phenomena can thus be noted. It can now be stated with some certainty that phrasing is related to prosodic structures, and that rhythmic patterns permit to establish a connection between temporal phenomena and the segmental content. That is the principal foundation upon which speech synthesis algorithms can be built.

The Automatic Generation of Durations: Algorithms

Once again, the reader will not find a complete overview of this area here. The following algorithms are, from our point of view, simply the most important attempts to generate durations automatically on the basis of text input. Two types of duration models can be distinguished: *rule-governed systems* and *statistical systems*.

Rule-Governed Systems

In these approaches, a number of rules — generally sequential rules — are applied to linguistic material which is characterised by an intrinsic duration. It results in an output duration. These output durations are supposed to take into account various phenomena such as linguistic constraints (like syntactic factors) or psycholinguistic constraints (like length).

The following algorithms (GGL, CPC, PHI, Bachenko and Fitzpatrick, and MG) are all built on the same basic notions, as they use a number of concepts from generative syntax.

Grosjean Grosjean and Lane (1979) — GGL. The aim of this algorithm was to predict performance structures. For each word boundary, this cyclic algorithm matches an index of linguistic complexity to a measure of the distance to the midpoint of the segment.

The mean correlation of 0.83 between predictions and observations leads to the conclusion that this simple algorithm is a relatively good predictor of durations, even of the pause data. However, the syntactic analysis tends to overestimate the importance of inter-lexical function words (Gee and Grosjean, 1983).

Cooper and Paccia Cooper (1980) — CPC. Their algorithm contains 14 rules to predict, for English, the probability of a pause occurring at each inter-lexical boundary, as well as segmental lengthening, pause and segment durations. It essentially accounts for the depth of syntactic nodes.

The mean correlation obtained between measures and predictions is about 0.75. When it is applied to French, the correlation decreases to 0.57. The main objections are that the rule application is not clear enough, and that there is no bisection compounds for mid–sized sentences (Gee and Grosjean, 1983).

Gee and Grosjean(1983) Phonological Phrase Algorithm — PHI. This algorithm suggests that two factors govern the temporal structure of the sentence: The syntactic structure and the information content-based distinction between function and lexical words. The function words are considered to be weak syllables. This algorithm does not require the whole tree structure of a sentence to start segmentation into prosodic units.

The mean correlation is reported to be very high (0.96), probably because this algorithm integrates phonological, syntactical and prosodic information. It demonstrates that performance structures reflect prosodic structures. When it is applied to French, the major prosodic boundaries are rather well predicted, except that the post–verbal boundary is overestimated.

Bachenko and Fitzpatrick (1990) — BF. Influenced by the former algorithm, these authors conceived a system for English capable of predicting phrasing by a process of localising phrase boundaries. First, phonological words and phrases are identified. Then, boundary salience rules are applied, assigning a relative strength — i.e., perceptibility — to each phrase boundary according to syntactic labelling, length, and adjacency.

Their results indicate that 80% of the primary boundaries — i.e., the most easily perceived boundaries — were correctly predicted. The system's limitation concerns its parsing errors. For example, incorrect part of speech assignments and incorrect analyses of pre–head modifiers have been identified.

Monnin and Grosjean (1993) — MG. This algorithm specifically developed for French is also promising, because the mean correlation between the performance structures of nine read sentences and the prediction of these structures with the algorithm is about 0.94. Major and minor prosodic boundaries are correctly predicted. Consequently, the sentence is segmented into prosodic units that are not necessarily equivalent to surface syntactic structures. However, the algorithm has not been extensively tested on other sentences.

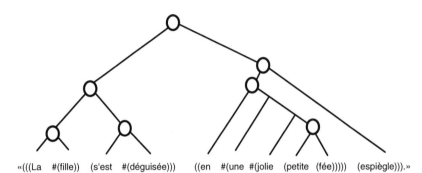

«(((La #(fille)) (s'est #(déguisée)))   ((en #(une #(jolie (petite (fée))))) (espiègle))).»

Figure 3. A performance structure tree according to the Monnin and Grosjean rules. A single node separates «petite» and «fée», which predicts a short final syllable and adjoining pause for «petite». By contrast, five nodes separate «déguisée» and «en», which predicts a much larger final syllable and pause duration at this major juncture. The #-mark specifies an attachment of grammatical to lexical words. Performance structure trees are quite different from syntactic structure trees, no matter the theoretical tradition.

The Keller-Zellner (KZ) Rules (1993): Initially derived from the MG algorithm and conceived for French, this algorithm is quite different in form as well as in content. Basically, the aims of these rules are to satisfy the criteria of *simplicity*, respect of *psycholinguistic plausibility*, and *high predictive capacity* for the data sets at hand.

Prosodic constituents are formed on the basis of simple proximal syntax. No syntactic structures more complex than those applying to a single phrase are required. Prosodic groups can be identified by the application of steps 1 and 2 of the Monnin-Grosjean rules.

Final syllable+pause durations increase in duration as the constituent proceeds. The increase proceeds from an empirical minimum to an empirical maximum. The initial hypothesis calls for equal steps. Increased durations correspond to a slowing down, which is a commonly observed phenomenon in speech.

Rhythmic alternance was observed for two locations: post-verbally and in the middle of 4-6 word constituents. Rhythmic alternance occurs when one element is lengthened more than strictly required. As a consequence, the following element must be shortened "in order to conclude the constituent in time". Concretely, this amounts to postulating an *inversion of durations* for the word pair involved in the alternance.

The resulting algorithm is quite simple and is reproduced at the end of this chapter. Correlations with the Caelen-Haumont and the Monnin-Grosjean data sets are reported in Table 4. It is found that correlations are quite regular. They never dip below a linear correlation of .7, and generally tend to be found in the 0.8 range.

Table 4. Linear correlations between predicted and measured final syllable+pause durations according to two sets of rules.

Caelen-Haumont Data Set	Monnin-Grosjean		Keller-Zellner	
	Normal	Slow	Normal	Slow
Sentence 1	.786	.895	.862	.845
Sentence 2	.289	.375	.811	.829
Sentence 3	.925	.808	.878	.751
Mean	**.667**	**.693**	**.850**	**.808**
Monnin-Grosjean Data Set	Normal	Slow	Normal	Slow
Sentence 1	.890	.674	.873	.835
Sentence 2	.914	.796	.886	.954
Sentence 3	.981	.886	.773	.892
Sentence 4	.961	.826	.798	.850
Sentence 5	.947	.736	.827	.872
Sentence 6	.984	.711	.812	.835
Sentence 7	.931	.841	.754	.906
Sentence 8	.940	.585	.870	.809
Sentence 9	.968	.808	.701	.818
Mean	**.946**	**.763**	**.810**	**.863**

An inspection of the evolution of F_0 and energy values at the end of prosodic constituents postulated here shows some regularities. F_0 values rise at the end of each constituent, except for the sentence-final constituent. Energy values fall regularly at the end of each constituent. This suggests that the temporal structure characterized here interacts directly with control over F_0 and energy.

As they cannot predict the *whole* temporal structure of an utterance, the previous models are obviously incomplete. Even if inter-lexical pauses and word-final lengthenings are generated satisfactorily, these algorithms neglect syllabic and segmental durations.

Statistical Systems

Within the perspective of text-to-speech systems, it is important to control speech timing at each level of the sentence generation process. The MITalk system — the English text-to-speech system developed at the Massachusetts Institute of Technology (Allen *et al.*, 1987) — satisfies this requirement and thus provides an excellent point of departure. Although this system belongs to an older generation of synthesizers and sounds quite artificial by today's standards, its temporal structure is based on an influential approach first developed by Klatt (1976). It is a statistical model built around segmental durations, *i.e.*, durations for individual phonemes.

On the basis of data collected in a variety of projects conducted by several authors, Klatt's vowel model begins by calculating an inherent phonological duration for a given segment. This duration is then shortened or lengthened as a function of the succeeding segment, its position within the phrase, the presence or absence of stress, and word length. Lehiste's non-sense word data (cf., Klatt, 1976) was re-analysed, and it was found that just four rules in Klatt's model can account for 97% of the total variance of the measured vowel durations.

A somewhat similar model was proposed by O'Shaughnessy (1981, 1984). This is probably the most important statistical model for spoken French text. On the basis of numerous readings of a short text containing all phonemes of French, a model of durations of acoustic; segments suitable for synthesis by rule was proposed. In this model, 33 rules specify basic durations for various classes of segments, as well as modifications to this basic duration as a function of phonetic context.

For sound classes that do not involve prepausal lengthening, the model was able to predict the durations for 281 segments of a text, with a standard deviation of 9 ms. But it was less accurate for the prediction of prepausal vowel durations, because of the greater variability of these segments in such positions. Moreover, this model was not able to predict silent inter-lexical pauses.

These two statistical models are constructed around the same essential hypothesis, an hypothesis which is open to an important critique. The authors assume that speech timing phenomena can be captured by the segment, as if this unit "possesses an inherent target value in terms of articulation or acoustic;manifestation" (Fujimura, 1981). However, recent measures have indicated that syllable-sized durations are generally less variable than subsyllabic durations, and thus represent more reliable anchor points for the calculation of subsyllabic durations (Barbosa and Bailly, 1993). This approach to duration receives further support from the observation that stress variations and variations of speech rate tend to modify at least syllable-sized units, certainly more than single segments. The durations of coarticulation phenomena could also profit from this reorientation of perspective. It may be more profitable to see segments and their coarticulatory phenomena from the perspective of integrating a number of segments into a *syllable*, than from that of the atomic durational measure represented by the phoneme.

Independent of whether the calculation begins with the segment or with the syllable, a statistical approach to duration is very promising.

Results of this type suggest that a likely next step in this area of research is the development of a robust statistical model, capable of predicting the entire durational structure of a sentence.

Conclusion

It is estimated that speech synthesis will sound more fluent, will be more pleasant to listen to, and will likely be more intelligible when silent and filled pauses are systematically integrated into the verbal stream. Since these pauses enclose prosodic units — which we have equated with performance structures — pauses can be predicted by the same mechanisms that let us predict performance structures. Algorithms have been developed that test these predictions, and which are presently being tested with respect to various types of speech material.

These advances are part of a larger effort to develop models capable of controlling various aspects of speech fluency in TTS systems. Issues in pausing and in speech error repair are also of importance to automatic speech recognition, since future systems for the understanding of spontaneous speech will have to show sufficient intelligence to deal with speech repair, and may well profit from the regularity of the pause and syllable duration patterns found in the temporal structure of speech.

The Keller-Zellner Algorithm

(1) Identification, from left to right, of the *nuclei* of the prosodic constituents: nouns, verbs and free-standing adjectives, adverbs and pronouns (such as "La chemise est *sale*", "c'est *bien*", "pense à *ça*").

(2) Creation of the *prosodic constituents* by grouping the words around the nucleus. All words to the left of the nucleus are attached to the right-lying nucleus, except for post-posed adjectives and post-posed pronouns which are attached to the left-lying nucleus ("la chemise *blanche*", "donne-*lui*").

(3) Calculation of *predictions for final syllable+pause durations*. Within each prosodic constituent, durations increase from a minimum to a maximum duration. Initially, the increase is assumed to occur in equal steps. (The minimum and maximum are assumed to be 50 and 350 ms in normal speech, 50 and 525 ms in slow speech.) The first final syllable in a constituent has a duration of minimum+step size ms.

(4) *Rhythmic tradeoffs:*

1. *Post-verbal trade-off:* When a constituent follows a verb and there are at least two words prior to the nucleus, the final syllable duration of the first word is lengthened with respect to that of the second word. (Exchange durations for words 1 and 2.)

2a. *Rhythmic alternance:* If a constituent is four or more words long, and if word 3 is two or more syllables long, word 2 is lengthened with respect to word 3. (Exchange durations for words 2 and 3.)

2b. *If rule 1 has already applied:* If a constituent is four or more words long, and if word 4 is two or more syllables long, word 3 is lengthened with respect to word 4. (Exchange durations for words 3 and 4.)

3. *Single-word constituents:* Constituents containing a single word show reduced final syllable durations. (Reduce durations for single word constituents by 50 ms.)

(5) *Measure of final syllable+pause.* The measure begins with the vowel of the final syllable and ends at the end of the pause. It includes whatever intervening consonant may occur, but it excludes the characteristic optional schwa of French méridional speakers (as in «biologiste»). Excluding the optional schwa permitted us to make direct comparisons of data sets from northern and méridional speakers. Resulting time measures were very similar. For a limited data set, the intervening consonant was suppressed. However, resulting durations were found to show greater variability than those that included the consonant. Measures for sentence-final words were only known for a few sentences and were thus set to 0 in all cases for statistical purposes.

References

Allen, G.D. (1975). Speech rhythm: Its relation to performance universals and articulatory timing. *Journal of Phonetics, 3,* 75-86.

Allen, J., Hunnicutt, M.S., & Klatt, D. (1987). *From text to speech. The MITalk system.* Cambridge, England: Cambridge University Press.

Bachenko J., & Fitzpatrick E. (1990). A computationnal grammar of discourse-neutral prosodic phrasing in English. *Computational Linguistics, 16,* 155-170.

Barbosa, P., & Bailly, G. (1993). Generation and evaluation of rhythmic patterns for text-to-speech synthesis. *Proceedings of an ESCA Workshop on Prosody* (pp. 66-69). *Lund, Sweden.*

Bloodstein, O. (1981). *Handbook on stuttering.* Chicago: National Easter Seal Society for Crippled Children and Adults.

Boomer, D.S., & Ditmann, A.T. (1962). Hesitation pauses and juncture pauses in speech. *Language and Speech, 5,* 215.

Botte, M.C., Canévet, G., Demany, L., & Sorin, C. (1989). *Psychoacoustique et perception auditive.* Série audition. Paris: Inserm/ Sfa / CNET.

Butcher, A. (1980). Pause and syntactic structure. In W. Dechert & M. Raupach (Eds.), *Temporal variables in speech* (pp. 86-90). Mouton.

Caelen-Haumont, G. (1991). *Stratégies des locuteurs et consignes de lecture d'un texte: analyse des interactions entre modèles syntaxiques, sémantiques, pragmatique et paramètres prosodiques.* Thèse d'Etat, Aix-en-Provence.

Chafe, W. (1980). Some reasons for hesitating. In W. Dechert & M. Raupach, (Eds.), *Temporal variables in speech* (pp. 169-180). Mouton.

Cook, M., Smith, J., & Lalljee, M. (1974). Filled pauses and syntactic complexity. *Language and Speech, 17,* 11-16.

Cooper,W., & Paccia Cooper, J. (1980). *Syntax and Speech.* Cambridge, MA: Harvard University Press.

Dauer, R.M. (1983). Stress-timing and syllable timing reanalyzed. *Journal of Phonetics, 11,* 51-62.

Dechert, W., & Raupach, M. (Eds.), *Temporal variables in speech.* Mouton.

Fraisse, P. (1974). *La psychologie du rythme.* PUF, Paris.

Ferreira, F. (1993). Creation of prosody during sentence production. *Psychological Review, 2,* 233-253.

Fónagy, I. (1992). Fonctions de la durée vocalique. In P. Martin (Ed.), *Mélanges Léon* (pp. 141-164). Editions Mélodie-Toronto.

Fujimura, O. (1981). Temporal organisation of articulatory movements as a multidimensional phrasal structure. *Phonetica, 38,* 66-83.

Gee, J.P., & Grosjean, F. (1983). Performance structures: A psycholinguistic and linguistic appraisal. *Cognitive Psychology, 15,* 411-458.

Goldman–Eisler, F. (1968). *Psycholinguistics: Experiments in spontaneous speech.* New York: Academic Press.

Goldman–Eisler, F. (1972). Pauses, clauses, sentences. *Language and Speech, 15,* 103-113.

Grégoire, A. (1899). Variation de la durée de la syllabe en français. *La Parole, 1,* 161-176.

Grosjean, F. (1980a). Linguistic structures and performance structures: Studies in pause distribution. In W. Dechert & M. Raupach (Eds.), *Temporal variables in speech* (pp. 91-106). Mouton.

Grosjean, F. (1980b). Comparative studies of temporal variables in spoken and sign languages: A short review. In W. Dechert & M. Raupach (Eds.), *Temporal variables in speech* (pp. 307-312). Mouton.

Grosjean, F., & Deschamps, A. (1975). Analyse contrastive des variables temporelles de l'anglais et du français. *Phonetica, 31*, 144-184.

Grosjean, F., & Dommergues, J.Y. (1983). Les structures de performance en psycholinguistique. *L'Année psychologique, 83*, 513-536.

Grosjean, F., Grosjean, L., & Lane, H. (1979). The patterns of silence: Performance structures in sentence production. *Cognitive Psychology, 11*, 58-81.

Hirst, D., & Di Cristo, A. (in press). *Intonation systems: A survey of twenty languages.*

Klatt, D. (1976). Linguistic uses of segmental duration in English: Acoustic and perceptual evidence. *Journal of the Acoustical Society of America, 59*, 1208–1221.

Keller, E. (1990). Speech motor timing. In W.J. Hardcastle & A. Marchal (Eds.), *Speech production and speech modelling* (pp. 343-364). Kluwer Academic Publishers.

Keller, E., Zellner, B., Werner, S., & Blanchoud, N. (1993). The prediction of prosodic timing: Rules for final syllable lenthening in French. *Proceedings ESCA Workshop on Prosody* (pp. 212-215). *September 27-29. Lund, Sweden.*

Lacheret–Dujour, A. (1991). Le débit de la parole: un filtre utilisé pour la génération des variantes de prononciation en français parisien. *Actes du XIIème Congrès International des Sciences Phonétiques* (pp. 194-197). *Aix en Provence.*

Lehiste, I. (1972). The timing of utterances and linguistic boundaries. *Journal of the Acoustical Society of America, 51*, 2018–2024.

Levelt, W. J. M. (1989). *Speaking: From intention to articulation.* Cambridge, MA: MIT Press.

Martin, Ph. (1980). L'intonation est-elle une structure congruente à la syntaxe? In M. Rossi et al. (Ed.), *L'intonation: de l'acoustique à la sémantique* (pp. 234-271). Klincksieck.

Martin, Ph. (1992). Il était deux fois l'intonation. In P. Martin (Ed.), *Mélanges Léon* (pp. 293-304). Editions Mélodie-Toronto.

Miller, J., Grosjean, F., & Lomanto, C. (1984). Articulation rate and its variability in spontaneous speech: A reanalysis and some implications. *Phonetica, 41*, 215-225.

Monnin, P, & Grosjean, F. (1993). Les structures de performance en français: caractérisation et prédiction. *L'Année Psychologique, 93*, 9-30.

O'Shaughnessy, D. (1981). A study of French vowel and consonant durations. *Journal of Phonetics, 9*, 385-406.

O'Shaughnessy, D. (1984). A multispeaker analysis of durations in read French paragraphs. *Journal of the Acoustical Society of America. 76*, 1664-1672.

Pfauwadel, M.-C. (1986). *Etre bègue.* Paris: Retz.

Selkirk, E.O. (1984). *Phonology and syntax: The relation between sound and structure.* MIT Press, Cambridge, MA.

Starkweather, W.C. (1987). *Fluency and stuttering.* Prentice Hall.

Zellner-Bechel, B. (1992). Le bé bégayage et euh... l'hésitation en français spontané. *Actes des 19eme J.E.P.* (pp. 481-487). Bruxelles.

Zwicker, E., & Feldkeller, R.(1981). *Psychoacoustique: l'oreille récepteur d'information.* Collection technique et scientifique des télécommuications. Paris: Masson.

SECTION
2

STATE OF THE
ART

SECTION 2:   STATE OF THE ART

E. Keller and Jean Caelen
Introduction to Section 2: State of the Art

P. Bhaskararao
Subphonemic Segment Inventories for Concatenative Speech Synthesis

B. Pfister and C. Traber
Text to Speech Synthesis: An Introduction and a Case Study

T. Styger and E. Keller
Formant Synthesis

G. Chollet
Automatic Speech Recognition: State of the Art, Current Issues and Perspectives

K. Torkkola
Stochastic Models and Artificial Neural Networks for Automatic Speech Recognition

Introduction to Section 2: State of the Art

Eric Keller[1] and Jean Caelen[2]

[1] Université de Lausanne, LAUSANNE, Switzerland
[2] Institut de la Communication Parlée, GRENOBLE, France

In speech synthesis and speech recognition, the "state of the art" is a moving target. For this reason, no attempt was made to provide extensive descriptions of existing synthesis and recognition systems in this book. Instead, it was decided to concentrate on the fundamental techniques of the field. While marketed systems evolve rapidly, and are often shrouded in commercial secrecy, the fundamental techniques they employ remain quite stable. The chapters of this section introduce these techniques, and they provide a great many useful references to further readings in the field.

The section begins with a number of chapters on speech synthesis. Synthesised speech is in essence "re-composed speech", i.e. speech reconstituted in one way or another from elements or portions of previously recorded speech. One of the crucial issues in synthesis concerns the elements that go into the reconstitution.

At the most banal level, one can simply record whole sentences and play them back as required. Indeed, for many common applications, this remains the simplest and most efficient solution (e.g. "4th floor: Household appliances"). At the next level, part of the recording is stable, and part is generated from recordings of single words — again a familiar solution for information systems. For example, telephone companies often provide phone numbers according to the pattern: "The number is: 9-8-7, 3-5-4-6". The initial portion of the message is recorded, and the numbers are generated from individual recordings. In order to facilitate comprehension, the number preceding the comma is chosen from a special set of numbers having "pause characteristics", i.e. lengthened final syllables and special intonation contours.

However, such solutions tend to be of marginal interest. The real challenge lies in reconstructing almost any speech from much smaller segments or even, from a set of abstract elements. The three initial chapters of this section discuss this issue from different perspectives.

In the first chapter, Bhaskararao describes experiments performed with minimalist or near-minimalist systems. In this case, exceedingly small segments of speech are stored and concatenated as required. This approach is appropriate to cases where computing power is weak and available storage is minimal (Bhaskararao's own segment inventory for Indian languages is just 1.6 Mb in uncompressed form). However, for reasons indicated in the previous section, coarticulatory information — and with it, a great deal of naturalness of speech — is all but lost in such minimalist systems. In the second part of his chapter, Bhaskararao explains how coarticulatory information is best incorporated into somewhat more powerful systems, while respecting, as best as possible, the combinatorial possibilities of various types of languages.

Pfister and Traber present the various choices that go into designing the synthesis architecture for a mature concatenative system, capable of dealing with free connected text. From the perspective of their own, highly respected SVOX system, they show that beyond the creation of a satisfactory concatenative segment inventory lies considerable additional footwork associated with developing the grammatical underpinnings of a synthesis system. Grammatical knowledge ("syntax" and "morphology"[1]) is required to disambiguate so-called homographs and to provide realistic-sounding prosodic information. A common example of an English homograph is the word "record" which has two different pronunciations depending on its grammatical class and function (e.g. "she rec'ords 'records"). Grammatical knowledge permits to identify which form of the word is present, and thus permits the selection of the correct pronunciation.

Styger and Keller present a totally different approach to the problem of speech synthesis. Instead of attempting to "glue together" pieces of pre-recorded speech, relatively abstract parameters, such as frication, formants and amplitudes, are stored away and recomposed as required. This approach is called "formant synthesis", and over short stretches of

---

[1] Syntax: The systematic order that language elements follow in an utterance to convey a particular grammatical sense. Example: The difference between normal (declarative) and inverted (interrogative) word order, as "are you" *vs.* "you are" in "are you/you are in a good mood". Morphology: Modifications of a base form designed to a convey specific grammatical sense. Example: "see"—"sees"—"seeing" or "rose"—"roses".

speech, it has been shown to be capable of generating utterances that are difficult to distinguish from those produced by human speakers.

The reason behind this outstanding performance again has much to do with coarticulation. Coarticulatory effects can extend over considerable periods of time, and often span more time than even the longest stored segments of a concatenative system. So even very good and extensive inventories of speech segments cannot account for all coarticulatory effects that are possible in a language. Advanced formant synthesis systems, on the other hand, contain their own rules for simulating coarticulatory effects, which are then applied to the calculation of the right combination of formants.

Another improvement comes from the generation of the intonational contour. Segment-based systems generally perform considerable signal-analytic sleight-of-hand[2] to stretch or squeeze the fundamental frequency periods of a speech signal into a shape that produces the auditory effects of higher or lower voice pitch. Although modern techniques of this sort can be very good, they do leave a distinct auditory trace. Formant synthesis, on the other hand, generates pitch from first principles, and thus has the potential of producing a much cleaner speech waveform.

However, the great promise of this approach is also its greatest pitfall. Typical formant synthesis systems manipulate arrays of between 40 and 60 parameters, and generate a new set of parameters every 5-10 ms. Opinions are still sharply divided on whether this is a practicable task. John Local (York University, UK, see Chapter 12) has shown that outstanding results are possible in the generation of any two-syllable English word by the application of a few hundred, well-designed rules. However some other authors remain exceedingly sceptical of the general viability and commercial applicability of this approach.

The final two chapters in this section by Chollet and Torkkola deal with speech recognition. Gérard Chollet has taken upon himself the considerable task of providing a first introduction — in just a few pages — to the enormous field of speech and speaker recognition. The essential question in recognition concerns the ultimate application. Command recognition to control a computer, a chirurgical instrument or aircraft operation is rather different from the recognition of connected speech in interactive information systems. Recognition without any or with very limited training involves quite different algorithms and currently, makes much more limited promises, than recognition after a more or less considerable training period. Finally, *speaker* recognition is quite different from *speech* recognition. Required computing power and algorithms, as

---

2 They apply a so-called PSOLA, a "pitch-synchronous overlap and add" operation to the signal (see Pfister and Traber's chapter).

well as the system's ultimate constraints are directly related to the specific purpose that the recognition capacity is supposed to satisfy.

Torkkola's chapter links up directly with these issues by discussing the two main computational approaches to recognition. In contrast to synthesis where phonetic and linguistic considerations are in the foreground, statistical and still to a lesser degree, neuro-computational algorithms are in the foreground in current-day speech recognition. Torkkola explains in some detail the advantages of both approaches. Statistical (or "Markovian") techniques predominate in current applications, but for a number of relatively technical reasons, neuro-mimetic approaches show considerable promise of being able to surpass statistical approaches. Their ascendancy in desktop computing has recently been reinforced by the mass production of affordable neurocomputing chips (Baran, 1994). It is likely that this type of computing capacity will soon be applied to speech recognition where it will no doubt have a massive impact.

Reference

Baran, N. (1994). Neural networks: Intel and Nestor to commercialize neural-net chip. *BYTE, 19 (March)*, 32.

Subphonemic Segment Inventories for Concatenative Speech Synthesis

4

Peri Bhaskararao

Deccan College, PUNE 6, India and
ILCAA, Tokyo University of Foreign Studies, TOKYO, Japan

Concatenative synthesis is based upon "stringing together" pieces of pre-recorded speech segments. What should constitute such a segment is the major concern of this paper. We shall examine different segment types used in synthesis systems. Segments of variable lengths are proposed for synthesising any language. General phonetic criteria for deciding the optimal segment sets for a given language are discussed.

Types of Speech Synthesis

Speech output systems are generally of two types: Non-interactive systems and interactive systems. For example, automatic announcement systems are usually non-interactive or minimally interactive, in the sense that the user does not interact with such a system. Text-to-speech (hereafter, TTS) systems, on the other hand, constitute a major type of interactive system, *i.e*, a system where a user often expects the output to be produced either in real time or nearly real time on the basis of written text. The input to a TTS system is a text in a particular language, and its output is the spoken form of the input text.

TTS systems can also be either restricted or unrestricted. A restricted TTS system can operate with a limited set of vocabulary or phrases, etc. An unrestricted TTS system can take any amount of text input in a language, and can generate corresponding speech output. A TTS system can be monolingual (catering to only one language), or it can be multilingual (catering to two or more languages). There are also multidialectal systems which allow the user to convert text into speech of different dialects of a language.

A TTS system has two main components, a text-to-segment conversion component and a segment-to-speech synthesizer. The first component converts the input text into strings of synthesis segments. These synthesis segments differ from system to system, and they depend on the basic approach to synthesis that has been chosen. The second component converts these segments into actual speech output.

The two major approaches to speech synthesis are parametric and concatenative. In a parametric synthesis system such as the Klatt synthesizer (Allen *et al.*, 1987), a phonological unit is first divided into several acoustic units, and each of these acoustic units is generated "according to a sequence of control signals" which "set up specific parameter values which depend upon the language to be synthesised, and the transitional effects between these values are provided by the dynamics of the system" (Peterson *et al.*, 1958). In a concatenative synthesis system, stored discrete segments are recalled and concatenated (chained together) to produce speech. These discrete segments generally are prerecorded and processed chunks of "actual human utterances or they may be discrete segments which are artificially generated to form basic units for the synthesis" (Peterson *et al.*, 1958).

Segments for Concatenative Synthesis

If we ignore very large units such as phrases or sentences, the next smaller unit for concatenation is a word. Words have indeed been used as concatenative units for synthesis (Buron, 1968; Chapman, 1971; Eady *et al.*, 1987). However, for an unlimited text-to-speech system of a language, it is practically impossible to store the digital information of all the words of a language. Hence, researchers have been experimenting with segments of various lengths for achieving better economy, generalisations based on phonetic criteria, and ultimately, output of better quality. Some of the systems that use segments of different lengths based on different segmentation principles are listed in Table 1.

Phonemes

At the other extreme from the phrase or the word, there is the phoneme. A "phoneme" is a minimally distinct, abstract class of sounds in a language. For instance, in English /p/ is a phoneme, as opposed to /b/, because it contrasts with other sounds in such words as "*pat*" and "*bat*". Although the phoneme appears to be an attractive linguistic unit for speech synthesis because of the limited number of phonemes that are necessary for any given language, "all efforts to string together phoneme-sized chunks of speech have failed" (Klatt, 1987). One of the major reasons for this failure is that the boundaries between phonemes usually correspond to areas that are acoustically volatile. Phoneme-sized building blocks were found to be unsatisfactory as synthesis segments because of the coarticulatory effects of the adjacent sounds (Harris, 1953). Even conventional allophones (i.e. variants of phonemes, specific to certain phonetic contexts) cannot serve as "ideal" concatenative segments, because they still do not account for a good number of such coarticulatory effects. Speech synthesized with phonemes as units "would hardly be intelligible, even if each phoneme was represented by several allophones in the segment inventory, one for each general type of phonological context" (Sivertsen, 1961).

Table 1. A list of segment types used in earlier implementations.

Segment Type	Some of the Implementations
Word	Buron, 1968; Chapman, 1971; Eady *et al.*, 1987
Syllable	Ouh-young *et al.*, 1986
CVC	Hayashi and Murakami, 1992
VCV	Sato, 1978; Sagisaka and Sato, 1981
Diphone/Dyad	Lefevre 1986; Isard and Miller,1986; Hakoda *et al.*, 1986
Pseudophoneme	Mikuni and Ohta, 1986
CV & V	Ohyama *et al.*, 1988; Rajesh Kumar *et al.*, 1989
Demisyllable	Lovins and Fujimura, 1976; Fujimura and Lovins, 1978; Lovins *et al.*, 1979; Eady *et al.*, 1987
Demi-syllable +Triphone	Bhaskararao *et al.*, 1991
Subphoneme	El-Imam, 1989; Dan and Dutta, 1991; Bhaskararao and Venkata, 1992

Diphones and Demi-syllables

It can thus be seen that the synthesis segment should satisfy a number of criteria. In addition to being part of a computationally manageable inventory of items, the segment in question should capture all the transient and transitional information that is usually present between conventional consonant and vowel phonemes. A segment that can satisfy this condition was found to be a "dyad". A dyad is generally composed of the final portion of one unit and the initial portion of a succeeding unit

(Wang and Peterson, 1958; Sivertsen, 1961; Dixon and Maxy, 1968). The term "diphone" is generally used as a synonym of the term "dyad". However in a strict sense, the two can be differentiated (Klatt, 1987). In essence a diphone stands for the transition between adjacent segments (Klatt, 1987; Olive and Spickenagel, 1976).

The "demi-syllable" is a unit that very closely resembles a diphone (Lovins and Fujimura, 1976; Fujimura and Lovins, 1978; Lovins *et al.*, 1979). The diphone boundary in a CVC (consonant-vowel-consonant type) syllable generally lies in the middle of the V. This results in two diphones — CV and VC — for each CVC syllable. Though the number of diphones and demi-syllables that are extracted from the CVC syllable seem to be the same, they differ in their relative lengths. A *diphonic* cut is made in the middle of the V of CVC, whereas a *demi-syllabic* cut is made at the place in the V where the C-to-V transition ends and the steady state of the vowel begins. Rajesh Kumar *et al.*, (1989), use a hybrid CV and V segment system in the synthesis of some Indian languages.

Triphones

Triphones are alternate units that are successfully used in speech recognition and that can also be used in speech synthesis. To generate a CVC syllable, one would require a triphone containing the CV transition, the V portion as well as the VC transition. However, the extremely large number of segments that would be required for a system that uses only triphones is a discouraging factor. Usage of a limited number of triphones within a demi-syllable system for improved synthesis of momentary sounds such as flaps and trills has been proposed (Bhaskararao *et al.*, 1991).

A system that is essentially based on triphone VCV segments was implemented for Japanese, as reported by Sato (1978), and by Sagisaka and Sato (1981). This system requires 768 segments to generate Japanese. Similarly, a system was developed for Japanese that is based on CVC segments, and that is optimised by including only the most frequent triphones and a few supplementary diphones (Sato, 1992). This hybrid system requires a total number of only 1300 segments, as opposed to the very large set of triphones that would be required if the system were entirely based on triphones. Saito (1992) points out that the shift from VCV segments to CVC segments is due to the underlying philosophy that "vowels are key components determining synthesised voice quality and should not be segmented or concatenated in their middle at all, and concatenation of units must be made in consonantal parts because they are small in amplitude so that the discontinuity introduced by the concatenation sounds less distinct".

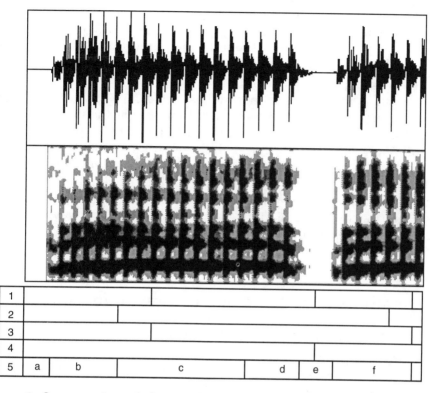

Figure 1. Segmentation of the word [pæpæ] using different segment types. 1=Diphones; 2=Demisyllables; 3=VCV segments; 4=CVC segments; 5=Subphonemic segments (**a** and **e**: plosive stricture, **b** and **f**: from plosive burst till the end of transition into the vowel, **c**: steady-state of vowel; **d** and **h**: vowel to consonant transition.

Subphonemic Segments

Diphones, demi-syllables and triphones aim at capturing the transitional as well as the transient information that is available between consonants and vowels, as well as between vowels and vowels, and between other continuant sounds. However, while capturing this information, one can simultaneously attempt to segment the stationary and non-varying portions of the signal, and to economise by suppressing repetitive elements.

El-Imam (1989) utilises such an approach for Arabic, and employs only 400 segments. Dan and Dutta (1991) use a segment inventory that contains segments of variable length. Their segments correspond to what they call phonemes, "partnemes" (partial phonemes), and transitions. This is a successful attempt at capturing some of the phonetic generalisations in deciding on the size of synthesis segment. Bhaskararao and Venkata (1992) describe the implementation of a system for text-to-speech conversion for Hindi and Urdu languages. This system incorporates a highly optimised segment inventory consisting of 450 subphonemic segments which can be used for the unlimited generation of speech in any of these languages.

Systems that use diphones, demisyllables, CVC or VCV units, etc., have segments of a more or less fixed length. On the other hand, the segments in a subphonemic-segment system are not of a fixed length. The flexibility of being able to choose the length of a segment makes such a system highly economical. Moreover, several phonetic generalisations can be captured in such a system, which render it more elegant. One of these is the technique of combining VC segments for all stops and fricatives of the same place of articulation. Figure 1 maps onto a waveform and corresponding spectrogram the segment boundaries of various major concatenative systems.

Preparation of a Subphonemic Segment Inventory

In the following section, we will examine some of the methods for developing an optimal segment inventory of subphonemic segments. These methods are general in nature, and are meant for synthesising the speech of any language. First, definitions of some essential terms are presented. This is followed by a classification of segments into groups, and a discussion on the method of preparation of these segments.

Definitions

We give below definitions of some of the essential terms that will be used in the later discussion on preparation of subphonemic segment inventories.

Stricture: Every speech sound produced in continuous speech results from the modification of the vocal tract shape. This is achieved by various means. One of them is creation of a *stricture* (a narrowing) in the supra-glottal area (i.e. an area that includes the pharynx and the oral cavity). Strictures are created by bringing together two articulators to a certain degree. Articulatory strictures are of two types — sustainable and momentary.

During a sustainable stricture the articulators may be closed:
    (a) completely (as in stops or plosives), e.g. [p], [b];

(b) partially (fricatives), e.g. [s],[f],[z];

(c) at the median line but with an opening on the sides of the oral cavity (laterals), e.g. [l];

(d) in the oral cavity but with an opening into the nasal cavity from the pharynx (nasals), e.g. [m],[n].

During a momentary stricture the articulators may be:

(a) closed for a very brief period of time (taps and flaps), e.g. [ɾ], [ʈ];

(b) closed intermittently (trills), e.g. [r];

(c) approximated but without complete closure (approximants), e.g. [w].

Burst: The period from the release of stricture of a stop sound till the onset of the first glottal pulse of the transition of the following vowel, if any.

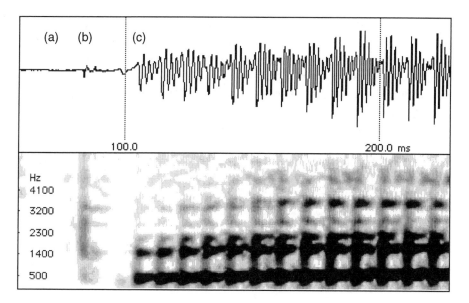

Figure 2. Waveform and spectrogram of the syllable [pæ] showing: (a) stricture, (b) burst, (c) transition from the stop into the vowel.

Transition: The highly varying portion of the signal that is usually available:

(a) between the end of the steady state of a vowel and the onset of a consonant

(b) from the first glottal pulse of a vowel after the release of a consonant stricture till the beginning of the steady state of a vowel. Some amount of transition is available during the aspiration portion of a burst also.

Figure 2 depicts a waveform illustrating the terms defined above.

Segment Types

For the purposes of concatenative synthesis, segments can be classified into *transitory* and *sustainable*. Transitory segments are those that are highly time-varying. They cannot be prolonged. Sustainable segments are prolongable for some time without undergoing much variation.

The *transitory segments* belong to three further types as listed below:

Type I. Consonant-Vowel Transitions. This class contains transitions that reflect movements from consonants to vowels belong here. It includes (i) the bursts of plosives (stop consonants), plus the transitions leading to the subsequent vowels (referred to as StV hereafter), and (ii) the releases of the strictures of non-plosive consonants, plus the transition leading to the following vowels.

Type II. Vowel-Consonant/Vowel Transitions. This class contains transitions that reflect movement from vowels to consonants, as well as from vowels to vowels. It includes transitions between (i) each vowel and all the plosives and fricatives of each homorganic[1] class, (ii) each vowel and each consonant (other than those covered in (i) above), and (iii) each vowel and each other vowel (available both in diphthongs and vowel-vowel sequences).

Type III. Variable Strictures. This class contains stricture periods of trills, flaps and taps. The members of this class vary continuously in their acoustic structure. Each trill, tap and flap of a language has to be represented by a separate segment.

Sustainable segments belong to two further types as listed below:

---

[1] Homorganic: produced in the same articulatory area. E.g. /n/ and /t/ are homorganic, since they both involve a prominent closure at the alveolar ridge.

Type IV. Vowel Steady-States. This class contains the steady-state portions of each vowel of a language. Separate steady-state segments are required for each oral vowel, each nasal vowel, and each vowel produced by a different phonation type (e.g. normal voice, creaky voice, murmur).

Type V. Consonant Steady-States. This class contains those stricture portions of voiceless plosives, voiced plosives, nasals (also known as nasal murmurs), laterals, and fricatives which are not listed under Type II.i).

The Preparation of Segments

In concatenative synthesis, segments of these various types are chained together in order to produce the final speech output. To create a satisfactory auditory impression, it is important to pay careful attention to the transition between segments, and it is useful to consider some further differentiations between types of segments. The nature of each of these segment types, as well as the different sets of segments that may be required for synthesising a language are discussed next.

Type I:

Plosives followed by vowels. When two consonants are produced with different manners of articulation (e.g. as a plosion or as a frication), yet with the same general vocal tract configuration, the resulting waveforms differ not only in the stretch characterised by the stricture, but also with respect to the overall spectral shape observed at the *release* of the stricture. E.g. a /t/ is different from an /s/ not only in the part of the signal related directly to the stricture, but also in terms of the spectral structure observed in the part immediately afterwards.

Stops (or plosives) differ drastically from the rest of the consonants with respect to their release. This is because the stricture of a stop sound is complete, and at the time of the release of the stricture, there is usually a burst with a good amount of turbulence and certain amount of aspiration. Stop bursts are acoustically highly complex, and are characterised by "considerable acoustic structure and dynamic spectral change" (Repp and Lin, 1990). A stop burst contains three phases — a *transient*, a *fricative* segment, and an *aspiration* segment (Fant, 1973).

It is tempting to separate the transient (called the "spike" in sound spectrography) from the rest of the burst, to be treated as a separate segment. By doing this, a segment with just the transient alone is obtained, which could be concatenated with the remaining portion of a burst. However in fact, this approach probably does not result in any real economy, since the characteristics of the whole burst (including the spike) are influenced by the following vowel. Repp and Lin (1989) have shown that "isolated transients contain information about both the consonant and the vowel of CV syllables, and that this information is contained in a very distinct formant structure". Similarly, the fricative and the aspiration portions also are heavily influenced by the subsequent vowel. Hence, a separation of the transient from the rest of the burst, and treating them as two separate segments, would not lead to any economy in the segment inventory. The whole of the burst (transient, frication, and aspiration), plus the CV transition, should thus be kept as a unitary segment. If these segments are called StV segments, one would require StV segments for all the possible combinations of each of the plosives with each of the vowels in the language under consideration.

The exact place where the transition ends depends to some degree on the degree of aspiration. If the stop is voiceless and is considerably aspirated, most of the transition may well be completed during the aspiration portion itself. That is, by the time voicing starts, the transition might be completed and the first glottal pulse of the vowel may lead directly into a steady-state of the vowel. Since the burst and the transition share several characteristics, and since in the case of heavily aspirated stops, the transition might be completed during the aspiration period, it is best to keep the burst and transition as a single unit, *viz.*, StV, and to perform the slice in the succeeding vocalic portion.

In many languages of the world, a minimal distinction between voiced and voiceless plosives exists (e.g. /p/ *vs.* /b/). Additionally, languages may possess distinctive sets of voiceless aspirated and voiceless unaspirated plosives (e.g. /pʰ/ *vs.* /p/). Such a distinction may be either at allophonic level, as in English ("pit" [pʰɪt] *vs.* "spit" [spɪt]), or at contrastive level, as found in several languages of South Asia. In both cases, aspirated and unaspirated voiceless plosives require different StV segments. Separate StV segments are thus required for each *consonantal phonation type* available in the language under consideration: Voiceless unaspirated stops, voiceless aspirated stops, voiced unaspirated stops, and voiced aspirated stops (i.e. murmured stops).

This portion of the signal also varies on the basis of the airstream type, *viz.*, an *egressive airstream*[2] as in the case of all the stop sounds of English, Japanese or German, or an *ingressive airstream* as in the case of certain sounds of Zulu or Sindhi. Hence in certain languages, separate StV segments are also required for each of the *airstream types* that are used in the production of stops. In some languages, one would for example require different StV segments for stops produced with pulmonic

---

[2] Egressive: "blowing out from the lungs", ingressive: "sucking into the lungs".

egressive airstream, glottal egressive airstream (ejectives), glottal ingressive airstream (implosives), and velar ingressive airstream (clicks).

Non-plosives followed by vowels: The consonants that fall into this category include all fricatives (other than those included in Type II(i) above), nasals, trills, flaps, taps, laterals, and approximants. Distinct segments are needed, consisting of the portion from the release of the stricture till the end of the transition into the following vowel.

Type II:

Vowel-to-Homorganic stop/fricative transitions. In the course of an extensive experimentation with various methods of economising segment inventories for speech synthesis, it was found that one requires only one transitional segment for a vowel followed by any stop that is a member of a given homorganic class (Bhaskararao and Venkat, 1992). This was successfully extended to include fricatives which are homorganic with the stops. The following homorganic classes of stops and fricatives were thus established for a majority of South Asian languages (Table 2).

Table 2. Homorganic sounds

Homorganic Class	*Consonants involved*	*Segment Name*
Labial class	(p, pʰ, b, bʰ)	Vowel-Bilabial
Dental class	(t, tʰ, d, dʰ, s, z)	Vowel-Dental
Retroflex class	(ʈ, ʈʰ, ɖ, ɖʰ, ʂ)	Vowel-Retroflex
Palatal class	(c, cʰ, j, jʰ, ʃ)	Vowel-Palatal
Velar class	(k, kʰ, g, gʰ, x, χ)	Vowel-Velar

A single transition segment would suffice for the sequence of a particular vowel followed by any of the stops or fricatives of a homorganic class. For instance, the same VC transition segment can be used for the generation of the following sequences of vowels and consonants: [ak], [akʰ], [ag], [agʰ], [ax], and [aχ].

When the articulators move from the position for a vowel to a plosive of a particular place of articulation, the movement is similar, even though the stop could be voiceless unaspirated or aspirated, plain voiced or murmured. Due to this fact, we require only one transition segment in this situation. Further, towards the end of a vowel transition, as the stricture for a fricative starts forming (in a vowel-fricative sequence), the acoustic energy is almost cut off. Even plosives produced with different airstream types (e.g. glottal egressive) fit into these homorganic classes. Thus a transition segment containing the vowel [a] leading into a bilabial plosive can be used as VC segment in the production of the following syllables: Pulmonic egressive [ap], [apʰ], [ab], [abʰ] and glottal ingressive [aɓ].

Vowel-to-Nonhomorganic Stops/Fricative Transitions. Transitions between vowels and consonants that do not belong to homorganic stops and fricatives belong to this category, and they include all the nasals, trills, flaps, taps, laterals, and fricatives in a language.

Vowel-to-Vowel Transitions. These include transitions between two vowels which might constitute vowel sequences or the two vocalic segments of a diphthong. For instance, for the vowel sequences or diphthongs [ai], [ia], [ae], [ea], and [ao] we would require the V-V transition segments [a-i], [i-a], [a-e], [e-a], and [a-o] respectively.

Type III

The stricture portions of trills, taps and flaps are characterised by momentary changes in their acoustic quality (Catford, 1977). The stricture period of a flap or a tap is so short in duration that any segmentation within the stretch of such a brief stricture might give rise to artefacts during concatenation. It was thus proposed by Bhaskararao *et al.*, (1991) that such strictures be kept as unitary segments only.

Type IV

Steady-state portions of each vowel fall under this type. Separate steady-state segments are required for each oral vowel, each nasal vowel, and each vowel produced by different phonation types, such as normal voice, creaky voice, murmur. Only one pitch pulse for each vowel type (with pitch normalised) needs to be stored (Dan and Dutta, 1991). This leads to considerable economies. A vowel of any duration can be produced by repeating the stored pitch pulse as required.

Type V

1. The stricture portion of a voiceless plosive is characterised by an absence of acoustic energy. Similarly, the stricture portion of a voiced plosive contains acoustic energy at the first formant level. The amount of voicing during the stricture period of a voiced stop depends upon the language. Plosives can differ in their "degree" of voicing. This difference is more temporal and depends upon how much of the stricture period + the post-stricture period is voiced. Following Ladefoged (1982), we can differentiate the following types of segments with reference to different degrees of voice-onset-time.

(i) A purely voiceless stop (either aspirated or unaspirated) has no voicing during its stricture period. Hence, the stricture segment of such a stop is characterised by absence of any acoustic energy (e.g. voiceless unaspirated and aspirated plosives of a majority of South Asian languages, English, French, Spanish, and Thai).

(ii) A plosive may be partially voiced as in English. The stricture segment of such a plosive has no voicing during the beginning but acquires voicing towards the end.

(iii) A plosive may be fully voiced as in French, Spanish, Thai, Hindi and several other South Asian languages. The stricture segment of such a plosive is voiced throughout.

Other differences in VOT (voice onset time) which depend upon degrees of aspiration will be catered to by StV type of segments, as the acoustic information of the aspiration is available in the signal that follows the release of the stricture.

2. After accounting for the stricture portions of plosives, the system has to take into consideration the stricture portions of the remaining consonantal manners of articulation.

Separate stricture segments for nasals (containing "nasal murmurs") are necessary for each nasal consonant of a language. In addition, separate structure segments for each fricative and each lateral are required. Bhaskararao and Venkata (1992) report an interesting fact about the segments necessary for fricatives and laterals. The stricture portions of these sounds are considerably affected by the coarticulatory effects from the succeeding vowel. Such coarticulatory effects are noticeable in the case of some of the other consonant types as well. Moreover, the coarticulatory effect of vowels during the stricture period of the preceding fricative or lateral is clearly noticeable (O'Connor, 1973). Figure 3 shows the difference in the waveform and corresponding spectrogram of a fricative followed by vowels that differ in their lip-rounding.

For this purpose, fricatives have to be divided into front lingual fricatives and back lingual fricatives. Isaard and Miller (1986) have shown that one would require allo-diphones to account for significant allophonic differences in a language. Similarly, a front lingual fricative is effected by the rounding of the vowel that follows it. Two broad allo-segments have to be maintained for these front fricatives — a rounded fricative allophone and an unrounded allophone. In the case of the back fricatives such as [x], [X] and [h], one would require one allo-segment each for the vowel that follows it. For instance, following is an illustrative list of the fricative and vowel sounds available in a language, and the list of allo-segments that would be required to be included in the segment inventory.

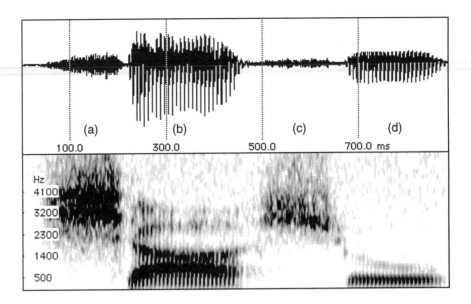

Figure 3. Differences in the fricative [ʃ] in the context of unrounded vowel [a] and rounded vowel [u]. (a) unrounded [ʃ] before [a], (b) vowel [a], (c) rounded [ʃ] before [u], (d) vowel [u].

If in a given language there are vowels [i], [e], [u], [o], [a] and fricatives [s], [ʃ], [χ], then one would require the following allo-segments to generate the respective syllables (Table 3).

Table 3. Allo-segments

Allo-segments required	For generating the syllables
unrounded-[s]	[si], [se], [sa]
rounded-[s]	[su], [so]
unrounded-[ʃ]	[ʃi], [ʃe], [ʃa]
rounded-[ʃ]	[ʃu], [ʃo]
[i]-coloured [χ]	[χi]
[e]-coloured [χ]	[χe]
[u]-coloured [χ]	[χu]
[o]-coloured [χ]	[χo]
[a]-coloured [χ]	[χa]

Conclusion

After looking at the main difference between parametric and concatenative synthesis methods, we have examined various types of concatenative segment types. The conventional linguistic units, such as phonemes and allophones, were found to be unsuitable as units for concatenative synthesis. However, either phonemes or allophones can be maintained as intermediary stages in the text-to-acoustic waveform transformation. Though sub-word units such as diphones and demisyllables can avoid some of the inherent problems of word-level synthesis units, sub-phonemic segment units have been evaluated to be the best alternative for small-scale systems. Such units not only bring about an optimisation of the segment inventory to be stored, they also capture some of the phonetic generalisations, such as unification of vowel-consonant transitions involving homorganic consonants. The need for allo-segments was also evaluated, in order to accommodate significant coarticulatory effects between vowels and consonants.

References

Allen, J.B., Hunnicut, M.S., & Klatt, D. (1987). *From text to speech: The MITalk system.* Cambridge, England: Cambridge University Press.

Bhaskararao, P., Eady, S.J., & Esling J.H. (1991). Use of triphones for demisyllable-based speech synthesis. *Proceedings of ICASSP-1991,* 11.S7.28.

Bhaskararao, P., Venkata, N.P. (1992). A report on an unlimited text-to-speech system for Hindi and Urdu. Manuscript.

Buron, R.H. (1968). Generation of a 1000-word vocabulary for a pulse-excited vocoder operating as an audio response unit. *IEEE Transactions on Audio and Electroacoustics AU-16,* 21-5.

Catford, J.C. (1977). *Fundamental Problems in Phonetics.* Bloomington: Indiana University Press.

Chapman, W.D. (1971). Techniques for computer voice response. *IEEE International Conference Record,* 98-9.

Dan, T.K., & Dutta, A.K. (1991). Speech synthesis: A time domain model. In A.K. Dutta (Ed.), *Proceedings of the international workshop on recent trends in speech, music, and allied signal processing.* Delhi: Indian Statistical Institute.

Dixon, R., & Maxy, H. (1968). Terminal analog synthesis of continuous speech using the diphone method of segment assembly. *IEEE Transactions on Audio and Electroacoustics. AU-16,* 40-50.

Eady, S.J., Dickson, B.C., Urbanczyk, S.C., Clayards, J.A.W., & Wynrib, A.G. (1987). Pitch assignment rules for speech synthesis by word concatenation. *Proceedings of ICASSP-1987.* 1473-6.

Eady, S.J., Hemphill, T.M.S., Woolsey, J.R.Clayards, J.A.W. (1987). Development of a demisyllable-based speech synthesis system. *Proceedings of the IEEE Pacific Rim Conference on Communications, Computers and Signal Processing,* 463-6.

El-Imam, Yousif A. (1989). An unrestricted vocabulary Arabic speech synthesis system. *IEEE Transactions on ASSP, 37:12,* 1829-45.

Fant, G. (1973). *Speech sounds and features.* Cambridge, MA: MITPress.

Fujimura, O., & Lovins, J. (1978). Syllables as concatenative phonetic elements. In A. Bell & J.B. Hooper (Ed.), *Syllables and segments* (pp. 107-20). New York: North-Holland.

Hakoda, K., Kabeya, K., Hirahara, T., & Nagakura, K. (1986). Japanese text-to-speech synthesizer based on residual excited speech synthesis. *Proceedings of ICASSP-86*, 2431-4.

Harris, C.M. (1953). A study of the building blocks in speech. *Journal of the Acoustical Society of America, 25*, 962-9.

Hayashi, T., & Murakami, K. (1992). Implementation of waveform files for synthesis-by-rule. *Proceedings of ICASSP-1992*, II.41-3.

Isard, S.D., & Miller, D.A. (1986). Diphone synthesis techniques. *IEE International conference on speech input/output techniques and applications. Conference publication no. 258*, 77-82.

Klatt, D.H. (1987). Review of text-to-speech conversion for English. *JASA, 82:3*, 737-93.

Ladefoged, P. (1982). *A course in phonetics*. New York: Harcourt Brace Jovanovich.

Lefevre, Jean-Paul. (1986). A diphone speech synthesis approach applicable to different languages. *Proceedings of ICASSP-1986*, 2443-6.

Lovins, H.B., & Fujimura, O. (1976). Synthesis of English monosyllables by demi-syllable concatenation. Presented at the 92nd Meeting of the Acoustical Society of America, San Diego.

Lovins, H.B., Machhi, M.J., & Fujimura, O. (1979). A demisyllable inventory for speech synthesis. In J.J. Wolf & D.H. Klatt (Eds.), *Speech communication papers presented at the 97th Meeting of the Acoustical Society of America* (pp. 519-22).

Mikuni, I., & Ohta, K. (1986). Phoneme based text-to-speech synthesis system. *Proceedings of ICASSP-1986*, 2435-8.

O'Connor, J.D. (1973). *Phonetics*. Harmondsworth, England: Penguin.

Ohyama, T., Kaseda, M., & Sato, Y. (1988). Speech synthesis by rule using CV&V segment and residual waveform. In *Proceedings of the second symposium on advanced man-machine interface through spoken language* (pp.16.1-7).

Ouh-young, M., Shie, C., Tseng, C., & Chiu-yu, L. (1986). A Chinese text-to-speech system based upon a syllable concatenation model. *Proceedings of ICASSP-86*, 2439-42.

Olive, J.P., & Spickenagle, N. (1976). Speech resynthesis from phoneme-related parameters. *JASA, 59*, 993-6.

Peterson, G.E., Wang, W.S-Y., & Sivertsen,E. (1958). Segmentation techniques in speech synthesis. *Journal of the Acoustical Society of America, 30:8*.

Rajesh Kumar, S.R., Sriram, R., & Yegnanarayana, B. (1989). A new approach to develop a text-to-speech conversion system for Indian languages. *In Proceedings of the regional workshop on computer processing of Asian languages, Bangkok.*

Repp, B., & Lin, H. (1990). Acoustic properties and perception of stop consonant release transients. *Journal of the Acoustical Society of America, 85*, 379-96.

Sagisaka, Y., & Sato, H. (1981). VCV compilation speech synthesis using prosodic elements extracted from original speech (in Japanese). *Transactions of Institute of Electron. Commun. Eng. Jpn. [Part A] 64*, 551. (Reported in Saito & Nakata 1985).

Saito, S., & Nakata, K. (1985). *Fundamentals of speech signal processing*. Tokyo: Academic Press.

Saito, S. (Ed.) (1992). *Speech science and technology*. Tokyo: Ohmsha.

Sato, H. (1978). Speech synthesis on the basis of PARCOR VCV concatenation units (in Japanese)*Transactions of Institute of Electron. Commun. Eng. Jpn. [Part AD 61, 868.* (Reported in Saito & Nakata 1985).

Sato, H. (1984). Speech synthesis using CVC concatenation units and excitation waveform elements (in Japanese). In *Transactions on the committee on speech research. Acoustical Society of Japan S83-69*. (Reported in Saito, S. (Ed.), 1992).

Sato, H. (1992). Text-to-speech synthesis for Japanese. In Saito, S. (Ed.), 1992.

Sivertsen, E. (1961). Segment inventories for speech synthesis. *Language and Speech, 4,* 27-90.

Tohkura, Y.,& Sagisaka, Y. (1980). Synthesis by rule using CV-syllable (In Japanese). Acoustic Society of Japan Meeting 3-4-3 (May 1980), pp. 623. (Reported in Sato, H., 1992).

Wang, W.S-Y., & Peterson, G.E. (1958). Segment inventory for speech synthesis. *Journal of the Acoustical Society of America, 30,* 743-6.

Text-to-Speech Synthesis: An Introduction and a Case Study

5

Beat Pfister and *Christof Traber*

Speech Processing Group, Computer Engineering and Networks Laboratory, Swiss Federal Institute of Technology, CH-8092 ZURICH, Switzerland

This chapter presents an introduction to text-to-speech synthesis, i.e. to systems that generate synthetic speech starting from orthographic text. Possible applications of such systems are reading machines for the blind and automatic information services over the telephone line. The first section of the chapter discusses the general problems of text-to-speech synthesis and shows different possible ways of solving them, and the second section gives a more detailed description of one particular realised modern text-to-speech system for German.

Speech synthesis systems are usually grouped into two classes: Concept-to-speech systems and text-to-speech (TTS) systems. Concept-to-speech systems synthesise speech departing from semantic/pragmatic concepts and have full knowledge of the purpose and meaning of the utterances to be synthesised. These systems are used when the contents of the utterances to be synthesised are generated by the system itself (e.g. in response to user queries in automatic dialog systems). TTS systems, on the other hand, simulate the human process of reading aloud given texts and are mainly used as aids for the blind or speaking-impaired and in automatic information services (e.g. reading weather forecasts, news, or mailbox contents over the telephone line). TTS systems must first analyse the text to be read aloud in terms of the underlying linguistic structure and then generate speech starting from the results of this analysis.

This chapter deals with TTS systems only. In the first part, we will give an overview of the major problems that TTS systems encounter and show possible solutions that can currently be found in various systems. Since TTS systems differ considerably in their internal processing, the second part presents one particular modern TTS system in more detail, namely the SVOX system for German which has been developed at our laboratory. The purpose of this second part is to give an idea of how TTS systems can be built and how their components interact.

Major Problems and Possible Solutions

Speech Production

The primary prerequisite of a TTS system is a speech generator, i.e. an apparatus or a piece of software which is capable of producing signals that sound like human speech. In the history of speech synthesis this was the first problem that was attacked. First attempts to produce speech by means of mechanical devices date from the end of the 18th century (Schroeder, 1993). Today, the speech production is generally realised as a computer program that generates artificial speech signals as sequences of numbers which are then played out via a digital-to-analog converter.

A large part of this book deals with different approaches to the generation of human-like speech. The different speech production methods can be divided into three major categories:

a) The articulatory models generate speech signals via the simulation of the acoustical properties of the human vocal tract. This is a very obvious approach and therefore has been investigated since the very beginning of speech processing research. However, given the achieved results in terms of speech quality, it is not clear whether this is a promising approach.

b) The speech signal models intend to capture the perceptually relevant time-variable features of the speech signal such as the formants, the spectral shape, the periodicity, etc. The most popular type of such a speech signal model is the formant synthesiser. Unfortunately, it is a very difficult task to control the formant transitions in a perceptually correct manner.

c) The concatenative approach tries to avoid the main problem of the above approaches, namely the lack of naturalness of the synthesised phones and phone transitions. It assumes that a speech signal can be generated by concatenation of speech segments (e.g. diphones, half-syllables, etc.) that have been extracted from natural speech. Of course, this approach inherently provides natural-sounding speech within the basic segments. However, the speech quality may be impaired by the mismatch at the segment boundaries and by the necessary modifications of the prosodic parameters. Different methods exist to carry out such modifications, most notably the LPC (linear predictive coding) scheme and the newer and very successful PSOLA approach (pitch-synchronous overlap-add; Moulines and Charpentier, 1990).

In order to control the speech production component of a TTS system, it is necessary to know what sounds are to be produced (spectral or segmental information), and how long, at what pitch, and with what intensity they are to be produced (prosodic or suprasegmental information). The following sections discuss how this information can be obtained in TTS systems.

Phonetic Transcription

Usually, the information about the sequence of sounds to be produced by the speech production module is taken from the phonetic transcription of an utterance, which itself must be derived from the orthographic input text. This derivation is usually done by a combination of looking up words in a phonetic dictionary and so-called grapheme-to-phoneme conversion or letter-to-sound rules.

Until recently, typical TTS systems contained a system of rules that tried to generate the phonetic transcription of words from their orthographic form (which is possible to a certain degree in alphabetical languages). Words that were not treated correctly by this conversion were stored together with their proper pronunciation in an "exceptions dictionary". With the increasing memory capacities of modern computers, there is a clear tendency in current TTS systems towards large dictionaries containing tens of thousands of entries (Coker *et al.*, 1990). The few exceptions, i.e. words that cannot be analysed using the dictionaries of the system, must, however, still be treated by letter-to-sound rules.

The structure of dictionaries depends to a certain extent on the language for which they are used. For English, a full-word dictionary may be sufficient, whereas for languages with more inflected, derived and composed forms (such as German or French) it is appropriate for the most part to store allomorphs in the dictionary and to morphologically decompose the input words.

Letter-to-sound rules are most commonly formulated as ordered sets of context-sensitive rewrite rules, which convert input letters into corresponding phonetic symbols depending on the context of each letter (e.g. Allen *et al.*, 1987). However, there are also other approaches to letter-to-sound conversion, including rhyming and analogy methods (Coker *et al.*, 1990; Dedina and Nusbaum, 1991), neural networks (Sejnowski and

Rosenberg, 1986), or grammar-based methods (Hunnicutt *et al.*, 1993; Traber, 1993).

Realisation of Speech Sounds

The phonetic transcription of an utterance is an abstract, canonical representation of the sound sequence to be realised. The acoustic manifestation of individual speech sounds is not only largely influenced by speaker characteristics and speaking style, but also to a very high degree by the neighbouring sounds (so-called coarticulation). A text-to-speech system must integrate these influences in order to achieve a high degree of naturalness and intelligibility. In concatenative synthesis systems, the problem is tackled by simply cutting out sample realisations of phoneme sequences from natural speech and by concatenating them into new utterances, where the basic elements are chosen so as to appropriately cover a large part of the coarticulation effects. In other synthesis approaches, e.g. rule-based formant synthesis, coarticulation must be modelled and generated explicitly. Chapter 12 by J. Local in the "Challenges" section of this volume describes a promising new approach to the mastering of coarticulation in formant synthesis.

Generation of Prosodic Parameters

In addition to segmental properties, prosodic parameters are required to drive the speech production component, i.e. duration, fundamental frequency (Fo) and intensity values. These parameters all have an intrinsic, articulatorily motivated and a more abstract linguistic component. TTS prosody research has dealt mostly with Fo and segmental duration as acoustic correlates of the more abstract concepts of intonation and rhythm. Intensity is generally regarded of lesser importance for the naturalness of synthetic utterances.

Intonation and rhythm are to a large extent language- and dialect-specific (different languages may be very different in their prosodic schemes) but also show some universal properties (e.g. the well-known declination phenomenon in intonation; Cohen *et al.*, 1982). Within a specific language, intonation and rhythm depend largely on accentuation and phrasing of an utterance. In many languages, high degrees of prominence of a syllable are expressed by a major Fo rise or fall and/or increased duration and intensity, and phrase boundaries are marked by pauses or lengthening of the syllable(s) before the phrase break and/or a rising continuation pattern in Fo. Therefore, what is needed in a TTS system is a component that generates the physical prosodic parameters on the basis of the accentuation and phrasing of an utterance, and of general (language-specific and universal) prosodic properties.

The methods used to generate Fo contours in TTS systems differ widely. Among the approaches are some that set up declination lines (base and top lines) and that generate movements between these lines according to a set of rules (Collier, 1991), or some that produce downstepping target points which are connected by standard patterns (Kohler, 1991; Pierrehumbert, 1981). Öhman (1967) and Fujisaki (1981) have described a quantitative model of Fo production, which is driven by accent and phrasing commands. Other (implicit) approaches directly use Fo patterns which were extracted from natural speech and which are concatenated to new Fo contours (Aubergé, 1992; Larreur *et al.*, 1989; Traber, 1992). Alternatively, Hidden Markov Models or neural networks are used to generate Fo contours (Ljolje and Fallside, 1986; Sagisaka, 1990; Traber, 1992).

Methods for generating segmental durations also vary considerably, but in general they are more statistics-oriented than Fo generators. Among these methods are rule systems (Carlson and Granström, 1986a; Klatt, 1979), decision trees (Pitrelli and Zue, 1989), or neural-network-based duration control (Campbell, 1990).

Accentuation and Phrasing

In order to control the acoustic prosodic parameters, accentuation and phrasing of an utterance must be known.

The task of an accentuation module in a TTS system is to assign a degree of prominence (accent strength) to each syllable of the utterance to be synthesised. A prerequisite for the proper accentuation of an utterance is the knowledge of the word stress positions and word accent types in tone languages like, e.g. Swedish. This information is derived in close conjunction with the phonetic transcription of the input words. The sentence accentuation process then weights the different word accents against each other.

In general, accentuation depends mostly on the pragmatic context and the semantic content of a text, which are not easily available in today's TTS systems. However, some of this higher-level linguistic information is reflected in the lexical and syntactic structure of a sentence. For example, function words — which usually remain unstressed in a "neutral" statement — can be distinguished lexically from content words, which are likely to be stressed; a noun within a noun phrase usually receives more weight than an adjective preceding it; the primary accent of the sentence very often falls on the last noun phrase in the sentence. One of the best examples of a reflection of semantic weight in syntax is the

French *mise en relief* using "c'est", in which the prominent item (and the strong accent connected with it) is marked explicitly:

il a cassé le verre *vs.* c'est <u>lui</u> qui a cassé le verre

The phrasing of a sentence, i.e. the grouping of words into speech groups or phrases is more dependent on the syntactic structure of an utterance than accentuation: Words that belong together syntactically also tend to be spoken together in one group. A phrasing procedure in general inserts boundaries of different strengths between neighbouring words.

Accentuation and phrasing in TTS systems are usually done by rule systems which are taken from, or at least motivated by, purely linguistic work (e.g. Bachenko *et al.*, 1986; Gee and Grosjean, 1983; Selkirk, 1984; Quené and Kager, 1992). An example of a different approach is the statistical decision-tree phrasing method described in Hirschberg (1991).

Lexical, Morphological and Syntactic Analysis

The purposes of a syntactic sentence analysis in a TTS system are manifold:

(a) to assign a hierarchical constituent structure to each sentence, which provides essential information to generate sentence accentuation and phrasing, which then control the prosody of the speech signal;

(b) to disambiguate homographs, i.e. words with identical spelling but different syntactic functions and pronunciations, e.g.
English: 'record (noun)   *vs.*   re'cord (verb)
German: 'modern (verb)   *vs.*   mo'dern (adjective)
     ich höre <u>zu</u> ("zu" as verb prefix; carries main sentence accent)
                    vs.
     ich gehöre <u>zu</u> ihnen ("zu" as preposition; unaccented);

(c) to obtain the proper pronunciation of abbreviations and numbers; for example, the pronunciation of German ordinal numbers depends on the case and number of the surrounding constituent, e.g.
     am 3. Oktober   *vs.*   der 3. Oktober
     (am dritt<u>en</u> ...; dative)   (der dritt<u>e</u> ...; nominative);

(d) in future TTS systems, the syntactic analysis may serve as a basis for semantic and pragmatic analysis.

The syntactic sentence analysis must know the syntactic categories and other syntactic information (e.g. case, number, and gender) of each word in the sentence in order to parse the whole sentence. This information could most easily be stored in a full-form word lexicon, in which each entry consists of the graphemic word form, syntactic attributes (word category and different additional attributes used in the syntactic analysis), and possibly the phonetic transcription of the word. However, in languages like German, which are rich in inflected forms, derivations and compounds, it is not desirable to store each word in each possible form in a full-form lexicon. Instead, a morphological analysis of each word should reveal its internal structure (e.g. a word like German "begehst" should be split up into the prefix "be", the verb stem "geh" and the inflection ending "st"). The morphological analysis therefore needs a lexicon of morphemes or allomorphs and a word grammar which defines legal decompositions of words into morphemes.

Virtually all TTS systems carry out morphological and syntactic analysis to a certain degree, but the various systems differ in the formalisms applied, the sizes of the lexicons used and the completeness of the syntactic analysis. Instead of trying to fully analyse a sentence syntactically, many systems only try to find the prosodically most important constituents within a whole sentence (phrase-level parsing; e.g. Allen *et al.*, 1987).

Higher-Level Text Analysis

In order to really imitate a human being in reading texts, a TTS system would have to go beyond the syntactic level and carry out semantic, pragmatic, and discourse analysis. For unrestricted input, this is not feasible for the time being. In the future, however, TTS research will surely try to treat higher levels of text analysis. First attempts to do so can be found in the attempts to model the given/new distinction: Objects which are already known (given) are less accented than newly introduced objects (Hirschberg, 1992; Horne *et al.*, 1993). The relationship between higher linguistic levels and prosody is further explained in Chapter 13 of this volume.

A Case Study: The SVOX TTS System for German

In this section, we present a particular TTS system in more detail, namely the SVOX system for German, which has been developed at our laboratory.

Comparing the two surface forms text and speech (as shown in Figure 1), one notices that their properties are very different: Text consists of discrete symbols (out of a small set) that form clearly separated words and sentences, whereas the speech signal properties vary continuously, i.e. phones in general neither have well-defined characteristics nor exact boundaries, and they are heavily influenced by neighbouring phones and by the prosodic context.

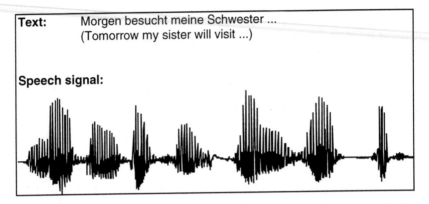

Figure 1. Surface forms: Text *vs.* speech. Text consists of discrete abstract symbols, whereas the speech signal varies continuously, and no clear boundaries are visible between speech sounds.

Apart from the phonetic content, speech signals also reflect speaker characteristics, whereas the corresponding text is speaker-independent. Therefore it seems reasonable to separate the text-to-speech task into a speaker-independent and a speaker-dependent part (Figure 2). The purpose of the speaker-independent part is to transform the input text into an abstract, i.e. speaker-independent representation of the speech to be produced. This phonological representation includes the phonetic transcription of the words, the word and sentence accents, and the phrase boundaries. This speaker-independent part of the text-to-speech system is called transcription.

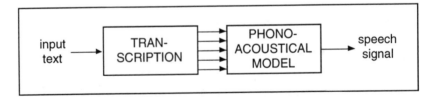

Figure 2. The two main parts of the SVOX system: The transcription performs the speaker-independent symbolic processing, and the phono-acoustical model converts the output of the transcription into the time-varying, speaker-dependent properties of the speech signal.

By means of a so-called phono-acoustical model that simulates an existing or a hypothetical speaker, the abstract linguistic representation is transformed into an adequate speech signal. Thus, the phono-acoustical model does not only implement some speech production mechanism, but also includes the generation of the prosodic parameters that determine the speech production substantially.

Speech Production Mechanism: Diphone Synthesis

Extraction of Speech Segments

In the SVOX system, diphones are used as speech segments to be concatenated. Diphones are speech segments that begin in the centre of one phone and end in the centre of the following one, and in particular include the transition between the two phones. The requirements for the extraction of such diphones from speech signals are as follows

a) It is obvious that the speech segments used for concatenation have to be extracted from carefully but naturally uttered high-quality speech signals. Therefore, most diphone segments have been extracted from the accented syllable of existing polysyllabic words (not nonsense words, as used in many projects).

b) The positions where the speech signal has to be cut, i.e. the boundaries of the resulting diphones, have to be selected in a way that the discontinuity caused by the concatenation of the diphones is minimal. The discontinuity is measured in terms of some spectral distance (the log area distance) across the concatenation.

Although both requirements are simple and clear, the second one is not easily met. The problem is that there exists no procedure that directly and reliably minimises the mean discontinuity between all neighbouring diphones. Therefore, so-called centroids have been used to determine the diphone boundaries. A centroid is a typical or averaged description of the spectral characteristics of a phone. With the help of the centroid, a diphone boundary, i.e. the centre of the phone concerned, is set at the position of minimum spectral distance between the signal and the respective centroid, as illustrated in Figure 3. The boundaries of most of the diphones in the SVOX system have been determined using this procedure. For diphones that start or end in a pause, however, the starting or ending point has been defined by means of a simple intensity criterion. (For further information, see Kaeslin, 1986).

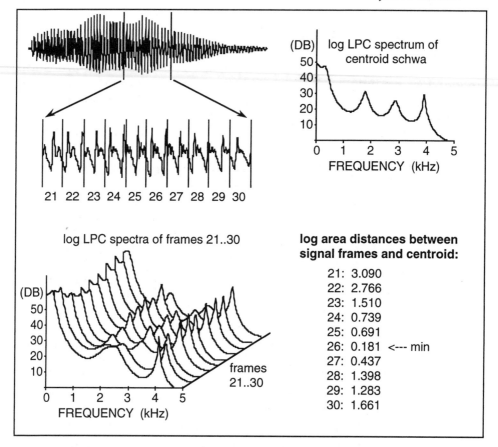

Figure 3. Locating the boundary between the two diphones [nə] and [ən] in a speech signal (top left) using the centroid of the [ə] phone (i.e. an average spectrum of the schwa sound): The diphone boundary is found at the point of minimum log area distance between the log LPC spectrum of the signal (bottom left) and the log LPC spectrum of the centroid (top right). The distance values (bottom right) show that the optimal diphone boundary lies between the signal frames 26 and 27.

Prosodic Manipulation of Speech Segments

The suprasegmental quality of synthesised speech signals depends on how the control of prosodic parameters is realised, i.e. the fundamental frequency, the intensity, and the duration of the segments. Therefore, speech synthesis based on the concatenation of diphones (or any other type of speech segments) must not simply put one segment after the other. The segments must rather be modified in terms of fundamental frequency, duration and intensity to meet the local prosodic requirements. These requirements are a function of where a segment is located in a word and in a sentence, of the accent level of the concerned syllable, of the speaking rate, of the speaker's intention, etc.

In SVOX, linear predictive coding (LPC) is applied to independently modify the different prosodic parameters of the segments. This allows the separation of the information concerning the spectral shape, the fundamental frequency, the intensity and the duration of short speech segments, and thus makes it possible to control the prosodic parameters individually. The linear predictive coding scheme (Makhoul, 1975) was originally used for source coding applications, i.e. to represent speech frames efficiently (short speech segments of some 10 to 20 ms length). This representation includes separate parameters for the description of the spectral shape (given in the form of a set of filter coefficients), of the intensity, of the periodicity and the duration of a speech frame.

From the LPC parameters, the corresponding speech frame may be approximatively reconstructed as shown in Figure 4: The periodicity parameter indicates which signal source has to be used: noise or periodic impulses (depending on whether the speech frame is unvoiced or voiced). The source signal of the required duration is multiplied with the intensity factor. The digital filter performs the required spectral shaping.

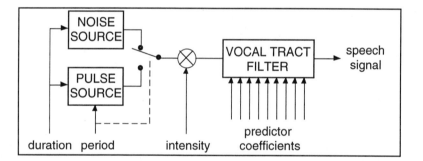

Figure 4. Speech signal generation by LPC synthesis: A source signal (white noise or a pulse sequence) is modified by a time-varying filter which is controlled by linear prediction coefficients.

It is possible to transform virtually any speech signal (regarded as a sequence of speech frames) into a corresponding sequence of LPC parameters and vice versa. Thus, transforming diphone segments into LPC parameters is an appropriate way of modifying prosodic parameters in natural speech: The fundamental frequency is easily controlled by adjusting the period of the impulses (for voiced frames only); the intensity is controlled by the appropriate factor; the duration is modified by reconstructing a longer or shorter frame of speech than the original frame size.

Transcription

The transcription transforms orthographic input text into an abstract phonological representation of the utterance to be synthesised. To achieve this, the input text is first subjected to a syntactic and morphological analysis. Higher-level linguistic analysis (semantics, pragmatics, discourse) is not feasible for a general-purpose TTS system for the time being. The text analysis stage is followed by a stage which generates the phonological representation of the utterance from the result of the previous analysis. The following sections describe the different transcription stages in more detail.

Text Pre-Processing

Most TTS systems carry out quite an elaborate text pre-processing at the start of the synthesis process, in which, for example, abbreviations are expanded to full words, numbers are converted into text form, and punctuation marks are separated from words. However, for a language like German, the appropriate place for such processing is in our view not before, but within a syntactic and morphological analysis. In our system, this kind of pre-processing has therefore been completely integrated with the syntactic and morphological analysis.

Syntactic and Morphological Analysis

One of the aims of our system was to have a common framework for the syntactic and morphological analysis of German sentences (Russi, 1992). The current system comprises a full-form lexicon (mainly function words, proper names, and abbreviations), a morpheme lexicon (prefixes, suffixes, stems, inflection endings), a sentence grammar, and a word grammar. The grammars were originally written in the UTN formalism (unification-based transition networks; Russi, 1992), a modified version of the well-known ATN formalism (Woods, 1970), but have recently been converted into the equally powerful but somewhat more concise and more easily readable DCG formalism (definite clause grammars; Pereira and Warren, 1980).

Since all lexicon entries in our system also contain phonetic transcriptions, the phonetic transcription of words is usually obtained by concatenation of the phonetic transcriptions of the individual parts of the words. In this regular case, we do not need to apply so-called letter-to-sound rules as many other TTS systems do in order to obtain the phonetic transcription of a word from the graphemic form. If, however, words are not regularly analysable in terms of known morphemes, we adopted a "fall-back" strategy which fits very smoothly into the regular word analysis environment: there is an additional "stem grammar" which defines the possible decompositions of German and foreign word stems into consonant and vowel clusters. The corresponding phonetic transcription of the vowel and consonant clusters then yields the phonetic transcription of the unknown stem. This additional stem grammar (which may be considered a formulation of the phonotactic and graphotactic rules of the German language) and the corresponding lexicon of consonant and vowel clusters have been written in the same formalism as the other lexicons and grammars (Traber, 1993).

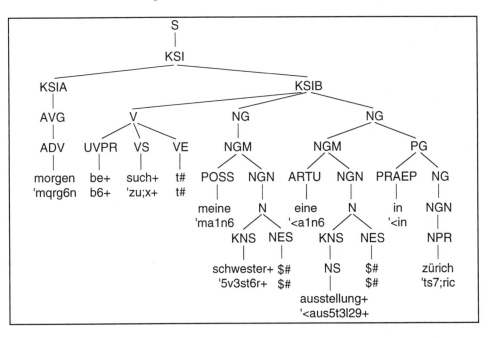

Figure 5. Syntax tree generated by SVOX for the sentence "Morgen besucht meine Schwester eine Ausstellung in Zürich." ("Tomorrow my sister will visit an exhibition in Zurich.") The leaves of the tree (words or morphemes) show the graphemic and the corresponding phonetic lexicon entries, where '+' denotes a morpheme boundary and '$#' denotes an empty inflection ending. The higher tree nodes represent morpho-syntactic categories (e.g. N = noun, VS = verb stem, UVPR = unaccented verb prefix, VE = verb ending, NG = noun group, PRAEP = preposition, PG = prepositional group, KSI = declarative sentence with subject in non-first position).

In addition to these lexicons and grammars, there are also some rules (so-called two-level rules) which convert graphemic and phonetic surface forms (i.e. the "normal" graphemic and phonetic forms as they are usually written) into the lexicon forms and vice versa (Russi, 1992). These rules handle different phenomena that occur at morpheme boundaries in German (such as the insertion or deletion of an 'e' or schwa between a verb stem and a verb ending), and they convert for example umlauts written as "ae", "oe", and "ue" into the lexical forms "ä", "ö", and "ü".

The output of the syntactic analysis in our TTS system is an annotated syntax tree which consists of the constituent hierarchy as well as the phonetic transcriptions of all words and morphemes of the sentence. Figure 5 shows an example of such a tree produced by the TTS system.

Accentuation

morgen be<u>such</u>t meine <u>Schwes</u>ter eine <u>Aus</u>stellung in <u>Zü</u>rich				
initial accents:				
(1)	(1)	(1)	(1)	(1)
after first cycle:				
(1)	(1)	(1)	(2	1)
after second cycle:				
(1)	(2	2	3	1)
preliminary sentence accentuation:				
(2	3	3	4	1)

Figure 6. Accentuation by cyclic application of the so-called nuclear stress rule. Initially, all content words receive a primary accent (1). The accentuation rules then specify one element in each syntactic constituent which retains the primary accent, whereas all other accents within the same constituent are reduced (i.e. increased in value).

To derive accentuation from syntactic and lexical information only (as most present TTS systems attempt to do) can clearly not be done perfectly, but the situation is not completely hopeless either. In the SVOX system, accents are derived from the syntactic structure of a sentence by applying two main rules (shown in Figure 6):

1) Some word categories (mostly function words) are declared to be unstressed; all other words initially receive a primary accent (accent level 1) on their word stress position.
2) The so-called nuclear stress rule is applied in cyclic fashion from the leaves of the syntactic tree to the root, thereby weighting accents against each other (Kiparsky, 1966; Selkirk, 1984); the nuclear stress rule states that each syntactic constituent has a nucleus (e.g. the noun within a noun phrase), which remains primary-accented, whereas all other accents within the same constituent are reduced (i.e. increased in

numeric value); in our system, a collection of syntactic subtree patterns define the nucleus position of each possible syntactic constituent.

The result of this accentuation procedure is a sentence in which each syllable carries a certain accent value. These values will then be modified again in a later step.

Phrasing

morgen	besucht	meine	Schwester	eine	Ausstellung	in	Zürich
initial boundaries:							
#0 #1	#2	#4	#2 #4	#3	#4 #0		
clitic word							
#0 #1	#2	#2	#3 #0				
rhythmic melting, cycle 1:							
#0 #1	#2	#2	#0				
rhythmic melting, cycle 2:							
#0 #1	#2	#0					
final phrasing:							
morgen # besucht	meine	Schwester # eine	Ausstellung	in	Zürich		

Figure 7. Phrasing by iterative deletion of initial phrase boundaries. The initial boundaries are set according to the syntactic separation strength between adjacent words (#0 denotes the strong sentence boundary, #1, #2, #3, etc., denote successively weaker boundaries). After removing the boundaries between clitic (i.e. completely unaccented) words and the closest neighbouring accented words, boundaries are further deleted in order of increasing strength under the condition that preliminary phrases around a boundary are too short to remain independent.

The phrasing algorithm that is used in our system is a slightly modified version of an algorithm described in Bierwisch (1966), which works in the following steps (shown in Figure 7):

1) An initial boundary is set between each pair of neighbouring words; the strength of this boundary is set to the level of the first common ancestor node of both words in the syntactic tree (i.e. the stronger the syntactic connection between words, the less the initial separation strength).

2) Unaccented (clitic) words are enclosed in that neighbouring phrase from which they are less separated; this is achieved by deleting the weaker one of the boundaries to the left and right of the unaccented word.

3) Boundaries are deleted further in the order of their strength (from weak boundaries to stronger ones) under the condition that preliminary phrases around a boundary are too short (in terms of number of accents

and syllables) to remain independent (rhythmic melting of neighbouring preliminary phrases); otherwise the boundaries remain.

The result of this algorithm is a sentence split up into syntactically motivated phrases.

Accent Renormalisation and Phonological Representation

The application of the nuclear stress rule in the accentuation procedure may lead to unnaturally many accentuation levels which are not phonetically meaningful (it is impossible to distinguish more than three or four accent levels in speech). The initial accentuation is therefore modified again after the phrasing of the sentence has been determined: Within each phrase, all accent strengths are increased as much as possible, but the original hierarchical ordering is maintained; this ensures that relative prominences of syllables within a phrase remain as predicted by the accentuation rules and that each phrase receives a primary accent (the phrase accent), while keeping the accent values in a reasonable range.

   The result of all steps in the transcription part of our TTS system is the phonological representation of an utterance, which comprises the phonetic transcription of all words, an accent value for each syllable, and phrase boundaries. An example of such a representation is depicted in Figure 8.

---

[1]mɔr-gən # bə-[2]zuˡxt maḭ-nə [1]ʃvɛs-tɐ # laḭnə [2]aus-ʃtɛ-luŋ ǀɪn [1]t̬sy:-rɪç

Figure 8. Phonological representation of an utterance consisting of the phonetic transcriptions of words (including syllable boundaries), accent values ([x]; otherwise unaccented syllable), and phrase boundaries (#).

Phono-Acoustical Model

The phono-acoustical model transforms the abstract phonological representation of an utterance into the physical parameters of the speech signal. In contrast to the speaker-independent transcription, the phono-acoustical model attempts to imitate one specific speaker as well as possible. The modules of the phono-acoustical model are described in the following sections.

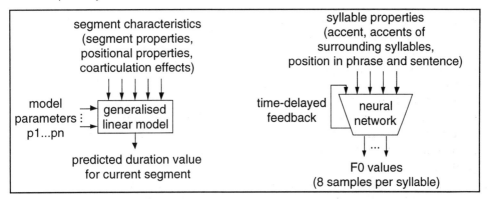

Figure 9. Trainable models for the realisation of phonological data in terms of acoustic prosodic parameters: A generalised linear model is applied to compute segmental durations from numerically encoded segment properties (left), and a recurrent neural network is used to generate fundamental frequency contours from encoded syllable properties (right). For the application in the TTS system, the model parameters were estimated automatically from natural-speech data.

Duration Control

The duration control module generates duration values for all segments of the artificial speech signal based on different factors, such as the kind of the current segment (fricative, sonorant, ...), the kind of the surrounding segments, accentuation, position of the segment within the syllable, the foot, the phrase, and the sentence. These factors, which are known to influence the segmental duration, can easily be derived from the phonological representation of an utterance. The duration values in our system are generated from a binary coding of these factors and combinations of these factors by applying a so-called generalised linear model (Figure 9). In this statistical model, the output value is a linear function of the input values. The coefficients used in this linear function are parameters that were statistically estimated such that the model optimally predicts the segmental durations of a set of given natural sentences (Huber, 1990).

Fundamental Frequency Control

In our system, the most successful fundamental frequency control was achieved using a recurrent neural network (Traber, 1992). Basically, a neural network can simply be regarded as a non-linear statistical model with a large number of parameters. These parameters (called weights) are estimated in a training procedure such that they optimally predict a set of given outputs from the corresponding inputs. This approach to Fo generation is therefore closely related to the approach taken for duration control.

Fo contours in our system are generated syllable-wise (Figure 9). For each syllable in the utterance, the accent value of the concerned syllable and the accent values of a number of surrounding syllables are fed into the network together with some attributes describing segmental properties of the syllable as well as the position of the syllable within the phrase and the sentence. The output of the network is the Fo pattern of the current syllable (represented by eight samples of the Fo contour). The concatenation of these syllable patterns yields the Fo contour of the whole utterance. The feedback in our neural network implements a short-term memory and is intended to model temporal phenomena such as declination. Figure 10 shows an example Fo contour generated by our TTS system.

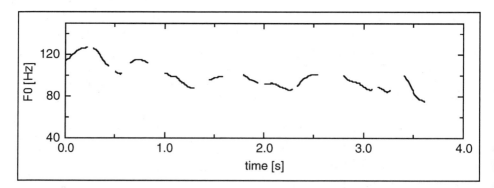

Figure 10. Fo contour generated by the neural network for the utterance "Morgen besucht meine Schwester eine Ausstellung in Zürich." (voiced signal parts shown only).

Signal Generation

In a last step, diphones (represented by their LPC coefficients) are concatenated according to the phonetic transcription of the utterance, and LPC synthesis is applied to generate the speech signal using the fundamental frequency and duration values generated by the corresponding modules.

Conclusion

Today, there exists a large number of different text-to-speech systems for a variety of languages. Although the overall structures of different systems may look quite alike, the internal processing can differ considerably. Therefore, instead of explaining many different solutions to the various text-to-speech processing stages, the aim of this chapter has been to show the internal structure of an example system in more detail. The reader is invited to compare the approaches taken in the present system with the different solutions adopted in, e.g. the MITalk system (Allen *et al.*, 1987), the KTH system (Carlson and Granström, 1986b), or the CNET system (Larreur *et al.*, 1989).

Although some existing TTS systems perform quite well at the task of reading aloud information in a "neutral" speaking style, the production of completely natural-sounding speech and the extraction of higher-level (semantic, pragmatic) information from orthographic text, and its appropriate realisation in terms of acoustic parameters, remain major challenges for the future.

References

Allen, J., Hunnicutt, M. S., & Klatt, D. (1987). *From text to speech: The MITalk system.* Cambridge, England: Cambridge University Press.

Aubergé, V. (1992). Developing a structured lexicon for synthesis of prosody. In G. Bailly & C. Benoît (Eds.), *Talking Machines: Theories, Models, and Designs* (pp. 307-322). Amsterdam: North-Holland.

Bachenko, J., Fitzpatrick, E., & Wright, C. E. (1986). The contribution of parsing to prosodic phrasing in an experimental text-to-speech system. *Proceedings of the 24th Annual Meeting of the Association for Computational Linguistics.*

Bierwisch, M. (1966). Regeln für die Intonation deutscher Sätze. *Studia Grammatica, VII* (pp. 99-201). Berlin: Akademie-Verlag.

Campbell, W. N. (1990). Analog I/O nets for syllable timing. *Speech Communication: Special Issue on Neural Nets and Speech, 9,* 57-61.

Carlson, R., & Granström, B. (1986a). A search for durational rules in a real-speech data base. *Phonetica, 43,* 140-154.

Carlson, R., & Granström, B. (1986b). Linguistic processing in the KTH multi-lingual text-to-speech system. *Proceedings of the International Conference on Acoustics, Speech, and Signal Processing (ICASSP)* (pp. 2403-2406). Tokyo, Japan.

Cohen, A., Collier, R., & 't Hart, J. (1982). Declination: Construct or intrinsic feature of speech pitch? *Phonetica, 39,* 254-273.

Coker, C. H., Church, K. W., & Liberman, M. Y. (1990). Morphology and rhyming: Two powerful alternatives to letter-to-sound rules for speech synthesis. *Proceedings of the ESCA Workshop on Speech Synthesis* (pp. 83-86). Autrans, France.

Collier, R. (1991). Multi-language intonation synthesis. *Journal of Phonetics, 19.*

Dedina, M. J., & Nusbaum, H. C. (1991). PRONOUNCE: A program for pronunciation by analogy. *Computer Speech and Language, 5,* 55-64.

Fujisaki, H. (1981). Dynamic characteristics of voice fundamental frequency in speech and singing. Acoustical analysis and physiological interpretations. *Speech Transmission Laboratory Quarterly Progress and Status Report STL-QPSR (KTH Stockholm), 1,* 1-20.

Gee, J. P., & Grosjean, F. (1983). Performance structures: A psycholinguistic and linguistic appraisal. *Cognitive Psychology, 15,* 411-458.

Hirschberg, J. (1991). Using text analysis to predict intonational boundaries. *Proceedings of the 2nd European Conference on Speech Communication and Technology (Eurospeech)* (pp. 1275-1278). Genova, Italy.

Hirschberg, J. (1992). Using discourse context to guide pitch accent decisions in synthetic speech. In G. Bailly & C. Benoît (Eds.), *Talking Machines: Theories, Models, and Designs* (pp. 367-376). Amsterdam: North-Holland.

Horne, M., Filipsson, M., Johansson, C., Ljungqvist, M., & Lindström, A. (1993). Improving the prosody in TTS systems: Morphological and lexical-semantic methods for the tracking of "new" *vs.* "given" information. *Proceedings of the ESCA Workshop on Prosody* (pp. 208-211). Lund, Sweden.

Huber, K. (1990). A statistical model of duration control for speech synthesis. *Proceedings of the 5th European Signal Processing Conference (EUSIPCO)* (pp. 1127-1130). Barcelona, Spain.

Hunnicutt, S., Meng, H., Seneff, S., & Zue, V. (1993). Reversible letter-to-sound sound-to-letter rules based on parsing word morphology. *Proceedings of the 3rd European Conference on Speech Communication and Technology (Eurospeech)* (pp. 763-766). Berlin Germany.

Kaeslin, H. (1986). A systematic approach to the extraction of diphone elements from natural speech. *IEEE Transactions on Acoustics, Speech, and Signal Processing (ASSP), 34,* 264-271.

Kiparsky, P. (1966). Über den deutschen Akzent. *Studia Grammatica, VII* (pp. 69-98). Berlin: Akademie-Verlag.

Klatt, D. H. (1979). Synthesis by rule of segmental durations in English sentences. In B. Lindblom and S. Öhman (Eds.), *Frontiers of Speech Communication Research* (pp. 287-301). London: Academic Press.

Kohler, K. J. (1991). Prosody in speech synthesis: The interplay between basic research and TTS application. *Journal of Phonetics, 19,* 121-138.

Larreur, D., Emerard, F., & Marty, F. (1989). Linguistic and prosodic processing for a text-to-speech synthesis system. *Proceedings of the First European Conference on Speech Communication and Technology (Eurospeech)* (pp. 510-513). Paris, France.

Ljolje, A., & Fallside, F. (1986). Synthesis of natural sounding pitch contours in isolated utterances using Hidden Markov Models. *IEEE Transactions on Acoustics, Speech, and Signal Processing (ASSP), 34,* 1074-1080.

Makhoul, J. (1975). Linear prediction: A tutorial review. *Proceedings of the IEEE, 63,* 561-580.

Moulines, E., & Charpentier, F. (1990). Pitch-synchronous waveform processing techniques for text-to-speech synthesis using diphones. *Speech Communication, 9,* 453-467.

Öhman, S. (1967). Word and sentence intonation: A quantitative model. *Speech Transmission Laboratory Quarterly Progress and Status Report STL-QPSR (KTH Stockholm), 2-3,* 20-54.

Pereira, F. C. N., & Warren, D. H. D. (1980). Definite clause grammars for language analysis — A survey of the formalism and a comparison with augmented transition networks. *Artificial Intelligence, 13,* 231-278.

Pierrehumbert, J. (1981). Synthesizing intonation. *Journal of the Acoustical Society of America, 70,* 985-995.

Pitrelli, J. F., & Zue, V. W. (1989). A hierarchical model for phoneme duration in American English. *Proceedings of the First European Conference on Speech Communication and Technology (Eurospeech)* (pp. 324-327). Paris, France.

Quené, H., & Kager, R. (1992). The derivation of prosody for text-to-speech from prosodic sentence structure. *Computer Speech and Language, 6,* 77-98.

Russi, T. (1992). A framework for morphological and syntactic analysis and its application in a text-to-speech system for German. In G. Bailly & C. Benoît (Eds.), *Talking Machines: Theories, Models, and Designs* (pp. 163-182). Amsterdam: North-Holland.

Sagisaka, Y. (1990). On the prediction of global Fo shape for Japanese text-to-speech. *Proceedings of the International Conference on Acoustics, Speech, and Signal Processing (ICASSP)* (pp. 325-328).

Schroeder, M. R. (1993). A brief history of synthetic speech. *Speech Communication, 13,* 231-237.

Sejnowski, T. J., & Rosenberg, C. R. (1986). *NETtalk: A Parallel Network That Learns to Read Aloud.* Johns Hopkins University Technical Report JHU/EECS-86/01.

Selkirk, E. O. (1984). *Phonology and syntax: The relation between sound and structure.* Cambridge, MA: MIT Press.

Traber, C. (1992). Fo generation with a database of natural Fo patterns and with a neural network. In G. Bailly & C. Benoît (Eds.), *Talking Machines: Theories, Models, and Designs* (pp. 287-304). Amsterdam: North-Holland.

Traber, C. (1993). Syntactic processing and prosody control in the SVOX TTS system for German. *Proceedings of the 3rd European Conference on Speech Communication and Technology (Eurospeech)* (pp. 2099-2102). Berlin, Germany.

Woods, W. A. (1970). Transition network grammars for natural language analysis. *Communications of the ACM, 13,* 591-606.

Formant Synthesis   6

Thomas Styger and *Eric Keller*

Laboratoire d'analyse informatique de la parole (LAIP)
Université de Lausanne, CH-1015 LAUSANNE, Switzerland

A simple approach to the basic "source-filter" model of speech production, as used for synthesis purposes, is presented in this chapter. In the introduction, a short review of the principal synthesis methods is given. Direct synthesis, synthesis using a production model and articulatory synthesis are introduced succinctly. The source-filter model is then described. Topics such as voicing and friction sources, vocal tract filter and lip radiation are summarised. Finally Klatt's formant synthesiser is presented as an application of this theory.

The purpose of the first section of this chapter is to provide an insight into the main speech synthesis techniques that are in common use. The principles of these approaches are exposed to give a short overview and to prepare the reader for the main topic of this chapter, which is formant synthesis. This synthesiser type is based on the source-filter theory of speech production, which will be introduced in the second section. The last section is dedicated to a specific implementation of the above-described theory: The Klatt formant synthesiser.

An Overview of Synthesis Techniques

Automatic speech signal generation on computers is commonly called "speech synthesis". The various generation techniques can be divided into three classes (Calliope, 1989):
— direct synthesis,
— synthesis using a production model,
— vocal tract simulation.

Direct Synthesis

In direct synthesis, the speech signal is generated by direct manipulation of its wave form representation. *Wave form concatenation;*is representative of this synthesis category (Cooper *et al.*, 1951). In this approach, several fundamental periods of pre-recorded phonemes are simply concatenated, or "glued together". The phonemes are then connected to form words and sentences.

This simple technique requires very little computing power or disk space. However, it results in relatively poor quality, which is only acceptable in a few applications, such as in toys. In this method, coarticulation phenomena[1] are not generally taken into account, which is likely to be the reason that speech produced by this technique is of limited intelligibility (Klatt, 1987).

Another direct synthesis technique is the *channel vocoder;*(Dudley, 1939). This procedure generates signals by activating a number of frequency channels, in proportion to the distribution of formant energy in the spectrum (i.e. according to the *vocal tract transfer function*). To simulate the voice fundamental frequency (F_0) source, an evenly-spaced train of impulses is applied. In fricative segments, a noise generator is substituted for this source.

The advantage of this technique is that synthesis proceeds by direct inversion of spectral analysis results, that it is entirely automatic, and that information relating to the excitation is completely independent of information about the transfer function. However, the quality obtained in this manner remains limited, due to the small number of channels used, i.e. because of the relatively gross quantification of the spectrum. For these reasons, the technique is no longer used in current speech synthesis.

Synthesis Using a Speech Production Model

Methods that simulate the speech production mechanisms are mainly based on the source-filter theory. In this approach, a linear filter simulates the vocal tract, which in turn is driven by an adequate source.

Two main techniques belong to this category: The formant synthesiser (Klatt, 1980) and diphone concatenation (O'Shaughnessy *et al.*, 1988), using a linear prediction coding technique (LPC) (Atal and Hanauer, 1971).

---

[1] That is, the fact that the same phoneme is produced quite differently, and has rather different spectral characteristics, when appearing in one phonetic context or in another.

Formant Synthesiser

In formant synthesis, the basic assumption is that the vocal tract transfer function can be satisfactorily modelled by simulating formant frequencies and formant amplitudes. The synthesis thus consists of the artificial reconstruction of the formant characteristics to be produced. This is done by exciting a set of resonators by a voicing source or noise generator to achieve the desired speech spectrum, and by controlling the excitation source to simulate either voicing and voicelessness. The addition of a set of anti-resonators furthermore allows the simulation of nasal tract effects, fricatives and plosives.

The specification of about 20 or more such parameters can lead to a satisfactory restitution of the speech signal. The advantage of this technique is that its parameters are highly correlated with the production and propagation of sound in the oral tract. The main current drawback of this approach is that automatic techniques of specifying formant parameters are still largely unsatisfactory, and that consequently, the majority of parameters must still be manually optimised.

Diphone Concatenation Synthesiser

Most current commercial applications use various concatenation techniques, i.e. techniques where segments of speech are tied together to form a complete speech chain. These techniques require a fair bit of manual preparation of the appropriate speech segments, but once the segment inventory is constituted, only moderate computational power is needed to chain the segments into an acceptable speech stream.

As indicated above, attempts at building utterances from *phoneme* wave forms have been of limited success, due to coarticulation problems. The use of larger concatenative units has been more successful. Particularly diphones (i.e. excised wave forms from the middle of one phoneme to the middle of the next one) appear to handle coarticulation problems reasonably well. Diphones are concatenated at points were there is a minimum degree of coarticulation, so that transitions at the diphone boundaries must be subjected to a minimum of smoothing.

The development of the linear predictive coding (LPC) technique for speech analysis and re-synthesis has made it possible to store relatively large inventories of high quality speech wave forms in limited space. This model describes a signal sample as a linear combination of the preceding samples. The algorithm calculates model coefficients by minimising the mean square error between the predicted signal and the original signal. These coefficients are recalculated every 5 to 20 ms. About 10 to 16 coefficients are necessary to obtain an acceptable synthesis quality. The system is in fact an all-pole linear filter that simulates the source spectrum and the vocal tract transfer function. The technique has many advantages, such as the automatic analysis of the original signal, fairly easy algorithmic integration, and fidelity to the original sound.

However, among the problems with diphone synthesis remains the danger of major discontinuities occurring at the interface between two halves of a vowel, in cases where dissimilar formant targets are used on the two sides of the interface. In severe cases of formant discontinuity, this produces a bi-vocalic sound quality and an audible discontinuity at the diphone boundary. Also, the model is not well-adapted to nasal and fricative simulation, because the vocal tract model contains only poles, while nasal and fricative spectra involve prominent zeroes, as well as poles.

Synthesis by Vocal Tract Simulation

The preceding techniques attempt, by simple computational techniques, to (re-)generate a signal that is perceptually optimal. They are intended to produce a wave whose spectrum is as close as possible to the real speech signal without simulating any aspect of the human vocal tract. As indicated, such techniques simply attempt to *limit* the negative effects of the coarticulation phenomenon.

A number of relatively recent vocal tract simulation techniques attempt to deal directly with the coarticulation problem by simulating the physical behaviour of the speech production apparatus (Scully, 1990; Maeda, 1990). Such an *articulatory model*;reconstitutes the shape of the vocal tract as a function of the position of the phonatory organs (lips, jaw, tongue, velum). The signal is calculated by a mathematical simulation of the air flow through the vocal tract. The control parameters of such a synthesiser are: sub-glottal pressure, vocal cord tension, and the relative position of the different articulatory organs.

This technique might seem seductive: A more physical model should be easier to control than a functional one. Indeed, in laboratory use, this approach has produced some good preliminary results. However, many problems remain to be solved. For example, articulatory data obtained by cineradiographic recordings are relatively imprecise, and do not produce a complete inventory of articulatory configurations to be used in synthesis. On the other hand, the vocal cord source is difficult to model for vowels, and the source is even more difficult to generate in the case of stops and obstruents. Currently, this kind of synthesiser is therefore still reserved for fundamental research.

A Classification of Synthesis Techniques

It is interesting to consider the classification presented in the preceding paragraphs in terms of a number of operational parameters (see Figure 1):

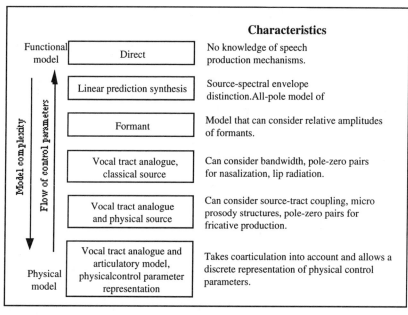

Figure 1. Classification of different synthesis techniques as a function of the model complexity and the flow of the control parameters.

— *decreasing information flow* required to generate the control parameters for synthesis. In direct synthesis, a new command is required each fundamental period cycle, while in the case of the articulatory model, a new command is generated only at the beginning of each articulatory gesture,

— *increasing model complexity* that integrates a progressive knowledge of the production mechanism,

— a progressive distinction between *functional models* that simulate speech by a set of global parameters, and *physical models* that simulate the details of the physical process.

Source-Filter Model

Since the most prominent synthesis techniques in use today are based on the *source-filter* concept, it is interesting to consider in some detail the different aspects of this theory. The source-filter theory states that the vocal tract can be modelled as a linear filter that varies over time. The filter (i.e. a set of resonators) is excited by a source, which can be either a simulation of vocal cord vibration for voicing, or a noise that simulates a constriction somewhere in the vocal tract. The sound wave is created in the vocal tract, then radiates trough the lips (Figure 2).

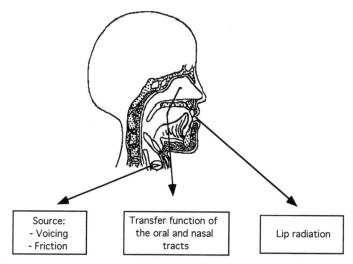

Figure 2. Concept of the source-filter model. The model is divided into tree separate parts, namely the source (voicing and friction), the filter (implementing the transfer function of oral and nasal tract), and lip radiation.

In this model, there is no interaction between the source and the filter, other than that the fact that the filter imposes its resonant characteristics on the source. Hence, the individual acoustic properties of the source and the filter can be separately simulated. The vocal tract filter can be modelled as an acoustic tube with a varying cross-sectional area formed by the pharynx, the oral cavity, the nasal cavity, and the lips. The resonance effects observed in this tube are in turn simulated by a linear filter.

Source Modelling

Let us consider each part of this model in detail.

Speech sounds may be divided into those produced with a periodic vibration of the vocal cords (voiced sounds), and those generated without vocal-cord vibrations, but with plosive or friction noise (voiceless sounds). For this reason, two excitation sources are needed for synthesis:

(i) a source producing a quasi-periodic wave, the voicing source, and

(ii) a noise generator, the friction source.

The Voicing Source

The excitation for voiced sounds provided by the vocal fold vibration can be represented by the general block diagram of Figure 3.

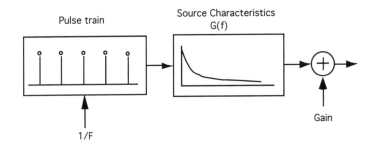

Figure 3. Block diagram of a basic voicing source model. It simulates the glottal wave by filtering an impulse train. A gain control allows the amplitude setting for voicing.

The model is composed of an impulse train generator that produces pulses at the rate of one per fundamental period. This impulse excitation simulates the generation of acoustic energy at the instant of the opening of the vocal cords. This signal then drives a linear filter whose frequency response G(f) approximates the glottal wave form. The function G(f) must be chosen so that it approximates accurately the spectrum of the source. At the end, a gain control device allows the adjustment of the voicing amplitude.

The *source spectral characteristics* are directly related to the type of vocal cord activity that is modelled (Klatt and Klatt, 1990). As shown in Figure 4.a, different maximal glottal openings (as in laryngealised, modal and breathy voice) result in various wave forms. The temporal characteristics of each signal are shown in Figure 4.b, and Figure 4.c shows their respective frequency characteristics. It can be seen that the transfer function has low-pass characteristics. The spectral slope can vary between approximately -12 dB/octave and -24 dB/octave. This value is directly related to the duration of glottal opening. For instance, spectral roll-off is smooth in the case of a short opening duration.

Different models have been proposed for characterising the *transfer function* G(f). The simplest consists of a low-pass filter whose spectral slope can be varied (Klatt, 1980). In the case of the model presented in Figure 3, the impulse train is simply sent through such a filter to obtain a good approximation of the glottal wave form.

Some more recent models represent G(f) with a more accurate mathematical function (Titze, 1989; Fant and Liljencrants, 1985) or a mechanical simulation of the vocal cord vibration (Ishizaka and Flanagan, 1972; Flanagan *et al.*, 1975). These models can introduce some irregularities into the fundamental period cycle, which adds more naturalness to the voice (Klatt, 1987).

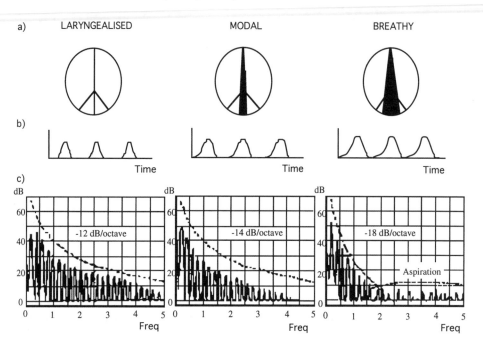

Figure 4. Various glottal source characteristics for laryngealised, modal and breathy vowels. a) Schematic glottal opening for different voice qualities. b) Glottal volume velocity waveform. An increasing opening at the arythenoids is characterised by a longer open period and a less abrupt closure event. c) Source spectra. A progressive opening of the vocal folds is characterised by an increased spectral slope. In case of breathy voicing, the weaker high-frequency harmonics are replaced by aspiration noise (Klatt and Klatt, 1990).

Friction Source

Voiceless sounds are generated when the vocal cords are in a non-vibrating mode and are held open. This allows the air to flow unobstructed through the vocal tract, where it is inhibited at some point to create friction or a plosion. This phenomenon is due to a pressure drop across a constriction formed in the vocal tract, where the flow of air becomes turbulent.

The usual model for the friction source consists of a pseudo-random white noise generator and a gain parameter to allow an adjustment of friction amplitude. Nevertheless this model is not very accurate, since the actual friction source is not located in the larynx as the model states, but at the location of the main constriction where the airflow becomes turbulent (Badin, 1989). The exact mechanisms involved in the creation of this acoustically complex phenomenon are still under discussion, so that a fully satisfying friction model for synthesis purposes is still some time away.

Vocal Tract Modelling

The source-filter modelling of *vocal tract behaviour* is intended to simulate the formant characteristics of the various speech sounds. It is an efficient approach allowing precise simulation of almost all phonemes. In the initial model that we will discuss here, the resonance characteristics depend only on their respective configuration and are independent of the source. In other words, it is assumed that no source-tract interaction occurs. Thus this supposition is not entirely realistic, because a non-linear coupling exists between the glottal source and the first vocal tract resonance modes (Fant, 1986; Stevens and Bickley, 1986).

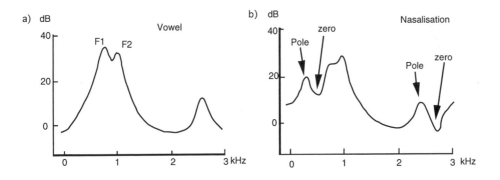

Figure 5. Example of the frequency spectrum of a vowel (a) and a nasalised vowel (b). Oral sounds, such as vowels, can be simulated with an all-pole system (formants), whereas nasalisation implies a pole and zero system (formants and anti-formants).

For oral sounds, such as vowels, the acoustic wave form generated by the source is propagated through the vocal tract. As the acoustic wave form moves through the vocal tract, some of its frequencies are augmented, whereas some others are depressed. Which of the frequencies undergo enhancement depends on the particular configuration of the speech organs, that is, on the position of the jaw, the tongue and the lips. The frequencies occurring at the main resonant areas of the vocal tract for a given sound are the formants. These resonances may be assumed to behave as a resonating all-pole filter, and can thus be modelled with a set of *poles*. These poles are identified as "peaks" in the frequency spectrum (Figure 5.a).

When the nasal cavities are coupled with the vocal tract, a certain number of anti-resonances (anti-formants) also appear in the spectrum, as a result of the sound-damping properties of the nasal cavity. Those are identified as "troughs" or *zeros* in the transfer function. Hence for nasals and nasalised vowels, the transfer function has to contain both poles and zeroes (Figure 5.b). It should be mentioned that zeroes also appear in the complex articulation of fricatives and stops.

It has been shown that a good approximation can be obtained by modelling each formant with an electrical resonator (Fant 1960). The latter is a band-pass filter (pole filter) whose characteristics are shown in Figure 6.a. Two parameters may be specified, the resonance frequency F and the bandwidth BW. An anti-formant can be modelled with a band-stop filter (zero filter) having the inverse characteristics. Figure 6.b shows the generation of the first four formants as a superposition of resonators at different frequencies.

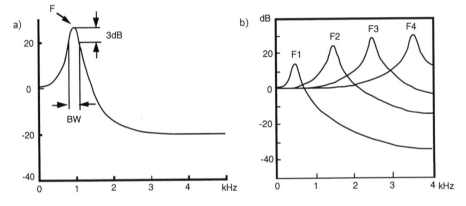

Figure 6. Transfer function of the formant resonators. a) Spectrum of a single formant resonator. The resonator is a second order low-pass filter characterised by its centre frequency F and its bandwidth BW. b) Contribution of each formant to the amplitude spectrum.

The transfer function of the entire tract is obtained by connecting these different circuits according to two possible combinations (Figure 7). In the first configuration, the resonators are combined in parallel. In practice, this corresponds to the successive *addition* of each filter's transfer function. Each resonator is preceded by a gain which adjusts the relative amplitude of the given spectral peak. In the second case, synthesis operates by connecting the resonators in cascade, a process which results in the *multiplication* of the spectrum by each of the successive transfer functions.

There are theoretical premises for these distinctions. A parallel formant synthesiser allows for the direct control of each formant amplitude and sums the outputs of the simultaneously excited formant resonators. While not an accurate acoustic imitation of vocal tract behaviour in speech, parallel synthesisers are better adapted at producing consonants than vowels (Holmes, 1983). The serial connection of the formant resonators adds the effect of each higher resonance to the final output, and thus produces a direct replica of the total formant energy distribution, which corresponds quite well to the natural resonance mode of the vocal tract. This approach constitutes a fairly faithful imitation of vocal tract behaviour, and as a result, serial synthesisers are particularly good for synthesising vowel sounds.

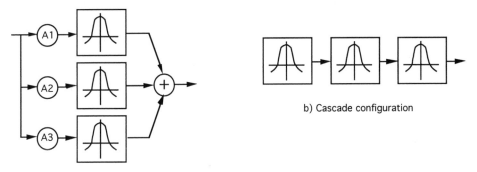

a) Parallel configuration

b) Cascade configuration

Figure 7. Two ways of combining formant resonators. a) Parallel configuration. b) Cascade configuration.

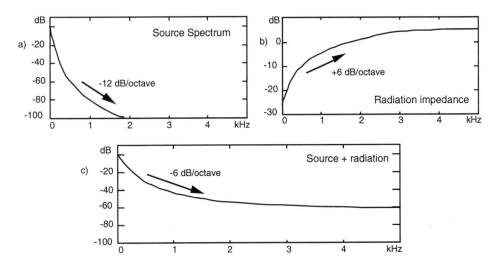

Figure 8. Spectral characteristics of the voicing source and lip radiation. a) Source spectrum with its approximate -12 dB roll off. b) Spectrum of the radiation characteristic. c) Combined effect of the source spectrum and radiation characteristic. The tilts caused by the combined -12 dB/octave roll-off in the glottal airflow and the +6 dB/octave lift of the radiation effect cause the voiced speech spectrum to fall off at an approximate rate of -6 dB/octave.

Lip Radiation

At the mouth opening, the acoustic wave ceases to be constrained in its propagation. This modification of the propagation medium leads to reaction forces that the wave has to counter. This is identified by the modification of the radiation impedance, whose characteristics vary with the wave frequency. The frequency spectrum of a radiated speech sound is tilted upward by approximately +6 dB/octave (Figure 8.b), since high frequency components are better transmitted through the opening than their low frequency counterparts. In synthesis practice, this can be simulated by the application of a high-pass filter.

It has to be noted that the tilts caused by the combined -12 dB/octave roll-off in the glottal airflow and the +6 dB/octave lift of the radiation effect cause the voiced speech spectrum to fall off at an approximate rate of -6 dB/octave (Figure 8.c).

Example of a Formant Synthesiser

To conclude this chapter, we shall outline a prominent implementation of the electrical analogue synthesis technique, i.e. the synthesiser proposed in 1979 by Dennis Klatt (Klatt 1980). This is a direct application of the source-filter theory, implemented by a computer simulation of an electrical structure, consisting of resonators combined in cascade or parallel. The electrical analogue has its historical roots in the first synthesisers that were built of discrete electrical elements. However nowadays, numerical systems are generally used to simulate the operation of these elements.

The Klatt implementation is a cascade/parallel synthesiser, which allows a choice between the formant resonator configurations according to the type of sound to be produced, and which permits the simulation of male and female voices. Its block diagram is shown in Figure 9. A set of 40 parameters determine the output wave. Their abbreviations are explained in Figure 10. Thirty-four of these can be varied dynamically (represented by the symbol "V"). The constant parameters in Figure 10 (symbol "C") control the general configuration of the synthesiser.

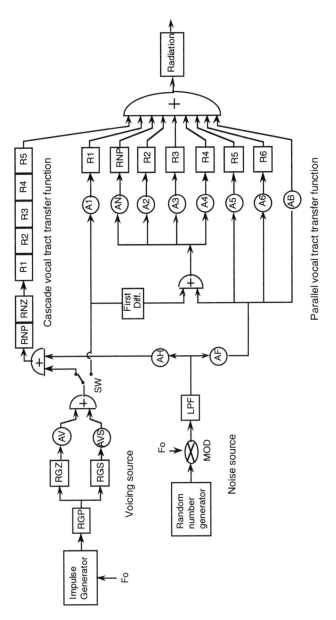

Figure 9. Block diagram of the Klatt 79 synthesiser (Klatt, 1980).

Sources

The synthesiser implements two voicing sources. The first is characterised by a -12 dB/octave spectral slope and is primarily destined for vowel synthesis. A low-pass filter (RGP) performs this function. An anti-resonator (RGZ) optionally modifies spectral details of the source to some degree. The second voicing source is a quasi-sinusoidal source required for voiced fricatives and voice bars[2]. Its spectral slope (-24 dB/oct.) is obtained with a second low-pass filter (RGS). The switch SW sends both voicing sources either to the cascade (Figure 9, top), or the parallel configuration (Figure 9, bottom).

Symbol	C/V	Min.	Max.	Name
DU	C	30	5000	Duration of the utterance (ms)
NWS	C	1	20	Update interval for parameter reset (ms)
SR	C	5000	20000	Output sampling rate (Hz)
NF	C	1	6	Number of formants in cascade branch
SW	C	0	1	0=Cascade, 1=Parallel tract excitation by AV
G0	C	0	80	Overall gain scale factor (dB)
F0	V	0	500	Fundamental frequency (Hz)
AV	V	0	80	Amplitude of voicing (dB)
AVS	V	0	80	Amplitude of quasi-sinusoidal voicing (dB)
FGP	V	0	600	Frequency of glottal resonator "RGP"
BGP	V	50	2000	Bandwidth of glottal resonator "RGP"
FGZ	V	0	5000	Frequency of glottal anti-resonator "RGZ"
BGZ	V	100	9000	Bandwidth of glottal anti-resonator "RGZ"
BGS	V	100	1000	Bandwidth of glottal resonator "RGS"
AH	V	0	80	Amplitude of aspiration (dB)
AF	V	0	80	Amplitude of frication (dB)
F1	V	180	1300	Frequency of 1st formant (Hz)
B1	V	30	1000	Bandwidth of 1st formant (Hz)
F2	V	550	3000	Frequency of 2nd formant (Hz)
B2	V	40	1000	Bandwidth of 2nd formant (Hz)
F3	V	1200	4800	Frequency of 3rd formant (Hz)
B3	V	60	1000	Bandwidth of 3rd formant (Hz)
F4	V	2400	4990	Frequency of 4th formant (Hz)
B4	V	100	1000	Bandwidth of 4th formant (Hz)
F5	V	3000	6000	Frequency of 5th formant (Hz)
B5	V	100	1500	Bandwidth of 5th formant (Hz)
F6	V	4000	6500	Frequency of 6th formant (Hz)
B6	V	100	4000	Bandwidth of 6th formant (Hz)
FNP	V	180	700	Frequency of nasal pole (Hz)
BNP	V	40	1000	Bandwidth of nasal pole (Hz)
FNZ	V	180	800	Frequency of nasal zero (Hz)
BNZ	V	40	1000	Bandwidth of nasal zero (Hz)
AN	V	0	80	Amplitude of nasal formant (dB)
A1	V	0	80	Amplitude of 1st formant (dB)
A2	V	0	80	Amplitude of 2nd formant (dB)
A3	V	0	80	Amplitude of 3rd formant (dB)
A4	V	0	80	Amplitude of 4th formant (dB)
A5	V	0	80	Amplitude of 5th formant (dB)
A6	V	0	80	Amplitude of 6th formant (dB)
AB	V	0	80	Amplitude of bypass path (dB)

Figure 10. Control parameters of the Klatt '79 synthesiser. A set of 40 parameters determine the output wave. Thirty-four can be varied dynamically (symbol "V"). The constant parameters (symbol "C") control the general configuration of the synthesiser.

---

[2] I.e. the low-frequency energy bands resulting in normal speech from the voice fundamental frequency.

A random noise generator is also available and furnishes the equivalent of a friction source controlled by the gain AF and an aspiration source, with gain AH, that is mixed with the voicing source. As the noise source spectrum must be approximately flat, a low pass filter (LPF) cancels the effect of lip radiation (represented in the last block in Figure 9). In the case of voiced sounds, the turbulence noise is modulated by the vocal fold vibration. This amplitude modulation (MOD) is controlled by the fundamental frequency. One may note that the friction source is only sent through the vocal tract in its parallel configuration.

Vocal Tract Simulation

The vocal tract, in its cascade configuration, is realised with five resonators (R1...R5), whose central frequency and bandwidth can be individually adjusted. The addition of a supplemental resonator (RNP) and anti-resonator (RNZ) allows synthesis of nasal sounds. The parallel configuration contains seven formant resonators (R1...R6, RNP), each having an individual gain control (A1...A6, AN). Moreover a bypass connection, containing only a volume control (AB), allows simulation of sounds that do not have prominent peaks in their spectrum.

Developments Since 1979

The synthesiser presented in this paragraph is not the latest version of Klatt's formant synthesiser. In the past 10 years, substantial improvements have been made to allow a better synthesis of male and female voices.

Perhaps the most significant improvements are related to the glottal source. Parametric source models, such as proposed by Fant and Liljencrants (Fant and Liljencrants, 1985), or the one proposed by Klatt (Klatt and Klatt, 1990), allow a better waveform shape generation than the impulse source presented earlier. To match the voice quality of different speakers, parameters such as the glottal opening time during a voicing period, and the velocity of the glottal closure, may be adjusted. Within an utterance by a given speaker, these parameters can be varied as active laryngeal adjustments are made to produce voiceless obstruents consonants or prosodic changes within phrases and sentences. The parameters can also be modified, as the laryngeal state reacts passively to the manipulation of constrictions in the airway, for example during voiced obstruents and or sonorant consonants produced with a narrow constriction. In addition, to improve naturalness of the synthesised speech, some glottal pulse timing irregularities, such as jitter and diplophonia, can now be added.

Proper adjustment of these parameters permits the generation of a glottal source with a spectrum that is a good approximation to the spectrum of glottal source for almost any male or female speaker. Nevertheless, a deeper understanding of the acoustic manifestations of variations in voice qualities and during the production of various types of sounds is needed. An important work that goes in this direction has been performed by Gobl (1988), who studied variations of the voice source in connected speech by means of inverse filtering and waveform parametrisation. This study showed significant changes in the glottal pulse shape found at the onset and at the termination of the voice source, and also at many of the boundaries between vowels and consonants. Re-synthesis of utterances using parameters from an acoustical analysis showed good results.

It has been stated above that the source-filter model is a linear system in which source and vocal tract interactions are neglected, on the assumption that the volume velocity waveform depends very little on the shape or impedance of the vocal tract. It is also known that this assumption is not entirely correct, since the vocal fold impedance can vary, due to different glottal openings, and because of constrictions that have a "retro-effect" on vocal fold vibration. The presumed relationship between glottal area and glottal flow is perturbed by standing wave-pressure fluctuations in the pharynx, which invalidate the assumed transglottal pressure over a cycle.

Some of these non-linear coupling effects can be simulated in Klatt's new synthesiser version (Klatt and Klatt, 1980). In the cascade branch, an additional pole-zero pair is inserted, which allows simulation of acoustical coupling to the trachea when the glottal opening is sufficiently large. In addition, these supplemental resonators can be used for better nasal sounds synthesis. Especially nasalised vowels can be simulated with a better accuracy. The time-varying glottal impedance affects the vocal tract transfer function primarily by causing increased losses at low frequencies when the glottis is open. It has also been observed that the first formant frequency may increase during the open phase of the glottal cycle. A method for synchronously changing first formant frequency and bandwidth pitch is thus provided.

Another improvement made by Cheng and Guérin (1987) to the parallel configuration consists in introducing a pole-zero pair in cascade with the first formant resonator. They have shown that the parallel configuration allows a better adjustment of the overall spectrum details for the synthesis of nasalised vowels. The introduction of a zero is necessary to provide the nasal percept.

The generation of speech with a formant synthesiser having a large set of control parameters requires that quantitative data and explicit models be developed in two areas of phonetics. One is concerned with constraints that the articulatory and aerodynamic systems impose on the sound. The other area involves the temporal control of the articulatory processes that determine the timing of the control parameters. Developing mapping relations requires that theories and models of glottal vibration and vocal-tract acoustics be refined, for example, by the estimation of the distribution of turbulence noise with vocal tract constrictions, by the determination of the time course of onsets and offsets of vocal fold vibration for voiced consonants, and by the modelling of acoustic losses with consonantal constrictions. Refinements in our understanding of articulatory control processes highlight the need for several types of data and models. Quantitative data must be obtained on rates of release and closure of articulators that form the primary consonantal constrictions for stops and fricatives. Furthermore, it is necessary to determine how articulatory parameters that are not directly involved in forming the consonantal constriction are timed in relation to the primary articulators.

Conclusion

In this chapter, a brief review of the principal speech synthesis methods has been presented. Diphone concatenation systems are currently the most widely used synthesis technique. Various commercial systems are available, which produce a fairly good synthesis.

The limitations of these systems are mainly related to the excessive size of diphone data bases that are required to deal with coarticulation problems. Relatively large speech segments (e.g. demi-syllables or syllables) are needed to handle coarticulation more or less satisfactorily. To attain even more satisfactory diphone speech, even larger segments may be necessary, which in turn would lead to even larger data bases.

One alternative is formant synthesis which operates on space-efficient, parametrised input. Given a coarticulatorily motivated string of input parameters, formant synthesisers solve the coarticulation problem quite elegantly. However, current problems concern the precise definition of, and the exact balance between these input parameters, which are quite delicate. However, recent work has shown that automatically generated formant synthesis can produce speech virtually indistinguishable from model utterances. The main disadvantage of these systems remains the considerable computational load which currently allows real-time synthesis only on powerful computers.

References

Atal, B.S., & Hanauer, S.L. (1971). Speech synthesis by linear prediction of the speech wave. *Journal of the Acoustical Society of America, 50,* 637-655.

Badin, P. (1989). Acoustics of voiceless fricatives: Production theory and data, *Speech Transmission Laboratory Quatrerly Progress and Status Report, 3,* 33-55.

Calliope (1989). *La parole et son traitement automatique.* Masson.

Cheng, Y.M., & Guérin, B. (1987). Nasal vowel study: Formant structure, perceptual evaluation and neural representation in a model of the peripherial auditory system. *Bulletin de la Communication Parlée, 1,* 91-132.

Cooper, F.S., Liberman, A.M., & Borst, J.M. (1951). The interconversion of audible and visible patterns as a basis for research in the perception of speech. *Proceedings of the National Academy of Sciences of the United States of America, 37,* 318-325.

Dudley, H. (1939). The vocoder. *Bell Laboratories Record, 17,* 122-126.

Fant, G. (1960). *Acoustic theory of speech production.* The Hague: Mouton.

Fant, G. (1986). Glottal flow: Models and interaction, *Journal of Phonetics, 14,* 393-399.

Fant, G., & Liljencrants, J. (1985). A four parameter model of glottal flow. *Speech Transmission Laboratory Quarterly Progress and Status Report, 2,* 18-24.

Flanagan, J.L, Ishizaka, K., & Shipley, K.L. (1975). Synthesis of speech from a dynamic model of the vocal cords and vocal tract. *Bell Systems Technical Journal, 54,* 485-506.

Gobl, C. (1988). Voice source dynamics in connected speech. *Speech Transmission Laboratory Quarterly Progress and Status Report, 1,* 123-159.

Gold, B., & Rabiner, L.R. (1968). Analysis of digital and analog formant synthesizers. *IEEE Transactions on Audio and Electroacoustics 16, 1,* 81-94.

Holmes, J.N. (1983). Formant synthesizers: Cascade or parallel. *Speech Communication, 2,* 251-273.

Ishizaka, K., & Flanagan, J.L. (1972). Synthesis of voiced sounds from a two-mass model of the vocal cords. *Bell Systems Technical Journal, 51,* 1233-1268.

Klatt, D.H. (1980). Software for a cascade/parallel formant synthesizer. *Journal of the Acoustical Society of America, 67,* 971-995.

Klatt, D.H. (1987). Review of text-to-speech conversion for English. *Journal of the Acoustical Society of America, 82,* 737-793.

Klatt, D.H., & Klatt, L.C. (1990). Analysis, synthesis and perception of voice quality variations among female and male talkers. *Journal of the Acoustical Society of America, 87,* 820-857.

Maeda, S. (1990). Compensatory articulation during speech: Evidence from the analysis and synthesis of vocal-tract shapes using an articulatory model. In W.J. Hardcastle & A. Marchal (Eds.), *Speech Production and Speech Modelling* (pp. 131-149). Amsterdam: Kluwer.

O'Shaughnessy, D., Barbeau, L., Bernardi, D., & Archambault, D. (1988). Diphone speech synthesis, *Speech Communication, 7,* 55-65.

Scully, C. (1990). Articulatory synthesis. In W.J. Hardcastle & A. Marchal (Eds.), *Speech Production and Speech Modelling* (pp. 151-186). Amsterdam: Kluwer.

Stevens, K.N., & Bickley, C.A. (1986). Effect of vocal tract constriction on the glottal source: Experimental and modeling studies. *Journal of Phonetics, 14,* 373-382.

Titze, I.R. (1989). A four parameter model of the glottis and vocal fold contact area. *Speech Communication, 8,* 191-201.

ANNEX: Terminal Analog Synthesiser

The terminal analog method (or formant synthesiser) simulates the speech production mechanism using an electrical structure consisting of the connection of several resonance (formant) and anti-resonance (anti-formants) circuits.

The complex frequency characteristics (Laplace transformation) of a resonance;(pole) circuit can be represented as (Gold and Rabiner, 1968):

$$H(s) = \frac{s_n \cdot s_n^*}{(s - s_n)(s - s_n^*)} \qquad (1)$$

where

$$s = -\sigma + j\omega$$

$$s_n = -\sigma_n + j\omega_n \quad \text{and} \quad s_n^* = -\sigma_n - j\omega_n \qquad (2)$$

Digital simulation of this circuit can be represented with its z-transformation:

$$H(z) = K_p \left(\frac{Az^{-1}}{1 + Cz^{-1} + Bz^{-2}} \right) \qquad (3)$$

where:

$$K_p = \frac{\sigma_n^2 + \omega_n^2}{\omega_n} \qquad A = e^{-\sigma_n T} \sin(\omega_n T)$$

$$B = e^{-2\sigma_n T} \quad \text{and} \quad C = 2e^{-\sigma_n T} \cos(\omega_n T) \qquad (4)$$

T is the sampling period. These equations imply that the digital simulation circuit can be represented as shown in Figure A.1(a). When the resonance frequency $f_n = w_n/2\pi$ [Hz] and bandwidth $b_n = s_n/\pi$ [Hz] are given, the circuit parameters can be obtained. The anti-resonance (zero) circuit indicated in Figure A.1(b) can easily be obtained from the resonance circuit, based on the inverse circuit relationship. Here, $K_z = \omega_n / \sigma_n^2 + \omega_n^2$.

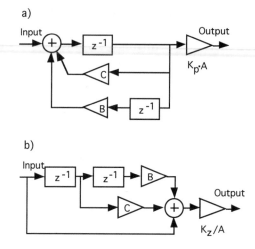

Figure A.1. Digital network implementing a second order resonator. a) Band-pass filter. b) Stop-band filter.

The complete formant network H(z) is obtained by connecting N formant or anti-formant resonators $H_n(z)$ in cascade:

$$H(z) = \prod_{n=1}^{N} H_n(z) \tag{5}$$

or in parallel:

$$H(z) = \sum_{n=1}^{N} A_n \cdot H_n(z) \tag{6}$$

The transfer function of the entire synthesiser can thus be given by:

$$F(z) = G(z) \cdot \left(1 - z^{-1}\right) \cdot H(z) \tag{7}$$

Where G(z) is a suitable source filter and H(z) is the formant network. In the early Klatt formant synthesizer version (Klatt, 1980) the voicing source transfer function is approximated with one or two second order resonators (3), where the resonance frequency f_n is set to zero to obtain a low-pass characteristic. The transfer function (1-z-1) approximates the lip radiation characteristics.

Automatic Speech and Speaker Recognition: 7
Overview, Current Issues and Perspectives

Gérard Chollet

Institut Dalle Molle d'Intelligence Artificielle Perceptive (IDIAP)
C.P. 609, CH-1920 MARTIGNY, Switzerland
and CNRS, URA 820, 46 rue Barrault, F-75634 PARIS CEDEX, France

"Intelligent" machines will soon be available to everyone at a reasonable cost. An important function of such machines is that they master speech input/output to communicate with us naturally. They should understand human speech, and they should be able to generate human-like speech messages. Although the ultimate goal of a totally human-like communication with computers may still be well beyond our reach, speech research has already produced a number of useful techniques for speech transmission and storage at low bit rates, speech synthesis from text, speaker verification, speech recognition and understanding. This chapter provides a short overview of the various fields contributing to the development of "Automatic Speech Recognition" (ASR) devices, of the problems that need to be solved in this domain, and of suggestions on how to these problems might be approached. The reader is systematically referred to relevant papers in the literature.

In the development of automatic communication techniques, phonetics is acknowledged as the scientific discipline most directly concerned with the production, perception, description, learning, and evolution of speech. The field of signal processing, as a counterpart, provides the tools to achieve adequate analytical descriptions of speech and its signal.

These two fields provide a number of tools and techniques for the description and the processing of speech. The selection and use of these tools, in turn, depend largely on the final application. In speech recognition, for example, the problem is to decide what has been said on the basis of measurements of the pressure wave (usually a sampled and quantised version of a microphone signal). This is, in fact, a problem of inverse system modelling. In order to solve this problem, the analysis must use techniques that apply knowledge about constraints operating on the speech production mechanism. Such knowledge can estimate the articulatory parameters that were in effect during the production of the analysed utterance, and ultimately, allows the reconstruction of the original speech event.

A complicating factor in solving this problem is that recorded speech is rarely complete in itself — a fact which is related to the very nature of speech as a human communicative tool. As our primary communication mode, speech is an activity that involves learning right from birth. Consequently, the speech signal itself may not contain all the information of the message, as most of it is *implied* and thus *shared* by the sender and the receiver.

To understand speech therefore, a machine would need a model of the world similar to ours, a problem that is properly speaking part of the field of artificial intelligence (AI). An adequate representation of speech knowledge and its relation to pragmatics is thus the key to the recognition of speech with unrestricted vocabulary, speaker, language, etc. More restricted cases of speech recognition (multi- or single-speaker speech, speech with limited vocabulary, pragmatic frame, topic, task, etc.) are more tractable, and do not require knowledge representations that are quite as extensive.

Another important pole in automatic speech recognition are advances in computer technology, which is an important driving force in speech research. This field furnishes the tools that render speech recognition and speech synthesis possible in the first place. Also, rapid progress in computer architecture and VLSI design are the keys to industrial developments in speech processing. However, despite the considerable recent advances in this field, some caution is advisable since many more years of fundamental speech research are needed before natural, unlimited speech I/O becomes a reality.

Speech processing is a rapidly developing field, driven by much-expected applications in telecommunication, man-machine interaction, information storage and retrieval, and the like. A better understanding of our speech production and perception mechanisms finds applications in the coding, synthesis and recognition of speech. Such models of human speech processing are most useful in speech recognition research, where observed data and measured parameters can be better explained through an understanding of how such signals are produced and of how they can be perceived.

In fact, speech is a very special type of signal that has received much attention, particularly from the phonetic sciences. But the analysis of speech also involves knowledge from many other fields: linguistics, physics, physiology, psychology, signal processing, computer science, and more. This will become even more evident in the next section, where an overview of current areas in ASR research and development will be attempted. The emphasis will be placed on some important issues with suggestions for further developments. All along, references to further reading are provided with comments on the issues discussed. These references do not necessarily point to original research, but to recent publications that can in turn be used to retrieve earlier work.

What are the Challenges in ASR?

One way of appreciating the difficulty of bringing speech communication to computers is to consider some of the complexities of human speech. Speech is the most natural way to communicate for humans. While this has been true since the dawn of civilisation, the invention and widespread use of the telephone, audiophonic storage media, radio, and television has given even further importance to speech communication and speech processing.

Speech is also the result of much *training* since birth, a training that is enhanced by what appears to be a natural ability to learn. This capacity is lost to some degree as we grow older, as shown by the fact that an adult non-native speaker of a language is most often recognised as such, and that true multilinguals were generally exposed to different languages in their early childhood.

Furthermore, speech is an essential part of any culture. For example, *social status* can be induced from a person's speech. In this sense, speech is produced by humans in order to be heard by other humans. Speakers and listeners share a common knowledge base. Information from this knowledge base is not necessarily conveyed via the signal, but it may be necessary for an understanding of the signal's message. It is important for engineers of computer speech to realise that their machines will only achieve performance similar to that of humans when human common sense, presuppositions, logic, and pragmatics can be made accessible to the machine.

ASR proceeds by the identification of *speech patterns* (the "building blocks of speech"). A finite set of such patterns must thus be defined. These could be "elementary speech sounds", more complex sounds (diphones, polyphones), words, groups of words, or some other units. Linguists and phoneticians often propose the use of phonemes or allophones. However, such units are difficult to localise in the signal, and most often are impossible to segment by automatic means. They are also highly variable, as well as context- and speaker-dependent. This is also to some extent true for other units. No optimal set has been identified so far, and the selection of a given set of units is application-dependent. In most cases, a lexicon (a set of words) is used, where each lexical entry can be represented in terms of the units that have been selected for representing the speech signal.

In most situations where pattern recognition is performed, the problem of *variability* is pervasive. Since the speech code is highly structured and redundant, speakers have much leeway for conveying their messages. The generality of messages are intended to communicate with other human beings, and may in fact pose too great a challenge for an automatic system. The decoding of messages essentially constructed for other human beings may be too complex, unless the user offers the machine some special "co-operation", such as control over speaking mode, the use of a restricted set of words, the application of a normalised syntax, and the like. By the same token, a recogniser may have to use quite a diverse set of knowledge sources to succeed in its decoding task, such as inferences about a speaker's original articulation, the phonology of the language employed, the speaker's individual speaking habits, the extent and type of the assumed lexicon, syntactic, semantic, and pragmatic competence, and more.

Paradoxically, the speech recognition process may not be completed once *recognition* has occurred. Most speech communication contexts (with the possible exception of the "automatic typewriter"), furthermore require an *understanding* of what has been said. Although some form of trivial "understanding" may be possible for simple tasks, the interpretation of unlimited speech discourse will require very complex mechanisms. Some of these mechanisms can be shared with text interpretation. But since speech contains much more information than text (in particular, prosodic information), it is likely that ASR will have to go far beyond text understanding in developing the foundations for a fairly complete interpretation of spoken material.

The Place of ASR within Speech Technology

It is useful to understand that automatic speech recognition is part of the larger field of *speech processing*. Three main areas can be distinguished in this field, although they overlap considerably: *Coding, recognition, and synthesis*. Figure 1 schematises the relationship between these areas. Speech enhancement and compression are useful for both recognition and coding.

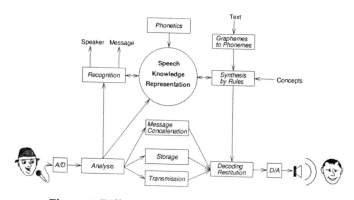

Figure 1: Different areas in automatic speech processing.

While speech carries information about the message, the speaker, and the recording environment, the purpose of speech recognition is to single out the message. On the other hand, in the identification or the verification of the speaker's identity, the aim is to isolate speaker-specific information. However, in all of these cases where input signals are analysed or coded, the key operation concerns the extraction of relevant from irrelevant information. At the signal analysis level, this involves the processes of speech enhancement and noise subtraction.

These isolating processes can be supported by higher-level rules. Since speech is a structured signal, our knowledge of that structure can be formalised as context-dependent variable rules. In particular, it is likely that observed intra- and inter-speaker variability can be predicted from such models.

Phonetics and ASR

Having delineated some of the main aspects of ASR, and after outlining the challenges that will have to be faced in the future, we now turn to the historical antecedents of this field.

The story begins with phonetics, the science of speech. One of the central concerns of the phonetic sciences is establishing the inventory, the description, and the comparison of speech sounds for all languages. Acoustic phonetics is a central part of this science. The development and use of the sound spectrograph (Bell, 1967) added considerable stimulus to this discipline. Among other topics, phonetics is also concerned with how humans produce and perceive speech. Introductory textbooks are Denes and Pinson (1973), Pickett (1980) and Marchal (1981). More advanced monographs are Fant (1973), Ladefoged (1975), and Lieberman (1977).

Some excellent collections of papers were edited in books by Cole (1980), Lass (1976), Lehiste (1967), and Lindblom and Ohman (1979). Fant (1970) is the prime reference for studies on acoustics and speech production. Jakobson *et al.* (1963) published their pioneer work on distinctive features of speech sounds which stimulated developments in phonology, speech perception, and automatic speech recognition.

Much of the early research in phonetics concerned the identification of a set of *basic units of speech*, the phonemes. A phoneme is a unit capable of inducing a minimal meaning difference between two utterances (e.g. *sun* vs. *fun*). Since languages differ somewhat with respect to their set of minimal phonemic differences, phonemes are language-dependent. They are best considered as abstract units with a perceptual reality. It has often been suggested that phonemes also serve as articulatory goals in speech production. However, since such goals (if they really exist) are context and speaker-dependent, the status of phonemes in speech production is contested (e.g. is the /k/ in "kit" and in "cot" really the same sound? Physical evidence shows two very different sounds (see Chapter 1, this volume). One way of dealing with this problem is to propose a set of so-called "allophones". Under this hypothesis, the basic form would still be the phoneme, but its physical manifestation in different contexts would involve a set of allophonic variants of the basic phonemic goal.

Prosody is a distinct branch of phonetics concerned with suprasegmental effects on parameters such as fundamental frequency, segmental intensity and duration. Its rules are to considerable degree language-specific. Prosody influences all levels of the speech generation and comprehension hierarchy.

Speech Analysis Techniques in ASR

A second thread leading to the current ASR research is the history of speech signal analysis, which starts with the invention of recording. A microphone converts a pressure wave into an electrical signal. The characteristics of this transducer and its position relative to the source are essential factors in ASR, since they influence the quality of the recording, and thus the results of the analysis.

Most current speech signal analyses are performed on a digital representation of the signal which provides the most flexible way of performing such analyses. For simplicity's sake, the analogue signal is sampled and quantised at a fixed rate. During this process, the speech signal is bandwidth-limited, preserving low frequency components. Low-pass filtering at about 7 kHz and sampling at 16 kHz permits later reconstruction with no loss in quality, while sampling at lower frequencies is only possible with a loss of high frequency components. Low-pass filtering at sampling and reconstruction are necessary, since components higher than the Nyquist rate (half the sampling frequency) must be eliminated to avoid frequency folding (superposition) during spectral analysis.

Many simple measurements on the signal provide useful information. The short-term energy envelope, for example, reflects the succession of vowels (high energy) and consonants (low energy). Zero-crossing counts and histograms on the signal and its derivatives provide some basic spectral information. In fact, most 1-D signal processing techniques have been applied to speech. The purpose is usually to obtain a different representation of the signal which is either better-suited for subsequent transformations, or which is amenable to some data reduction technique.

A time *vs.* frequency *vs.* amplitude representation (a "spectrogram" or "spectral relief") has proved to be a visually attractive representation of speech. The spectrogram necessitates a computational definition of a spectrum to be applied at each time instant, but it induces no data reduction. The choice of a particular spectral analysis technique is generally determined by the specific application.

Signal Pre-Processing: Parametric *vs.* Non-parametric Techniques

The next step in preparing the speech signal for ASR is the establishment of a model of the underlying speech event. Both parametric and non-parametric techniques are used for this purpose. A *parametric technique* attempts to model a speech production system by estimating the parameters of a transfer function relating the input (usually unknown, but hypothesised) to the output (the speech signal). Linear parametric techniques assume an ARMA (autoregressive, moving-average) model. Linear prediction is a subtype of these autoregressive models.

A *non-parametric* technique performs some transformation on a window of the signal (see also Rabiner and Schafer, 1978). The length and the shape of that window is adjusted to favour a given interpretation. A typical example is the Fourier transform. Further processing, such as smoothing or peak picking, is necessary to reduce the data rate.

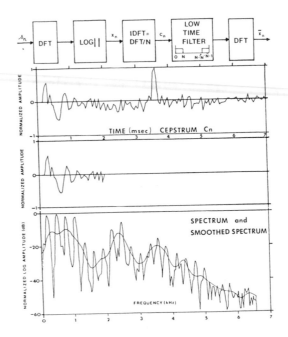

Figure 2. Spectral and cepstral analysis. From to top to bottom: The sequence of operations for cepstral smoothing, the cepstrum, the truncated cepstrum, and the superimposed power spectrum and cepstrally smoothed spectrum.

A common signal preparation technique is to estimate the spectral content by simple bandpass filtering. A filter bank can be simulated using the discrete Fourier transform (DFT) or the fast Fourier transform (FFT) on the windowed signal. If the window contains several fundamental periods of the signal (voiced speech), the log-power spectrum exhibits harmonic components. Figure 2 illustrates a technique to estimate simultaneously a spectral envelope and the signal's fundamental frequency (Verhelst and Steenhout, 1986). The cepstrum c_n is obtained as the Fourier transform of the power spectrum. The peak at 3.6 ms corresponds to the fundamental period T_0. The cepstrum can be truncated to retain only the slowly varying components of the spectrum, and Fourier transforms to obtain a smoothed spectrum.

Linear Prediction of Speech

Another signal preparation technique involves obtaining LPC ("Linear Predictive Coding") coefficients. To this effect, the output s_n of an ARMA(p, q) model is expressed as a linear sum of p past samples and (q+1) input values u_n:

$$s_n = a_i \, s_{n-i} + b_j \, u_{n-j}$$

In speech processing, the input values u_n are unknown; therefore much development has focused on AR(p) models:

$$s_n = a_i s_{n-i} + e_n$$

The residual error e_n can be used as the input sequence to the synthesis filter $1/A(z)$ with $A(z) = -a_i z_{-i}$ and $-a_0 = 1$:

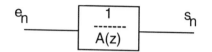

Ideally, the filter $1/A(z)$ corresponds to the vocal tract and the excitation e_n to a glottal waveform and/or a frication noise. The prediction coefficients a_i can be updated on every sample (sequential recursive or adaptive techniques), at regular intervals (global or blockwise stationary modelling), or can be estimated as time-dependent functions (non-stationary modelling). Gueguen (1985) gives an overview of the different techniques, while Makhoul (1975) and Markel and Gray (1976) focus primarily on global methods.

Non-Stationary Models

Since the filter (vocal tract) changes continuously during the production of a sentence, the filter's temporal evolution should be described and modelled. Several approaches are being investigated in this context (Chollet *et al.*, 1986). Since the filter parameters are time-dependent, they can be expressed as linear combinations of *a-priori* chosen or computed functions, or they can be modelled as a two-dimensional process. The main application is an improved description of spectral transitions for speech storage, synthesis and recognition.

Noise Subtraction, Speech Enhancement

Speech is often produced in a noisy environment. In fact, any unwanted component of a signal is considered to be "noise". In many speech recognition applications (industrial, military, transport, etc.), the noise component can be quite strong. Different speakers can even talk simultaneously ("cocktail party effect"). Therefore, speech enhancement from single or multiple microphones is of considerable theoretical and practical interest (Lim, 1983). If speech is captured from a single microphone, it may be more efficient to adapt the recogniser to the environment, rather than to attempt noise subtraction.

Digital Signal Processors

Speech has a relatively low bandwidth. Except for signal acquisition from multiple microphones, most of the algorithms described above can be processed in real time on a single VLSI chip. Most VLSI manufacturers propose general purpose digital signal processors that are quite adequate for prototyping. The Texas Instrument family TMS 320C2x, C3x, C40, C50, the Motorola 56xxx and 96xxx, and the AT&T DSP-16 and 32C are most popular for this purpose. Custom design may be more profitable for series production (Barral and Moreau, 1986).

The Variability of Acoustic Parameters and the Problem of Speaker Recognition

The result of a signal analysis is usually a set of measurements associated with speech segments. Important questions for speech coding and recognition applications concern the possible values observed, their statistical distribution, the influence of the phonetic context, of the speaker, of his speaking rate, of his language, and of the environment, etc.

To what extent is the observed variability *perceptually relevant*? The answer probably depends on the application. In ASR, the objective is to *reduce* variability. In the search for invariant features (Stevens, 1972), some transformations may become necessary to compensate for contextual effects and speaker differences. Further research must be undertaken to define the rules underlying these transformations.

Our ability to identify familiar voices (Nolan, 1983), on the other hand, justifies work on what has become known as *"automatic speaker recognition"* (Doddington, 1985). Here, inter-speaker variability is *exploited*, rather than minimised.

One of the central problems in this field is that the potential identification of a speaker is always limited to a closed set, since only a limited number of speakers is available to the system at any point. A speaker that does not belong to this set may not be detected as such, and could be misclassified as a member of the set. Speaker verification is more attractive in active identification situations. Here the speaker claims his identity (using speech or some other means), and the machine matches the person's individual speech (or handwriting) characteristics to a pre-stored template.

Since the detection of impostors may require very fine distinctions, verification should theoretically be just as difficult as identification, and the resulting misclassifications should be just as likely. However in practice (as in security applications), speakers are more co-operative when they need to have their identity verified to access a service, and thus use particularly clear speech. This reduces the number of misclassifications. Speaker classification techniques developed in the context of verification and identification could possibly also end up being useful in the context of a speaker-independent ASR system, for which a number of speaker templates have been established (Rosenberg and Shipley, 1981).

Finally in this line of inquiry, research on techniques to transform the voice of a given speaker into that of another should be actively pursued. Success with such techniques would have important applications to speech coding (preserving or modifying a given identity), synthesis (with several speakers), and recognition (adaptation of reference templates or knowledge to new speakers).

Speech Recognition

The speech signal conveys linguistic information that a recognition algorithm intends to retrieve. During the past 40 years, many such algorithms have been proposed with increasing, but still rather limited performance. An important milestone was demonstrated by a system developed at IBM (Jelinek, 1985). It is able to recognise, in real time, isolated words from a set of 20 000 after a 20-minute training session, and that with an error rate of less than 5%. However as it turns out, this performance was still insufficient for the intended application, which was an automatic typewriter. In the past 10 years, research has focused on several dimensions of possible improvement, such as limitation of training time, acceptance of more natural speaking styles (continuous speech), adaptation to the environment, etc.

Why is it so difficult to recognise speech automatically? What are the main technical issues? What are current capabilities? These are some of the questions we wish to develop in the subsequent sections, with many references to the specialised literature for more detailed information.

There is a large spectrum of possible recognition capabilities, including:
- *isolated* word recognisers for segments separated by pauses,
- word *spotting* algorithms that detect occurrences of key words in continuous speech,
- *connected* word recognisers that identify uninterrupted, but strictly formatted, sequences of words (e.g. recognition of telephone numbers),
- restricted speech *understanding* systems that handle sentences relevant to a specific task, and
- *task-independent continuous* speech recognisers, which is the ultimate goal in this field.

Generally speaking, automatic speech recognition algorithms use statistical and structural pattern recognition techniques (Levinson, 1985;

Moore, 1985; Rabiner and Juang, 1993), and/or knowledge-based (phonetic and linguistic) principles (Zue, 1985). Either whole segments (words) are directly recognised (global method), or an intermediate phonetic labelling is used before lexical search (analytic method).

Among *global* methods, direct pattern matching techniques were substantially improved with the development of dynamic time warping (DTW) for proper time alignment. DTW is quite efficient for isolated word recognition (Sakoe and Chiba, 1978) and can be adapted to connected word recognition (Bridle *et al.*, 1982; Ney, 1984). Markov modelling (Levinson *et al.*, 1983; Bourlard and Wellekens, 1986) offer even better efficiency at the expense of a lengthy training (remember the IBM system!). Most commercial recognisers implement global techniques.

The success of global techniques reflect our inability to integrate the variability of speech. *Analytic* techniques are more scientifically attractive. They recognise the validity of distinctive features and phonetic distinctions (Cole *et al.*, 1985), and they can be integrated in knowledge-based systems. The rules that govern such systems can either be conceived from human expertise or inferred from examples. Artificial neural networks offer a promising alternative for the classification of fine phonetic distinctions (Waibel and Lee, 1990). A challenge of the coming years is to combine these analytic and stochastically based approaches (see Chapter 8, this volume).

For many applications, like interactive voice servers over the telephone, speaker independence is a necessity. This is currently achieved by a lengthy training of word models over large speech data bases. An alternative consists of training phonetic models and specifying words models from these. An application could then be designed from text allowing a "flexible" vocabulary for new applications.

Learning from Examples

It is probably impossible to control all the parameters responsible for speech variability. Under such conditions, a statistical approach offers the best chances of success. Such an approach requires a statistically valid sample of all the speech patterns our system should recognise. This sample is obtained from very large speech data bases. The availability of low cost, digital storage media such as Compact Disks (CDROMs) permits a wide dissemination of these data bases. The value of speech corpora has been recognised and co-ordination is being organised internationally. The COCOSDA (Co-ordinating Committee for Speech Data bases and Assessment) is steering this effort (Chiavari, 1991). The "Polyphone" project was launched by COCOSDA in 1992. Its goal is the recording of a large number of speakers (5000) over the telephone network for as many languages as possible. As of December 1993, recordings are being collected in American English, American Spanish, Japanese, Dutch, Spanish, and Swiss French. Other languages are being considered. The LDC (Linguistic Data Consortium) has taken on the responsibility of distributing a large number of these CDROMs.

Hidden Markov Models (HMMs) and Artificial Neural Networks (ANNs) have been used with some success for speech pattern classification tasks (see the chapter by Torkkola in this volume). These models still require a lot of expertise to define an optimal structure for a given application. Stochastic grammars with the help of grammatical inference techniques (Vidal and Casacuberta, 1993) may offer a general solution to this problem. We may be able to use such grammars in co-operation with knowledge-based system, and therefore for unifying speech recognition techniques.

Adaptation to New Speakers

Many applications require the possibility of using a speech recogniser without preliminary training of the machine for each new user. Stochastic techniques (such as Markov modelling) allow training on a large population at the expense of discriminative power. Using multi-reference templates with a DTW-based pattern matching approach would be inadequate for large vocabularies. If invariant features could be found (Stevens *et al.*, 1986), they should be used. Other features or parameters need to be adapted (Choukri and Chollet, 1987). This adaptation should be applied dynamically (during actual use of the recogniser), and under user supervision.

Speech Understanding Systems and Dialogues

A speaker articulates his message in order to be *understood*. Recognition places an emphasis on the identification of acoustic patterns and access on to the lexicon. *Understanding* is more directly concerned with higher levels, including meaning and strategies. In many practical situations, a specific task is assigned to the machine, and speech input must concern this task. Semantic, syntactic and pragmatic constraints play a role at least equivalent to that of phonetics. Strategies to control and combine these diverse sources of knowledge become a major issue (Wood, 1985).

The speaker's intent is reflected in the *prosody* of his message. Speech is much richer in this respect than text, and understanding should be facilitated through an exploitation of prosodic information. It may be the case that technology would have to perform better at the acoustic level, before complex applications (in which prosody plays a major role) can be processed successfully. It should be possible to make a better use of this neglected information (Langlais and Méloni, 1993). A man-machine dialogue system seems to be a good platform to study these phenomena. Information servers via the telephone are being developed and being tested world-wide. They can offer useful services and should be a major market in the coming decade.

Evaluation

Testing the performance of different algorithms and systems has become a major issue in the development of ASR systems (Pallett, 1985), since systems are costly and are of very divergent quality and task applicability. For this purpose, data bases and algorithms should be shared by independent testing teams. COCOSDA, the National Bureau of Standards in the US, NATO and the European Economic Commissions are very much concerned with these standardisation issues. The ESPRIT-SAM (Speech input/output Assessment Methodology) project has resulted in useful recommendations that ought to be recognised internationally (e.g. by CCITT, ISO, and the like).

We have already mentioned that many factors contribute to the variability of speech. They affect the performance of recognisers (Pallett, 1985). Speech data bases could hardly cover all possible conditions. Speech transformation and synthesis techniques have been proposed to better control the variability of speech and therefore the testing conditions (Chollet, 1993).

Finally, it must be remembered that the recognition performance of a given system provides only a partial indication of user satisfaction. *User-friendliness, response time* and *other man-machine interface* issues should also be considered. Ergonomists clearly have an important role to play in the success of this technology.

Conclusions and Future Outlook

Speech processing is a mature science with well-defined objectives and applications. Advances in computer technology and microelectronics stimulate progress, but the real bottleneck still lies in our incomplete understanding of human speech and language communication mechanisms. In particular, our knowledge of the speech code or phonetic code relating linguistic units to acoustic speech events is still incomplete. We cannot predict (synthesise) the speech signal that a given speaker (of known dialect, anatomy, mood, etc.) would produce during the utterance of a given sentence in a specific situation. New experimental approaches must be adopted for confronting large data bases with adequate speech models. Knowledge-based systems should be developed to offer such capabilities.

The very real need for computer speech I/O will be the driving force of future developments. Digital telephony, voice mail, vocal output for various information systems, etc., will be consumers of this technology. Office systems offer a huge market. Speech processing has been and will increasingly be applied in the medical field. The detection of voice and speech pathology, speech rehabilitation, speech training, speech audiometry, adaptive hearing aids and cochlear implants are potential applications. Continuing research on a voice-activated typewriter and a translating telephone will no doubt lead to useful subproducts.

Many other areas of speech processing should have been discussed here, but can only be mentioned due to limited space. Most of them use knowledge from the above-mentioned techniques. Some areas have been scarcely sketched. One is multi-sensor measurements of speech (laryngeal microphone, electroglottograph, nose sensor, close-mouth mike, ambient noise mike, microphone arrays, synchronised lip image, etc.). A multi-sensor approach may well provide a better chance of solving the above-mentioned inverse problem. It would also allow better speech enhancement, and it would help to differentiate voices in a cocktail-party effect situation.

References and Further Reading

Ahlbom, G., Bimbot, F., & Chollet, G. (1987). Modeling spectral speech transitions using temporal decomposition techniques. *Proceedings ICASSP*, Dallas, 13-16.

Ainsworth, W.A. (1988). *Speech recognition by machine*. Peter Peregrinus.

Ainsworth, W.A. (Ed.) (1990). *Advances in speech, hearing and language Processing*. JAI Press.

Barral, H., & Moreau, N. (1986). VLSI architectures for a real-time LPC-based feature extractor. *Proceedings ICASSP*, Tokyo, 381-384.

Bell, A.M. (1967). *Visible speech: The science of universal alphabetics*. London: Simpkin, Marshall.

Bimbot, F., Ahlbom, G., & Chollet, G. (1987). From segmental synthesis to acoustic rules using temporal decomposition. *IX-ICPhS*, Talliin.

Bimbot, F., Chollet, G., & Tubach, J.P. (1990). Phonetic features extraction using time-delay neural networks. *International Conference on Speech and LanguageProcessing*, Kobe, Japan.

Boite, R., & Kunt, M. (1987). *Traitement de la parole*. Presses Polytechniques Romandes.

Borden, G.J., & Harris, K.S. (1980). *Speech science primer: Physiology, acoustics, and perception of speech*. Williams and Wilkins.

Bourlard, H., & Wellekens, C.J. (1986). Connected speech recognition by statistical methods. *Eurasip short course on speech processing*, Brussels.

Bridle, J.S., Brown, M.D., & Chamberlin, R.M. (1982). An algorithm for connected word recognition. *Proceedings ICASSP*, Paris, 899-902.

Calliope. (1989). *La parole et son traitement automatique*. Masson.

Carré, R., Degremont, J.F., Gross, M., Pierrel, J.M., & Sabah, G. (1991). *Langage humain et machine*. Presses du CNRS.

Chiavari (1991). *Workshop on International Cooperation and Standardization of Speech Databases and Speech I/O Assessment methods*. Chiavari: CSELT and CEC DGXIII.

Chollet, G., Galliano, J.F., Lefevre, J.P., & Viarra E. (1983). On the generation and use of a segment dictionary for speech coding, synthesis and recognition. *Proceedings ICASSP*, Boston, 1328-1331.

Chollet, G., Grenier, Y., & Marcus, S.M. (1986). Temporal decomposition and non-stationary modeling of speech. *EUSIPCO*, The Hague.

Chollet, G., & Montacié, C. (1988). A PC-based workstation for the evaluation of speech recognizers and data-bases. *SPEECH-88 (FASE)*, Edinburgh.

Chollet, G. (1993). Evaluation of ASR systems, algorithms and data-bases. *NATO-ASI*, Bubion.

Choukri, K., & Chollet, G. (1987). Adaptation of automatic speech recognizers to new speakers using canonical correlation analysis techniques. *Computer, Speech and Language*, Vol 1-2.

Cole, R.A. (Ed.) (1980). *Perception and production of fluent speech*. Lawrence Erlbaum Associates.

Cole, R.A., Stern, R.M., & Lasry M.J. (1985). Performing fine phonetic distinctions: Templates versus features, In J.S. Perkell & D.H. Klatt (Eds.), *Variability and invariance in speech processes*. Lawrence Erlbaum Associates.

De Mori, R. (1983). *Computer models of speech using fuzzy algorithms*. Plenum Press.

Denes, P.B., & Pinson, E.N. (1973). *The speech chain*. Double Day: Anchor Press.

Dilts, M.R., & Milne, S. (1989). The conversational computer: A vision of the future. *Speech Tech '89*, 90-94.

Doddington, G.R. (1985). Speaker recognition: Identifying people by their voices. *Proceedings of the IEEE*, 73.

Fallside, F., & Woods, W.A. (Eds.) (1983). *Computer Speech Processing*. Prentice Hall.

Fant, G. (1970). *Acoustic theory of speech production* (2nd ed.). The Hague: Mouton.

Fant, G. (1973). *Speech sounds and features*. Cambridge: MIT Press.

Flanagan, J.L. (1972). *Speech analysis, synthesis and perception* (2nd ed.). Springer Verlag.

Fry, D.B. (1980). *The physics of speech*. Cambridge University Press.

Furui, S., & Sondhi, M.M. (Eds.) (1992). *Advances in speech signal processing*. Marcel Dekker.

Gagnoulet, C., & Jouvet, D. (1989). Développements récents en reconnaissance de la parole. *L'Écho des Recherches*, 135.

Gueguen, C. (1985). Analyse de la parole par les méthodes paramétriques. *Annales des Télécoms*.

Haton, J.P., Pierrel, J.M., Perennou, G., Caelen, J., & Gauvain, J.L. (1991). *Reconnaissance automatique de la parole*. Dunod Informatique, AFCET.

Jakobson, R., Fant, G., & Halle, M. (1963). *Preliminaries to speech analysis: The distinctive features and their correlates*. Cambridge, MA: MIT Press.

Jelinek, F. (1985). The development of an experimental discrete dictation recognizer. *Proceedings of the IEEE*, 73.

Ladefoged, P. (1975). *A course in phonetics*. Harcourt Brace Jovanovich.

Langlais, Ph., & Méloni, H. (1993). Integration of a prosodic component in an automatic speech recognition system. *EUROSPEECH*, Berlin, 2007-2010.

Lass, N.J. (ed.) (1976). *Contemporary issues in experimental phonetics*. Academic Press.

Lea, W.A., Medress, M.F., & Skinner, T.E. (1975). A prosodically guided speech understanding strategy. *IEEE Trans. ASSP, 23,* 30-38.

Lee, K.F. (1989). *Automatic Speech Recognition. The development of the SPHINX system.* Kluwer.

Lehiste, I. (ed.) (1967). *Readings in acoustic phonetics.* Cambridge, MA: MIT Press.

Levinson, S.E., Rabiner, L.R., & Sondhi, M.M. (1983). An introduction to the application of the theory of probabilistic functions of a Markov process to automatic speech recognition. *Bell System Tech. J., 62,* 1035-1074.

Levinson, S.E. (1985). Structural methods in automatic speech recognition. *Proceedings of the IEEE, 73,* 1625-1650.

Lieberman, P. (1977). *Speech physiology and acoustic phonetics: An introduction.* Collier Macmillan.

Lienard, J.S. (1977). *Les processus de la communication parlée.* Masson.

Lim, J.S.(Ed.) (1983). *Speech enhancement.* Prentice-Hall.

Lindblom, B.E.F., & Sunberg, J.E.F. (1971). Acoustical consequences of lip, tongue, jaw, and larynx movements. *Journal of the Acoustical Society of America, 50,* 1116-1179.

Lindblom, B., & Ohman, S. (Eds.) (1979). *Frontiers of speech communication research.* Academic Press.

Longuet-Higgins, C. (1983). Tones of voice: The role of intonation in computer speech understanding. In F. Fallside & W.A. Woods (Eds.), *Computer speech processing.* Prentice Hall.

Maeda, S. (1982). A digital simulation method of the vocal tract system. *Speech Communication, 1,* 199-229.

Makhoul, J. (1975). Linear prediction: A tutorial review. *Proceedings of the IEEE, 63,* 561-580.

Marchal, A. (1981). *Les sons et la parole.* Montreal: Guerin.

Markel, J.D., & Gray, A.H. jr. (1976). *Linear prediction of speech.* Springer Verlag.

Moore, R.K. (1985). Systems for isolated and connected word recognition. In R. De Mori & C.Y. Suen (Eds.), *New systems and architectures for automatic speech recognition and synthesis.* Springer-Verlag.

Newell, A., Barnett, J., Forgie, J., Grenn, C., Klatt, D., Licklider, C.R., Munson, J., Reddy, R., & Woods, W. (1973). *Speech understanding systems: Final report of a study group.* Amsterdam, The Netherlands: North Holland.

Ney, H. (1984). The use of a one-stage dynamic programming algorithm for connected word recognition. *IEEE Trans. ASSP, 29,* 263-271.

Niemann, H., Lang, M., & Sagerer, G. (Eds.) (1988). *Recent advances in speech understanding and dialog systems.* Springer Verlag.

Nolan, F. (1983). *The phonetic bases for speaker recognition.* Cambridge, England: Cambridge University Press.

Pallett, D.S. (1985). *Automatic speech recognizer performance assessment,* Washington, D.C.: National Bureau of Standards.

Pickett, J.M. (1980). *The sounds of speech communication: A primer of acoustic phonetics and speech perception.* University Park Press.

Pierrel, J.M. (1987). *Dialogue oral homme-machine.* Hermes.

Rabiner, L.R., & Schafer, R.W. (1978). *Digital processing of speech signals.* Prentice Hall.

Rabiner, L.R., & Juang, B.-J. (1993). *Fundamentals of speech recognition.* Prentice Hall.

Rosenberg, A.E., & Shipley, K.L. (1981). Speaker identification and verification combined with speaker independent word recognition. *Proceedings ICASSP,* Atlanta, 184-187.

Saito, S. (Ed.). (1991). *Speech Science and Technology.* Amsterdam: IOS Press.

Sakoe, H., & Chiba, S. (1978). Dynamic programming algorithm optimization for spoken word recognition. *IEEE Trans. ASSP, 26*, 43-49.

Sakoe, H. (1979). Two level DP-matching: A dynamic programming based pattern matching algorithm for connected word recognition. *IEEE Trans. ASSP, 27*, 588-595.

Schroeder, M.R. (Ed.) (1985). *Speech and speaker recognition*. Berlin: Karger.

Shirai, K., Kobayashi, T., & Yazawa, J. (1986). Estimation of articulatory parameters by table look-up method and its application for speaker-independent phoneme recognition. *Proceedings ICASSP*, Tokyo, 2247-2250.

Stevens, K.N. (1972). The quantal nature of speech: Evidence from articulatory-acoustic data. In E.E. David Jr. & P.B. Denes (Eds.), *Human communication: A unified view*. N.Y.

Stevens, K.N., Keyser, S.J., & Kawasaki, H. (1986). Toward a phonetic and phonological theory of redundant features. In J. Perkell & D.H. Klatt (Eds.), *Variability and invariance in speech processes*. Erlbaum.

Verhelst, W., & Steenhaut, O. (1986). On short-time cepstra and deconvolution of voiced speech. In I.T. Young et al. (Eds.), *Signal Processing III: Theories and Applications*. Elsevier Science Pub. B.V., Eurasip.

Vidal, E., & Casacuberta, F. (1993). Syntactic Learning Techniques for Language Modeling and Acoustic-Phonetic decoding, *NATO-ASI*, Bubion.

Waibel, A., Hanazawa, T., Hinton, G., Shikano, K., & Lang, K. (1988). Phoneme recognition: Neural netwoks *vs.* Hidden Markov models. *IEEE-ICASSP*, New York, 107-110.

Waibel, A., & Lee, K-F. (Eds.). (1990). *Readings in Speech Recognition*. San Mateo, CA: Morgan Kaufmann.

Wakita, H. (1979). Estimation of vocal-tract shapes from acoustical analysis of the speech wave: The state of the art. *IEEE Trans. ASSP, 27*, 282-285.

Witten, I.H. (1982). *Principles of computer speech*. Academic Press.

Wood, W.A. (1985). Language processing for speech understanding. In F. Fallside & W.A. Woods (Eds.), *Computer speech processing*. Prentice Hall.

Zue, V.W. (1985). The use of speech knowledge in Automatic Speech Recognition. *Proceedings IEEE, 73*, 1602-1615.

Other Sources of References

Journals

- IEEE Journals: Trans. on Audio and Speech, Proceedings
- Speech Communication (North Holland, ed.)
- Computer Speech and Language
- Journal of the Acoustical Society of America
- Journal of Phonetics
- Phonetica
- Journal of the Japan Acoustical Society
- Speech Technology (Media Dimension)

International Conferences

- ICASSP (IEEE Conf. on Acoustics, Speech and Signal Processing)
- IEEE Workshops
- ASA (Acoustical Society of America)
- ICPhS (Int. Cong. of Phonetic Sciences)
- ICSLP (International Conference on Speech and Language Processing)
- EUROSPEECH (European Speech Communication Association)
- ESCA ARW
- NATO ASI
- EUSIPCO (European Signal Processing Conference)
- GRETSI
- RFIA (AFCET)
- ICPR (International Conference on Pattern Recognition)
- NIPS
- Japan Acoustical Society
- Speech Tech
- AVIOS (American Voice I/O Society)
- JEP (Journées d'Etudes sur la Parole, Société Française d'Acoustique)

Stochastic Models and Artificial Neural Networks for Automatic Speech Recognition

8

Kari Torkkola

Institut Dalle Molle d'Intelligence Artificielle Perceptive (IDIAP)
C.P. 609, CH-1920 MARTIGNY, Switzerland

This chapter concentrates on the data-based approach to automatic speech recognition. The speech signal is modelled by algorithms that can extract knowledge from speech data automatically. We describe some of the basic principles behind two approaches of this kind, hidden Markov models and artificial neural networks, and we discuss their applicability to speech recognition. We also review some of the current research aimed at overcoming the limitations of these techniques.

Knowledge-Based *vs.* Data-Based Approaches

There are two primary approaches to research in automatic speech recognition (ASR), a knowledge-based approach and a data-based approach. In the knowledge-based approach, the aim is to express human knowledge of speech in terms of explicit rules: Acoustic-phonetic rules, rules describing words of the lexicon, rules describing the syntax of the language, and so on.

Data-based statistical approaches have achieved considerable success recently. In these approaches, the speech signal is modelled by algorithms that can extract knowledge from speech data automatically. Two approaches of this kind, hidden Markov models (HMMs) and artificial neural networks (ANNs), as well as combinations of these, are presented in this chapter in an introductory manner. In the knowledge-based approach, heuristic rules are acquired from human experts. In HMMs or ANNs, learning is achieved by presenting speech data to the algorithm, and by having the data improve the models automatically. In general, the more data presented to the model, the better the performance of the resulting recogniser.

Over the last few years, most ASR research in has concentrated on the statistical approach. As a result, notable improvements in performance have been observed. Statistical approaches are also gaining a foothold in other domains, such as optical character recognition, or grammar construction for natural language processing.

We begin this presentation by an introduction to HMMs. Next, we shall take a quick look at ANNs, and we shall conclude by studying the approaches to combine the best features of both approaches.

Stochastic Models for Speech Recognition

From Templates to Probabilistic Models

The simplest working approach to isolated utterance recognition is template matching: storing parameterised forms of utterances and matching new utterances against these templates. Nonlinear *time variations* in acoustic patterns can be absorbed in matching by dynamic time warping (DTW) procedures (Godin and Lockwood, 1989).

DTW stretches and compresses various sections of the utterance so as to find the alignment that results in the best possible match between the template and the utterance on a frame-by-frame basis. By "frame" we mean a short segment (10-30ms) of speech signal which is the basis of parameter vector computation (spectra, cepstra, LPC-coefficients, etc.), and a "match" is defined as the sum of frame-by-frame distances between the template and the input utterance. The template with the closest match defined in this manner is chosen as the recognised word.

To absorb *acoustic variations*, statistical methods can be integrated into DTW approaches. To this end, we shall call the template frames *states*. A first step is to replace the frame-by-frame distance by a probability that the input frame can be produced by a template state. To achieve robust probabilistic models, and to be able to estimate their parameters, the hundreds of states in a template must be reduced to just a few states. This leads to a tradeoff between obtaining a good probabilistic model and losing the time information in the template (Huang *et al.*, 1990).

We now take a closer look at the principles behind hidden Markov models. This presentation will be informal, intuitive and introductory, written from an engineer's point of view. For more detailed information about HMMs, several texts can be recommended, such as Rabiner (1989), and Huang*et al.,* (1990). A good collection of papers about all aspects of speech recognition is Waibel and Lee (1990), and an excellent textbook is Rabiner and Juang (1993).

Fundamentals of Hidden Markov Models

Markov Chains

A natural language often exhibits significant structure. In English for example, the letter Q is almost always followed by a U. Therefore, the probability of seeing the letter U at a particular instant of time very much depends on the preceeding letter. Similarly, the initial part of a message often greatly influences subsequent events. Such a stochastic process (a process whose outcome is random) can be described by a *j*th order *Markov* process, in which the current event depends only on the *j* most recent events (the Markov property).

In line with an often-cited example (Rabiner, 1989), we construct a simple first order three-state Markov model of the weather. Assume that the weather is in one of the following: state 1: rain, state 2: cloudy, or state 3: sunny. We could define a state transition probability matrix as follows:

$$A = \{a_{ij}\} = \begin{matrix} 0.4 & 0.2 & 0.1 \\ 0.3 & 0.6 & 0.1 \\ 0.3 & 0.2 & 0.8 \end{matrix}$$

which expresses, for example, that if today is sunny (state 3 = column 3), the probability that tomorrow is rainy (state 1 = row 1) is expessed by a_{31} = 0.1. In addition to predicting tomorrow's weather, such a model can be used to compute, for example, how probable a given weather sequence, like "sun-sun-rain-rain-rain-sun" could be.

In this kind of model, each state corresponds to an observable event. Such models can thus be used to study observed symbols arranged in a discrete time series. In a *hidden* Markov model, the observation attached to each state corresponds to an output *probability distribution* instead of a *deterministic event*. The underlying stochastic process, the state sequence, is hidden, we can only observe it through another set of stochastic processes that produce the sequence of observations. In the next section we shall look at an example of this kind of model.

A Simple Hidden Markov Model

Figure 1 shows an example of a hidden Markov process with two states. It consists of two mugs that contain pebbles marked either with "1" or "2", and of two boxes that contain black and white balls. Mugs correspond to transition probabilities from the states and boxes correspond to output distributions attached to the two possible states.

According to some random process, an initial mug is chosen. From there, a pebble is picked at random. This determines the next state of the model (either "1" or "2"). From a box carrying the same number as the pebble, an observation is picked at random. Next, from a mug carrying the same number, a new pebble is picked to determine the next state transition, and so on.

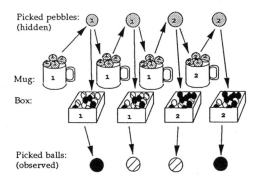

Figure 1. An example of a hidden Markov model.

Now, only the ball sequence is observable, the generated state number sequence is hidden to the observer. Such a model could be used to generate ball sequences, but an interesting question concerning practical applications is how to build a model on the basis of sample ball sequences to describe and explain regularities (states) of the sequence.

In general, there are three basic problems that must be solved before using HMMs (Rabiner, 1989). (1) The *evaluation problem*. Given a model and an observation sequence, determine how likely it is that the model has generated a given set of observations. (2) The *state assignment problem*, in which one has to determine the most likely state sequence corresponding to an observation sequence. (3) The *estimation problem*. Given the model structure and observations, determine the most likely parameters of the model (state transition probabilities, state output probabilities, initial state distribution). How these problems relate to speech will be addressed in the following sections.

Evaluation Problem — Isolated Word Recognition

The first of the three problems can be viewed as scoring how well a given model matches a given observation sequence. If we have several competing models, the solution to this problem allows us to choose the model which best matches the observations. We look at this problem in light of the simple two-state model of Figure 2.

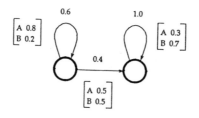

Figure 2. Another simple hidden Markov model. Observations are now attached to state transitions instead of state occupancies. The probabilities of transitions from one state to another are given, as well as the probabilites of each transition generating one of the two possible observable symbols (A or B).

Figure 3 illustrates how to compute the probability of the observation sequence "AAB", using the state model of Figure 2. Let us assume that the initial state is 1. Each state at each time step is depicted with the probability of being in this particular state at that particular time while generating the given observation. These probabilities are computed by summing up all possible transitions from the previous time step to this particular state. The total probability is the sum of probabilities over all (two) states at the final time step 3. This algorithm is called *the forward algorithm*. Similar computations can be done starting from the final state toward the starting state, in which case the algorithm is called *the backward algorithm*.

How probable it is for the HMM of Figure 2 to produce a sequence like "AAB"? In Figure 3, each possible state transition is depicted with its probability multiplied by the probability of generating the observed symbol when taking the transition (see Figure 2 for these probabilities). Each state is also depicted with the probability of being at this particular state while generating the given observations up to that time step. These state probabilities are derived by summing up all transitions leading to the state, each multiplied by the probability of the preceeding state. The total "forward probability" a_F is the sum of the state probabilities over all final states. Here it is 0.19 (0.03 + 0.16).

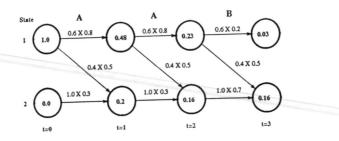

Figure 3. Computing forward probability a_F for an observation sequence "AAB". The total a_F is the sum of the probabilities over all final states. Here it is 0.19 (0.03 + 0.16).

To apply these concepts, consider isolated word recognition. For each word of the vocabulary, we design a separate HMM. A speech signal is represented as a time sequence of spectral (or other feature) vectors, which are coded using a spectral codebook with M codevectors. The observations are thus a sequence of indices of those codebook vectors that were closest to the speech feature vectors. This is called *vector quantisation*. First, we can use the solution to problem 3 to train the word models on the basis of recorded examples. Recognition of an unknown utterance is now performed by evaluating the probability that each model generates this utterance, and by selecting the model with the highest score.

At this point we note that the output processes need not be discrete, that is, coming from a finite alphabet, but they can also be continuous probability densities, such as Gaussian distributions (see Figure 8).

Determining The Best State Sequence — Connected Word Recognition

To illustrate the second problem, finding the best state sequence through a single HMM, we take an example from connected-word recognition. Assume as above that we have HMMs for words of the vocabulary, but that now, we can construct sentences from these words, according to some restrictions, such as the graph depicted in Figure 6. Finding the most probable (hidden) state path through a large composite model enables us to determine the most probable word sequence corresponding to the observation sequence.

The algorithm, called *Viterbi-algorithm* (Forney, 1973; Rabiner, 1989), is illustrated in Figure 4. The algorithm is quite similar to the forward algorithm. The only difference is that instead of summing the probabilities of transitions from all states of the previous time step, only the most probable transition is left, and the rest is discarded. Tracing back from the most probable final state reveals the most probable state sequence. For our example, the best sequence is 1-1-2-2. Note that for partial sequences, the best state sequence might not be the same as for the whole, for example, for "AA", the best state sequence would be 1-1-1.

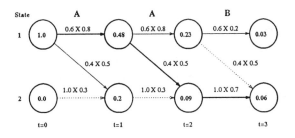

Figure 4. An illustration of the Viterbi-algorithm: Finding the best state sequence corresponding to the observed sequence "AAB". The most probable path is thickened and the discarded transitions are drawn as dotted lines.

Training

The most difficult problem of HMMs is how to adjust model parameters to maximise the probability of training observation sequences given a model structure. There is no known way of solving this analytically. We can, however, choose the parameters in such a way that this probability is locally maximised using an iterative procedure called *Baum-Welch re-estimation* (Baum and Petrie, 1966; Rabiner, 1989). Old parameters are replaced by new ones, that are computed on the basis of previous ones as well as from training observations. It can be shown that the new ones are more likely to produce the given observations (Huang*et al.*, 1990). Figure 5 illustrates parameter estimation. Assuming that M represents current parameter values, new values M make observations more likely, resulting in higher forward probability a$_F$. It is also possible to get stuck on a local maximum before reaching the true maximum likelihood estimate M.

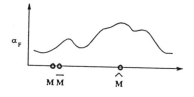

Figure 5. The space of parameters in training HMMs. Horizontal axis depicts the parameter values, and vertical axis shows the likelihood of the HMM to produce the training data. M is the maximum likelihood estimate.

Applying HMMs to Speech Recognition

We have already noted that HMMs can be used to model words, but in fact, it is possible to use HMMs to represent any unit of speech. A good strategy is to represent as HMM any knowledge that can be represented in that way (such as a phonetic or syntactic knowledge source). This is because such an HMM can be automatically trained from data, which results in improved accuracies if training and decoding are treated in the same framework.

For example, if subword models with a grammar are used, word and sentence knowledge can be incorporated by representing each word as a network of subword models, which expresses every way in which the word could be pronounced. The grammar can be represented as a network of words, encoding grammatically acceptable sentences (Figure 6). A huge HMM modelling all acceptable sentences is thus obtained. A basic Viterbi search might be too slow with such large networks, since it enumerates all possible states. Advanced techniques such as beam search or A* search should be used in such cases (Nilsson, 1982; Paul, 1991).

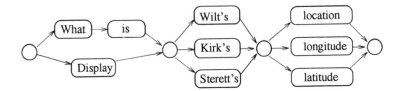

Figure 6. A model for a sentence. Each ellipse corresponds to a word model which may be composed of phone models, for example.

Choosing words as sub-units is practical for small vocabulary applications. Large vocabularies require that word models be composed of smaller units, because without the sharing of data between word models, a prohibitively large amount of training data would be required. Typically, the choice of subword model (phones, diphones, or triphones) is based on linguistic considerations, where each word can be represented by a concatenation of such elements.

To model coarticulation, phones can be modelled according to their immediate right and/or left phone context. Both within-word and between-word coarticulation can be taken into account by such triphone modelling (Lee, 1990). However, having a separate model for each context results in an excessively large number of models, which would require too much training data for reliable parameter estimation. The number of free parameters must thus be reduced or smoothed.

A solution to this is *parameter tying* (Young, 1992). For example, if phones are modeled with three-state models (states corresponding roughly to the beginning, middle and end of the phone), the middle states of triphones can be tied together, that is, they are shared by all triphone models of this phone. In general, similar output distributions can be automatically clustered to reduce their number (Hwang and Huang, 1991). A small number of distributions is then shared among all states of all models. Another solution is to estimate more robust monophone and/or diphone parameters and interpolate triphone parameters with these (Jelinek and Mercer, 1980).

This problem illustrates well one of the most important issues in designing a HMM-based system: How to estimate a huge number of parameters with only a limited amount of training data at hand.

An advantage of hidden Markov modelling is that training data need not be labelled, that is, word or phone boundaries need not be indicated. Word models, corresponding to the words of the written sentence, are concatenated. The resulting long string of models is trained as an entity, using the spoken sentence as a whole. Word boundary information is automatically absorbed in the model (embedded training). Other techniques, such as some neural network models, may face some problems in training for continuous speech, since word boundaries cannot be detected easily. Thus hand-labelling of the training data might be required in some cases.

Language Modelling for HMMs

The role of language models is to constrain possible words to be considered at each decision point. Without such a model, the entire vocabulary must be considered at each point in time; with a model, many candidates can be eliminated. Alternatively, it is possible to assign higher probabilities to some word candidates than others.

There is a multitude of methods to express permissible word sequences. Regular and context-free grammars have been widely used for this purpose. On the other hand, stochastic grammars assign an estimated probability to any word that can follow a given word (digram) or two given words (trigram) (Bahl *et al.*, 1983). Such modelling can contain both syntactic and semantic information, but these probabilities must be trained on a very large text corpus. Similarly, word pair grammars specify those words that can legally follow any given word with uniform probabilities.

About Model Structures

Everything cannot be inferred from training data, at least the modelling methodology must be predetermined (like the use of HMMs). Determination of the structure of sub-unit models may also be guided by our knowledge of phonetics, although some methods have been reported for constructing the model structure automatically on the basis of appropriate data (Takami and Sagayama, 1992). As examples of sub-unit structures, two practical phone models are depicted in Figures 7 and 8.

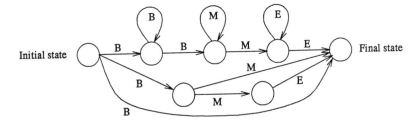

Figure 7. An example of a phone topology.

In the first figure, letters refer to output distributions that are tied together within the model. Here, output distributions are attached to state transitions (Lee, 1989). In the second picture, they are attached to states. This figure also illustrates the use of continuous observation densities. In this case, output distributions might be parametric distributions, such as Gaussians, or mixtures of multiple distributions (Bahl *et al.*, 1988). In this figure, there is only one observation dimension, but in practice, the dimension of the feature vector is used. According to the rationale of continuous HMMs, continuous observations can be modelled directly without any degradation or distortion associated with vector quantisation or any other kind of discretisation.

Finally, it may be noted that the (Gaussian) distributions that form the basis of continuous mixture modelling can be shared or tied among all states. This results in so called semi-continuous HMMs (Huang and Jack, 1989).

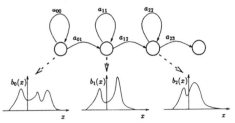

Figure 8. Another example of a phone topology with continuous density observations: a_{ij} denotes transition probabilities from state i to state j and b_i denotes the output distribution of state i.

Limitations of Basic HMMs and Some Solutions

Basic HMMs are subject to several limitations. One concerns the state occupancy duration which is implicitly exponential. It is possible to add state *duration models*, but at the cost of increased computational complexity (Guédon and Cocozza-Thivent, 1990). A major further limitation is the assumption that successive observations are independent (i.e. that observations depend only on the current state and not on a set of previous states). However, it is clearly the case that successive frames of speech are not independent from each other. One attempt to ameliorate this problem is to use differential and acceleration coefficients computed from a longer sequence of speech frames (Lee, 1989). A better solution may be to construct stochastic models of entire segments, and to model speech as a concatenation of such segments (Roucos and Dunham, 1987).

Finally, speech certainly is not a genuine first-order Markov process. Maximum likelihood estimation produces parameters that converge towards their true values, but these might be true values of wrong models. Therefore, an estimation criterion that works well in spite of these inaccurate assumptions should result in an improved recognition accuracy. Several such criteria have been introduced, among others the maximum mutual information criterion (Bahl *et al.*, 1986). Instead of trying to identify true model parameters, this criterion proceeds by minimising the average uncertainty of the word sequence to be recognised, given the acoustic observations.

The strengths of HMMs are their capability of dealing with the sequential nature of speech, the existence of well-founded training methods without a need for preliminary segmentation of training data, and their decoding efficiency in explaining an observation sequence in terms of a sequence of HMMs. These strengths have made HMMs the predominant method in current automatic speech recognition technology and research.

Artificial Neural Networks for Speech Recognition

In this section, we give an overview of artificial neural networks (ANNs), with special reference to speech recognition. From the multitude of excellent references on this topic, we shall mention the following: Hertz *et al.* (1991), Kohonen (1988), Lippmann (1987), McClelland *et al.*, (1986), Pao (1990). Some texts that concentrate on speech recognition and neural networks are Fallside (1992), Lippmann (1989), Morgan and Scofield (1992), and Robinson (1993).

What Are Artificial Neural Networks?

Artificial neural networks can be defined as a collection of simple adaptive processing elements (nodes, units, or neuron models) that collectively can accomplish something of interest. Each element computes a function of the output activations of other processing elements, and the resulting activation is made available to yet other computing elements. This function is usually a weighted sum of the inputs, passed through a sigmoid-like nonlinearity. An example of such an element is depicted in Figure 9.

The field of artificial neural networks (or *connectionism*, or *neural computation*) is concerned with wide varieties of ways of interconnecting these elements, as well as with techniques to determine the values of the weights in the network on the basis of available training data (learning).

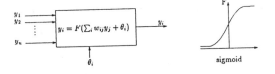

Figure 9. A simple neuron model and an illustration of a sigmoid function (F).

The ways that neural computation differs from more convential computation can be characterised as follows:

— the use of many similar and simple processing elements,
— the massively parallel operation of these elements,
— knowledge is not stored in individual units or as rules, but distributed as connections and interactions across the network.

Biological plausibility is often mentioned in connection with neural computation. However, it must be kept in mind that the above-mentioned model of a neuron is an extreme simplification, far removed from biological reality. Nevertheless, interesting collective effects emerge from a network of such artificial elements which exhibit certain similarities to the collective behaviour of biological neurons. While the question of how information is processed in the brain is no doubt intriguing, we are more directly interested in how neural computation can be utilised for speech recognition. In this sense, our viewpoint remains that of an engineer, not that of a biologist.

An Example of an ANN Architecture:
Feed-Forward Nets and Back-Propagation

To illustrate the ANN architectures, we shall have a look at feed-forward networks. Figure 10 depicts a simple feed-forward network. Each circle is a "neuron-like" computing unit with a weighted sum of its inputs, passed through a nonlinear function, usually a sigmoid.

It has been shown that this kind of network, also known as "multi-layer perceptrons" (MLPs), can be trained to produce (almost) any desired outputs for a given set of inputs.

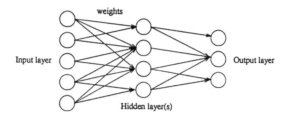

Figure 10. A simple feed-forward network.

The net is initialised with random weights. An input example is presented to the network, and the corresponding output vector is calculated. This is then compared to the desired output.

The error between desired and actual outputs can be considered as a function of the weights, and the weights can be modified so as to decrease the error. It is convenient to start weight update computations at the output layer, after which the computations for the following layer can be based on those of the previous layer. Thus the error computation propagates backwards from the output layer towards the input layer. This kind of training algorithm based on gradient descent is called *error back propagation* (McClelland *et al.*, 1986).

There are many variations on this basic algorithm to speed up the convergence towards a low-error solution. This remains a subject of active research, as the training typically requires many iterations, and thus involves a great deal of computing.

There are two major classes of training paradigms for ANNs, supervised and unsupervised training. Back-propagation is an example of the former type, where the training set consists of pairs of input and desired output patterns. In unsupervised learning, there is no information at all about the ideal output for a given input. Instead, learning is guided by the inherent structure in the training data, or by some general principle, such as the minimising of information loss through the model.

What Can ANNs Do for Speech Recognition?

Since ANNs can in principle be trained to approximate any mapping, they can be used for pattern classification (Lippmann and Gold, 1987) (Leung and Zue, 1988). They are especially amenable to this, because many classification tasks require the construction of complex decision surfaces.

A possible configuration for a feed-forward network used as a classifier is to have as many output units as there are pattern classes. The desired output for each class is such that only the output unit of a particular class is kept active, while the activation of other output units is increasingly suppressed. In an extension to this classifying function, one can use artificial neural networks to estimate the probability density function over observed classes of objects. A network can thus be used as a component in a system that incorporates other probabilistic evidence, such as an HMM system.

In case of speech, input to the network may be a short-time spectral representation of speech, which may include some context.

A problem with this kind of a scheme is that the input, if it includes context, is a fixed-time window without any possibility for alignment or time-stretching. So called "Time Delay Neural Networks" (TDNNs) solve a part of the problem by tying the weights from every frame of input to the hidden layer. The same can be done with a range of hidden-layer units. Sections of the network can be made to perform the same computations, which makes the network time-shift invariant (Waibel *et al.*, 1989). This form of weight sharing and this imposition of constraints on the connectivity can be seen as the incorporation of prior knowledge into the ANN design.

Specifically, to avoid the problem of fixed time windows, one can introduce cycles into the network graph. This lets the net keep information about past inputs for an amount of time that is not fixed *a priori*, but that depends on weights and on the input data. Variations of the back-propagation algorithm have been developed to train this kind of recurrent ANNs (Robinson, 1989).

In addition to feed-forward or recurrent nets trained by error back propagation, there are different ANN architectures for classification tasks. Two approaches that can be mentioned briefly are "Learning Vector Quantization" (LVQ) (Kohonen *et al.*, 1988), which is an algorithm to train a two-layer network for optimum discrimination between pattern classes, and "Radial Basis Function" (RBF) networks (Moody and Darken, 1989).

Furthermore, there are ANN architectures that are appropriate for producing new kind of representations of complex data, for example, of speech data. An example of such networks are Kohonen nets, or "Self Organizing Maps" (SOMs) (Kohonen, 1989; Kohonen, 1990). This kind of net organises itself automatically by so-called competitive learning, according to the structure of the input data (unsupervised training). An example of a two-dimensional representation of Finnish phonemes is depicted in Figure 11. Incoming speech can be mapped as the path of best-responding cells of the SOM. Such a mapping can be used as a basis of speech recognition (Torkkola and Kokkonen, 1991).

In addition, SOMs can also be used to illustrate, analyse and characterise speech, for example to diagnose phonation disorders (Leinonen *et al.*, 1992).

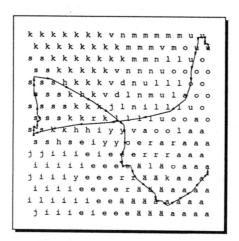

Figure 11. Mapping speech onto a two-dimensional SOM grid. Pronouncing the Finnish word "usea".

A Major Weakness of ANNs — The Time-Sequential Nature of Speech

Although ANNs with delays and recurrent connections can in theory model any temporal structure, current architectures are inefficient in capturing some important aspects of temporal structure. Pure ANNs are currently at their best when recognising short utterances or smaller speech sub-units. However, the mapping ability of ANNs can be used to derive new representations of the speech signal. Combinations of ANNs with other tools that have been proven useful in modelling the temporal structure of speech are thus of interest. Such combinations, in particular with DTW and HMMs, are discussed in the next section.

Another weakness of most current ANN models is the relatively long training time. A great deal of research effort is devoted to improving convergence times of current algorithms and to the development of faster algorithms.

Hybrid Methods for Speech Recognition

There are several possible approaches to the integration of ANNs with either HMMs or DTW. From a theoretical point of view, it has been shown that HMMs are a specific instance of certain type of recurrent ANNs. In this case, the forward-backward algorithm is equivalent to backpropagation (Bridle, 1990). The application of competitive or error-correcting training to HMMs shows how HMMs can be improved by means of a connectionist viewpoint. It is also possible to combine the strong features of each methodology to achieve a better performance than either could on its own. We shall take a quick look at these hybrid methods now.

ANNs as Vector Quantisers or Classifiers for HMMs

One way to combine HMMs with ANNs is to use ANN models as vector quantisers. While traditional vector quantisers aim to represent speech parameter vectors with minimum distortion, ANNs can be trained to discriminate.specific features relevant to the task. For example, if the task is phoneme recognition, LVQ-type of networks can be trained as frame-level (or using a wider context) phoneme classifiers. These ANNs then provide a stream of information to HMMs consisting of phoneme labels (Iwamida et al., 1990; Torkkola et al., 1991; Le Cerf and Van Compernolle, 1993). Since HMMs can combine the outputs of independent streams, information from other parallel networks computing some other relevant aspects of the task can be integrated (Mäntysalo et al., 1992; Torkkola, 1994).

ANNs Used to Compute Observation Probabilities for HMMs or Local Distance Scores for DTW

Another hybrid approach is the use of multi-layer perceptrons (MLPs) to act as discriminant local probability generators for HMMs (Bourlard et al., 1992), instead of using, for example, mixtures of Gaussians to generate observation probabilities. The training of HMMs is reduced to training transition probabilities.

This kind of hybrid combines several advantages of MLPs and HMMs: HMMs furnish their temporal processing abilities and provide embedded training procedures (thus obviating the need to segment training data), while MLPs are employed for their strong discriminative abilities, and to eliminate the need to formulate assumptions about likely observation probability densities. Further, when an MLP uses context in addition to its current frame (factors that are ignored in pure HMMs), the correlation between consecutive acoustic observations can be taken into account.

MLPs can also be used as local distance generators for dynamic time warping (DTW). In this architecture, the discrimination power of MLPs is combined with the time alignment abilities of DTW (Sakoe *et al.*, 1989).

ANNs to Replace Subword Models

One step further from an ANN-DTW hybrid is to construct subword models by ANNs. The idea is to find out which concatenation of these subword models best matches incoming speech. Again, to overcome the HMM assumption of independence between successive observations, researchers have tried to construct models that take a longer duration of speech signal into account. These *segmental* models classify or model entire segments of speech, instead of short-time observations. It is possible to use MLPs or LVQ as the basis of such models (Cheng *et al.*, 1992; Leung *et al.*, 1992). Similarly, *predictive* subword models aim at being able to predict the next frame of a particular subword unit (a phone, for example). As such predictors, MLPs can be used, with input that includes the phonetic context (Iso and Watanabe, 1991; Tebelskis *et al.*, 1991).

Connectionist Training of HMM Parameters or DTW Templates

Inspired by error-driven training methods developed for ANNs, several researchers have applied the same philosophy to HMM training, as well as to the training of ANN-HMM and ANN-DTW hybrids. This involves finding a suitable cost or error function whose derivatives with respect to parameters can be easily computed. Gradient descent can then be used to minimise this function. For example, in Young (1991), a cost function based on a maximum mutual information criterion is used to train pure HMMs. Driancourt and Gallinari (1992) furthermore show how different kinds of ANN modules can be combined with DTW and can be trained using the same principles. This training could even be extended to DTW templates. Similarly, Bengio *et al.*, (1992) show how ANN parameters and HMM parameters can be trained within the same framework.

Conclusion

We have taken a brief look at the two techniques that currently receive most of the attention in speech recognition research, hidden Markov models and artificial neural networks. Their popularity in the speech engineering community can be explained by their relatively effortless application: All that is needed is a great deal of training data. Most of the commercial speech recognition systems that go beyond small vocabulary isolated word recognition are based on HMMs, and the best systems in research laboratories are based on either HMMs alone, or on a combination of both HMMs and ANNs.

Though the best current systems based on these methods are already useful in restricted tasks, human performance is still far superior to the current state of the art. Integrating (human) linguistic knowledge easily and efficiently into these systems thus remains an important topic for future research.

Acknowledgements

This text owes a lot to the following references: Fallside (1992), Huang *et al.* (1990), Rabiner (1989) and Robinson (1993).

References

Bahl, L., Brown, P., de Souza, P., & Mercer, R. (1986). Maximum mutual information estimation of hidden Markov model parameters for speech recognition. In *Proceedings of the IEEE ICASSP* (pp. 49-52). Tokyo, Japan.

Bahl, L.R., Brown, P.F., de Souza, P.V., & Mercer, R.L. (1988). Speech recognition with continuous parameter hidden Markov models. In *Proceeding of the IEEE ICASSP* (pp. 40-43). New York City, USA.

Bahl, L.R., Jelinek, F., & Mercer, R.L. (1983). A maximum likelihood approach to continuous speech recognition. *IEEE Trans. on Pattern Analysis and Machine Intelligence, 5,* 179-190.

Baum, L. & Petrie, T. (1966). Statistical inference for probabilistic functions of finite state Markov chains. *Ann. Math. Stat., 37,* 1554-1563.

Bengio, Y., de Mori, R., Flammia, G., & Kompe, R. (1992). Global optimization of a neural network - hidden Markov model hybrids. *IEEE Trans. on Neural networks, 3,* 252-259.

Bourlard, H., Morgan, N., & Renals, S. (1992). Neural nets and hidden Markov models: Review and generalizations. *Speech Communication, 11,* 237-246.

Bridle, J. S. (1990). Alphanets: A recurrent neural network architecture with a hidden Markov model interpretation. *Speech Communication, 9,* 83-92.

Cheng, Y., O'Shaughnessy, D., Gupta, V., Kenny, P., Lenning, M., Mermelstein, P., & Parthasarathy, S. (1992). Hybrid segmental-LVQ/HMM for large vocabulary speech recognition. In *Proceedings of the IEEE ICASSP* (Vol. 1, pp. 593-596). San Francisco, CA, USA.

Driancourt, X. & Gallinari, P. (1992). A speech recognizer optimally combining learning vector quantization, dynamic programming and multi-layer perceptron. In *Proceedings of the IEEE ICASSP* (Vol. 1, pp. 609-612). San Francisco, CA, USA.

Fallside, F. (1992). Issues in speech recognition using neural networks. In *Proceedings of the Int. Conf. on Artificial Neural Networks.* (Vol. 1, pp. 765-773). Brighton, U.K.

Forney, G. (1973). The Viterbi algorithm. *Proc. IEEE, 61,* 268-278.

Godin, C. & Lockwood, P. (1989). DTW schemes for continuous speech recognition: A unified view. *Computer Speech and Language, 3,* 169-198.

Guédon, Y. & Cocozza-Thivent, C. (1990). Explicit state occupancy modelling by hidden semi-Markov models: Application of Derin's scheme. *Computer Speech and Language, 4,* 167-192.

Hertz, J., Krogh, A., & Palmer, R.G. (1991). *Introduction to the theory of neural computation.* Addison-Wesley.

Huang, X.D., Ariki, Y., & Jack, M.A. (1990). *Hidden Markov models for speech recognition.* Edinburgh University Press.

Huang, X.D. & Jack, M.A. (1989). Unified techniques for vector quantization and hidden Markov modelling using semi-continuous models. In *Proceedings of IEEE ICASSP* (Vol. 1, pp. 639-642).

Hwang, M.-Y. & Huang, X. (1991). Shared distribution hidden Markov models for speech recognition. *Technical Report CMU-CS-91-124,* School of Computer Science, Carnegie Mellon University.

Iso, K. & Watanabe, T. (1991). Large vocabulary speech recognition using neural prediction model. In *Proceedings of the IEEE ICASSP* (Vol. 1, pp. 57-60). Toronto, Canada.

Iwamida, H., Katagiri, S., McDermott, E., & Tohkura, Y. (1990). A hybrid speech recognition system using HMMs with an LVQ-trained codebook. In *Proceedings of the IEEE ICASSP* (Vol. 1, pp. 489-492). Albuquerque, NM, USA.

Jelinek, F. & Mercer, R. (1980). Interpolated estimation of Markov source parameters from sparse data. In *Proc. of the workshop on pattern recognition in practice.* North-Holland.

Kohonen, T. (1988). An introduction to neural computing. *Neural Networks, 1,* 3-16.

Kohonen, T. (1989). *Self-Organization and Associative Memory* (3rd ed.). Berlin: Springer

Kohonen, T. (1990). The self-organizing map. *Proceedings of the IEEE, 78,* 1464-1480.

Kohonen, T., Barna, G., & Chrisley, R. (1988). Statistical pattern recognition with neural networks: Benchmarking studies. In *Proceedings of the IEEE Int. Conf. on Neural Networks* (Vol. 1, pp. 61-68). San Diego, USA.

Le Cerf, P. & Van Compernolle, D. (1993). Using parallel MLPs as labelers for multiple codebook HMMs. In *Proceedings of the IEEE ICASSP93* (Vol. 1, pp. 561-564). Minneapolis, MN, USA.

Lee, K.-F. (1989). *Automatic speech recognition: The development of the SPHINX system.* Boston, MA: Kluwer Academic Publishers

Lee, K.-F. (1990). Context-dependent phonetic hidden Markov models for speaker-independent continuous speech recognition. *IEEE Trans. on Acoustics, Speech, and Signal Processing, 38,* 599-609.

Leinonen, L., Kangas, J., Torkkola, K., & Juvas, A. (1992). Dysphonia detected by pattern recognition of spectral composition. *Journal of Speech and Hearing Research, 35,* 287-295.

Leung, H., Hetherington, I., & Zue, V. (1992). Speech recognition using stochastic segmental neural networks. In *Proceedings of the IEEE ICASSP92* (Vol. 1, pp. 613-616). San Francisco, CA, USA.

Leung, H.C. & Zue, V.W. (1988). Some phonetic recognition experiments using artificial neural nets. In *Proceedings of the IEEE ICASSP88* (pp. 422-425). New York City, USA.

Lippmann, R.P. (1987). An introduction to computing with neural nets. *IEEE ASSP Magazine, 4*, 4-22.

Lippmann, R.P. (1989). Review of neural networks for speech recognition. *Neural Computation, 1*, 1-38.

Lippmann, R.P. & Gold, B. (1987). Neural-net classifiers useful for speech recognition. In *Proceedings of the 1st Int. Conf. on Neural Networks* (Vol IV, pp 417-425). San Diego, USA.

Mäntysalo, J., Torkkola, K., & Kohonen, T. (1992). LVQ-based speech recognition with high-dimensional context vectors. In *Proceedings of ICSLP* (Vol. 1, pp. 539-542). Banff, Alberta, Canada.

McClelland, J. L., Rumelhart, D. E., & the PDP Research Group Editors (1986). *Parallel distributed processing: Explorations in the microstructure of cognition.* MIT Press/Bradford.

Moody, J. & Darken, C. (1989). Fast learning in networks of locally tuned processing units. *Neural Computation, 1*, 281-294.

Morgan, D.P. & Scofield, C.L. (1992). *Neural networks and speech processing.* Kluwer Academic Publishers.

Nilsson, N. (1982). *Principles of artificial intelligence.* Tioga publishing company.

Pao, Y. (1990). *Adaptive pattern recognition and neural networks.* Addison-Wesley.

Paul, D. B. (1991). Algorithms for an optimal A* search and linearizing the search in the stack decoder. In *Proceedings of the IEEE ICASSP* (Vol. 1, pp. 693-696). Toronto, Canada.

Rabiner, L. (1989). A tutorial on Hidden Markov Models and selected applications in speech recognition. *Proceedings of the IEEE, 77*, 257-286.

Rabiner, L. & Juang B-H. (1993). *Fundamentals of speech recognition.* Prentice Hall.

Robinson, A.J. (1989). *Dynamic error propagation networks.* Ph.D. thesis, Cambridge University Engineering Department, England.

Robinson, T. (1993). Artificial neural networks: The mole-grips of the speech scientist. In M. Cooke, S. Beet, & M. Crawford (Eds.), *Visual representations of speech signals* (pp. 83-94). John Wiley.

Roucos, S. & Dunham, M. (1987). A stochastic segment model for phoneme based continuous speech recognition. In *Proceedings of the IEEE ICASSP* (Vol. 1, pp. 73-76). Dallas, TX, USA.

Sakoe, H., Isotani, R., Yoshida, K., Ichi Iso, K., & Watanabe, T. (1989). Speaker-independent word recognition using dynamic programming neural networks. In *Proceedings of the IEEE ICASSP* (pp. 29-32). Glasgow, Scotland.

Takami, J. & Sagayama, S. (1992). A successive state splitting algorithm for efficient allophone modeling. In *Proceedings of the IEEE ICASSP* (Vol. 1, pp. 573-576). San Francisco, CA, USA.

Tebelskis, J., Waibel, A., Petek, B., & Schmidbauer, O. (1991). Continuous speech recognition using linked predictive neural networks. In *Proceedings of the IEEE ICASSP* (Vol. 1, pp. 61-64). Toronto, Canada.

Torkkola, K., Kangas, J., Utela, P., Kaski, S., Kokkonen, M., Kurimo, M., & Kohonen, T. (1991). Status report of the Finnish phonetic typewriter project. In *Proc. Int. Conf. on Artificial Neural Networks* (pp. 771-776). Espoo, Finland.

Torkkola, K. & Kokkonen, M. (1991). Using the topology-preserving properties of SOFMs in speech recognition. In *Proceedings of the IEEE ICASSP* (Vol. 1, pp. 261-264). Toronto, Canada.

Torkkola, K. (1994). New ways to use LVQ-codebooks together with hidden Markov models. In *Proceedings of the IEEE ICASSP*. Adelaide, Australia.

Waibel, A., Hanazawa, T., Hinton, G., Shikano, K., & Lang, K. (1989). Phoneme Recognition Using Time-Delay Neural Networks. *IEEE, Trans. on Acoustics, Speech and Signal Processing, 37,* 328-339.

Waibel, A. & Lee, K.-F. (Eds.) (1990). *Readings in speech recognition,* San Mateo, CA: Morgan Kaufman Publishers,

Young, S. (1991). Competitive training: A connectionist approach to discriminative training of hidden Markov models. *Proc. IEE, 138,* 61-68.

Young, S. (1992). The general use of tying in phoneme-based HMM speech recognisers. In *Proceedings of the IEEE ICASSP* (Vol. 1, pp. 569-572). San Francisco, CA, USA.

SECTION
3

CHALLENGES

SECTION 3: CHALLENGES

Introduction to Section 3: Challenges

Eric Keller[1] and *Jean Caelen*[2]

[1] Université de Lausanne, LAUSANNE, Switzerland
[2] Institut de la Communication Parlée, GRENOBLE, France

The "Challenges" section of this book occupies about half of its chapters. The reader is warned that there is a substantial jump in difficulty as one moves from the first to the second half of this volume. If the subsequent chapters define some "future challenges" for our field in general, they may also represent a "more immediate comprehension challenge" for the new reader.

For this reason, we begin the section with a somewhat more detailed discussion of the central issue which inspired the assembling of the "Challenges" chapters in the first place. *It is the question of how much knowledge about human speech processing is required for developing speech synthesis and speech recognition devices.* Many of the arguments in the first half of this book have already demonstrated that *speech synthesis* cannot operate without direct reference to the human model. Without being a carbon copy of human speech production, synthesis must necessarily be structured along parameters and principles that are similar to those that govern human speech. However, is the same true of *speech recognition*? Many observers resolutely maintain that that is not so.

In automatic speech recognition, a difference can be made between systems based on artificial intelligence (AI), and those that emerge from various techniques of pattern recognition and thus proceed by the identification of prototypes (DTW: "Dynamic Time Warping", HMM: "Hidden Markov Model", NN: "Neural" or "Neuromimetic Network"). Overall, the latter systems (e.g. the Markovian models) have shown better performance than AI-type systems, without being by any means inspired or necessarily similar in operation to human perceptual and cognitive processes. Indeed, judging exclusively by results obtained, or by systems in current use, it would seem that reference to the human cognitive model is not at all required for good performance in speech recognition. As a consequence, much cognitively-, linguistically- or AI-oriented research in speech recognition has been totally abandoned over the last few years.

We would argue that this is a regrettable and short-sighted policy. It would seem to us that over the long term, the systematic neglect of issues surrounding human communicative, cognitive and linguistic behaviour is likely to lead to substantial confusion and to major limitations in recognition systems. Systems that recognise by a set of "magic black boxes" (e.g. large arrays of markovian chains or neuromimetic pattern recognisers, dealing in global fashion with speech input) cannot be expected to produce more than the correct recognition of pre-stored speech sequences and the rejection of non-stored patterns. Unless a system is designed to learn specific types of cognitive or linguistic information, it cannot be expected to generalise, or to "learn" parameters in terms of familiar cognitive and linguistic categories. Consequently, when such systems fail, debugging is severely hampered by a lack of evident coherence, and by the lack of explicitness of system parameters. Much like reptilians that never evolved beyond a certain highly efficient pattern recognition, pattern-driven speech recognition cannot be expected to evolve much beyond a fairly focused, and thus admittedly highly efficient, recognition performance.

This is not to say that human computation cannot be efficient as well. Current knowledge on the computations that humans perform in order to understand complex communicative interactions, for example, provide ample reason to argue that human computations, while very complex, can also be highly efficient (for some appreciation of the details of this argument, see Chapter 16). The supposed inadequacies of human computation is therefore insufficient reason for rejecting all anthropomorphic computer models of speech recognition. Quite the contrary. Studies of human communicative behaviour suggest that human speaker-listeners operate with exceeding efficiency, and take into account complex interactions between supporting forms of evidence, in order to recognise and interpret spoken information. The issue is not so much one of efficiency of computation, as it is an issue of knowing *exactly what* human computations are performed in a given situation to arrive at a specific recognition or interpretation performance.

To further cement this argument, let us examine the various aspects of human recognition performance. This may guide us in establishing which human-type computations might be of interest when creating similar computer-based algorithms.

1. Human perception is relatively robust in the parameter extraction of relevant acoustic data from noisy acoustic input (cf. Chapters 14 and 15).

2. Human perception is fairly successful at calculating distinctive features (be they articulatorily or acoustically-based) for the discrimination of specific sounds or sound patterns (see Chapter 9).

3. Human listeners show good performance at the identification (sometimes "the active reconstruction") of those phonological and lexical events that are most helpful in understanding a given passage — and that despite the fact that such events may be coarticulatorily and prosodically encoded in literally thousands of different ways (see also Chapter 9).

4. Human listeners appear to maintain sets of local identification hypotheses, which indicates that they are capable of dealing in an efficient manner with uncertain and incompletely-decoded material.

5. Humans can exercise complex reasoning in evaluating, completing or rejecting such partial hypotheses on the basis of multiple sources of heterogeneous knowledge (acoustic, phonetic, lexical, syntactic, semantic or pragmatic knowledge).

6. Humans can apply sophisticated decision-making and control strategies in order to coordinate processing, and to resolve coreferential language phenomena such as anaphoras, deictics, hesitations, error corrections, ellipses, incomplete sentences, etc. Even more sophisticated coordinate processing occurs when multi-modal input is analysed (see Chapter 16).

7. Humans are well-equipped to adapt their perceptual mechanisms to novel situations and to new speakers, or to new and complex tasks. Also, humans show exceptional ability to learn new vocabulary and even new language structures throughout their lives.

8. Current artificial recognition systems are comparatively ill-prepared and easily derouted in face of a series of higher-level tasks. For example, they cannot "guess" at the meaning of a new, unfamiliar word the way human language users can, they cannot coalesce information from multiple sources (e.g. when several speakers talk at the same time), nor can they compensate for erroneous pronunciations, or adjust to a strong foreign accent. The best current systems (the statistically-based systems) are not advanced enough to be able to draw inferences from and to improve upon their own performance; both of these are abilities in which humans excel. Consider also that humans can reason about events that have never even occurred, and which are therefore (by definition) beyond the grasp of statistical systems.

Reflections such as these amply motivate the position we've taken in this volume. In our perspective, development on synthesis *as well as* recognition devices can profit from looking at human speech performance. However, this position must be understood correctly. We do not propose that machines should be constructed exactly like humans. As proponents of the non-cognitive approach like to point out, when humans learned to fly, the winning design was not an articulated, highly flexible, bird-like wing, but it was a relatively simple, fixed-wing design. For a variety of excellent reasons, recognition devices built for machines will necessarily operate differently than those of humans.

However, consider also that it wasn't by avoiding the force of lift and the law of gravity that flight was mastered. In terms of the flight analogy, the current status of automatic speech recognition bears greater resemblance to the achievements of the Wright brothers than to current fixed- or rotary-wing flight. The "thing" flies, often just barely, but a great deal more theory needs to be understood and intelligently applied to operational systems to insure "secure flight" under the most exacting conditions. With this in mind, let us examine in some more detail a number of current approaches to speech recognition.

Which Speech Recognition System?

Outside of the statistical systems, the principles of which are explained in Torkkola's chapter (Chapter 8), the majority of current knowledge-oriented systems are constituted of a community of "experts" (or "agents") that exchange information in a proposal/verification mode. For example, there might exist an "expert" on fundamental frequency whose job is to identify different prosodic structures in the input stream. These recognition systems are mainly distinguished by the *strategy* that they employ, more than by the *knowledge sources* that they use. In fact, all of these systems manipulate knowledge about roughly the same acoustic, phonetic, lexical, prosodic, syntactic and semantic information.

In such systems, the "experts" — each related to one or several knowlege sources — operate either in *coordinated* fashion under the direction of an external supervisor, in *autonomous* fashion, or in *distributed* fashion. In the case of *coordinated operation under a supervisor*, the recognition strategy is determined by a centralised process which activates the experts according to a hierarchical (Sacerdotti, 1977) or an "opportunist"[1] plan (Hayes-Roth and Hayes-Roth, 1979). Several layers of experts, and thus several supervisors, are also possible (Gong and Haton, 1987; Sabah, 1988, 1990).

In the cases of *autonomous* and *distributed* systems, the agents cooperate actively to resolve the problems with which they are confronted. They not only communicate to exchange data and knowledge which they require to solve a problem, but they also maintain control information about their own status. In these latter systems, a level of

---

[1] In the sense of "exploiting opportunities when they present themselves".

metacommunication is thus required where agents must inform each other about their internal status. We will examine the major types of these autonomous or distributed models next.

The Multi-expert Models

In the so-called "blackboard"[2] systems, such as Hearsay II (Erman *et al.*, 1980), the processing modules called "experts" are guided by the data. In contrast to the hierarchical systems where expected solutions are made available by higher-level processes, here solutions "rise spontaneously to the surface", and are assembled into a complete interpretation as different experts complete their analysis on the basis of available data.

This type of organisation appears the most attractive of all major model types, since at least in theory, coordination becomes unnecessary. In reality however, errors and uncertainties are not checked by higher-level processes and are thus allowed to propagate across levels. To impede such error propagation, an expert module must therefore be able to question its own results at all times, and must be given the power to refine or modify its predictions. Since it cannot always make these decisions alone and at the right moment, it must be able to refer to other "experts" to resolve open issues. For example, some phonetic decisions depend on lexical and prosodic information, and vice versa, some lexical decisions depend on phonetic information. In Hearsay II, as in all "autonomous" systems, data must thus be corrected, and hypotheses must be enlarged. This is where the problem occurs. The same experts may thus be reactivated several times, which in turn can create infinite loop conditions, since knowledge sources are no longer independent of each other.

In systems with a hierarchical strategy, such as HWIN, this type of problem does not arise, but as a consequence of the hierarchical schema, the general strategy remains static — which sometimes leads to a processing inadequacy with respect to available data and to a certain lack of subtleness in the management of hypotheses and tests. Improvements thus consist of either creating a "focussing strategy", whose purpose is to activate experts that stand the greatest chance of advancing the understanding process, or of implementing an "opportunist strategy", where some form of metaknowledge is applied to the problem and to the performance of the experts.

---

2 In these systems, a "blackboard", or a central exchange for ongoing hypotheses is maintained where experts deposit information to support or reject the hypotheses.

The Multi-agent Models

As in general application programming, large recognition systems become close to unmanageable when constructed entirely according to traditional procedural programming principles. Object-oriented (OO) models were thus introduced in order to improve on the structure of recognition systems. From the start, the notion of "frame" (Minsky, 1975), and later, the object-oriented approach proved to be a powerful representational tool, since it offered a rich and explicit organisational structure for the various operating elements. OO techniques have since been applied extensively to so-called "high-level" problems in visual recognition and in natural language processing.

Despite the success of OO-based systems, procedural or rule-based systems have also proved to be useful in a complementary role to OO-based models (Nazif and Levine, 1984; McKeown, 1985). Procedural approaches are "action-centered", i.e. have an organisation focused on the "reasoning process" required to explain a particular activity. Such techniques have thus turned out to be successful at low-level types of processing, such as feature detection. Altogether, a variety of multi-agent architectures have been tested, representing various compromises between object-oriented and task- or rule-oriented types of processing on the one hand, and between spatial exploration, coordination and planning strategies on the other (VISIONS system, Hanson & Riseman, 1978; SIGMA system, Matsuyama and Hwang, 1985).

In terms of their theoretical orientation, these multi-agent systems are based on two different organisational paradigms, a sociopsychological and a neuropsychological paradigm. In systems based on sociopsychological notions, agents must have "beliefs" and "intentions", in order to solve a given problem in collective and coordinated fashion. These "beliefs" are cognitive operations that provide more or less well-defined representations of their environment, while the "intentions" are premises of illocutory language acts (Searle, 1969; Searle and Vanderveken, 1985) which they entertain in their communications. In this type of organisation, each agent is of sufficient size to detain a certain "intelligence" of its own. It is therefore capable of reacting to itself and to its environment. Its behaviour is the consequence of its observations, its knowledge, its particular competence and its intentions. Currently, systems based on this type of schema have not grown much beyond ten agents because of the extensive flow of information that must be maintained between all agents of the system.

In systems based on neuropsychological notions, agents are microscopic reactive system ("feature detectors") that respond in automatic fashion to certain stimuli. They are conceived as specialised modules, similar to neural response columns or Fodor's (1983) "modules". Such systems can comprise up to several hundred agents, each of whose individual competence is rather limited, but whose global behaviour "appears intelligent" (Minsky, 1986). The advantage of this architecture is that communicative paths between such units can remain rather limited.

In Search of a "Guided Dynamic Organisation"

Both, multi-expert and multi-agent approaches to speech recognition pose some major philosophical problems. Even though it is possible to conceive of a competence distributed over a large number of agents, the emergence of a "self" (in the sense of "awareness of self and its actions") is more likely the result of a centralised than a distributed organisation. This is because a structure needs a central focus of operation in order to be able to judge the value of its input processes. This appears to typify human behaviour. As we saw above, the ability to draw inferences from and to improve upon one's own performance is an important attribute of human speech recognition performance.

In fact, the weakness of a strongly distributed organisation arises from its strict separation into levels and from the entirely ascendant nature of the modules, as well as from the attendant problems of synchronous processing and inter-module communication. "Detectors" in the strict sense are autonomous. To maintain this autonomy, a process must often duplicate processing that is also required elsewhere. The alternative is waiting for another module to finish its own processing and to pass its result. However as was indicated above, this can lead to unacceptable delays or to infinite loop conditions.

So the essential difficulty is to develop a dynamic organisational structure which can profit from specialised knowledge processing encapsuled in separate layers, at the same time as it can be guided by a "stronger self" which knows when to pursue an analysis path and when to abandon it. Technically speaking, such an organisation may well be modelled by neuromimetic networks — which are probably more subtle in use and certainly more adaptive than rule-governed structures — but much more importantly, the structure must contain a considerable array of interdependent communicative paths that can be selectively inhibited by higher command. The crucial issue — one that has been insufficiently addressed by current systems and which appears to be admirably solved in human processing — is exactly how such a "higher command" and its interaction with lower modules should be structured.

Further Question Marks

Current connected-speech recognition systems are subject to a series of further critiques, some of which may again find some interesting resolutions by a consideration of the human analogy.

All current systems suffer from considerable *slowness*. Hearsay II, for example, was not able to meet the original goal of real-time performance, as it had been set out by the U.S. Government-sponsored DARPA project. Part of the problem again appears to be related to its centralised control (which in the case of Hearsay II operated on a single process at a time). However, even parallel processing methods have not been able to improve its speed of operation (Nii, 1986). Consider by contrast human connected-speech processing which can run well ahead of real time. Quite often, listeners can instantaneously complete well-formed sentences that are stopped in mid-stream. This indicates that their recognition processing is running minimally in parallel with the perceived speech chain, and quite often formulates completion hypotheses well ahead of the speaker.

Some aspects of the internal functioning of current recognition systems are also "counter-intuitive", when the human analog is considered. For example, automatic recognition systems often operate by backward consultation and by the full-depth development of all alternative solutions (comparable to the typical computer chess strategy). However, there is considerable psycholinguistic evidence that for human listeners, the identification of the first word of an utterance (and even the first syllable of the first word) reduces the recognition uncertainty for the remainder of the sentence, and that human processing proceeds largely left-to-right. Furthermore, sentence complexity does not seem to be related in any systematic fashion to the type of reasoning used, which appears more in tune with the capacities of the human system which is characterised by a relatively limited short-term memory span (i.e. one type of processing where computers do better than humans). Clearly, if computers are to aspire to human levels of speech recognition performance, the implications of choosing a non-human like processing architecture must be weighed carefully.

Challenges

It is evident from this short overview that there is considerable richness in the human model. Only few of the challenges mentioned here are covered in the succeeding chapters. Nevertheless, there is ample material for some initial discussion of several of the central issues of speech synthesis and speech recognition of the coming years.

The section begins with an article by *Boë, Schwartz and Vallée* who address the question of how the human vowel space is subdivided in human speech processing. This problem is representative of a whole class of typical speech processing problems, since it poses the problem of dealing with the high variability of speech parameters. For example, formant values for a given vowel are not always the same, nor are they rigorously differentiated from those of another vowel, particularly in fast speech, and thus pose major detection difficulty to acoustico-phonetic input processors. The authors of this chapter present the current thinking and some original experimentation to determine how this problem is to be addressed.

The next chapter by *Gabioud* takes us to the core of the question of how a direct human analog of a speech processing unit could be modelled. The relatively complex chain of processes and calculations required to produce speech synthesis by a direct model of speech articulation is described. Gabioud indicates that the current limits of this approach are in part rooted in the circumscribed availability of precise empirical information about human articulatory behaviour, and thus points out one of the characteristic weaknesses of direct models of human speech behaviour.

The chapter by *Perrier and Ostry* addresses the question of the direct model of articulation from a dynamic perspective. They indicate that models rooted in the study of human movement can be generalised to speech articulations. They demonstrate that without being complete algorithmic descriptions of speech articulation, such models can nevertheless offer some interesting perspectives on traditional areas of difficulty in the simulation of human speech, such as how to handle the so-called "vowel reduction" phenomena occurring in fast speech.

The chapter by *Local* illuminates another problem of developing synthesis devices from an interesting and unusual perspective. The question is how to model the time stream of the considerable number of parameters in a formant synthesiser (42 parameters in Klatt's original synthesiser, around 60 parameters in current, updated versions). Issuing from principles rooted in phonetic science and phonology, Local develops an original theory (whose validity is demonstrated by a fully operational implementation) of how to structure these parameters over the duration of a complete syllable.

With Geneviève *Caelen-Haumont's* chapter, an entirely different set of questions is raised. At issue is high-level control over prosodic parameters. Do human speakers place emphasis and intonational contours in terms of their syntactic knowledge, or do they apply semantic and pragmatic principles? Caelen-Haumont's data suggest that both principles have their importance, probably at different points in the development of a theme. Even though the transfer to computational algorithms appears fraught with particular difficulties in the case of such higher-level control (especially in the case of semantic or pragmatic principles), the demonstration of their relevance to speech organisation poses a valid challenge for developers of natural-sounding speech synthesis devices.

The next two chapters are probably best considered as a pair, since they both address the issue of how speech can be identified against a competing background of speech or noise. Both issue from the same base literature, yet offer complementary sets of solutions. *Cooke and Brown* first go over the basic issues of sound separation and then enter into a detailed description of the principles that separating devices can follow to attain similar performance. *Summerfield and Culling* provide detailed illustrations of two processes which illustrate the advantages of exploring the human model. They arrive at logical, yet computationally surprising solutions that not only appear to do the job of separating speech sources, but also minimise the effects of potential hearing loss and exploit the partial duplication and complementary information available from the two acoustic inputs arriving via the two ears.

The chapter by Jean *Caelen* closes out the volume with a detailed illustration of the problems that arise when speech recognition is integrated into an operational application (in this case, a simple graphics editor) that can also respond to mouse and keyboard input. The problems surrounding this integration run the gamut from how to define the extent of a series of objects, to how to reconcile the different ways of pointing to a set of objects by speech and by mouse action. Caelen's article demonstrates that issues such as these will require a whole new set of conventions and intelligent application design for their successful resolution.

Altogether, the motivated reader will find a rich set of materials here which amply demonstrates the dynamic vibrancy of current efforts of bringing speech to the computer.

References

Erman, L.D., Hayes-Roth, F., Lesser, V.R., & Reddy, D.R., (1980). The Hearsay-II speech understanding system: Integrating knowledge to resolve uncertainty. *Computer Survey, 12*, 213-253.

Fodor, J.A. (1983). *The modularity of Mind: An essay on faculty psychology.* Cambridge (Mass.): MIT Press.

Gong, L.Y., & Haton, J.P. (1987). *A society of specialists for speech understanding.* IEEE-ICASSP, San Diego.

Hanson, A. R., & Riseman, E. M. (1978). VISIONS: a computer vision system for

Hayes-Roth, B., & Hayes-Roth, F. (1979). A cognitive model of planning. *Cognitive Science, 3,* 275-310.

interpreting scenes, in *Computer Vision System* (pp. 303-334), New York: Academic Press.

Matsuyama, T., & Hwang, V. (1985). SIGMA: A framework for image understanding-integration of bottom-up and top-down analyses. *Proceedings IJCAI, 2,* 908-915.

McKeown, D. M., Wilson, J. R., & McDermott, J. (1985). Rule-based interpretation of aerial imagery. *IEEE Transactions of Pattern Analysis and Machine Intelligence, PAMI-7,* 570-585.

Minsky, M. (1975). A Framework for Representing Knowledge. In P.H. Winston (Ed.), *The Psychology of Computer Vision* (pp. 142-157). New York, N.Y.: McGraw-Hill.

Minsky, M. (1986). *The society of mind.* Cambridge, MA: MIT Press.

Nazif, A. M., & Levine, M. D. (1984). Low level image segmentation: An expert system. *IEEE Transactions in Pattern Analysis and Machine Intelligence, PAMI-6,* 555-577.

Nii, H.P. (1986). Cage and poligon: Two frameworks for blackboard-based concurrent problem-solving. *Technical Report KSL-86-41.* Stanford University.

Sabah, G. (1988). *L'intelligence artificielle et le langage.* Paris: Hermès.

Sabah, G. (1990). A model for interaction between cognitive processes. Proceedings of COLING'90, Vol. 3, Helsinki, pp. 446-448.

Sacerdotti, E.D. (1977). *A structure for plans and behavior.* New York: Elsevier.

Searle, J. R., (1969). *Speech acts.* Cambridge: Cambridge University Press.

Searle, J.R., & Vanderveken, D. (1985). *Foundations of illocutionary logic.* Cambridge University Press.

The Prediction of Vowel Systems: Perceptual Contrast and Stability

9

Louis-Jean Boë
Jean-Luc Schwartz
Nathalie Vallée

Institut de la Communication Parlée, CNRS URA 368
INPG and Université Stendhal, GRENOBLE, France

Since the beginning of the 1970s, several attempts have been made to explain the phonetic structure of vowel systems by introducing extralinguistic principles, be they listener-oriented (perceptual contrast and stability) or speaker-oriented (articulatory contrast and economy). The best predictions have emerged from the perceptual contrast theory, however two principal problems remain: The excessive number of high non-peripheral vowels, and the impossibility of predicting the [i, y, u] series within the high vowel set. We try to eliminate these difficulties while remaining within the domain of listener-oriented principles. First, we study the perceptual contrast in the F1-F2-F3 space, in order to better account for the role of higher formants in the perception of front vowels. In this space, we show that the problem of high non-peripheral vowels can be solved by increasing the weight of F1. However the case of [y] can only be understood by reinforcing the stability of the [i, y] pair. This is done by means of a "focalisation" principle, according to which vowels with strong formant convergence would be perceptually preferred: [i] is characterised by a strong F3-F4 convergence, and [y] is characterised by a strong F2-F3 convergence.

The automatised generation of vowels or the recognition of vowels in an acoustic signal depends crucially upon our understanding of how and where the acoustic energy is distributed in the frequency *vs.* time *vs.*

amplitude space. The great variability in the exact placement of the prominent frequency bands associated with vowels ("the vowel formants") is well-documented. Consequently, the question has been raised whether the ear responds, not to the specific frequencies, durations or amplitudes of vowel formants, but rather to their contrasting distribution or organisation. If automatic speech recognition is to perform as well as the ear, or if speech synthesis is to sound as natural as a human speaker, the issue of the organisation of vowel systems is likely to be of direct concern to speech technology.

Since the beginning of the '70s, several attempts have been made to explain the phonetic structure of vowel systems by introducing non-linguistic principles, be they listener-oriented (perceptual contrast and stability) or speaker-oriented (articulatory contrast and economy). The best predictions have been obtained with the so-called "perceptual contrast theory" (Liljencrants and Lindblom, 1972), but two main problems remain: The excessive number of high, non-peripheral vowels in the model predictions, and the impossibility of predicting the [i, y, u] series within the high vowel set. In the present study, we attempt to eliminate these difficulties, while remaining within the field of listener-oriented principles.

We began by a simple replication of the seminal Liljencrants and Lindblom 1972 study. However, we performed this replication in a 3-D acoustic space, namely the F_1-F_2-F_3 domain, in order to better account for the role of higher formants in the perception of high vowels. Moreover, we introduced a parameter enabling control over the respective weights of F_1 on one hand and the higher formants on the other, in order to better deal with the case of peripheral vowels. We then introduced an additional local perceptual cost, controlled by a second parameter, in order to deal with the case of front rounded vowels. We will discuss these innovations and modifications, describe the phonetic material that constituted our "experimental corpus", and present the prediction results together with our methodology for choosing the best values of control parameters and evaluating the goodness of fit of our model.

Apart from its general interest to the study of speech and language ("how does the ear — and the neural machinery hidden behind it — constrain language?"), this work has some practical relevance for speech technology, mainly in the field of automatic speech recognition, since:

1. It shows that speech objects have been "designed" by the human brain on the basis of *auditory distances*, among other factors;

2. It gives some insight into the *content* of these auditory distances for vowels, which seem to involve mainly two parameters, namely F1 and some integrated value of F2 and the higher formants, called F'2, with a relatively greater weight assigned to F1.

The Framework

In the recent special issue of the *Journal of Phonetics* devoted to "Linguistic Approaches to Phonetics", two contributions by Lindblom (1990) and Ohala (1990) make clearer than ever the importance of what Beddor and Toon (1990) call in their introduction to that issue "phonetic approaches to linguistics". They also highlight the need to reconsider the relationship between the linguistic system and the peripheral systems which enable the communication of a linguistic structure, namely the speech production and perception systems. Ohala (1990, p. 153) notices that:

> phonology and phonetics must (...) be closely integrated

since

> some of the pitfalls of practising phonology as an autonomous discipline are (...) circularity, reification, projection and myopia (...while...) integrating the two disciplines allow us to explain sound patterns in language in terms that have greater simplicity, generality, empirical verifiability, fruitfulness and convergence.

Lindblom (1990) focuses his contribution on the notion of "possible speech sounds" with the problems of finiteness and circularity, and emphasises the need for a deductive approach which looks at the primary language-specific facts from an *external* point of view, considering *non-linguistic constraints* on possible speech sounds. This is the framework adopted in the present paper. By an exploration of the vowel systems' regularities, we try to investigate some of the possible constraints arising from the perceptual system.

Two famous papers published in 1972 respectively by Stevens and by Liljencrants and Lindblom introduced the basic categories of arguments about the nature of the listener-speaker interaction, and its role in shaping phonological systems. All subsequent studies in this area were merely more systematic investigations into these categories. Let us briefly recall them.

Lindblom's Structural Constraints of Distinctiveness

The major criterion proposed by Lindblom under slightly different forms in a number of papers (beginning by the Liljencrants and Lindblom's 1972 seminal proposal) is that speech sounds must be *easy to distinguish* in order to be used as a support for linguistic content. This led Liljencrants and Lindblom to propose a criterion of *maximal perceptual contrasts* for vowel systems. For each vowel system, a "perceptual global cost" was developed on the basis of the summing of all inter-vowel distances. This cost was minimised in order to find the best system for a fixed number of vowels.

The results obtained with this principle were quite promising, despite some limitations that we shall consider later. On this exciting basis, Lindblom introduced two new and important ideas. First, the perceptual contrast should not be maximal, but *sufficient* (Lindblom and Maddieson, 1988; Lindblom *et al.*, forthcoming), considering that an articulatory demand for economy of gestures could counterbalance the perceptual demand for contrast; hence, the possibility of obtaining several different configurations for a given number of vowels. Second, the demand for contrast could also be introduced in the articulatory space, considering that vowels should also evolve so as to *"feel"* sufficiently different (Lindblom, forthcoming).

Throughout the theoretical and technical evolution of these ideas (*e.g.* the refinement of the concept of perceptual cost and the comparison of several auditory differences: Lindblom, 1986a), Lindblom has maintained a major *credo*. According to him, systems of sounds used for linguistic purposes are constrained by *systemic* and *relational*, rather than by *local* and *absolute* principles (Lindblom and Engstrand, 1989). Hence, it is because of a *structural* equilibrium between articulatory and perceptual demands that, for a given number of vowels, the corresponding sounds occupy definite — though possibly quite large — regions in the acoustic or articulatory space. It is as a result of this that phonetic alphabets are finite (Lindblom, 1990).

Stevens' Local Constraints of Contrast and Stability

In his famous "quantal theory of speech", Stevens (1972, 1989) looks for regions in which

> articulatory-acoustic relations are quantal in the sense that the acoustic patterns shows a change from one state to another as the articulatory parameter is varied through a range of values

and for similar kinds of relations between acoustic and auditory parameters (Figure 1), with the claim that this quantal relationship

> is a principal factor shaping the inventory of acoustic and articulatory attributes that are used to signal distinctions in language.

Most of Stevens' proposals for such quantal relationships concern the articulatory-to-acoustic transform. However in the case of the acoustic-to-auditory transform, Abry *et al.*, (1989) pointed out that there was a risk of *circularity*. Specifically, certain non-linearities in the acoustic-to-auditory transformation could be interpreted as a *consequence* of the role of linguistic representations in the perceptual task involved in the estimation of a given auditory parameter, instead of an extralinguistic factor acting as a condition of existence for a linguistic contrast. This concerns particularly the categorical perception paradigm (Massaro and Cohen, 1983), mentioned by Stevens (1972) as the prototypical case of an acoustic-to-auditory quantal relationship. Stevens' later proposals in 1989 are less amenable to such criticisms, since they are based on general and low-level properties of the auditory system (see also Ehret, 1992).

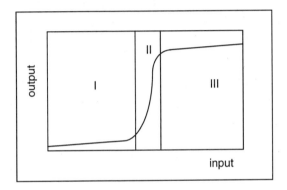

Figure 1. A typical quantal input-to-output relationship with two zones of stability (I and III) and one non-linear zone (II) (after Stevens, 1989).

Though not explicitly introduced as such by Stevens, quantal relationships could also be posited in the relationship between neurological commands and articulatory gestures. This is the case of muscular constraints likely to increase the stability of peripheral vowels by a *saturation mechanism* (Perrier, 1990). In this condition, the command-to-gesture relationship is stable (since whatever the command above a given threshold, the articulatory configuration remains the same), which results in good physical control for the production of the corresponding vowel. This enables good control over the vocal tract constriction in [i] due to genioglossus action (Kakita and Fujimura, 1977), or in [a] because of a saturation of the stiffness-length hyoglossus characteristics (Perkell and Cohen, 1989). It also enables good control of the lip area in [y] or [u], due to a saturation of the closure-protrusion action on lip rounding (Stevens, 1989). At even higher levels, the simultaneous gradient and qualitative structure of dynamical systems discussed by Browman and Goldstein (1990) is an important case of quantal behaviour, and has crucial implications in discussing the physical *vs.* cognitive dichotomy.

Extrinsic *vs.* Intrinsic Stability

Stevens' constraints are obviously *local*, with a "tendency toward particular regions within (the acoustic) space" (Stevens, 1989, p. 42), as opposed to Lindblom's relational ones. However, it is important to remember that these principles are always based on the relationship between two spaces, namely an input and an output space, with the emergence of a strong nonlinearity in the passage from input-to-output leading to a *structure in both spaces* with the *non-linearity acting as a boundary* (see Petitot Cocorda, 1985, for a discussion of this theory in the light of the *catastrophe theory*, and of the global structure that can be provided by local arguments in that framework). We (Schwartz, 1987; Abry and Schwartz, 1987) introduced the distinction between the *extrinsic stability* used by Stevens in his quantal theory, and the *intrinsic stability* due to the low cost that could be associated with a given articulatory, acoustic or auditory pattern, within its own space, and independently of any external control of that space.

A local criterion of low intrinsic articulatory cost has been used by ten Bosch (1991) in addition to the Liljencrants and Lindblom' relational auditory cost, in the prediction of vowel systems. This criterion consisted of the introduction of various tests of the departure of a given four-tube configuration from the neutral configuration as an index of the articulatory effort for uttering the corresponding formant structure. One could also introduce a criterion of intrinsic perceptual stability. This will be the topic of the second part of this study.

Strategy

It is reasonable to say that much more is known about auditory representations of vowel spectra than about articulatory representations of vowel configurations. Such concepts as auditory distances or spectral integration are easier to define in quantitative terms than are articulatory distances or articulatory costs. Hence it is the aim of the present study to try to go as far as possible in the *perceptual domain*, in order to test what can and cannot be explained in the structure of vowel systems by listener-oriented theories. It will also be an opportunity to point out some possible relevant characteristics of auditory processing of vowel spectra, in the light of the present study.

The first simulation based upon the perceptual contrast theory introduced by Liljencrants and Lindblom (1972) furnished promising results. Further developments by Crothers (1978), Lindblom (1986a) and Disner (1984) showed that the main trends of vocalic systems are well captured by the theory. However, a few problems remain. We shall consider here only those that are linked to high vowels, assuming that most other difficulties could be avoided by introducing regularisation principles. We shall outline what proposals have been or could be advanced in order to solve these problems by adding articulatory constraints, but our substantive proposals will focus on perceptual constraints. Our modelling work will consist in trying to apply some modifications and corrections to the basic principles introduced by Liljencrants and Lindblom in order to solve these problems: *This will lead us to try to combine systemic (relational) constraints "à la Lindblom" with local (absolute) constraints "à la Stevens".*

The Case of Peripheral Vowels

One of the main weaknesses of the first simulation by Liljencrants and Lindblom concerns the respective number of "peripheral" (front unrounded or back rounded) *vs.* "non-peripheral" (front rounded, central or back unrounded) vowels: The six-vowel prediction contained three high vowels [i, ɨ, u] and the predictions with seven or more vowels contained four high vowels [i, y, ɯ, u]. However, phonological inventories show that systems with only two high vowels are common for six- or seven-vowel systems (namely [i, e, ɛ, u, o, ɔ] and [i, e, ɛ, u, o, ɔ, a]), and that [i, y, ɯ, u] appear together only with a total of at least nine vowels. Hence the front-back dimension is over-represented in the simulations at the expense of the open-close dimension.

This severe problem has led Lindblom to suggest that there was a need for a vertical shrinking of the acoustic vowel space, leading to an increase of the weight of F_1 at the expense of the importance of F_2 or F'_2[1]. This proposal formed the basis for the introduction of new distances based on psychoacoustic concepts (Lindblom, 1986a). However, the results were not really conclusive. More recently, he has proposed that the close-open dimension could be better represented in proprioception than could the front-back parameter (Lindblom and Lubker, 1985). He has obtained good results by combining perceptual and articulatory contrast costs, and by assuming that vowels tend to evolve so as to both *sound* and *feel* sufficiently different (Lindblom, forthcoming).

---

[1] While vowel spectra are classically described in terms of formant values F_1, F_2, F_3 and possibly F_4, which are the first resonances of the vocal tract transfer function, a number of perceptual experiments (see e.g. Carlson *et al.*, 1970, 1975; Bladon and Fant, 1978) have led to the introduction of a "perceptual second formant" F'_2 which is defined as some combined value of F_2, F_3 and F_4 through complex non-linear computations (see later, and Figure 3).

The Case of Front Rounded Vowels

A fact that has generally received little consideration in studies on vocalic systems concerns differences among non-peripheral high vowels. A first statistical study on the UCLA Phonological Segment Inventory Database UPSID (Maddieson, 1984) shows that 24 of the 317 languages in the base (7.7%) contain [y], 23 (7.2%) contain [ɯ] and 44 (14.1%) contain [ʉ] or [ɨ]. This seems to fit well with the Perceptual Contrast Theory: vowels which are at the centre of the available F_2 region for the lowest F_1 are the most probable, while vowels displaced towards higher (namely [y]) or lower (namely [ɯ]) F_2 values have almost equally-lowered probabilities of appearance.

However, a closer inspection of the database reveals strong asymmetries between [y] (rounded front vowel) and [ɯ] (unrounded back vowel). Of 23 occurrences (i.e. 23 languages where this sound has been repertoried), [ɯ] co-occurs ten times with [i] only, eight times with [i, u] and five times with [i,y,u]. Yet this latter [i, y, ɯ, u] structure is the one that is best predicted by the theory, since the corresponding F'_2-values are respectively around 16, 13, 10 and 7 bark[2], and therefore optimally exploit the $F'2$ dimension. As was noticed by Crothers (1978), the [i, ɯ, u] structure is also acceptable, considering that F_2 for [ɯ] can reach about 1400 Hz, which gives an F'_2-series of 16, 11 and 7 bark. Finally, the [i, ɯ] structure with no rounded vowel is the least predicted. Its high frequency of occurrence can perhaps be interpreted by a low structural articulatory cost, or by a cultural pressure in favour of a system involving no lip action.

By contrast, in 24 occurrences in the database, [y] never co-occurs with [u] alone, but appears 14 times with [i, u] and ten times with [i, u], and one vowel from the [ɨ, ʉ, ɯ] set. The rather large number of [i, y, u] structures is not predicted by a hypothesis of maximal perceptual contrast with corresponding F'_2s of 16, 13 and 7 bark. It conflicts with the theory of adaptive dispersion (Lindblom and Engstrand, 1989), considering that [y] with its strong lip action is unlikely to be a vowel realised with a particularly low articulatory cost — though the possible "stability" of the relationship between the neurological rounding command and the articulatory result could be invoked (see above). The existence of this [i,y,u] structure thus constitutes a major problem, with which we have tried to deal in our simulations.

---

[2] The bark scale is a perceptual frequency scale defined on the basis of a number of psychoacoustical experiments (see e.g. Zwicker and Feldtkeller, 1969). Throughout this study, it is defined by the formula proposed by Schroeder *et al.* (1979): bark = 7 ArgSh (Hz / 650)

The Model

We first began by a simple replication of the seminal Liljencrants and Lindblom 1972 study. However, we attempted to perform this replication in a 3-D acoustic space, namely in the F_1-F_2-F_3 domain, in order to better account for the role of higher formants in the perception of high vowels. Moreover, we introduced a parameter enabling control of the respective weights of F_1 on the one hand, and the higher formants on the other. This was to deal with the case of peripheral vowels. We then introduced an additional local perceptual cost, controlled by a second parameter, so as to be able to deal with the case of front rounded vowels. In order to contextualise our results, we will first discuss these innovations and modifications, explain our "experimental corpus", our methodology for choosing the best values of both parameters, and our evaluation of the goodness of fit of the model.

3-D Replication of the Liljencrants and Lindblom's Study

A model similar to the one proposed by Liljencrants and Lindblom is defined by (1) an acoustic domain where vowels must be confined, due to articulatory constraints, (2) a distance defined on the considered acoustic parameters — formants or effective formants — (3) a criterion to select the "best" configurations for a fixed number of vowels. Let us consider our choice for each of these three points.

Definition of an Acoustic F_1-F_2-F_3 Domain

Extensive work in our laboratory (Perrier *et al.*, 1985; Boë *et al.*, 1992) on the articulatory model elaborated by Maeda (1979, 1988) has allowed us define a "maximal vowel space" (Boë, Perrier, Guérin and Schwartz, 1989), in which all of the 60 000 items of our articulatory-acoustic dictionary are located (Figure 2). This maximum vowel space was parametrised by F_3 in a rather efficient manner. Hence we dispose of a set of analytic equations that allow us decide whether a given (F_1, F_2, F_3) configuration is acceptable or not.

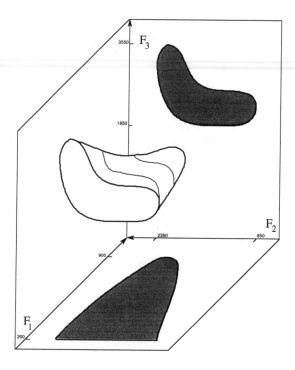

Figure 2. A maximal vowel space obtained by the 7-parameter Maeda's model.

Distances in the F_1-F_2-F_3 Space

These distances are necessary for computing an energy function:

$$E_o = \sum_{i,j} (1/d_{ij})^2 \tag{1}$$

where d_{ij} describes the spectral distance between two vowel prototypes in the simulation. E_o must then be minimised for optimal contrast. Since the global spectral distances used by Lindblom (1986a) were not really convincing, we limited ourselves to direct computation on the formant values. Let us consider two points P^a (F_1^a, F_2^a, F_3^a) and P^b (F_1^b, F_2^b, F_3^b) with all F values in bark. One could first propose an (F_1, F_2, F_3) Euclidian distance d_I, namely:

$$d_I = [(F_1^b—F_1^a)^2 + (F_2^b—F_2^a)^2 + (F_3^b—F_3^a)^2]^{1/2} \tag{2}$$

However, preliminary research (Schwartz et al., 1989) showed that results with d_I are unsatisfactory, since the unweighted F_3 dimension allowed two vowels to be distinguished only on this dimension, which produced completely unacceptable configurations. Hence F_3 must somehow be weighted. This weighting must be strongly non-linear, considering that F_3 plays an almost negligible perceptual role for back vowels, while it is quite important for front vowels. We decided to use an (F_1, F'_2) Euclidian distance d_{II}, namely:

$$d_{II} = [(F_1^b - F_1^a)^2 + (F'_2{}^b - F'_2{}^a)^2]^{1/2} \qquad (3)$$

where F'_2 was computed from F_2, F_3 and F_4 on the basis of a model we proposed in a study of the [i]-[y] contrast in French (Mantakas *et al.*, 1986; 1993). This model (Figure 3) is based on the concepts of a centre of gravity and a 3.5-bark critical distance d_c introduced by Chistovich and colleagues (Chistovich and Lublinskaya, 1979; Chistovich *et al.*, 1979). It assumes that as long as F_3 is far enough from F_2 (the distance between F_2 and F_3 is higher than d_c), F'_2 equals F_2, hence F_3 does not play any part. If F_3 is closer (distance between F_2 and F_3 lower than d_c), the distance between F_2 and F_4 — arbitrarily set at 3350 Hz for all vowels — is considered. If F_4 is further away (distance between F_2 and F_4 higher than d_c), then F'_2 is set between F_2 and F_3. If F_4 is closer (distance between F_2 and F_4 lower than d_c), then F'_2 is set either between F_2 and F_3, if F_3 is closer from F_2 than from F_4, or between F_3 and F_4, if F_3 is closer from F_4 than from F_2. This model has been shown to give quite good results in the prediction of F'_2 values, when compared to experimental data (Mantakas *et al.*, 1986; 1993).

Finally, in order to deal with the first of the two problems raised previously (the excessive number of high non-peripheral vowels), we decided to introduce Lindblom's proposal of a "stretching" of the acoustic space in the F_1 dimension by using an (F_1, F'_2) weighted Euclidian distance d_{III}, namely:

$$d_{III} = [(F_1^b - F_1^a)^2 + \lambda (F'_2{}^b - F'_2{}^a)^2]^{1/2} \qquad (4)$$

where λ could be chosen at any value lower than 1, assuming that higher formants are weighted by a $\sqrt{\lambda}$ factor and hence play a lesser part in vowel phonetic quality than do lower ones. This last distance was introduced as an easy way of implementing Lindblom's suggestion that F_1 weight was underestimated in the original simulations by Liljencrants and Lindblom. Though less related to experimental knowledge in auditory perception than are the distances tested by Lindblom, d_{III} is not completely ad hoc, and we shall discuss some possible experimental support for this parameter later.

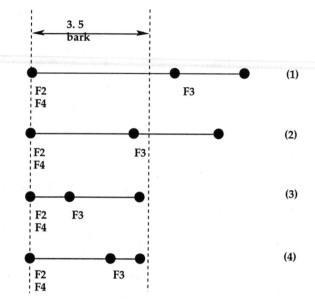

Figure 3. A model for the computation of F'$_2$ from F$_2$, F$_3$ and F$_4$.
Case (1)   F'2 = F2
Case (2) and (3)   F'2 = (IL2 * F2 + IL3 * F3) / (IL2 + IL3)
Case (4)   F'2 = (IL3 * F3 + IL4 * F4) / (IL3+ IL4)
with IL the intensity level of formants in dB and F in bark.

Criterion for the Selection of Preferred Vowel Configurations

Various criteria have been proposed in the literature for selecting vowel
configurations. Among them are: For a given number of vowels, select the
system with the *highest contrast* (Liljencrants and Lindblom, 1972), a set of
systems with the *highest contrasts* (Lindblom, 1986a), or systems with
sufficiently high contrast (Crothers, 1978). One could also think of another
criterion: select only those systems that are associated with *locally highest
contrasts* (i.e. local minima in the energy function), and hence which are
structurally stable when small acoustic modifications are applied. Since
various configurations of that kind can be obtained, one could then
imagine that the characteristics of such a system are provided by the
extent of the region in which all configurations are less stable (the
attraction basin). However, that width cannot be easily defined and
estimated in such a multidimensional problem, hence we decided to
combine two criteria, namely the local stability of a given system — the
fact that it is a local minimum for the energy landscape — together with
its global energy defined by equation (1) or its further modifications.

Formant Convergence: An Additional Cost of Local Intrinsic Stability

Introduction of the Focalisation Principle

The existence of the [i, y, u] structure shows that the [i]-[y] pair must be associated with a lower level of energy than one would predict on the basis of (F_1, F'_2) distances, and hence that we must introduce a new term into the energy function.

An important acoustic characteristic of vowels [i], [y] and [u] is the existence of a convergence of two formants, namely F_1 and F_2 for [u], F_2 and F_3 for [y] and F_3 and F_4 for [i]. A number of studies in vowel perception, beginning with the one- and two-formant approximations of vowel spectra by Delattre *et al.* (1952) and including the series of studies about F'_2 by Fant and colleagues (Fant and Risberg, 1963; Carlson, Granström and Fant, 1970; Carlson, Fant and Granström, 1975) have demonstrated the importance of formant convergence in the perceptual processing of vowel spectra. This concept has received support and some quantitative specification from the work of Chistovich and colleagues, who have demonstrated the existence of a critical integration distance of roughly 3.5 bark (Chistovich and Lublinskaya, 1979; Chistovich *et al.*, 1979).

Formant convergence also seems to provide a guide for phonetic classification (see Fant, 1983; Stevens, 1985). In our laboratory, Boë and Abry (1986), and later Badin *et al.* (1991), suggested that "focal points" — articulatory configurations with maximum formant convergence due to an exchange of affiliation of acoustic resonances — were indeed preferred points in vowel space. Furthermore, Schwartz and Escudier (1989) showed in a discrimination experiment in the [i]-[y] region that patterns with the greatest formant convergence were associated with a better perceptual stability, while patterns with less convergence, namely with F_3 at an equal distance from both F_2 and F_4, were more difficult to memorise. Schwartz (1987) attempted to relate this behaviour to the concept of "good and bad patterns" in the framework of Gestalt theory. Finally, Abry and Schwartz (1987) noticed that there was a region between [u] and [ɯ] where F_2 was at a great distance from both F_1 and F_3, and that this region seemed to be avoided by vowel systems. Stevens (1985) suggests, however, that the American English [u] might be found in that region, and wonders if the region of distant F_1, F_2 and F_3 could receive some common phonological status. All this has led us to introduce a "focalisation principle" aimed at providing some perceptual preference to vowels showing a *convergence between two formants*.

Formalisation

We decided to add to the classical terms in the energy function (namely E_o) a new set of terms for focalisation, diminishing the energy of configurations with vowels with close F_1 and F_2, F_2 and F_3 or F_3 and F_4, and hence making such configurations more stable. Our new energy function was now:

$$E = E_o + \alpha \, (E_{12} + E_{23} + E_{34}) \tag{5}$$

with

$$E_{12} = -\sum_i 1/(F_2{}^i - F_1{}^i)^2 \tag{6}$$

$$E_{23} = -\sum_i 1/(F_3{}^i - F_2{}^i)^2 \tag{7}$$

$$E_{34} = -\sum_i 1/(F_4{}^i - F_3{}^i)^2 \tag{8}$$

E_o was computed with distance d_{III}, which is a generalisation of distance d_{II}. We thus obtain a formula depending on two parameters, namely λ, which sets the weighting between F_1 and F'_2, and α, which determines the weighting between the structural E_o cost and the local E_{12}, E_{23} and E_{34} additional costs. Notice that these additional costs are likely to have three effects, namely (1) stabilise the [i, y] pair, (2) attract vowels towards the periphery of the vowel space, which could contribute to improve the "case of peripheral vowels", and (3) pull vowels away from the region between [u] and [ɯ] where F_2 is far from both F_1 and F_3.

Results

We have tested the model on systems of the database UPSID. We have selected 25 systems among the sample of 317 systems collected by Maddieson (1984). Each captures the most frequent configuration for a given number of vowels ranging between 3 and 9 (Figure 4).

number of vowels	Vowel systems and number of occurrence				
3	11	2			
4	12	6	2	2	
5	88	6	2		
6	22	10	9	5	
7	20	5	5	3	2
8	6	3	3	2	
9	7	2	2		

i	y	ɨ	ʉ	ɯ	u
ɪ	ʏ	ɨ̩	ʉ̩	ɯ̩	ω
e	ø	ə	ɵ	ɤ	o
'e'	'ø'	'ə'	'ɵ'	'ɤ'	'o'
ɛ	œ	ɜ	ʌ	ɔ	
æ	ɐ	ɑ̩	ɒ̩		
a̩	a	ɑ	ɒ		

Figure 4. The most frequent vowel systems derived from the UPSID database (above) and the 37 phonological symbols (below).

Above this limit, it has been shown (Vallée, 1990) that systems adopt new dimensions, mainly nasality and quantity. In Figure 5 we have associated the 37 phonological symbols used to describe the UPSID database, with formant frequencies inside the Maximal Vowel Space obtained with the articulatory model of Maeda (see Figure 2). These values have been selected, taking into account acoustic studies for different languages (American-English, Beyonde, Danish, Dutch, English, Finnish, French, German, Italian, Lamba, Norwegian, Swedish, Yoruba, etc.) (Vallée and Boë, 1992).

We can hypothesise that the pair of values λ and α can be slightly different for each language. However, our aim is to look for a single set of values that fit the most frequent systems as well as possible. So we have tested the 25 selected systems with 3 values for λ (0.25, 0.5, 1) and with five values for α (0, 0.25, 0.5, 0.75, 1), with a total of 375 simulations.

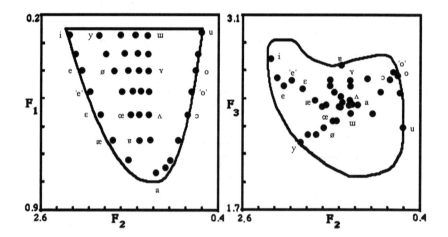

Figure 5. The vowel prototypes associated with the 37 phonological symbols of UPSID.

Notice that setting λ at 1 and α at 0 would perfectly replicate the original simulations by Liljencrants and Lindblom, except for the choice of a three- instead of two-dimensional acoustic space.

It appears that there is no unique pair of values (λ, α) which predict the stability of all of the most frequent systems. However, with $\lambda = 0.25$ and $\alpha = 0.50$, it is possible to stabilise 64% of our selection, which corresponds to 60% of the entire UPSID database. The most stable systems in our prediction are mainly those with peripheral vowels. They are also the most frequent (54% for UPSID).

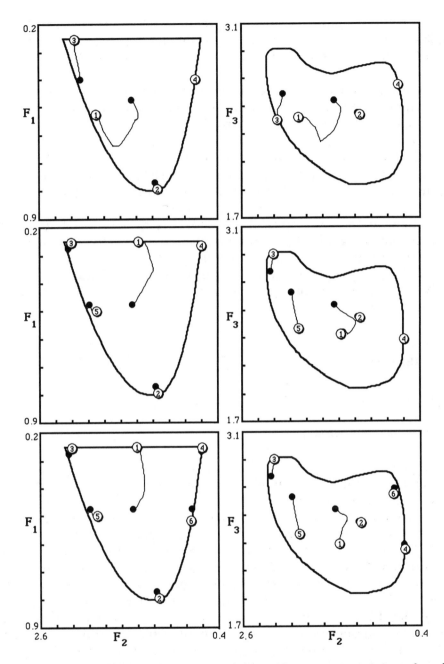

Figure 6. The impossibility of attaining stability with systems containing schwa [ə], without a close vowel between [i] and [u]: cases of [e ˈəˈ o a] (top), [iˈeˈˈəˈ a u] (middle) and [iˈeˈˈəˈa ˈoˈu] (bottom). Left: F1/F2, right: F2/F3. Initial positions are the blank circles, final stabilized positions are the white numbered circles.

The model improves on the previous results (Liljencrants and Lindblom, 1972; Lindblom, 1986a; Lindblom and Engstrand, 1990) in two respects, which correspond to the two problems we wanted to address:

I. Role of the λ parameter. Setting the F'_2 weighting value λ lower than 1 limits the number of vowels between [i] and [u] and allows the prediction of peripheral systems for $n > 5$.

II. Role of the α parameter. Setting the coefficient α higher than 0 produces stability for systems ($n > 7$) with [y]: The [i y e ɛ a ɔ o u] system is quite stable with $α > 0$, while with $α = 0$, [y] shifts towards [ɨ].

But, whatever the conditions, it is impossible to obtain stability with systems containing schwa ['ə'] without a close vowel between [i] and [u]. This is true for the [e 'ə' o a], [i 'e' 'ə' a u], [i 'e''ə'a 'o'u], [i 'e' 'ə' æ a 'o' u], [i 'e''ə'ɛ a ɔ 'o' u] systems which have been tested (Figure 6). These systems appear with a non-negligible frequency of occurrence (18% of the total of UPSID).

Discussion

Representations of Vowel Spectra

Formants and global distances

One of the criticisms raised by Lindblom (1986a) in his revision of the Liljencrants and Lindblom model concerns the adoption of a formant-based distance measure. A number of arguments, developed in more detail by Bladon (1982), lead him to conjecture that a distance based on the entire spectrum, as processed by the peripheral auditory system, would be more appropriate. However, the perceptual study by Carlson, Granström and Klatt (1979) showed that listeners were able to perform two very different kinds of estimations of perceptual distances between vowel spectra, namely a "psychoacoustic" estimation, where they attend to any modification of the sound timbre, and a "phonetic" estimation, where they concentrate on any modification of the vowel quality. When the two distances were experimentally manipulated, rather divergent results were obtained, and only the psychoacoustic distances were well-modelled by classical sone/bark or phon/bark distances (Carlson and Granström, 1979). By contrast, the phonetic distances could be simulated only with models that strongly reinforced formant representations, either by temporal coding in the so-called DOMIN model (Carlson and Granström, 1979), or by some kind of lateral inhibition mechanism in the spectral slope metrics (Klatt, 1982). This shows that formants do play a special role in vowel distances, which is the reason why we preferred to use formant distances in the present study.

Weighting of Low vs. High Formants

Another reason that Lindblom (1986a) gave for the introduction of distances based on the entire spectrum was that such distances are sensitive both to formant frequencies *and to levels*, which results in increasing the weight of F_1 in relation to the other formants, since it has a higher level in a typical vowel spectrum (Fant, 1960). Furthermore, some data suggest that lower formants may be better perceived than higher formants. Indeed, some of the identification results obtained by Delattre *et al.* (1952) with variations of formant intensities in synthetic two-formant vowels seem to show that the first formant does play a more prominent role than the second formant.

The authors first assumed "that the ear effectively averages two vowel formants which are close together, receiving from these two formants an impression which is highly similar to that which would be heard from one formant placed at a position somewhere intermediate between them" (p. 203), and then noticed that "in the case of the vowels [o] and [u], the correct average is at a value very close to the first formant" (p. 205). (Notice however that data obtained by Chistovich and Lublinskaya (1979) and Chistovich *et al.* (1979) are somewhat contradictory in this respect.) Also relevant in this discussion are data we obtained about F'_2 dependency on F_3 in the [i]-[y] or [e]-[ø] regions (Schwartz and Escudier, 1989). They show that for front vowels, when F_3 is close to F_2, F'_2 is determined by some average of F_2 and F_3, and depends more on F_2 than on F_3. When F_3 is close to F_4, F'_2 is determined by some average of F_3 and F_4, and depends more on F_3 than on F_4.

These perceptual data can be related to psychoacoustic data about auditory representations of vowels or complex sounds obtained by masking techniques, which provide some evidence of remote suppression of higher-frequency by low-frequency components (see e.g. Moore and Glasberg, 1983; Stelmachowicz *et al.*, 1982; Tyler and Lindblom, 1982). Potentially, this could be interpreted in terms of two-tone suppression phenomena in the auditory nerve (see Abbas and Sachs, 1979; Sachs and Young, 1979). In general terms, all these factors provide some support for the introduction of a λ factor lower than 1 in Equation (4).

Relationship Between Perceptual and Articulatory Representations

To date, two kinds of proposals have been introduced to explain the preference for a "vertical" exploitation of the vowel space, resulting in a greater number of degrees of height per series than the number of series in most phonological systems (Vallée, 1989): (1) Lindblom's exploitation of articulatory contrast (Lindblom, forthcoming) and our present suggestion that low formants somehow suppress higher ones in the perceptual representations of vowel spectra. We might thus ask if the two assumptions are related. It could be the case that a poor representation of F_2 as compared with F_1 leads to a poor articulatory representation of the front-back dimension, or that the fact that this dimension "feels" less important, plays a part on the poor perceptual representation of F'_2 when compared with F_1. These assumptions are of course impossible to test at present, but they signal a possible interesting case of interaction between motor and perceptual representations, as postulated for other perceptuo-motor human systems (Viviani and Stucchi, 1992).

An auditory framework for speech recognition

The reasonable success of our predictions of vowel inventories validates the nature of the representations used in our simulations. This has two main implications for any work involved with the representation of speech sounds, and mainly for automatic speech recognition.

   1. It shows that speech objects are mainly constrained by *auditory distances*, and that phonological categories emerge from *auditory representations*. This point is particularly relevant in a number of discussions about the nature of speech invariance (Perkell and Klatt, 1986), and in relationship to the Motor Theory of Speech Perception (Liberman and Mattingly, 1985). In a recent conference about Motor Theory (Mattingly and Studdert-Kennedy, 1991), Summerfield asked the question: "Suppose that somebody started to implement Stevens' view of lexical access on the computer, and simultaneously somebody attempted to form and implement algorithms to recover the gestures produced in the vocal tract. Would either of them solve the problem? Which of them would succeed first?" Our work shows that the *ultimate* stage of acoustic-to-phonetic decoding probably involves auditory rather than articulatory representations, even if articulatory representations could intervene somewhere along the decoding process.

   Moreover in the light of our simulations, it is likely that vowels should be conceived as static targets hidden in the signal, and should be defined by relational properties rather than as dynamic objects (Strange, 1989) (which does by no way mean that dynamic information plays no role in vowel identification, see Beautemps, 1993).

2. The nature of these representations is largely constrained by our work, which shows that F_1 and F'_2 are likely to be the two main correlates of auditory dimensions of oral vowels. Furthermore, Equation (4) can be used as an acceptable estimation of the auditory distance between two vowel spectra — or between an unknown incoming spectrum and a given prototype — with the λ factor set at a rather low value around 0.25.

Local and Relational Perceptual Constraints in the Region of High Front Vowels

While a *local criterion of intrinsic stability*, such as the focalisation principle, may provide a basis for a rounding contrast in front vowels, the region of high front vowels seems to be under the control of the three sets of constraints that were previously introduced.

The F'$_2$(F$_3$) Quantal Behaviour in the [i]-[y] Region

It is known from the perceptual study by Carlson *et al.* (1970) that the dependency of the "second effective formant" F'_2 on F_3 in synthetic four-formant stimuli with F_1, F_2 and F_4 respectively fixed at 250, 2000 and 3350 Hz — hence in the [i]-[y] region — is strongly non-linear. Indeed, F'_2 is first quite stable slightly above F_2, for F_3 varying between 2300 and 2500 Hz. Then F'_2 increases three times more quickly than F_3 when F_3 varies from 2600 to 2800 Hz, and F'_2 becomes stable again around 3000-3200 Hz when F_3 approaches F_4. More precisely, the results obtained by Schwartz and Escudier (1987) with the same corpus for French listeners reveal consecutive mean slopes of the F'_2(F_3) relationship of 0.5, 3 and 1, which would correspond, respectively, to regions I, II and III in Stevens' description of quantal relationships (Figure 7a).

This behaviour seems to be a sign of a specific auditory process of wide-band spectral integration, and not the consequence of a pre-existing phonological contrast (Schwartz and Escudier, 1987, 1989): The quick F'_2 increase derives from a change of focus. In fact, an F_2-F_3 convergence, which establishes F'_2 as the centre of gravity between F_2 *and* F_3, becomes an F_3-F_4 convergence that establishes F'_2 as the centre of gravity between F_3 *and* F_4. The mid-point on the bark scale between F_2 and F_4 (around 2650 Hz) provides a boundary between these two regions (Figure 7b).

The role of [ʉ] in shaping the [i]-[y] contrast

While the [i]-[y] boundary seems to be defined by a quantal relationship *à la Stevens*, the precise acoustic and articulatory realisations of [i] and [y] are also determined by relational contrast arguments *à la Lindblom*. Remote influences of the whole vowel systems on the precise formant values for [i] have been demonstrated by Disner (1978) in a cross-linguistic study.

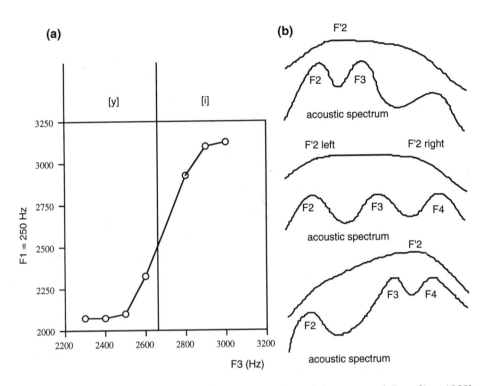

Figure 7. The complex dependency of F′₂ on F₃ (from Schwartz and Escudier, 1989): (a) experimental data for F′₂ estimates with French subjects and four-formant synthetic stimuli with $F_1 = 250$ Hz, $F_2 = 2000$ Hz and $F_4 = 3350$ Hz; (b) interpretation of the corresponding data.

In the case of [y], it appears (Schwartz *et al.*, 1993) that the existence of a concurrent [ʉ] has a consequence, namely that [y] is less rounded, so that the resonance of the front cavity does not reach values lower than the resonance of the back cavity (around 2000 Hz for male configurations). In other words, there seems to exist a second quantal point where the F_2 value begins to decrease because of an exchange of affiliation of F_2 and F_3, with the risk of [y] becoming confounded with [ʉ], if it exists in the system. The role of [ʉ] can be clearly seen in a comparison of Danish, which has no [ʉ], and Swedish and Norwegian, which do have a [ʉ]. In Danish, we find values of F_2 and F_3 for [y] for male speakers around 1700 and 2000 Hz, and in Swedish and Norwegian, around 2000 and 2500 Hz.

Although a structural pressure à la Lindblom seems to modify the reference position of [y] under the influence of [ʉ], the quantal [i]-[y] boundary resists this pressure. Compare Swedish which has [ʉ] in its phonological system besides the [i]-[y] pair, and French which does not. The Swedish reference formant values for [y] are different from those for French (which in fact are similar to those for Danish). However, the F_3 value where listeners switch from [i] to [y] is the same in both cases, namely around 2650 Hz, which is the mid-point on the bark scale between F_2 and F_4 (compare Carlson *et al.*, 1970, and Schwartz and Escudier, 1987 and 1989). This is summarised on Figure 8, which displays typical positions of [i], [y] in French and Swedish (namely [y/F] and [y/S]) and [ʉ], together with the common [y] *vs.* [i] boundary in both languages, namely B(y-i), and the two "quantal points" on the lip area-to-formants relationship, one at the mid-point between F_2 and F_4, the other at the crossing of F_2 and F_3.

To sum up, it appears that

(1) the [i]-[y] pair is stabilised by the intrinsic perceptual stability of both vowels,

(2) its boundary is set by the quantal acoustic-to-auditory $F'_2(F_3)$ behaviour, and

(3) the precise [i] and [y] reference positions are defined by the structural perceptual costs of the whole vowel system.

Hence it looks like all constraints operate concurrently.

From Implicit to Explicit Structure: The Series Principle

Since our work on front vowels focused on the highest exemplar of each series, the question remains as to whether some principle could explain a whole series, with one of the members acting as a kind of *key* for the rest of the series. However, from the perspective of the present study, *extra-linguistic* principles do not appear powerful enough to explain all of the regularities of vowel systems. For example, it is quite difficult to understand the existence of vowels like [ø] or [œ] in systems with a complete series of front rounded vowels, unless one assumes that the stabilisation of [y] enables the existence of a feature structure (+rounded, +front), which can then be exploited at various degrees of lip opening.

Another problem is that opening degrees are generally of equal value in all oral series of a given system. This is not well-predicted by the available models. Thus, the typical five-vowel system in Liljencrants and Lindblom (1972) is [i, e, a, ɔ, u], rather than [i, 'e', a, 'o', u] or its variants [i, e, a, o, u] or [i, ɛ, a, ɔ, u]. The F-model which gives the best predictions in Lindblom (1986a) predicts a nine-vowel system with three front unrounded vowels [i, e, æ] against two back rounded vowels [u, ɔ]. The symmetry in the nine-vowel system in the most recent predictions by Lindblom and Engstrand (1989) is still not perfect, with [i, e, ɛ] on the front unrounded side and [u, o, ɑ] on the back rounded side.

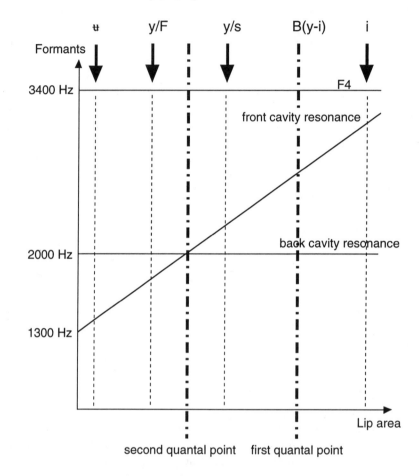

Figure 8. Formants, quantal points, phonemes and phonetic boundaries in French and Swedish in the region of high central or front vowels for varying lip area.

The systematically occurring *odd* number of peripheral vowels, including [a] and as many front unrounded and back rounded vowels, is also difficult to predict by implicit principles. This trend results in the fact that systems with an odd number of oral vowels generally have 0 or 2 interior vowels, while systems with an even number of vowels generally have 1 or sometimes 3 interior ones (Vallée, 1989). Though the combination of perceptual and articulatory contrasts in Lindblom and

Engstrand (1989) provides good results in this respect, it seems likely that in this second set of examples, the implicit structure is regularised by an explicit structure in which the feature (α high) is combined with other vowel features such as ($\pm$rounded), (front), (central) or (back) in a systematic manner.

Perceptual *vs.* Articulatory Constraints

Perceptual structural contrast for the *foundations*, quantal articulatory-to-perceptual relationship and intrinsic perceptual stability for *local reorganisations*, and explicit structure by feature combination for the *global equilibrium*: What other principles can be advocated? The present work indicates that articulatory constraints do not seem especially important in the shaping of vowel systems, while they are likely to be crucial for consonantal systems (Lindblom, 1986b). Still, an economy of articulatory gestures could have three main consequences, namely:

- to restrict vowel categories to "basic" articulations (Lindblom *et al.*, in press) as much as possible. "Elaborated" and "complex" articulations would be introduced only for a high number of vowels;

- to induce a facilitation term for the existence of schwa, which is the great loser in our simulations. Criteria of low articulatory cost, such as those introduced by ten Bosch (1991), are able to compensate this disadvantage very efficiently;

- to produce *diversity* and *evolution*. When a *maximal* perceptual contrast is replaced by a merely *sufficient* contrast, this could lead to a reduction of articulatory expense, and thus enable perceptually sub-optimal structures to survive. In that sense, articulatory economy could play the role of a *"temperature"* that stabilises sub-optimal structures, just as non-zero temperatures enable non-optimal organisations to exist in physical systems.

Conclusion

We have now obtained a reasonably good level of prediction of vocalic systems by means of listener-oriented principles, namely perceptual contrast and focalisation. The main trends observed in the UPSID inventory are well-captured. In the case of high front vowels, we have shown that three sets of constraints are at work, namely structural distinctions, extrinsic local contrast and intrinsic stability. Taken together, this evidence shows that implicit structure in linguistic systems involves both relational and local arguments. Regularisation principles should then suffice to allow a good systematic prediction.

This investigation shows the interest of exploiting auditory representations and auditory distances to describe speech objects, and hence it has a potential implication for automatic speech recognition. Speaker-oriented principles could of course modify our predictions. They could also be used to provide selection and evolution criteria between all stable systems. However, quantitative models still represent a major challenge for further research.

References

Abbas, P.J., & Sachs, M.B. (1979). Two-tone suppression in auditory-nerve fibers: Extension of a stimulus-response relationship. *Journal of the Acoustical Society of America, 59*, 112-122.

Abry, C., Boë, L.J., & Schwartz, J.L. (1989). Plateaus, catastrophes and the structuring of vowel systems. *Journal of Phonetics, 17*, 47-54.

Abry, C., & Schwartz, J.L. (1987). Quelques éléments pour une théorie des objets phonétiques du langage... autour d'une voyelle inconnue. [Elements for a theory of phonetic objects of language... around an unknown vowel]. *Bulletin du Laboratoire de la Communication Parlée, (Grenoble), 1A*, 191-210.

Badin, P., Perrier, P., Boë, L.J., & Abry, C. (1991). Vocalic nomograms: Acoustic and articulatory considerations upon formant convergences. *Journal of the Acoustical Society of America, 87*, 1290-1300.

Beautemps, D. (1993). *Récupération des gestes de la parole à partir de trajectoires formantiques: identification de cibles vocaliques non atteintes et modèles pour les profils sagittaux des consonnes fricatives.* Doctoral Thesis, Institut National Polytechnique de Grenoble.

Beddor, P.S., & Toon, T.E. (1990). Linguistic approaches to Phonetics. *Journal of Phonetics, 18*, 77-78.

Bladon, A. (1982). Arguments against formants in the auditory representation of speech. In R. Carlson & B. Granstrom (Eds.), *The representation of speech in the peripheral auditory system* (pp. 95-102). Amsterdam: Elsevier Biomedical Press.

Bladon, A., & Fant, G. (1978). A two-formant model and the cardinal vowels. *STL-QPSR, 1*, 1-8.

Boë, L.J., & Abry, C. (1986). Nomogrammes et systèmes vocaliques. [Nomograms and vowel systems]. *15th JEP, Sociéte Française d'Acoustique*, 303-306.

Boë, L.J., Perrier, P., & Bailly, G. (1992). The geometric vocal tract variables controlled for vowel production: Proposals for constraining acoustic-to-articulatory inversion. *Journal of Phonetics, 20*, 27-38.

Boë, L.J., Perrier, P., Guérin, B., & Schwartz, J.L. (1989). Maximal Vowel Space. *Eurospeech, 2*, 281-284.

Bosch, L. ten (1991). *On the structure of vowel systems. Aspects of an extended vowel model using effort and contrast.* Thesis, Amsterdam University.

Browman, C.P., & Goldstein, L. (1990). Gestural specification using dynamically-defined articulatory structures. *Journal of Phonetics, 18*, 299-320.

Carlson, R., Fant, G., & Granström, B. (1975). Two-formant models, pitch and vowel perception. In G. Fant & M.A.A. Tatham (Eds.), *Auditory Analysis and Perception of Speech* (pp. 55-82), London: Academic Press.

Carlson, R., & Granström, B. (1979). Model predictions of vowel dissimilarity. *STL-QPSR, 3-4,* 84-104.

Carlson, R., & Granström, B. eds. (1982). *The representation of speech in the peripheral auditory system.* Amsterdam: Elsevier Biomedical Press.

Carlson, R., Granström, B., & Fant, G. (1970). Some studies concerning perception of isolated vowels. *STL-QPSR, 2-3,* 19-35.

Carlson, R., Granström, B., & Klatt, D. (1979). Vowel perception: The relative salience of selected acoustic manipulations. *STL-QPSR, 3-4,* 73-83.

Chistovich, L.A., & Lublinskaya, V.V. (1979). The center of gravity effect in vowel spectra and critical distance between the formants. *Hearing Research, 1,* 185-195.

Chistovich, L.A., Sheikin, R.L., & Lublinskaya, V.V. (1979). 'Centers of gravity' and the spectral peaks as the determinants of vowel quality. In B. Lindblom & S. Ohman (Eds.), *Frontiers of Speech Communication Research* (pp. 143-158). London: Academic Press.

Crothers, J. (1978). Typology and universals in vowel systems. In J.H. Greenberg, C.A. Ferguson & E.A. Moravcsik (Eds.), *Universals of human language* (pp. 93-152). Stanford: Stanford University Press.

Delattre, P., Liberman, A.M., Cooper, F.S., & Gertsman, J. (1952). An experimental study of the acoustic determinants of vowel color; observations on one- and two-formant vowels synthesized from spectrographic patterns. *Word, 8,* 195-210.

Disner, S.F. (1978). Vowels in Gemanic languages. *UCLA Working Papers in Phonetics, 40,* 1-79.

Disner, S.F. (1984). Insights on vowel spacing. In I. Maddieson (Ed.), *Patterns of sounds* (pp. 136-155). Cambridge: Cambridge University Press.

Ehret, G. (1992). Preadaptations in the auditory system of mammals for phonetic recognition. In M.E.H. Schouten (Ed.), *The Auditory Processing of Speech — From Sounds to Words,* 99-112. Berlin: Mouton de Gruyter.

Fant, G. (1960). *Acoustic theory of speech production.* The Hague: Mouton.

Fant, G. (1983). Feature analysis of Swedish vowels - a revisit. *STL-QPSR, 2-3,* 1-19.

Fant, G., & Risberg, A. (1963). Auditory matching of vowels with two-formant synthetic sounds. *STL-QPSR, 4,* 7-11.

Klatt, D. (1982). Prediction of perceived phonetic distance from critical-band spectra: A first step. *Proceedings IEEE ICASSP,* 1278-1281.

Kakita, Y., & Fujimura, O. (1977). Computational model of the tongue: A revised version. *Journal of the Acoustical Society of America, 62,* S15(A).

Liberman, A.M., & Mattingly, I.G. (1985). The motor theory of speech perception revised. *Cognition, 21,* 1-36.

Liljencrants, J., & Lindblom, B. (1972). Numerical simulations of vowel quality systems: The role of perceptual contrast. *Language, 48,* 839-862.

Lindblom, B. (1986a). Phonetic universals in vowel systems. In J.J. Ohala (Ed.), *Experimental phonology* (pp. 13-44). New-York: Academic Press.

Lindblom, B. (1986b). On the origin and purpose of discreteness and invariance in sound patterns. In J. Perkell & D. Klatt (Eds.), *Invariance and variability of Speech Processes* (pp. 493-510). New-Jersey: Lawrence Erlbaum.

Lindblom, B. (1990). On the notion of possible speech sound. *Journal of Phonetics, 18,* 135-152.

Lindblom, B. (forthcoming). A model of phonetic variation and selection and the evolution of vowel systems. In S.-Y. Wang (Ed.), *Language transmission and change.* New-York: Blackwell.

Lindblom, B., & Engstrand, O. (1989). In what sense is speech quantal? *Journal of Phonetics 17,* 107-121.

Lindblom, B., & Lubker, J. (1985). The speech homonculus and a problem of phonetic linguistics. In V.A.Fromkin (Ed.), *Phonetic linguistics,* 169-192. Orlando, FL: Academic Press.

Lindblom, B., MacNeilage, P., & Studdert-Kennedy, M. (forthcoming) *Evolution of Spoken Language,* Orlando, FL: Academic Press.

Lindblom, B., & Maddieson, I. (1988). Phonetic universals in consonant systems. In L.M. Hyman & C.N. Li (Eds.), *Language, speech and mind* (pp. 62-78). London: Routledge.

Maddieson, I. (1984). *Patterns of sounds.* Cambridge studies in speech science and communication, Cambridge: Cambridge University Press.

Maeda, S. (1979). An articulatory model of the tongue based on a statistical analysis. *Journal of the Acoustical Society of America, 65,* S1, S22, 1979.

Maeda, S. (1988). Improved articulatory model. *Journal of the Acoustical Society of America, 84, Suppl. 1,* S146.

Mantakas, M., Schwartz, J.L., & Escudier, P. (1986). Modèle de prédiction du 'deuxième formant effectif' F'$_2$– application à l'étude de la labialité des voyelles avant du français. [Model of prediction of the "effective second formant F'$_2$" — Application to the study of front French vowels]. *15th JEP, Société Française d'Acoustique,* 157-161.

Mantakas, M., Schwartz, J.L., & Escudier, P. (1993). Center of gravity effect and classification of French front vowels in the roundedness opposition. Submitted to the *Journal of the Acoustical Society of America.*

Mattingly, I.G., & Studdert-Kennedy, M. (eds.) (1991). *Modularity and The Motor Theory of Speech Perception.* Hillsdale: Lawrence Erlbaum Associates.

Massaro, D., & Cohen, M. (1983). Categorical or continuous speech perception: A new test. *Speech Communication, 2,* 15-35.

Moore, B.C.J., & Glasberg, B.R. (1983). Masking patterns for synthetic vowels in simultaneous and forward masking. *Journal of the Acoustical Society of America, 73,* 906-917.

Ohala, J. (1990). There is no interface between phonology and phonetics: A personal view. *Journal of Phonetics, 18,* 153-171.

Perkell, J.S., & Klatt, D. (eds.) (1986). *Invariance and Variability in Speech Processes.* New-York: Lawrence Erlbaum Associates.

Perkell, J.S., & Cohen, M.H. (1989). An indirect test of the quantal nature of speech in the production of the vowels /i/, /a/, /u/. *Journal of Phonetics, 17,* 123-133.

Perrier, P. (1990). *De l'usage des modèles pour l'étude de la production de la parole [On the use of models for the study of speech production].* Habilitation à diriger des recherches, Institut National Polytechnique de Grenoble.

Perrier, P., Boë, L.J., Majid Shihab, R., & Guérin, B. (1985). Modélisation articulatoire du conduit vocal — exploration et exploitation. [Articulatory model of the vocal tract — test and capability]. *14th JEP, Société Française d'Acoustique,* 55-58.

Petitot Cocorda, J. (1985). *Les catastrophes de la parole. [Catastrophes of speech].* Collection Recherches Interdisciplinaires. Paris: Maloine.

Sachs, M.B., & Young, E.D. (1979). Encoding of steady-state vowels in the auditory nerve: Representation in terms of discharge rate. *Journal of the Acoustical Society of America, 66,* 470-479.

Schroeder, M.R., Atal, B.S., & Hall, J.L. (1979). Objective measure of certain speech signal degradations based on masking properties of human auditory perception. In B. Lindblom, S. Ohman (Eds.), *Frontiers of Speech Communication Research*, 217-229. London: Academic Press.

Schwartz, J.L. (1987). A propos des notions de forme et de stabilité dans la perception des voyelles. [About notions of shape and stability in the perception of vowels]. *Bulletin du Laboratoire de la Communication Parlée, (Grenoble), 1A*, 159-190.

Schwartz, J.L., Beautemps, D., Abry, C., & Escudier, P. (1993). Interindividual and cross-linguistic strategies for the production of the [i] vs [y] contrast. *Journal of Phonetics, 21*, 411-425.

Schwartz, J.L., Boë, L.J., Perrier, P., Guérin, B., & Escudier, P. (1989). Perceptual contrast and stability in vowel systems: A 3-D simulation study. *Eurospeech, 1*, 63-66.

Schwartz, J.L., & Escudier, P. (1987). Does the human auditory system include large scale spectral integration? In M.E.H. Schouten (Ed.), *The Psychophysics of Speech Perception* (pp. 284-292). Nato Asi Series, Dordrecht: Martinus Nijhoff Publishers.

Schwartz, J.L., & Escudier, P. (1989). A strong evidence for the existence of a large-scale integrated spectral representation in vowel perception. *Speech Communication, 8*, 235-259.

Stelmachowicz, P.G., Small, A.M., & Abbas, P.J. (1982). Suppression effects for complex stimuli. *Journal of the Acoustical Society of America, 71*, 410-420.

Stevens, K.N. (1972). The quantal nature of speech: Evidence from articulatory-acoustic data. In E.E. Davis Jr. & P.B. Denes (Eds.), *Human Communication: A unified view* (pp. 51-66). New-York: Mc Graw-Hill.

Stevens, K.N. (1985). Spectral prominences and phonetic distinctions in language. *Speech Communication, 4*, 137-144.

Stevens, K.N. (1989). On the quantal nature of speech. *Journal of Phonetics, 17*, 3-45.

Strange, W. (1989). Evolving theories of speech perception. *Journal of the Acoustical Society of America, 85*, 2081-2087.

Tyler, R.S., & Lindblom, B. (1982). Preliminary study of simultaneous-masking and pulsation-threshold patterns of vowels. *Journal of the Acoustical Society of America, 71*, 220-224.

Vallée, N. (1989). *Typologie des systèmes vocaliques. [Typology of vowel systems]*. Travail d'Etudes et de Recherche, Université Stendhal, Grenoble.

Vallée, N. (1990). *Structure et prédiction des systèmes vocaliques. [Structure and prediction of vowel systems]* Diplôme d'Etudes Approfondies, Sciences du Langage, Université Stendhal, Grenoble.

Vallée, N., & Boë, L.J. (1992). Vers des prototypes acoustiques et articulatoires des 37 phonèmes vocaliques d'UPSID. [Towards acoustic and articulatory prototypes for the 37 vocalic phonemes of UPSID] *19th JEP, Société Française d'Acoustique*, 53-58.

Viviani, P., & Stucchi N. (1992). Biological movements look uniform: Evidence of motor-perceptual interactions. *Journal of Experimental Psychology: Human Perception & Performance, 18, 3*, 603-623.

Zwicker, E., & Feldtkeller, R. (1969). *Das Ohr als Nachrichtenempfänger*. Stuttgart: S. Hirzel Verlag.

Articulatory Models in Speech Synthesis

10

Bernard Gabioud

Laboratoire d'analyse informatique de la parole (LAIP)
Université de Lausanne, CH-1015 LAUSANNE, Switzerland

This chapter is about articulatory models used in speech synthesis. After a first section where the need for articulatory models is explained, the chain of models required to perform an articulatory synthesis is described. The next section gives examples of the different kinds of articulatory models considered until now. Then S. Maeda's vocal tract model is described in some detail: How the shape of a vocal tract can be realistically described with a small number of parameters. Finally, the shortcomings of the present statistical approach are mentioned, and directions for future developments are proposed.

The primary goal of an articulatory synthesis model is to reproduce the voice signal by modelling the mechanisms of its natural production. Speech is produced in a human vocal tract, and is the result of the vibration of the vocal chords, modulated by the movement of the tongue, the lips, and other articulators. But modelling this entire process is a complex task: As there are many bones, muscles, hard and soft walls and cavities involved, simplifications are necessary. Many different models have been proposed, based generally on similar, but sometimes on very different assumptions. This chapter deals with the static aspect of articulatory models. (See Chapter 11 for the dynamic aspects.)

At present, articulatory synthesis should be considered more as a basic research tool for the understanding of speech production than as a method to produce commercial speech synthesis applications. Nevertheless, by giving us a better understanding of the speech production mechanisms, articulatory synthesis has the long-term potential to solve problems affecting the current approaches in speech synthesis.

The Need for Articulatory Models

It can be argued that articulatory models are not a necessary step for speech synthesis. Since the goals of speech production are largely acoustic (see Stevens, 1989), one could be tempted to conclude that the articulatory intermediary is an unnecessary complication. Good synthesis has been obtained either by segment concatenation (see Chapters 4 and 5), or by a rule-based phonology-to-acoustics approach (see Chapter 13).

However, both of these approaches are limited. Concatenation techniques are based on dictionaries which are speaker- and speech-rate dependent, because coarticulation changes with speech rate. At the present time, it is not known how samples are to be translated from one rate and one speaker into another coherent voice, with correct coarticulation. It can be argued that it would be much better to work at the level of the underlying causes, than at the level of the consequences of the articulation.

Rule-based phonology-to-acoustic models are limited in the sense that many rules are needed to produce the correct results. Even if these rules are well-founded phonologically, their phonetic interpretation is very empirical. This also shows the need for a good articulatory theory as the proper foundation of phonetic phenomena.

Approaches based on the sole description of the vocal tract as a set of n tubes do not seem to furnish a correct and adequate modelling of speech production either: If the number of tubes is small, as in Fant (1960), the modelling is anthropomorphically unrealistic; if the number of tubes is adequate, their parameters are insufficiently constrained. In the sense that it allows the analysis and simulation of acoustically relevant phenomena, it is more judicious to consider the n-tube approach as an adequate tool for the transition from the geometry of the vocal tract to the acoustic level, than to consider it as a true production model.

Speech synthesisers which use formants as input (e.g. Klatt, 1980) have no built-in constraints to link formant values with each other. Yet any particular shape of the vocal tract imposes a complex relationship between all formants, their frequencies and amplitudes. The inclusion of this speaker-dependent relationship is necessary for high-quality synthesis. This relationship is implicit in an articulatory model, and its predictive quality depends on the overall quality of the model.

In principle, articulatory models integrate, globally and to varying degrees, morphological and articulatory constraints. Such models also offer the possibility of varying the vocal tract shape coherently by acting on the control parameters of these models. It thus becomes possible to relate these geometric variations and associated formant changes to real behaviours in the speech production system.

A Chain of Models

By definition, articulatory models, while trying to reproduce as well as possible the speech signal, tend to simulate the natural mechanisms which cause this signal. This kind of modelling is a simplified representation of what actually happens between the glottis vibration and the sound radiation at the lips.

The problem can be divided into different steps. Although these steps are not entirely independent of each other, such a division renders the problem much more manageable.

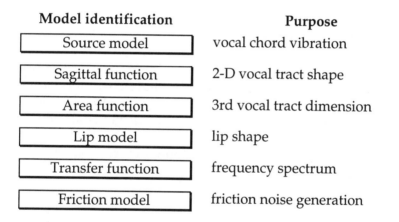

Model identification	Purpose
Source model	vocal chord vibration
Sagittal function	2-D vocal tract shape
Area function	3rd vocal tract dimension
Lip model	lip shape
Transfer function	frequency spectrum
Friction model	friction noise generation

Figure 1. The articulatory synthesis production chain, not including the synthesis itself.

First of all, one has to model the primary source of the human voice, the vibration of the vocal chords. Many studies have been devoted to this aspect of speech production (for example, see Ishizaka and Flanagan, 1972; Fant and Liljencrants, 1985; Fant, 1986; Titze, 1989). There are also extra noise sources and bursts when the constrictions are small, as for fricative and plosive consonants (see for example Klatt, 1980; Stevens and Bickley, 1986; Badin, 1989).

Secondly, a model for the shape of the vocal tract is needed. This step is itself divided into two steps: First, a two-dimensional model of the vocal tract sagittal section is established (e.g. on the basis of X-ray observations, see references in the next section). Then an area function is calculated, which adds the third dimension by converting the section width into a section area (see Chiba and Kajiyama, 1941; Heinz and Stevens, 1964; Perrier *et al.*, 1992; Beautemps *et al.*, 1993).

Finally, to finish with the mechanical aspect of the modelling process, a lip model is required, especially if the synthesis purports to include the visual synthesis of the lip movement, which contributes significantly to human speech recognition in noisy situations (see Lindblom and Sundberg, 1971; Abry and Boë, 1986; Guiard-Marigny, 1992).

With all the articulatory pieces in place, we are ready for the acoustic modelling procedure, which again consists of a number of steps: Source signal generation at the glottis, wave transmission along the vocal tract, generation of resonances and formants, calculation of the losses in the soft walls, opening of the nasal tract, and finally, sound radiation from the lips (see Fant 1960; Badin and Fant 1984; Chapter 6).

The present chapter concentrates on just one central piece of this chain: The modelling of the sagittal section of the vocal tract.

A Convergence of Ideas

Since a large number of models have been proposed, it is clearly beyond the scope of this book to give a review of all that has been done in this field. We need to restrict ourselves to a few examples to show the three main trends, which we could name *geometrical* models, *physiological* models, and *statistical* models. Also, in this historical section, we shall put the emphasis on the origin of the ideas adopted by current articulatory models.

Geometrical Models

An important early work is Öhman's (1966, 1967), based on cineradiographic films, in which tongue movement is described by three independent mechanical systems corresponding to an *apical articulator*, a *dorsal articulator*, and a *tongue body articulator*. The vowels are results of linear combinations of the extreme vocalic positions of /i/, /a/ and /u/. However, the tongue shape is represented as a circle of constant radius, and the articulator movements are not realistic enough to reproduce the tongue dorsum movement.

In Coker and Fujimura's work (1966), five parameters define the vocal tract configuration. The tongue shape is also a circle of constant radius, but an additional parameter allows for a better simulation of the tongue tip position, by deviating from the circle. The lip movements are described by an opening parameter and by a protrusion parameter. The values of this *small number of parameters* are used by a computer program to calculate area functions and formant frequencies.

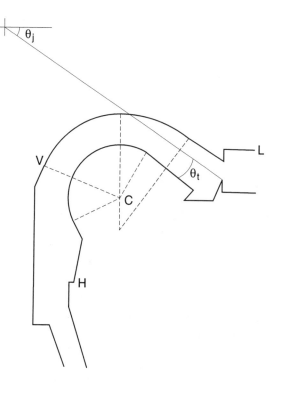

Figure 2. A simplified view of Mermelstein's model. The solid line shows the sagittal section, which consists of 3 arcs and 18 line segments. The dotted lines show the first and the last radius of the arcs. The hard palate and the external pharyngeal wall are fixed, the other structures are mobile. The various letters refer to the angles and points used as command parameters.

In 1973, Mermelstein proposed his articulatory, rule-based speech synthesiser. The shape of the sagittal section of the vocal tract is given by 3 arcs and 18 line segments. For the vowels, a set of articulatory parameters is defined, the values for which are determined from X-rays, completed by a set of acoustic parameters from natural speech data. Consonants are introduced as transition states between vowels satisfying specific constraints, and thus are coarticulated with the vowels. However, while allowing for a more detailed description of the vocal tract shape than Coker and Fujimura's model, this model has difficulties predicting a coherent movement for the large number of parameters needed.

Physiological Models

The physiological trend is exemplified by Perkell (1969, 1974), who represents the tongue by "16 mass-bearing flesh points which are connected to one another and to body attachments by 38 active and 47 passive generating elements". The advantage of physiological models is that they establish a link between the action of specific muscles and the articulations of the tongue.

In the same trend of muscle modelling, one should also cite work by Hiki and Oizumi (1974) and by Kiritani *et al.* (1975). However, such models are too complex to be mastered in most forms of contemporary speech synthesis.

Statistical Models

In order to take into account the importance of the place of constriction, Lindblom and Sundberg (1971) use the idea of modelling shape and positions of the tongue body by *factors explaining deviations from a neutral base configuration*. A factor C, which varies from 0 to 1, affects the shape of the tongue and the degree of constriction. A factor D determines the front-back position of the tongue: The vowel /i/ corresponds to $C = 1$, $D = -1$, the vowel /u/ corresponds to $C = 1$, $D = 0$, the vowel /a/ corresponds to $C = 1$, $D = +1$. All other shapes are obtained by interpolation. After calculating the formant frequencies using Fant's (1960) electric analogue circuit, Lindblom and Sundberg establish the sensitivities of the formants to the parameters of the model.

This type of model incorporates the basic idea that factors are to be specified which explain deviations from a neutral base configuration. This idea has since then been adopted by many other researchers, among them Kiritani and Sekimoto (1977), Shirai and Honda (1977), Harshman *et al.* (1977), and Maeda (1979, 1988).

In 1977, Harshman, Ladefoged, Goldstein and Rice proposed a factor analysis of ten English vowels pronounced by five speakers. All tongue movements are described by two parameters: the *front raising* component, which accounts for the advancing of the tongue root and the elevation of the tongue front, and the *back raising* component, which follows the elevation of the tongue toward the velum. The anatomic interspeaker differences are associated with different ranges of these factors. In their 1978 work (Ladefoged *et al.*, 1978), the same authors reconstruct the vocal tract sagittal shape from the first three formants; for this, a lip opening parameter is added to the model.

The main weakness of this model is an imprecise modelling of the movements of the tongue tip, which is necessary for consonants. On the positive side, this model proves how successful the factor analysis technique can be in producing a model with a small number of factors and a good data fit.

Although physiological models have the merit of proposing a fine description of the mechanical structures of the articulators and of their interactions, their control parameters are too complex. Pure geometrical models are relatively simple, but their input parameters are, unfortunately, difficult to interpret in physical terms. Statistical models have a clear advantage, if they are based on enough data to adequately represent all the vowels and consonants of a language, and have a small number of command parameters clearly associated with all the significant movements of the articulators.

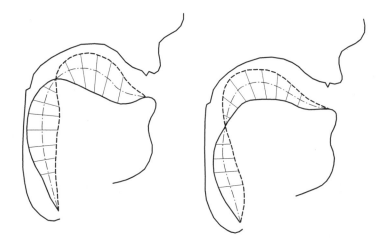

Figure 3. The effect of the two factors on the tongue shape, as predicted by the Harshman, Ladefoged, Goldstein and Rice model. The solid line represents the lowest value of the factor, the dashed lines the highest value, and the dot-dashed line the neutral position of the tongue.

Such a model has been presented by S. Maeda in 1979, and again in 1988, with a different set of data. The following section is devoted to Maeda's most recent model.

Maeda's Statistical Model

Maeda's 1988 linear component model is based on the analysis of cineradiographic data from the Phonetic Institute of Strasbourg, by Bothorel *et al.*, published in 1986. A corpus of 10.4 seconds of real speech, consisting of ten sentences from a French female speaker has been used. With 50 frames per second, this makes a total of 519 frames.

Using a semipolar coordinate system, the sagittal profile is measured along 30 grid lines on the digitised, hand-drawn X-rays (Figure 4). Unlike previously-used grids, the 1988 grid has a straight section for a better description of the front part of the tongue.

Here is a brief description of how the linear component model of the tongue is established. Basically it follows the model proposed by Lindblom and Sundberg in 1971. First of all, the average of the data is determined, and only the deviations from this neutral shape are

modelled. The sum of the squares of the normalised deviations is called
the *total variance of the data*.

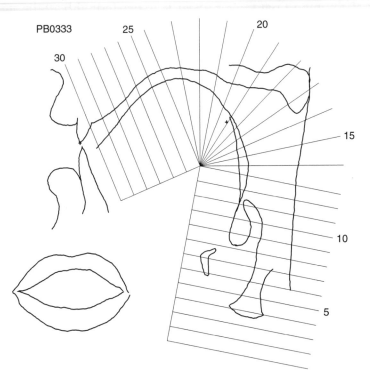

Figure 4. A hand-traced vocal tract radiographic profile with Maeda's semipolar
coordinate grid. On the bottom left, the frontal view of the lips. The vowel is an /i/
just before the palatal occlusion of a /k/ in the French sentence "Donne un petịt coup"
/dɔnœ̃ptịku/.

   Then, as the lower lip and the tongue are attached to the jaw, it is
justifiable to take into account the jaw movement before considering the
other movements. Thus, the effect of the jaw opening is first subtracted
from the data. In this corpus, this parameter explains only 15% of the
variance, because the selected speaker does not move the jaw very much
when she speaks.
   Thereafter, a principal component analysis of the tongue data is
performed, leading to three significant factors. The most important factor
follows the front-back position of the tongue body, and explains 43% of
the variance (see Figure 5). The second factor, interpreted as the height of
the tongue dorsum, explains 23% of the variance. The third factor is
related to the height of the tongue apex, and explains 7% of the variance.
The model thus explains a total of 88% of the variance of the tongue data.
Most importantly, the factors that Maeda obtains have an interpretation

which corresponds to what is expected from the other studies of the tongue movement (Öhman, 1966; Coker and Fujimura, 1966).

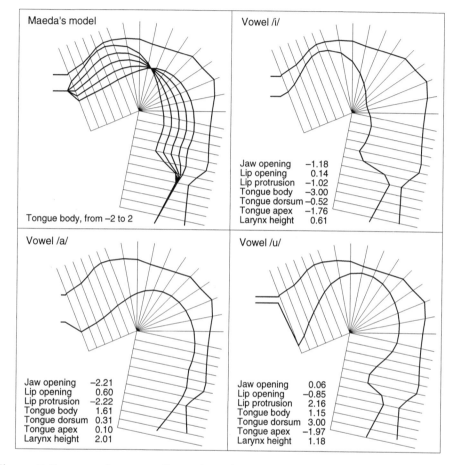

Figure 5. Four vocal tract configurations drawn using Maeda's model. The top left picture shows the effect of the tongue body parameter varying from –2 to +2. The others show examples of the vowels /i/, /a/ and /u/. The vowel /i/ has a tongue body in the front, and a low apex. The vowel /a/ has the tongue body in the back position, the jaw opened. The vowel /u/ has a strong protrusion, and the tongue dorsum is at its highest position.

The lip data, including the width, can be described adequately by two parameters: lip opening and lip protrusion. The height of the larynx is followed by one parameter. The movement of the velum is not included, nor is the nasal tract.

With Maeda's model, any shape of the vocal tract can be defined by the values of the seven normalised parameters, which typically lie between –3 and +3 (see Figure 5).

In his 1990 paper, using data from two speakers, Maeda observes the time variation of his model's parameters, interpreted as the basic speech articulators. The most important result is the evidence of articulatory compensation. Different configurations of the articulators are used to produce the same sound. The adjustment of tongue-dorsal positions compensate for different jaw openings. In the case of rounded vowels, the different jaw openings are compensated by an appropriate adjustment of the lip opening. This shows clearly that the speech production targets are acoustic, not articulatory; the articulators adjust within their constraints to produce the target sounds.

Although resulting from the analysis of a female speaker's vocal tract, Maeda's model has been shown to be well-suited to the production of French vowels, as pronounced by a male speaker. By simply applying a global increase of the vocal tract dimensions (except for the length of the hard palate), Boë *et al.* (1992) produce a good male voice, with the formants of all French cardinal vowels at the right place. In fact, Figure 5 uses this "male" version of the model.

Maeda's articulatory model successfully captures the essential features of one real human being's vocal tract, leading to the synthesis of a coherent voice. All vowels generated by this model sound as if they are really pronounced by the same voice.

Trends for the Future

First of all, it would be very interesting to generalise this single-speaker model to other individuals, by having extra parameters added, allowing for changes in the length and the width of the different parts of the vocal tract.

Another major project would be to use Maeda's model in a speech synthesiser. However, in our own attempts to resynthesise the original sentences used in Maeda's analysis, we encountered several unsolved problems, some of which are not too hard to solve, but others which are much harder. As a complement to Maeda's sagittal function model, we used the area function by Perrier *et al.* (1992), and the acoustic vocal tract response function is calculated using Badin and Fant's model (1984).

The Tongue Tip is Neglected by Statistics

Principal component analysis is iterative. It finds the factor (i.e. the linear combination of variables) which explains ("takes out") the most variance; then it finds another factor which again "takes out" most of the residual variance, and so on. Usually after a small number of iterations, most of the variance of the data is explained, and one can stop the process. This method has the advantage of explaining the most variance with the least number of factors.

However, to be used in an articulatory model, factors need to have a good physical interpretation, so that one can predict a sensible dynamic behaviour for them. After the subtraction of the effect of the jaw movement, Maeda had no problem with that requirement, so he kept the first three principal components as tongue shape factors.

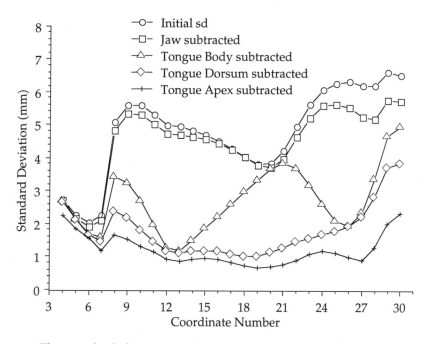

Figure 6. The standard deviations of Maeda's tongue model in function of the coordinate number (low coordinate numbers: pharynx; high coordinate numbers: tongue tip). The top line shows the initial standard deviation. The other lines show the cumulative effect of the factors taken into account. The difference between two lines show the effect of including a new factor. The bottom line is the final residual standard deviation for Maeda's model.

Unfortunately, the precision of the tongue tip position obtained by the model is poor. While doing a perfect job of explaining most of the variance of the data at the middle of the tongue, the three-factor solution neglects both ends. The residuals are not equally distributed along the vocal tract. They are extremely small in the middle and symmetrically large at both ends of the tongue. While an imprecision in the pharyngeal region does not have much acoustic effect, an imprecise front cavity affects significantly the quality of the front vowels.

The bottom line in Figure 6 shows the RMS residuals as a function of the coordinate number. The resolution at the tongue tip (coordinate 30) is worse by a factor of 3 than at the middle of the tongue (coordinate 19). A 2 mm resolution means in essence that 95% of the data falls within −4 mm and +4 mm.

The reason for this behaviour is that the coordinates have a strong local correlation. Figure 7 shows a part of the correlation matrix in the middle section of the tongue. Statistical theory assumes randomness: observations are not supposed to depend on each other. In the data analysed here, the strong correlation between neighbouring points induces strong constraints, and hence a better fit in the middle of tongue than at both ends, where the constraints are weaker. Consequently, an extra principal component would be needed for the tongue ends.

	d10	d12	d14	d16	d18	d20	d22	d24	d26
d10	1.000								
d12	0.924	1.000							
d14	0.766	0.936	1.000						
d16	0.600	0.820	0.960	1.000					
d18	0.346	0.604	0.809	0.929	1.000				
d20	-0.170	0.069	0.331	0.540	0.791	1.000			
d22	-0.714	-0.607	-0.398	-0.186	0.123	0.668	1.000		
d24	-0.833	-0.845	-0.735	-0.586	-0.333	0.246	0.867	1.000	
d26	-0.740	-0.847	-0.826	-0.741	-0.561	-0.039	0.667	0.929	1.000

Figure 7. Pearson Product-Moment Correlation of (part of) the tongue coordinates, skipping every second line. In addition to the very strong local correlation of the data, we can also observe (around d12-d24) the very strong anticorrelation which results from the physical tongue body front-back movement.

As Maeda himself argues, one does not need to use principal components as factors. Arbitrary components, which have a clear physical meaning, can be used instead. This is what Maeda did in his 1979 model for all the tongue factors, and in his 1988 model for the jaw opening factor. Such factors result from direct measurements instead of resulting from the statistical analysis. The disadvantage of arbitrary factors, however, is that they do not usually explain as much variance as principal components. But this is not our main concern.

Following Maeda's 1979 reasoning, it is possible to build a tongue model with three arbitrary factors, which have the same physical interpretation as the principal components, but which in addition minimise the residual error in the region where we need the best fit.

Here is one method. After the subtraction of the effect of the jaw, the front-back movement of the tongue body can be measured by a difference of the coordinates 11 and 25 (this is better than using only a measurement in the back). Then, after removing from the data the effect of this parameter, the raising of the tongue body can be followed by the coordinate 18. Finally, the tongue tip height can be followed by coordinate 29. Furthermore, to lower the effect of the imprecision of the measurements, one can average several neighbouring coordinates instead of using just one.

An even better solution is the following. After the subtraction of the effect of the jaw, a principal component analysis of the tongue using the coordinates 9 to 27 (excluding the tongue tip) is performed, leading to a tongue body and a tongue dorsum factor. Then, after the subtraction of the combined effect of these two factors, a reliable tongue tip factor can be extracted from the coordinates 27 to 30.

Using either of these two solutions, we bring the tongue tip resolution down to 1 mm. When the original sentences used for the analysis are resynthesised, the difference is unambiguously perceptible, especially in the front vowels such as /i/ and /y/.

It should be mentioned that for the sole purpose of direct production of the speech signal, the improvement presented in this section is not significant compared with Maeda's analysis. As the fitting imprecision can be compensated by a slightly different value of the parameters, the same vocal tracts can be generated by both models. Still, the new model has a better interpretation of the parameters: Instead of linear combinations of all the measurements, the new factors are based on the most relevant measurements of the articulators. In this way, the movement of the tongue can be clearly described as a movement of the jaw, plus a front-back movement of the tongue body relative to the jaw, plus a raising of the tongue back relative to the tongue body, plus a final adjustment of the apex. For the dynamics of the tongue movement, this is significant.

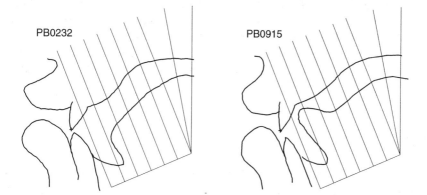

Figure 8. Two examples showing the tongue tip in a position the current model is unable to treat properly. The left picture is a /u/ and the right picture is just after the alveolar tap of a /l/. See also Figure 4 for comparison with the normal (and most frequent) case.

The Shape of the Tongue Tip

Even with the above improvements, we have not yet achieved a truly satisfactory sagittal model: the tongue tip needs more work. The above analysis assumes that the tongue contour crosses all the grid lines. The following two pictures show that it is obviously not always the case.

If it exists, the cavity shape in front of the tongue tip can be grossly miscalculated and misused in the analysis. To remedy this, one should probably stop using the grid at least 1 cm before the teeth, and use the real tongue tip x and y positions in the analysis. This could not be done with the Strasbourg data, because the tongue tip is not determined well enough from the X-rays. We should notice that Ladefoged in 1979 in his list of 17 necessary and sufficient parameters includes tip advancing, tongue bunching, tongue narrowing and tongue hollowing. Clearly, 15 years later, work still remains to be done in this direction.

The Control of Friction

Another question concerns fricative consonants: how precise is the model for predicting small constriction areas? The answer is: Certainly not precise enough (Beautemps, 1993). The inherent imprecision of the analysis and prediction method prevents this.

We should remember that this is difficult for us humans, too. Producing the right fricative is the last articulatory skill that children acquire, and sometimes even some adults cannot master it entirely. Also, our movement control system is not just a direct production system. It uses a combination of different techniques to reach its goals, such as the perception of the consequences of the movement, as well as learned movements. Moreover, various tricks are used, like leaning the tongue sides onto the hard palate in order to exert fine motor control over an alveolar fricative.

Conclusions

The statistical technique brings both power and simplicity to articulatory modelling: With a large matrix of coefficients established once and for all, using real data, a small number of parameters allows for an adequate description of all the shapes that a vocal tract can take.

The articulatory model presented here gives very good results in the production of the French vowels, in conjunction with state-of-the-art area functions, acoustic transfer functions and formant synthesis. Especially noteworthy is the coherence of the prediction of the formant frequencies.

Our resynthesis exercise has shown that a fixed grid is too limited as a way of getting measurements from cineradiographic data. Also, the use of principal components from the fixed grid coordinates fails to provide a good resolution at the places in the vocal tract where we need it.

More work needs to be done for the production of the consonants. Also, if the generalisation to other speakers and other languages is one objective for the future, an advanced articulatory models is certainly the right tool.

Scientists dream of a simple equation to explain all observations. Maybe there is one yet to be discovered, the basic physical principle of the universe. But as for speech, one is forced to accept the fact that this is a very complicated human activity. A simple, symmetrically beautiful model is simply not enough.

References

Abry, C., & Boë, L.-J. (1986) "Laws" for Lips. *Speech Communication, 5,* 97-104.

Badin, P., & Fant, G. (1984). Notes on vocal tract computation. *STQL-QPSR, 2-3,* 53-108.

Badin, P. (1989). Acoustics of voiceless fricatives: Production theory and data. *Speech Transmission Lab. QPSR, 3,* 33-55.

Beautemps, D., Badin, P., & Laboissière, R. (1993). Recovery of vocal-tract midsagittal and area functions from speech signal for vowels and fricative consonants. In Eurospeech '93 Proceedings, *3rd European Conference on Speech Communication and Technology, 1,* 279-302. Berlin.

Boë, L.-J., Perrier, P., & Bailly, G. (1992). The geometric vocal tract variables controlled for vowel production: Proposals for constraining acoustic-to-articulatory inversion. *Journal of Phonetics, 20,* 27-38.

Bothorel, A., Simon, P., Wioland, F., & Zerling, J.-P. (1986). *Cinéradiographie des voyelles et des consonnes du français. Recueil de documents synchronisés pour quatre sujets: vues latérales du conduit vocal, vues frontales de l'orifice labial, données acoustiques.* Strasbourg, France: Institut de Phonétique.

Chiba, T., & Kajiyama, M. (1941). *The vowel, its nature and structure.* Tokyo: Tokyo-Kaseidan Pub. Co.

Coker, C., & Fujimura, O. (1966) Model for the specification of the vocal tract area function. *Journal of the Acoustical Society of America,40,* 1271.

Fant, G. (1960). *Acoustic theory of speech production.* The Hague: Mouton.

Fant, G., & Liljencrants, J. (1985). A four parameter model of glottal flow. *Speech Transmission Lab. QPSR 2,* 18-24.

Fant, G. (1986). Glottal flow: Models and interaction. *Journal of Phonetics, 14,* 393-399.

Guiard-Marigny T. (1992) *Modélisation des lèvres.* DEA Signal Image Parole, INP, Grenoble.

Harshman, R., Ladefoged, P., & Goldstein, L. (1977). Factor analysis of tongue shapes. *Journal of the Acoustical Society of America, 62,* 693-707.

Heinz, J.M., & Stevens, K.N. (1964). On the derivation of area functions and acoustic spectra from cineradiographic films of speech. *Journal of the Acoustical Society of America, 36,* 1037-1038.

Hiki, S., & Oizumi, J. (1974). Speech synthesis by rule from neurophysiological parameters. In *Speech Communication Seminar*. Stockholm, Vol. 1-2, pp. 219-225.

Ishizaka, K., & Flanagan, J.L. (1972). Synthesis of voiced sounds from a two mass model of the vocal chords, *Bell Systems Tech. Journal, 51*, 1233-1268.

Kiritani, S., Itoh, S.K., & Fujimura, O. (1975). Tongue-pellet tracking by a computer controlled X-ray microbeam system. *Journal of the Acoustical Society of America, 57*, 1516-1520.

Kiritani, S., & Sekimoto, S. (1977). Parameter description of the tongue movements in vowel production. In *Modèles articulatoire et Phonétique*. GALF - Actes du Symposium de Grenoble, pp. 202-222.

Klatt, D.H. (1980). Software for a cascade/parallel formant synthesiser. *Journal of the Acoustical Society of America, 67*, 971-995.

Ladefoged, P. (1979). Articulatory parameters. *9th International Congress of Phonetic Sciences, Copenhagen, U.C.L.A. WPP 45*, 25-52.

Ladefoged, P., Harshman, R., Goldstein, L., & Rice, L. (1978). Generating vocal tract shapes from formant frequencies. *Journal of the Acoustical Society of America, 64*, 1027-1035.

Lindblom, B., & Sundberg, J. (1971). Acoustical consequences of lip, tongue, jaw and larynx movement. *Journal of the Acoustical Society of America, 50*, 1166-1179.

Maeda, S. (1979). An articulatory model based on statistical analysis. *Journal of the Acoustical Society of America, 65*, S1, S22(A).

Maeda, S. (1988). Improved articulatory model. *Journal of the Acoustical Society of America, 84*, Sup. 1, S146.

Maeda, S. (1989). Compensatory articulation during speech: Evidence from the analysis and synthesis of vocal-tract shapes using an articulatory model. In W.J. Hardcastle & A. Marchal (Eds.), *Speech Production and Modelling* (pp. 131-149). Kluwer: Academic Publishers.

Mermelstein, P. (1973). Articulatory model for the study of speech production. *Journal of the Acoustical Society of America, 53*, 1073-1082.

Öhman, S.E. (1966). Coarticulation in VCV utterances: Spectrographic measurements. *Journal of the Acoustical Society of America, 41*, 310-320.

Öhman, S.E. (1967). Numerical model for coarticulation. *Journal of the Acoustical Society of America, 36*, 1038.

Perkell, J.S. (1969). Physiology of speech production: Results and implications of a quantitative cineradiographic study. *Res. Monogr. 53*. Cambridge, MA: M.I.T. Press.

Perkell, J.S. (1974). *A physiologically oriented model of tongue activity in speech production*. Ph. D. Thesis. M.I.T. Cambridge, MA: M.I.T. Press.

Perrier, P., Boë, L.-J., & Sock, R. (1992). Vocal tract area functions estimation from midsagittal dimensions with CT scans and a vocal tract cast: Modelling the transition with two sets of coefficients. *Journal of Speech and Hearing Research, 35*, 53-67.

Shirai, K., & Honda, M. (1977). Estimation of articulatory motion. In Masayuki, Sawashima & Cooper (Eds.), *Dynamic aspects of speech production* (pp. 279-302). Tokyo: University of Tokyo Press.

Stevens, K. N. (1989). On the quantal nature of speech. *Journal of Phonetics, 17*, 3-45.

Stevens, K. N., & Bickley, C.A. (1986). Effect of vocal tract constriction on the glottal source: Experimental and modelling studies. *Journal of Phonetics, 14*, 373-382.

Titze, I.R. (1989). A four parameter model of the glottis and vocal fold contact area. *Speech Communication, 8*, 191-201.

Dynamic Modelling and Control of Speech Articulators: Application to Vowel Reduction

11

Application to Vowel Reduction

Pascal Perrier[1] and David J. Ostry[2]

[1] Institut de la Communication Parlée - URA CNRS 368
INPG and Université Stendhal, GRENOBLE, France
[2] Psychology Department, McGill University
MONTREAL, Québec, Canada

Some current thinking on the dynamic aspects of a speech motor control model useful in articulatory synthesis is presented. In the first part, the chapter outlines some dynamic and kinematic properties of skeletal limbs, supporting the idea of *a second-order modelling* of skilled movements of these limbs. Specific data on speech movements are then described, and an extension of this model to speech articulators is proposed. In the second part, the fundamentals of the *Equilibrium-Point hypothesis* proposed by Feldman for the control of human skilled movements are detailed. Finally, the interest of both above mentioned approaches for the understanding of the relationships between linguistic and physical levels in speech, is explained with respect to the vowel reduction phenomenon.

The transmission of linguistic messages by speaking is a complex process which involves encoding a discrete phonological sequence into a continuous acoustic signal. One of the most noticeable characteristics of this process is the variability that can be observed at the acoustical (and of course articulatory) levels between the productions of the same phoneme by the same speaker, in different conditions, or from one repetition to the other. The variability depends on both the phonetic context and on prosodic factors, such as speech rate and stress. Thus part of the variability is due to coarticulatory phenomena that originate in the fact that speaking is not a discrete and sequential, but a continuous and parallel task. For example, in the word "cat" ([kœt]), the motor commands for the vowel [œ] can start before the articulatory target of [k] is reached and, in same way, the commands for the consonant [t] can partially overlap the commands for the vowel [œ]. This example shows that it is possible for the realisation of the vowel [œ] to be influenced by both adjacent consonants and that, depending on the timing of the commands, such influence can be more or less strong.

For speech-synthesis systems, which today must generate output of very high quality to be competitive, it is essential to be able to reproduce coarticulatory phenomena accurately. Two strategies are currently being used to achieve this goal. The first consists of conducting an extensive analysis of speech signals in order to derive rules that describe coarticulatory effects for many combinations of phonemes in acoustical terms. An example of this approach is given in Chapter 12 which integrates classical phonological descriptions with high-quality speech synthesis.

The second approach attempts to infer basic principles that are able to explain the strategies involved in the acoustical production of phonological sequences at the motor control level. A background to the latter approach is contained in the widely cited proposals for an "articulatory phonology" made by Browman and Goldstein (1986) at Haskins Laboratories. Obviously, rather different philosophies underlie the two approaches and, therefore, important differences can be seen in the results. By generating coarticulatory effects at the signal level, it is now possible to generate high-quality synthetic sentences, whereas, as yet, research on motor-control strategies allows acceptable synthesis only of VCV nonsense syllables. But whereas the former approach will only be able to reproduce already observed coarticulatory effects, the latter has the potential of incorporating *basic principles*, and therefore, of predicting new effects. Such effects might be associated with new articulatory conditions, such as speech production perturbed by a bite block (as when a pipe-smoker talks), or with different pragmatic conditions (e.g. clear speech *vs.* spontaneous speech). In other words, the "motor control approach" should not only reproduce observed coarticulatory phenomena, but also have the potential for generating natural-sounding speech in novel situations.

Up to now, the quest for correlations between properties of acoustical speech signals and phonological units has been disappointing (see Perkell and Klatt, 1986). This failure attests to the great complexity of the translation from phonology to acoustics. Indeed, following Liberman and Studdert-Kennedy (1978), some authors have not hesitated to speak of a "drastic restructuring" between phonological description and acoustic realisation. Nevertheless under normal conditions, listeners can recover the phonological units of a spoken message from the acoustical signal alone.

Detailed consideration of the process of coarticulation at the motor-control level seems to be a good manner of achieving a better understanding of this perceptual feat. The comparison between, on the one hand, the strategies developed by talkers in order to limit acoustical variability, and the capabilities of the production apparatus on the other hand, can provide useful information about the demands on perception and, hence, about the process of perception. As Fowler *et al.* wrote in 1980, "[...]the style of control of any activity must reflect the contingencies of the execution while complying with the aim of the activity." For all these reasons, our topic here deals with the "motor control approach" to understanding coarticulation.

Before inferring the global control strategies used in speech production, it is necessary to characterise and to model the production apparatus and its possible control parameters. The fundamental concepts underlying the theory on the relations between the geometry of the vocal tract and acoustics were presented by Fant in his famous book entitled *Acoustic Theory of Speech Production* (Fant, 1960). Gabioud proposes in the present book an overview of the articulatory models useful for the study of the relations between articulatory positions and the geometry of the vocal tract. The present chapter moves one level higher in the speech production process, and considers the *dynamic properties* of speech articulators and their control.

In the first part of the chapter, the dynamic properties of speech-articulators will be presented, and the rationale for the view of the mass-spring model in speech research will be outlined. The second part of the chapter consists of a short description of the motor control system of the limbs and of the speech-articulators and the presentation of two models derived from the "Equilibrium-Point hypothesis". In the final section, we propose an application of these motor-control principles as an explanation of the well-known and important speech phenomenon called "vowel reduction".

Dynamic Properties of Speech Articulators

Speech articulators are formed of either hard tissues or cartilages, which are set in motion by muscles (in the case of the hyoid bone, jaw and laryngeal apparatus), or are themselves made up of different muscles (in the case of the tongue, lips and the velum). Speech articulator dynamic properties are therefore largely determined by the associated muscular characteristics, which are similar to those of all skeletal muscles whose contraction is responsible for the generation of forces. The internal structure of the muscles is complex (Rothwell, 1987, for an introduction). Our interest in the present chapter is directed at a functional characterisation of the dynamic behaviour of speech articulators, and at the neurophysiological principles of their control. Throughout the movement of a limb, the length of a muscle is modified, depending on the forces generated by the muscle itself, or by other muscles and forces acting on the limb. The ability to accommodate deformation is a typical property of elastic materials. For this kind of material, the relationship between length and the return force associated with both muscles properties and reflex mechanisms is an important characteristic.

A Spring–like Length–Force[1] Relationship

These relationships were illustrated by Asatryan and Feldman (1965) (see also Feldman, 1966, 1980), who presented data from human subjects whose forearm was constrained to move only in the horizontal plane against a load. The subjects adopted a specified initial joint angle, under load. Suddenly, the load was removed; the mechanical equilibrium was therefore upset, and the forearm was set in motion. The subjects had been instructed "not to intervene voluntarily" to correct the forearm deflections. The induced torques were measured in relation to the elbow angle and the results are shown in Figure 1.

Both for flexor and extensor muscles, the torque decreased with muscle shortening, until it became equal to the torque produced by passive elbow muscles (muscles without any activation). Moreover, for a given starting position and for a given load, the length-force curve remained fairly constant over several repetitions. Feldman therefore called the curves the *Invariant Characteristics* (IC) of the muscle, and proposed that each of them was related to a specified level of descending efferent influence onto the motoneuron pool. This conclusion was supported by measurements made by Feldman and Orlovsky (1972) in cat gastrocnemius muscle which was held at different lengths through forces controlled by a transducer, and whose activation by the central nervous system was simulated by electrical stimulation in the brain stem. The observed curves were similar to Feldman's ICs, and each of them was related to a given rate of the electrical stimulation (corresponding to a specified level of descending control).

---

[1] If the movement is a linear translation, force-length curves are considered; if there is a angular rotation, torque-angle curves are considered.

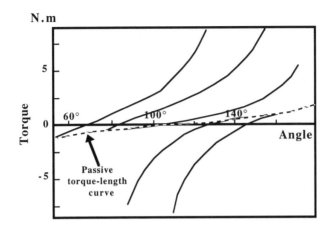

Figure 1. Forearm Torque-angle Invariant Characteristics (adapted from Feldman, 1986). Each curve corresponds to all unloading trials from a given initial position and load; different curves corresponded to different initial limb positions and different central commands.

In both experiments, the observed length-force relationships (or torque-angle relationships) were similar to those of a *damped mass-spring system*. For such a system (also called a *second-order system*), if stiffness k remains constant, and if l_0 (or λ) is the resting length, the length-force curve corresponds to a straight line with a slope k, crossing the X-axis at the length l_0 (or λ). Feldman's ICs (in Figure 1) are not straight lines: their derivative increases with muscle length. The dynamic behaviour of skeletal muscles, together with their control mechanisms, must therefore be described, over a specified length-range and for a specified level of descending control, as a non-linear second-order system, whose stiffness varies with muscle length.

Bell-shaped Velocity Profiles

Several kinematic properties of limb movement can be better interpreted when keeping in mind the typical kinematic behaviour of a simple undamped second-order system. Typically, the equation governing the motion of an undamped and time-invariant mass-spring system is:

$$m\frac{\partial^2 x(t)}{\partial t^2} = -k\left(x(t) - l_0\right)$$

where l_0, k and m are constants describing the resting length of the spring, the spring stiffness and the value of the mass. Therefore, if the initial position of the mass m is $l_0 + A/2$, and if there is no initial velocity, the movement and the velocity of the mass are given by the equations:

$$x(t) = \frac{A}{2} \cos\left(\sqrt{\frac{k}{m}}\, t\right) + l_0 \quad \text{and} \quad \frac{\partial x(t)}{\partial t} = -\frac{A}{2}\sqrt{\frac{k}{m}} \sin\left(\sqrt{\frac{k}{m}}\, t\right)$$

The movement of the mass is therefore periodic with a period T_0 given by:

$$T_0 = 2T = 2\pi\sqrt{\frac{m}{k}}$$

For t=0,

$$x = l_0 + \frac{A}{2} \quad \text{and} \quad \frac{\partial x}{\partial t} = 0.$$

The next zero-velocity position is reached for

$$t = \frac{T_0}{2} = T, \quad x = l_0 - \frac{A}{2}.$$

Between these two consecutive zero-velocity positions, the mass necessarily moves in a monotonic fashion though an extent A over a duration T. The associated velocity-profile (the velocity as a function of time t) is sinusoidal, and is usually called a *"bell-shaped velocity-profile"*. In the course of this displacement, the maximum-velocity, V_{max}, is given by:

$$V_{max} = -\frac{A}{2}\sqrt{\frac{k}{m}}$$

Two important characteristics of such a second-order system can now be emphasised:

(1) The ratio between the maximum-velocity and the movement amplitude (V_{max}/A) is directly proportional to the mass-normalised stiffness (k/m); for a given value of the mass m, the variations of this ratio can be explained by the variations of the stiffness k[2].

(2) The maximum-velocity (V_{max}), the movement amplitude A, and the movement duration T, are linked through the relation:

$$\frac{V_{max}}{V_{av}} = c \quad \text{or} \quad \frac{V_{max}}{A} = \frac{c}{T}$$

where c depends on the form of the velocity profile ($c = \pi/2 = 1.5708$ for an undamped harmonic oscillator).

These properties have been the focus of many kinematic studies of human skilled[3] movements. Within this perspective, for example, Nelson (1983) studied the up-down jaw movements in six English sentences pronounced by one native speaker. Maximum-velocity, considered as a function of movement duration and amplitude, was similar to idealised movements of second-order systems: The jerk was minimal. Taking a similar approach, Ostry and Munhall (1985) analysed tongue movement patterns in Consonant-Vowel syllables at two different speech rates for three native English speakers, and they showed that the function:

---

[2] If l_0 is not constant , V_{max} would depend on both stiffness and l_0.

[3] *"Skilled movements are developed through training and practice to achieve certain objectives associated with the particular task"* (Nelson, 1983).

$$\frac{V_{max}}{A} = \frac{c}{T}$$

provided a good fit to the measured data; moreover, values of c were not significantly different from 1.57. Similar observations were made by Munhall, Ostry and Parush (1985) for laryngeal adduction gestures in Vowel-Consonant-Vowel utterances.

Therefore its seems that the kinematic properties of simple cyclical speech movements can, at a first approximation, be simulated by an undamped time-invariant mass-spring system.

Second-order Modelling for Speech Movements

Both at the dynamic level of the length-force relationship and at the kinematic level of velocity profiles, much data argues in favour of a second-order (spring-like) modelling of skilled movements in general, and of speech movements in particular. The fairly good ability of second-order models to account for observed articulatory trajectories attests the validity of this approach. Moreover, Browman and Goldstein (1985) obtained suitable simulations of lower lip trajectories in [b'abëbab] in this manner. They fitted empirical trajectories with sinusoidal functions whose amplitude and frequency could change at each maximum-velocity point. Similarly, Perrier *et al.* (1991) demonstrated a fairly good fit of a distributed second-order model (Perrier *et al.*, 1990) to up-down jaw movements observed at two rates and for two speakers in CVCV sequences.

Therefore, second-order dynamics are probably a good approximation to speech dynamics. However in many cases, the need to introduce a damping factor into the second-order system has been emphasised in order to obtain a good fit between simulations and data (see e.g. Smith *et al.*, 1993). Moreover, Ostry and Flanagan (1989) observed for jaw movements, in a speech task as well as mastication tasks, that velocity profiles are not always exactly bell-shaped. They could be asymmetrical, with the acceleration phase being shorter than the deceleration phase (see Figure 2). The authors could model these skewed profiles with a damped linear second-order system, but only by taking into account "the properties of the load-opposing movement", that is, the viscous and elastic properties of the antagonist closing muscles. To explain speech dynamics, it is thus necessary not only to consider biomechanical properties of individual muscles, but also to address the question of what coordination and/or linkage strategies govern the behaviour of groups of muscles; in particular, how are agonist-antagonist muscles coordinated.

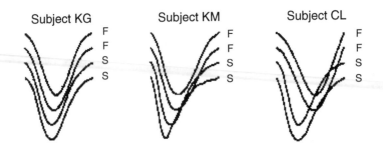

Figure 2. Velocity functions for jaw-opening movements at two rates. F indicates fast movements; S indicates movements at the subject's preferred rate (adapted from Ostry and Munhall, 1985).

These questions are currently provoking an important debate in the motor-control field concerning the parameters that are controlled and the strategies used to control them. To obtain the flavour of these discussions, the reader is referred to target papers by Stein (1982) or Bizzi *et al.* (1992), and to the corresponding commentaries. The following parts of this chapter will only attempt to explain one hypothesis for the control of skilled movements, namely the *Equilibrium-Point*[4] *hypothesis* as proposed by Feldman (1966). In fact, the basic concepts of this approach can be very helpful in understanding the control of speech production.

Control of Speech Articulators

The production of a limb movement arises from central commands (the *efferent information*) and is directed to α and γ motoneurones. *Afferent information* is sent back to the brain from muscle- and mechano-receptors, as well as from other sources. A range of experiments has demonstrated that high-level processing of feedback information by the CNS involves a latency in excess of 150 ms (Schmidt, 1982). In American English, the mean duration of a vowel is around 120 ms (Umeda, 1975), whereas stop-consonants can be shorter than 40 ms (Umeda, 1977). Similar observations have been made for French (O'Shaughnessy, 1981). Thus, the control of fluent speech cannot involve the on-line high-level processing of the feedback by the CNS.

Nevertheless, speech gestures are sufficiently precise to ensure the accurate perception of the intended phonological segment. Moreover, Folkins and Abbs (1975) observed that in spite of perturbations applied to the jaw during the production of a bilabial stop [p], the required lip closure could be achieved without significant disruption of the timing

---

4 An equilibrium-point corresponds to the position where the sum of the forces (or torques) acting on the system are zero.

pattern. The speech production process can therefore take into account peripheral information (in this case, the jaw perturbation), and compensate for it within a very short latency. The problem of how this compensation can be achieved might be solved by proposing that during the speech-learning phase, the speaker generates a representation of the motor objectives in terms of simple but efficient parameters, which can be stored and recalled at the appropriate time. Still, no compensation is possible without feedback, and because of the demonstrably short latencies, such feedback must occur at a low level. In other words, feedback must be reflexive. From this perspective, Feldman's *Equilibrium-Point hypothesis* is very appealing.

Feldman proposes a physiologically well-grounded, theoretical framework which sheds an interesting light on the two points mentioned above. (1) Movements are controlled by altering the equilibrium conditions between agonist and antagonist muscles; (2) this control involves α and γ *motoneurones* (Mns), as well as an afferent feedback via segmental and brain stem mechanisms. Let us examine this hypothesis in some more detail.

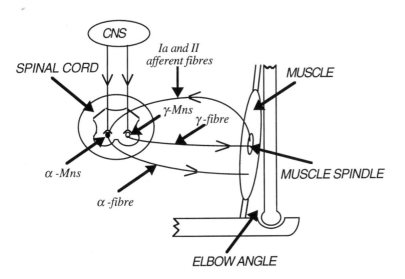

Figure 3. A schematic representation of muscle control.

α- and γ-motoneurones

The CNS sends efferent information to the muscles via the spinal cord, and receives afferent information arising from motion, force and pressure. Efferent information is sent both to α-*Mns* and γ-*Mns*. α-Mns are responsible for the contraction of the large-diameter extrafusal fibres that constitute the main part of a muscle, whereas γ-Mns innervate the muscle spindles. Muscle spindles are small fusiform structures situated in parallel with extrafusal muscle fibres. Because of their small diameter, muscle spindles have no direct effect on the contraction of the muscles but, thanks to sensory receptors located in their central region (the *equatorial* region), they send afferent information to the spinal cord via Ia and II afferent fibres (see Figure 3). A stretching of the equatorial region (due to either γ-activation or to the stretch in the long fibres) contributes to the activation of the α-Mns, and thus contributes indirectly to the contraction of the muscle. The activation of the α-Mns, followed by the contraction of the muscle, is therefore due both to central commands and to afferent feedback

Feldman's Equilibrium-Point Hypothesis: The "λ model"

Feldman (1966) assumed that movements are produced by a shift of the equilibrium-point of the muscle-load system. Remember also that Asatryan and Feldman noted that for a specified central command, muscle behaviour is described by an invariant and unique force-length (or torque-angle) relationship, called "Invariant Characteristic" (IC). For a given external load applied to the limb and for a specified central command, there is only *one* muscle length (or angle) for which the force (or the torque) generated in the muscle can counteract the load. Of course, another equilibrium position can be achieved for the same external load, but only if the behaviour of the muscle follows another IC. The CNS can therefore specify the desired equilibrium-position by selecting the appropriate IC. Moreover, as shown in Figure 1, the muscle follows the force-length (or torque-angle) relationship described by the IC only if the muscle length is greater than a given value λ, which is different and specific for each IC. If the muscle length is less than λ, no force is generated by the CNS in the muscle, whose behaviour is then similar to a passive elastic material. The parameter λ can therefore be considered as the *recruitment threshold* of the muscle, and the choice of this threshold completely determines the IC. Feldman thus proposed that the CNS determines the equilibrium-position reached by the limb for a given external load, by specifying the recruitment threshold λ, in terms of the central commands sent to the α- and γ-Mns.

Figure 4 (Flanagan *et al.*, 1992) is useful for a good understanding of the respective contributions of efferent and afferent information in the control of posture and movement. The system considered here is very simple: It consists of a limb with one degree of freedom and with only one muscle, which acts against a specified external load. Moreover we suppose that, independent of limb angle, the same muscle-torque is required to balance the load. Panel A of Figure 4 shows four limb postures, and panel B presents the corresponding α-Mns activation. In panel C, the associated length-force relationship is presented.

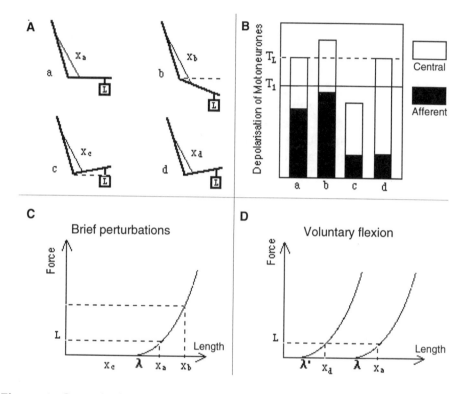

Figure 4. Control of a single-muscle, single-joint system following Feldman's Equilibrium-Point hypothesis (Flanagan *et al.*, 1992).

For limb posture *a*, a combination of central and afferent information produces the activation necessary for the generation of torque T_L in the muscle, which balances the load at length X_a. In limb posture *b*, the central activation remains the same as in posture a (left part of panel C), but the muscle is stretched ($X_b > X_a$). Afferent activation, and therefore global activation, increase. The torque generated in the muscle is greater than T_L in this condition, and it induces a movement in the direction of posture a. In limb posture *c*, the limb is suddenly unloaded, whereas central activation remains identical (panel C); activation falls below the recruitment threshold (T_1), and the load returns the limb to equilibrium. These two last cases illustrate how Feldman's Equilibrium-Point hypothesis explains the *maintenance* of a particular posture. Finally, a *voluntary movement* is possible from posture *a* to posture *d* by increasing the central contribution responsible for the generation of torque T_L in the muscle. This change corresponds to the shift of the recruitment threshold from λ to λ' (panel D).

In the case of a single joint limb moved by two antagonist muscles (flexor versus extensor), the movement can be controlled as illustrated in Figure 5. At point A (angle θ_1), the flexor and extensor recruitment thresholds are so selected (respectively λ_1 and λ_3) that agonist and antagonist forces are balanced. At a given time, the CNS specifies a new recruitment threshold λ_2 for the flexor. The torque-angle relationship for this muscle is shifted such that at angle θ_1, the flexor-torque increases (point B). The mechanical equilibrium is disturbed, and the limb moves in the direction imposed by the larger torque, inducing a reduction of limb angle. This change brings about a decrease of flexor torque, and an increase of extensor torque as specified by the selected ICs. A new equilibrium-position is achieved when flexor and extensor torques are again equivalent (point C). In this way, a *displacement* from angle θ_1 to angle θ_2 is produced.

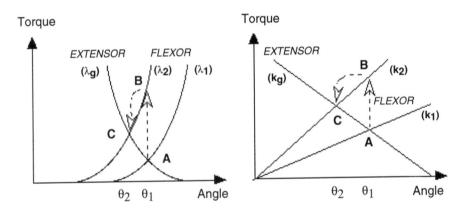

Figure 5 (left) and **Figure 6** (right). Movement between A and C, following respectively the λ-model and the α-model.

The two single-joint examples presented above show, in a simple way, how the Equilibrium-Point hypothesis can be exploited in order to understand the control strategies of human skilled movements. Many other movement conditions can be predicted in the same way, as for example movements with a constant stiffness (for more details, see Feldman, 1986). Moreover, Feldman and his colleagues propose an explanation for classical electromyographic patterns observed in such movements (Feldman *et al.*, 1990). More specifically for speech articulators, Flanagan and colleagues have elaborated a jaw model, where opener, closer and protruder muscles were modelled as non-linear second-order systems, controlled following the Equilibrium-Point hypothesis. The model produced realistic simulations of jaw movements in the sagittal plane by shifting the recruitment thresholds of the muscles linearly over time (Flanagan *et al.*, 1990).

Equilibrium Shift Through Stiffness Control: The "α Model"

Following Feldman's proposals, Bizzi and his colleagues performed experiments with monkeys in which they studied learned, visually-triggered head and arm movements (Bizzi *et al.*, 1978; Polit and Bizzi, 1979; Bizzi *et al.*, 1982). The common objective of these experiments was to generate evidence that the execution of such skilled movements is achieved with a motor program which is parameterised by the specification of the equilibrium-point. Intact adult monkeys were trained to point to a target light with the forearm and to hold the arm in that position for about one second; the forearm was fastened to an elbow apparatus, which permitted flexion and extension of the forearm about the elbow in the horizontal plane, and at no time could the monkeys see their arm. After training, the correct position was regularly reached with a good precision.

Next, the monkeys were de-afferented through surgery. Feedback was thus no longer available, and in particular, no more Ia afferent information was available. Bizzi and colleagues stated that, in spite of de-afferentation, the monkeys still raised their arms to the intended position. The authors concluded that the arm trajectory is effectively stored in the CNS independently of any afferent information. They have more recently argued that "the reflex apparatus contributes in a modest way to force generation" (Bizzi *et al.*, 1992). They do not dispute, of course, the existence of afferent influence, but they minimise the importance of the Ia afferent fibre gain and thus the α-activity induced in this way. They thus assume that the CNS acts essentially on "alpha activity to both agonists and antagonists which determines the stiffness of these muscles" (Bizzi, 1980). This approach corresponds to the so-called α-model for motor control.

Remember that for a second-order model, in which stiffness is constant, the length-force curve is a straight line, whose slope corresponds to stiffness. In Bizzi's perspective, a movement is therefore controlled as shown in Figure 6. For point A (angle θ_1), the flexor and extensor stiffnesses are so selected (respectively k_1 and k_3) that agonist and antagonist forces are equivalent. Shifts in the equilibrium positions (from A to C) are achieved by changing the stiffness of one or both muscles. Note that the λ-model and the α-model have in common the idea that the equilibrium-position is defined by the intersection of force-length (or torque-angle) curves for agonist and antagonist muscles and any external load. But these models are in fact very different: (1) In the α-model, the α-activity corresponds only to the central command, whereas in the λ-model, this activity is the consequence of a combination of central commands and feedback information; (2) the force-length relationships are linear in the α-model, but have a parabolic shape in the λ-model; (3) the α-model does not allow the simulation of movements with a constant stiffness, nor can it explain the same EMG level at two different equilibrium-positions.

Currently, there is intense debate about the merits of these two models (see *Behavioural and Brain Sciences*, 15, 1992). To us, Feldman's hypothesis seems to be more correct from a physiological point of view, and seems to be able to predict a wider range of movements, but on the other hand, Bizzi's approach provides a simple explanation for the functional behaviours of some gestures, in particular in the case of de-afferentiation.

Regardless of which approach proves to be favoured in the long run, both approaches are grounded in the idea that movements are made toward an equilibrium-point. It is possible to imagine that, if a movement consists of a sequence of gestures toward different equilibrium positions, *some* equilibrium-points might not be achieved because of dynamic and/or temporal constraints. This phenomenon has interesting implications for speech, where, depending on the phonetic context and/or prosodic conditions, some phonemes can have variable acoustical and articulatory realisations. The concept of the equilibrium-point allows us to introduce into our speech modelling the notion of an *intended gesture* toward a *virtual* (or *ideal*) *target*. The intended gesture would be the *ideal (or virtual) trajectory* from one equilibrium-point to the other (the virtual targets), and, depending on the dynamic and/or temporal constrains, its execution could induce various actual trajectories, across various positions (the *actual targets*). The last part of this chapter is devoted to the presentation of a simple example of speech processing, which exploits this idea.

The Equilibrium-Point Hypothesis and Vowel Reduction

In the 1960s, Lindblom (1963) studied the acoustical patterns of vowel [u] in three different consonantal contexts ([dud], [bub], [gug]), and for various rates of speech. With rate increases, he observed variations in formant frequencies. This was especially true for [dud], where the second formant of [u] varied from 700 Hz at a normal speech rate, to 1500 Hz at the fastest rate. Represented in the vowel triangle F_1-F_2, this change in formant frequency forms a trajectory that starts from one edge of the triangle (the extreme position for [u]), and moves toward the central part of the triangle. At the fast speech rate, the vowel triangle is reduced to a smaller triangle, located in the schwa region. That is why this phenomenon is called "vowel reduction" (for "vowel space reduction").

Lindblom explained this acoustic variability by the notion of "gesture undershoot"; that is, by the inability of the articulatory system to achieve the required vocalic gesture. Lindblom first attributed this phenomenon to time constraints: The articulatory system does not have enough time to perform the full, required gesture. He proposed that the invariant phonological command [u] underlying each of these various acoustical vocalic patterns could be recovered by an exponential "duration and locus" law. In accordance with this law, the second vowel formant in Consonant-Vowel-Consonant (CVC) syllables changes from the standard locus for the vowel to a consonantal locus with increases in the speech rate. At the same time, Öhman (1967) developed a model for the prediction of coarticulation in CVC syllables, based on the superimposition of a consonantal and a vocalic gesture (Öhman, 1966). He could thus predict Lindblom's observations simply by decreasing the duration of the inter-consonantal vowel (Öhman, 1967). It seemed that vowel reduction could be explained by a vocalic gesture toward an invariant vocalic target, which cannot be actually reached, owing to the shortness of the vowel duration.

In contrast to these results and explanations, Gay (1978) presented vocalic formant patterns that remained constant in spite of a large increase in speech rate. Moreover, Lindblom *et al.* (1987) required Swedish speakers to pronounce the sequence ['bab:abab] while constraining the amplitude of lingual movement with bite-blocks inserted between the teeth. They stated that in spite of the different movement amplitudes, the acoustical timing remained fairly constant. These two sets of data provide evidence that the dynamic properties of speech articulators are not constant, but are explicitly controlled by the CNS in order to achieve the required goal. Lindblom proposed that speech production be considered an "adaptative" process, whose variability is controlled depending on the conditions in which the speaker expresses himself: Specificities of the listener (same education level? stranger?), pragmatic conditions (oration? informal discussion?) (Lindblom, 1988, 1990). In this perspective, the speaker would control the dynamic properties of his speech articulation in different ways, depending on the style of speech which he wanted to produce. Lindblom *et al.* (1992) presented interesting data supporting this hypothesis.

Equilibrium-Point and Vowel Reduction

It can be informative to look at vowel reduction from the perspective of
the perspective of articulatory modelling described in the first two parts
of this chapter. The concept of the equilibrium-point provides a well-
motivated definition of the notion of "desired vocalic target" toward
which the vocalic gesture is directed. Second-order modelling provides a
simple manner of controlling the gesture's dynamic parameters. These
advantages can be illustrated with results recently obtained at the Institut
de la Communication Parlée (Loevenbruck and Perrier, 1993). The vocalic
sequence [iai] was studied in the French sentence "Il y a immédiatement"
([iliaimediatmã]), in three different conditions: (1) Slow speech rate and
stressed [a]; (2) slow speech rate and unstressed [a]; (3) fast speech rate
and stressed [a]. Data from one French native speaker were analysed.
Condition (1) is supposed to be the "ideal" one, in the sense that the
formant patterns achieved by the speaker correspond to ideal targets. In
both other cases, the formant patterns measured for vowel [i] were similar
to those of condition (1), but the formant patterns observed for [a]
demonstrated vowel reduction: The first formant, F_1, decreased, and the
second formant, F_2, increased in frequency.

Starting from formant trajectories measured in the recorded speech
signal, the successive vocal tract shapes in the sagittal plane were inferred
using the following approach. The non-linear relationships between the
articulatory configurations of the vocal tract and the formant patterns
were described by a polynomial relation, obtained by optimised curve
fitting to a database using Maeda's articulatory model (Maeda, 1990).
Derived vocal-tract shapes were computed by minimising, over the
sequence [iai], the mean-square error between the formant frequencies
generated by the model and measured formant frequencies, using the
back-propagation algorithm (Williams and Zipser, 1990). After that, for
each vocal-tract shape, four relevant points were extracted, showing the
movements in different parts of the vocal-tract. The most important
difference between the three speech conditions involved a movement in
the pharyngeal cavity. The backward movement of the tongue in the
gesture from [i] to [a] is less prominent in conditions (2) and (3) than in
condition (1) (see Figure 7, Panel A). This inference is compatible with the
phonetic context: The front vowel [i] tends to induce a more anterior
articulation for vowel [a]. The trajectory of the pharyngeal part of the
tongue was then simulated by using a distributed second-order model,
consisting of two damped springs acting on a normalised mass m, and
representing the agonist and antagonist muscle sets. This model was
controlled by two parameters: The stiffness ratio of both springs, and the
co-contraction level (sum of the spring-stiffnesses); the equilibrium-

level specifies the global dynamic behaviour of the model[5]. The command values of this model were inferred by minimising the global mean-square error using the same back-propagation techniques as above.

Loevenbruck and Perrier could thus show that the three different articulatory trajectories, and thus the three different formant patterns, could be generated from the same stiffness-ratio sequence, that is, with the same successive "virtual targets" corresponding to [i], [a] and [i] (Figure 7, Panel B). The differences between the trajectories obtained in the three studied conditions could be obtained by modifying both the timing and the dynamic parametrisation of the movement. Between conditions (1) (Panel B.1) and (2) (Panel B.2), no reliable difference was observed in the timing, whereas the co-contraction-level was much higher for the stressed vowel than for the unstressed one. On the other hand, the most important discrepancy between conditions (1) and (3) (Panel B.3) lay in the timing, whereas the co-contraction levels were almost identical. These outcomes are consistent with the idea that, at the same speech rate, the timing of the commands should remain fairly constant, and that a stressed movement should essentially involve more force than an unstressed one.

Conclusion

This simple example illustrates the power of the Equilibrium-Point hypothesis for understanding and reproducing of one aspect of variability in speech. Moreover the notion of a "virtual target" brings an interesting insight into the debate about speech invariance and variability, which is central to problems encountered in speech synthesis and speech recognition.

---

[5] This choice does not amount to a decision in favour of Bizzi's model; what is important here is the notion of *movement toward an equilibrium-point*, and of *dynamic parametrization* of this movement, more than the physiological adequacy of the model.

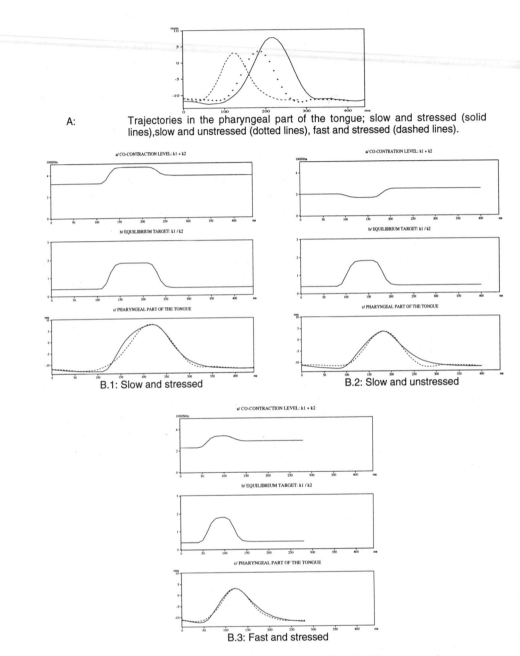

Figure 7. Inversion from articulatory trajectories [Panel A] to control parameters [Panel B: a/ Co-contraction; b/ Equilibrium targets; c/ Desired (dashed lines) and computed (solid lines) trajectories]: Equilibrium targets are identical, but differently parametrised in time and co-contraction (Loevenbruck and Perrier, 1993).

References

Asatryan, D.G., & Feldman, A.G. (1965). Functional tuning of the nervous system which control of movement or maintenance of a steady posture – I. Mechanographic analysis of the work of the joint on execution of a postural task. *Biophysics*, *10*, 925–935.

Bizzi, E. (1980). Central and peripheral mechanisms in motor control. In G.E. Stelmach & J. Requin (Eds.), *Tutorials in motor behavior*. Amsterdam, The Netherlands: North-Holland

Bizzi, E., Dev, P., Morasso, P., & Polit, A. (1978). Effect of load disturbances during centrally initiated movements. *Journal of Neurophysiology*, *39*, 435-444.

Bizzi, E., Accornero, N., Chapple, W., & Hogan, N. (1982). Arm trajectory formation in monkeys. *Experimental Brain Research*, *46*, 139-143.

Bizzi, E., Hogan, N., Mussa-Ivaldi, F.A., & Giszter, S. (1992). Does the nervous system use the equilibrium-point control to guide single and multiple joint movements? *Behavioral and Brain Sciences*, *15*, 603-613.

Browman, C., & Goldstein, L. (1985). Dynamic modeling of phonetic structure. In V.A. Fromkin (Ed.), *Phonetic Linguistics* (pp. 35-53). Orlando, Florida: Academic Press.

Browman, C., & Goldstein, L. (1986). Towards an articulatory phonology. *Phonology Yearbook*, *1*, 212-252.

Fant G. (1960). *Acoustic Theory of Speech Production*. The Hague: Mouton

Feldman, A.G. (1966). Functional tuning of the nervous system which control of movement or maintenance of a steady posture – II. Controllable parameters of the muscles. *Biophysics*, *11*, 565-578.

Feldman, A.G. (1980). Superposition of motor programs – I. Rythmic forearm movements in man. *Neurosciences*, *Vol. 5*, 80–92

Feldman, A.G. (1986). Once more on the Equilibrium-Point hypothesis (l model) for motor controL. *Journal of Motor Behavior*, *18*, *1*, 17-54.

Feldman A.G. & Orlovsky G.N. (1972). The influence of different descending systems on the tonic reflex in the cat. *Experimental Neurology*, *37*, 481-494.

Feldman, A.G., Adamovich, S.V., Ostry, D.J., & Flanagan, J.R. (1990). The origins of electromyograms - explanations based on the Equilibrium-Point hypothesis. In J.M. Winters and S.L-Y. Woo (Eds.), *Multiple muscle systems: Biomechanics and movement organization*. London: Springer- Verlag.

Flanagan, J.R., Ostry, D.J., & Feldman, A.G. (1990). Control of human jaw and multi-joint arm movements. In G.E. Hammond (Ed.), *Cerebral control of speech and limb movements* (pp. 29-58). Amsterdam, The Netherlands: Elsevier Science Publishers B.V. (North-Holland).

Flanagan, J.R., Feldman, A.G., & Ostry D.J. (1992). Equilibrium trajectories underlying rapid target-directed arm movements. In G.E. Stelmach & J. Requin (Eds.), *Tutorials in motor behavior II*. Amsterdam, The Netherlands: North-Holland

Folkins, J.W., & Abbs, J.H. (1975). Lip and jaw motor control during speech: Responses to resistive loading of the jaw. *Journal of Speech and Hearing Research*, *18*, 207-220.

Fowler, C.A., Rubin, P., Remez, R.E., & Turvey, M.T. (1980). Implications for speech production of a general theory of action. In B. Butterworth (Ed.), *Language Production, Vol. 1, Speech and Talk* (pp. 373-420). London, England: Academic Press.

Gay, T. (1978). Effect of speaking rate on vowel formant movements. *Journal of the Acoustical Society of America*, *63*, 223-230.

Liberman, A.M., & Studdert-Kennedy, M. (1978). Phonetic perception. In R. Held, H. Leibowitz & H.L. Teuber (Eds.), *Handbook of Sensory Physiology, Vol. III, Perception.* Heidelberg, Germany: Springer Verlag.

Lindblom, B.E.F. (1963). Spectrographic study of vowel reduction. *Journal of the Acoustical Society of America, 35,* 1773-1781.

Lindblom, B.E.F. (1988). Phonetic invariance and the adaptative nature of speech. In *Working models of human perception* (pp. 139-173). London, England: Academic Press.

Lindblom, B. (1990). Explaining phonetic variation: A sketch of the H&H theory. In W.J. Hardcastle & A. Marchal, *Speech production and speech modelling* (pp. 403-439). Dordrecht, The Netherlands: Kluwer Academic Publishers.

Lindblom, B., Lubker, J., Gay, T., Lyberg, B., Branderud P., & Holmgren K. (1987). The concept of target and speech timing. In R. Channon & L. Shockey (Eds.), *In honor of Ilse Lehiste* (pp. 161-182). Dordrecht, The Netherlands: Foris Publication.

Lindblom, B., Brownlee, S., Davis B., & Moon S.-J. (1992). Speech transforms. *Speech Communication, 11,* 357-368.

Loevenbruck, H., & Perrier, P. (1993). Vocalic reduction: prediction of acoustic and articulatory variabilities with invariant motor commands. *Proceedings of the 3rd European Conference on Speech Communication and Technology* (pp. 85-88), Berlin, Germany.

Maeda, S. (1990). Compensatory articulation during speech: Evidence from the analysis and synthesis of vocal-tract shapes using an articulatory model. In W.J. Hardcastle & A. Marchal (Eds.), *Speech production and speech modelling* (pp. 131-149). Dordrecht, The Netherlands: Kluwer Academic Publishers.

Munhall, K.G., Ostry, D.J., & Parush, A. (1985). Characteristics of velocity profiles of speech movements. *Journal of Experimental Psychology: Human Perception and Performance, Vol. 11, 4,* 457-474.

Nelson, W.L. (1983). Physical principles for economies of skilled movements. *Biological Cybernetics, 46,* 135-147.

Öhman, S.E.G. (1966). Numerical model of coarticulation. *Journal of the Acoustical Society of America, 41,* 310-320.

Öhman, S.E.G. (1967). Studies of articulatory coordination. *Speech Transmission Laboratory-Quaterly Progress and Status Report, 1,* 15-20, University of Stockholm

O'Shaughnessy, D. (1981). A study of French vowel and consonant durations. *Journal of Phonetics, 9,* 385-406.

Ostry, D.J., & Munhall, K.G. (1985). Control of rate and duration of speech movements. *Journal of the Acoustical Society of America, 77,* 640-648.

Ostry, D.J., & Flanagan, J.R. (1989). Human jaw movement in mastication and speech. *Archives of Oral Biology, 34, 9,* 685-693.

Polit, A. & Bizzi, E. (1979). Characteristics of motor programs underlying arm movements in monkeys. *Journal of Physiology, 240,* 331-350.

Perkell, J.S., & Klatt, D.H. (1986). *Invariance and variability in speech processes.* Hillsdale, New-Jersey: Lawrence Erlbaum Associates.

Perrier, P., Laboissière, R., & Eck, L. (1991). Modelling of speech motor control and articulatory trajectories. *Proceedings of the XIIth International Congress of Phonetic Sciences, 2* (pp. 62-65). Aix-en-Provence, France: Université de Provence.

Perrier, P., Abry, C. & Keller, E. (1990). Vers une modélisation des mouvements du dos de la langue. *Journal d'Acoustique, 2,* 69-77.

Rothwell, J.C. (1987). *Control of human voluntary movement.* London, England: Croom Helm.

Schmidt, R.A. (1982). *Motor control and learning.* Champaign, Illinois: Human Kinetics Publishers.

Smith, C.L., Browman,C.P., McGowan, R.S., & Kay, B. (1993). Extracting dynamic parameters from speech movement data. *Journal of the Acoustical Society of America, 93*, 1580-1588.

Stein, R.B. (1982). What muscle variable(s) does the nervous system control in limb movements? *The Behavioral and Brain Sciences,5*, 535-577.

Umeda, N. (1975). Vowel duration in American English. *Journal of the Acoustical Society of America, 58*, 434-455.

Umeda, N. (1977). Consonant duration in American English. *Journal of the Acoustical Society of America, 61* 846-858.

Williams, R.J, & Zipser, D. (1990). Gradient-based learning alogorithms for recurrent connectionist networks. In Y. Chauvin & D.E. Rumelhart (Eds.), *Back-propagation: Theory, architectures and application*. Hillsdale, New-Jersey: Erlbaum.

Phonological Structure, Parametric Phonetic Interpretation and Natural-Sounding Synthesis

12

John Local

Experimental Phonetics Laboratory
Department of Language and Linguistic Science, University of York,
YORK YO1 5DD, United Kingdom

This chapter presents an introduction to a novel approach to speech synthesis and discusses the kinds of linguistic knowledge-based structures which may be employed to generate high-quality natural sounding synthetic speech. The approach described here does not involve anything like segmental phonological or phonetic units. Rather, different levels of phonological structure are used, and the acoustic interpretation of such structures is determined by a simple constraint-satisfaction technique, rather than by a set of derivational transformational rules.

On the whole text-to-speech synthesis is not very good. Leaving aside complex issues such as naturalness, most synthesis fares rather badly even in terms of basic intelligibility. In a recent paper, which examines in detail a wide range of studies concerned with the perception and comprehension of synthetic speech, Duffy and Pisoni (1992) observe that "it is clear that even the best speech synthesisers are not comparable in segmental intelligibility to natural speech under the same testing conditions."[1]

The design of speech-based systems is usually regarded as an engineering problem rather than, say, as an exercise in cognitive and physical modelling. Thus, most extant text-to-speech systems use remarkably little linguistic knowledge at the control level, and the "audio end" usually employs signal generation techniques which are not particularly faithful models of human speech production. Often the extent of the knowledge component of such a system is the fact that words can be "split up" into different parts such as prefixes and suffixes, and that there needs to be some function to relate syntactic structures and prosodic parameters. The most widely used output techniques (waveform concatenation, LPC and formant synthesis) model the acoustic signal more-or-less directly, rather than in the manner of its production in humans.

Although this kind of approach continues and has achieved some success, researchers are now in general agreement that the quality of synthetic speech will only be improved by closer attention to human speech production. At the audio-output end considerable effort is now being invested in analysis of human speech production and articulatory modelling (Coker, 1976; Browman and Goldstein, 1985; Sondhi and Schroeter, 1987). However, it would be mistaken to assume that only the *output model* needs improvement. The *linguistic control* models used in speech synthesis have remained largely unchanged since the early 1960s. The theory and understanding of human linguistic competence, however, has changed significantly since that time. It seems timely therefore to reassess the assumptions underlying the linguistic control component of synthesis systems.

Synthesis by Rule: The Standard Model

In order to contextualise what follows, I will briefly outline the standard rule-based segmental model of speech synthesis control and highlight some of the practical and theoretical problems it presents. The standard model which is implemented in synthesis-by-rule-systems such as DecTalk, MITalk (Allen *et al.*, 1987), and SRS (Hertz, 1982) is that which can be found in most introductory phonology textbooks. This model holds that the information about the pronunciation of words and phrases

---

[1] However, the results of recent intelligibility tests (Local, 1993) on the YorkTalk synthesis system described below, suggest that Duffy and Pisoni's claim is prematurely pessimistic.

is adequately represented as strings of segmental units usually called phonemes. This assumption also underlies so-called non-linear approaches such as autosegmental phonology. Although phonemes are units of information coding which representing the *meaningful distinctions* between speech sounds, they are often erroneously treated as if they *were* speech sounds, classes of similar speech sounds or representations of speech sounds. The symbolic abstraction phoneme, however, corresponds to a variety of different speech sounds, depending on the context in which it occurs.

In order to select the appropriate speech sound in a particular context (i.e. the right *allophone*) the standard segmental model employs rules which map strings of phonemes onto strings of allophones. Strings of allophones are then mapped onto the control parameters of the particular synthesiser by another set of rules. This does not mean that the composition of these mappings is simple to compute, since each rule is intended to describe a single phonological "adjustment" to the phonemic representation, and the number of such adjustments to be made in the mapping from phonemic representations to allophonic representations is very large.

Although some rules do not interact with other rules and thus could logically be applied in parallel (simultaneously), most rules *do* interact and, in order to make the rules as simple as possible, are applied in a particular sequence. It is therefore not possible to determine the form of such rules independently of the order in which they apply. The task of constructing and debugging such a rule set is thus time-consuming, labour-intensive and requires great skill, as any speech synthesis researcher will affirm. The standard model, in its text-to-speech implementation, rests on the unquestioned assumption that it is possible in principle, however difficult in practice, to produce a rule-set which is simple, consistent, and which actually works. Mathematical-linguistic research into the formal properties of rule systems of this kind has shown that although some such sets are tractable (Johnson, 1972), rule sets of this kind needed to account for some phonological phenomena are not, in general, computationally tractable. For example, a rule system which permits both the insertion and removal of segments in a string does not in general have an algorithmic solution.

Insertion and removal of segments from strings are standard and common in text-to-speech rule systems. For example, the English phrase "idea of it" is pronounced by many people with an "intrusive r" between "idea" and "of". In contrast, in "it's my idea", there is no "intrusive r". So, the argument runs, an "r" is inserted in the first case (or, alternatively, an "r" is deleted in the second from a dictionary representation which includes the "r"). Similarly in the pronunciation of the phrase such as "next time" as "nex-time" the "t" sound at the end of "next" has been deleted. The normal descriptions of these facts in a rewrite rule-based system are:

(i) $0 \rightarrow r$ / ea _Vowel   (ii) $t \rightarrow 0$ / x _ t

where "$\rightarrow$" denotes "rewrite as", " 0 " denotes the empty string; "/ A _ B" denotes "in the context between A and B". In these examples I have used the conventional orthographic "r", "ea", "t" and "x", although in a speech synthesis system special phonemic and allophonic symbols might be used instead.

Taken individually, each of these rules may look like a plausible description of some natural-language phenomenon — although work on the phonetic detail of speech suggests that such rules grossly misrepresent the phonetic detail present in the acoustic waveform (Fourakis and Port, 1986; Kelly and Local, 1989; Manuel *et al.*, 1992). However, for speech synthesis to be algorithmically tractable, the model of human phonological competence employed cannot be a rule system of quite this kind. The complexity of these rule systems contrasts strikingly with the simplicity of the data structures (strings) and the single combinatorial operation which they employ (concatenation). Perhaps the phonological model (i.e. the rule system) can be simplified and constrained if a slightly more complex data structure is used in place of strings.

Non-Segmental Phonological Representation

For the last few years, along with colleagues and the University of York, I have been exploring a novel approach to the linguistic control of a speech synthesis system which is "knowledge-based" in that the emphasis is on the representation of invariant phonological information and phonetic variance, rather than on manipulation of strings[2]. The purpose of building the system, in the first instance, was to test a new theory of (i.e. a different data structure for) the representation of phonological information. Specifically we were interested in the possibility of elaborating a computationally tractable version of Firthian prosodic phonology (Firth, 1948). This we have done. Importantly, our success has not been achieved

2 Particular thanks to John Coleman, Richard Ogden, Adrian Simpson and Steve Harlow for work in the development of the YorkTalk system. None of them is responsible for any inadequacies in this chapter. Funding for this work has been provided by British Telecom Plc.

by any modifications to the *signal-generation model*, which is a standard formant synthesiser (Klatt, 1980), but by directing our attention to improvement of the *linguistic control model*.

In the approach we have developed, we take the view that phonological information is best encoded using graph structures (in particular directed acyclic graphs) rather than strings of segments. Let me give some uncontroversial examples of this hypothesis.

Firstly, even if the phonemic hypothesis were accepted, the distinctive units required to describe speech are often not of phoneme "size". For example, distinctions may be "bigger" than phonemes: "reJECT" (verb) *vs.* "REject" (noun) are distinguished by the relative prominence of their two syllables, as well as by holistic differences in the way in which those syllables are pronounced. Although this information could be encoded segmentally, a theory of phonological representation which uses labelled tree graphs provides a simpler and more predictive account (Lass, 1988).

Other kinds of observable acoustic differences are less easily modelled in such a framework. For example, the vocalic portions of the final syllable of words such as "whinny" and "windy" typically differ in terms of both quality and duration. This is a consequence of the structure (the phonological weight) of the *first* syllable (Local, 1990). Distinctive units may also be "smaller" than phonemes. For example, "tip" and "dip" differ in terms of only one phonological feature (usually called "voice"), and "tip" and "chip" differ in terms of the subphonemic structure of their first consonant.

Secondly, syllables are not just made up of strings of phonemes, but have an internal structure which is efficiently and usefully represented using graphs. For example in English, syllables consisting of some initial consonants, some vowels and some final consonants (e.g. "splint"), the vowel(s) group with the final consonants, rather than with the initial consonants. This claim is supported by various kinds of observations, including the following:

(1) the placement of stress in a word depends on the number of vowels or final consonants in a word; the number of initial consonants is not relevant.

(2) the contrast between a pair of words such as "bat" and "bad" is not limited to the final consonantal portions alone. The vocalic portion of such words are different in various ways as well.

(3) the conjugation of certain words in English, such as "bring"/ "brought" involves a difference in the vowel(s) and final consonant(s) *together*, although the initial consonant(s) are unaffected.

Thus there is substantial and varied evidence that syllables are internally structured. If this structure is represented by a graph, then these phonological facts can be encoded as properties of the representation. Graphs provide a data structure for the representation of distinctions between units of various sizes, from smaller than vowels and consonants, to larger than syllables and words. With such a variety of "sizes" of phonological units, the special status traditionally given to phonemes is completely undermined and rendered irrelevant. Consequently, graphs of this kind are sometimes called "non-segmental" or "non-concatenative" representations.

Firthian Non-Segmental Synthesis: The YorkTalk Model

Phonological and Phonetic Representations

As indicated earlier, YorkTalk is a computationally explicit version of Firthian prosodic analysis (Firth 1948). The Firthian approach to phonological analysis is distinctive in its complete rejection of "segments" at any level of analysis, by an emphasis on both paradigmatic *and* syntagmatic relationships, and by an insistence on explicitly stated parameters of phonetic interpretation for (parts of) phonological structure. In accordance with these Firthian prosodic principles, we make a strict distinction between *phonological* and *phonetic* representations. This distinction is reflected in the two main components of the system: phonotactic and metrical parsing on one hand, and phonetic interpretation on the other. The parsers are employed to construct non-segmental phonological representations from regularised orthographic input. These phonological representations are structured, directed acyclical graphs, rather than the more usual strings of segment symbols. The nodes of these graphs are labelled with *complex phonological categories*.

Figure 1 provides a simplified example, which reflects our non-segmental analysis of generalised English monosyllables (Whitley, 1955-1969). The syllable structure adopted is a reasonably conventional one with internal constituency (e.g. Fudge, 1969): The meaning of the phonological category labels is as follows:

- [heavy / light] represents the structural distinction between syllables with branching rimes and/or branching codas and those with non-branching rimes and codas;

- [±bck] and [rnd] operating at the syllable node together represent the phonological distinction between forms such as *pit* and *put;* or *geese* and *goose;*
- the feature [±voi] represents the distinction operating at onset between forms such as *pit* and *bit,* and at rime between forms such as *bit* and *bid.*
- [±nas] operating at the rimal structural constituent represents the distinction between forms such as *bet* and *bent* or *bed* and *bend;*
- [±chk] represents the distinction between checked and unchecked rimes (Whitley, 1959-1969; Wells, 1990);
- [close / mid / open] represent the terms in a "height" contrastivity system.

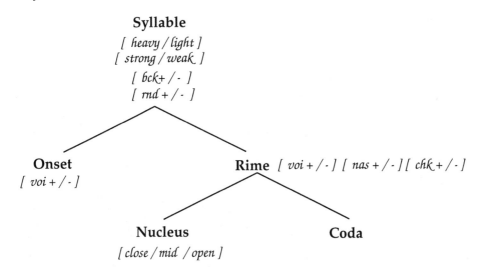

Figure 1. Partial phonological graph for generalised English monosyllables

The graphs which we use for phonological representation are defined by statements of a more restricted kind than the context-sensitive rewrite rules discussed earlier. Specifically they can be defined using context-free phrase structure rules of the form "A → B, C, ...", which denote the fact that a unit of type "A" consists of units of types "B, C, ...", etc. For example, in a syllable such as "bring", the vowel "i" and following consonant "ng" form a sub-syllable unit called the "rime". The syllable-initial consonant (or consonant sequence), the "onset" combines with the rime to form a syllable. Syllable structure can be described by context-free phrase-structure rules such as the following:

syllable → (onset), rime

onset → consonant, (consonant, (consonant))
rime → nucleus, (coda)
nucleus → vowel, (vowel)
coda → consonant, (consonant, (consonant))

Here "(...)" denotes optional constituents. These rules are simplified and partial for the purposes of illustration and focus on syllable structure only. (Coleman, forthcoming provides a fuller description). Other linguistic domains such as words, rhythmical units (feet), and sentences can be defined by similar phrase structure rule-sets (Church, 1985; Coleman, 1990; Ogden, 1992).

The Grammar

The actual grammar of phonological structure in the YorkTalk model employs a more sophisticated context-free grammar augmented with unification (*cf.* Shieber, 1986). This augmentation allows us to use bundles of phonological features as the units in the grammar-rules, rather than simple unstructured atomic labels such as "consonant", "syllable", "vowel", for instance, and to enforce constraints between sisters in a rule, mother-daughter constraints, and constraints on the linking of the daughter of one rule to the mother of another.

One benefit which falls out of this approach is the ability to share structure in phonological representations. This makes the expression of notions such as "co-articulation" straightforward, in that it may be viewed as the *sharing* (rather than procedural *feature copying* or *feature changing*) of a phonologically relevant feature between parts of a syllables. A further benefit of this, not shared by standard text-to-speech systems, is that it is only possible to generate possible English words. Words which break the phonotactic rules of English (such as "gwowpfz" or the actual, but non-English place-name "Brno") cannot be parsed, and therefore cannot normally be synthesised. This is a benefit in that it provides an explicit criterion for determining whether a word should be treated as an exception to be listed in an "exceptions dictionary", rather than assigned a structure by the parser.

Context-free phrase structure rules show two notable differences from the context-sensitive rule-systems discussed above. Firstly (with the exclusion of true ambiguity), employing a context-free rule-set for the analysis of a string yields the same analysis-tree, irrespective of the order in which the rules are applied: Order of application is inconsequential (Chomsky, 1957). Secondly, context-free phrase structure grammars have a simple logical interpretation and computational implementation as a logic grammar (Abramson and Dahl, 1989), such as a Prolog Definite Clause Grammar (Pereira and Shieber, 1987). One immediate benefit of this is that it makes the implementation, testing and debugging of context-free rule systems generally easier and more tractable than is the case with ordered "context-sensitive style" rule systems.

The graphs we employ are *abstract relational structures* and are treated as *having no intrinsic phonetic denotation*. This view differs from that in many other approaches to phonological statement, where features in the phonology are deemed to embody a transparent phonetic interpretation (typically cued by the featural *name*). The position we take does not mean that we see no interesting or "explanatory" links between phonetic phenomena and phonological structures. Rather we take the view that if we wish to develop a sophisticated understanding of the relationships between the meaning systems of a language and their instantiation in speech, then being forced to provide an explicit statement of the detailed parametric phonetic exponents of phonological structure is an essential prerequisite to such an understanding.

The feature labels for phonological units in YorkTalk are given mnemonic names, but their relation to phonic substance is not simple. Because they are distributed over different parts of the graph, their interpretation is essentially polysystemic. For example, the interpretation of the feature [+voice] at an onset is not necessarily the same as the interpretation of the feature [+voice] at a rime. Moreover, the occurrence of the feature [+voice] at some point in the phonological graph may generalise over many more phonetic parameters than those having to do simply with vocal cord vibration. Similarly, the absence of a feature such as [+voice] does not necessarily mean that the representation generalises over tokens where there is no phonetic voicing parameter. Vocalic, nasal and liquid portions typically have phonetic voicing, but the phonological representation to which such portions refer does not necessarily involve the contrastivity [+voice]. Phonological representations, then, are given an explicit phonetic interpretation in order to generate parameter files for synthesis, i.e. they are *interpreted*.

The Interpretation

The interpretation has two aspects: a temporal phonetic interpretation and a parametric phonetic interpretation. This interpretative view of phonetic exponency is grounded in the work of prosodic analysts for whom phonological representations are entirely *relational*, and thus do not contain information about temporal or parametric (articulatory/acoustic) phonetic events (Carnochan, 1957; Firth, 1948; Sprigg, 1957). The temporal interpretation (driven by statements of constraint on constituent timings) instantiates a version of the co-production hypothesis (Firth, 1948; Fowler, 1980), and the parametric phonetic interpretation states the relationships between features or bundles of features at nodes in the phonological graph and the relevant parameters for a Klatt formant synthesiser (Klatt, 1980).

The resulting "parameter strips" are sequences of ordered pairs, where any pair denotes the value of a particular parameter at a particular (linguistically relevant) time, like {node (Category, T_start, T_end, parameter section}. (Ladefoged, 1980, argues for a similar formulation of the mapping from phonological categories to phonetic parameters). The parametric phonetic interpretation of the phonological representations is constrained by the principle of compositionality (Partee, 1984) which states that the "meaning" of a complex expression is a function of the meaning of its parts and the rules, whereby the parts are combined. Thus the phonological "meaning" of a syllables equals the "meaning" of its constituents. In YorkTalk, this principle is instantiated by requiring any given feature or bundle of features at a given place in the phonological structure to only have one possible interpretation.

More complete and more technical descriptions of the phonological theory and the compositional phonetic interpretation in YorkTalk can be found in Coleman (1990, 1992), Local (1992a, b), and Ogden (1992). The YorkTalk system is an all-software implementation written in Prolog (the Klatt synthesis engine employed is written in Pascal), and runs on a Digital Equipment MicroVax 3400.

From Phonology to Acoustics

How does this approach, which proposes relatively abstract graphical representations for phonology, interface with the acoustic speech synthesis model? This amounts to solving the problem of how graphical phonological representations are mapped onto the parameter files which are the input to the speech synthesis model.

The phonetic parameter files are made up of a two-dimensional matrix consisting of a sequence of n-dimensional vectors of parameter values. Each such vector describes n characteristics of the speech waveform at 5-ms time intervals. Although these phonetic parameter files have a two-dimensional organisation, they can be analysed as consisting of sub-matrices of varying sizes which relate to the units of the hierarchical phonological structure (e.g. syllables, words, phrases) described earlier. Thus the task of phonetic interpretation of the phonological graphs devolves to (i.e. translates into a task of) mapping the objects and relations of the phonological representation onto descriptions of the phonetic sub-matrices and their arrangement with respect to each other in the parameter file.

This is achieved as follows. The phonological graphs have some information about phonological contrasts encoded at every node. Each contrast is represented by a feature and its value; for example, the distinction between "pit" and "bit" is encoded as using the feature [-voice] at the onset node of the representation of "pit" and [+voice] at the onset node of the representation of "bit". The phonetic interpretation of [-voice] at the onset node consists of a small number of statements which describe sub-matrices of the phonetic parameter file. For example, the amplitude of voicing and aspiration (AV and AH parameters) for voiceless onsets are described by the following kind of parametric descriptions:

> AV=0 from t=onset_start to t=onset_end
> AH=58 from t=onset_end-10 to t= onset_end
> AH=40 from t=onset_end to t=onset_end+10
> AH=0 from t=onset_end+20 to t=onset_end +30

The precise details of such "exponency statements" have been painstakingly developed by ourselves and other researchers (Klatt, 1980; Kewley-Port, 1982).

Applying the Algorithm

In order to perform the mapping from nodes and features in the phonological graphs to the sub-matrices of the phonetic parameter files, each node must be visited in some order. The process of phonetic interpretation is accomplished by a graph-traversal algorithm which visits every node "head-first" fashion, constructing parametric interpretations of each node as it proceeds. This structure-driven, parametric, co-production approach provides a simple model, amongst other things, for the coarticulatory characteristics of onset consonants and rimes. Since the rime is the head of the syllable, the phonetic interpretation of the rime is performed before the phonetic interpretation of the onset. This means that the phonetic parameters of the onset are dependent on the phonetic parameters of the rime — as they are in natural speech production. The implication of this is that the phonetic parameters, which expone various parts of structure are not concatenated, but "overlaid" in time.

A good deal of the naturalness of the speech generated by the York model derives from the modelling of coarticulation, etc., as *"overlays"* deriving from the interaction of temporal constraints with head-first interpretation. A clear demonstration of this overlaying model can be found in the phonetic interpretation of a maximally complex onset cluster, such as **spl/spr**. Here the liquid is deemed to be the head of the constituent, because any plosive or fricative in such an onset cluster shares the resonance characteristics of the liquid. In the variety of English modelled by YorkTalk, l is "clear" and r is "dark". Figure 2 below gives a graphical representation of this compositional parametric overlaying.

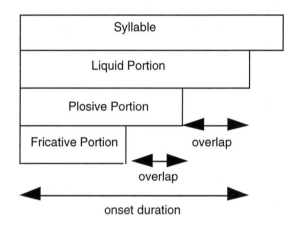

Figure 2. Graphical representation of overlaying of exponents in **spl/spr** onsets.

Figure 3, below, shows spectrograms of YorkTalk synthetic versions of the words "split" and "sprit". As in natural spoken English, it is possible to observe that the periods of initial frication differ appropriately in their resonance characteristics, as do the release and transition portions of the plosion.

Figure 4 shows spectrograms of DECtalk synthetic versions of the same two words. In comparison with the YorkTalk output, the fricative portions are strikingly similar, showing little — if any — evidence of the resonance colouring of the liquid in the onset cluster.

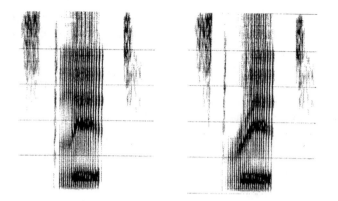

Figure 3. Spectrograms of YorkTalk synthesis of *split* (left) and *sprit* (right).

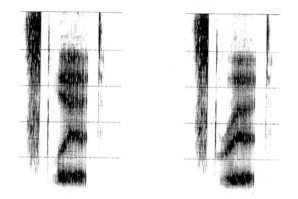

Figure 4. Spectrograms of DECtalk synthesis of *split* (left) and *sprit* (right).

Combining Syllables

Ambisyllabicity provides another important example of the principle of parametric phonetic interpretation in the YorkTalk model. Rather than simply stringing syllables together, we adopt the hypothesis of *maximal ambisyllabicity*, that is, as far as possible, the coda and onset of adjacent syllables are treated as *shared pieces of structure* (Shieber, 1986). These pieces of structure are then given an appropriate compositional interpretation (Local, 1992b, forthcoming).

A straightforward way of instantiating the parametric exponents of these ambisyllabic pieces of structure is to construct the relevant first syllable parameters up to the coda closure, construct those for the second syllable from onset closure, and then to overlay the parameters for the second syllable on those of the first at an appropriate point. The phonetic consequences of this are, for example, the affiliation of coda and onset exponents with their appropriate syllables. Transitions *into* the ambisyllabic portion are part of the *coda* exponents, and transitions *out* are part of the *onset* exponents. Notice that this approach to phonetic interpretation involves the overlaying of syllables. Figure 5 below gives a schematic representation of syllable overlaying.

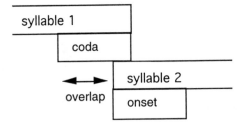

Figure 5. Temporal relations between two overlaid syllables.

The spectrograms in Figure 6 illustrate the acoustic consequences of parametric interpretation of the ambisyllabic portions of plosivity and laterality in the word *happily*.

These spectrograms also illustrate the implementation of "deletion" as a *phonetic*, rather than as a phonological phenomenon. The Firthian approach to phonology requires inalterability of phonological representations. Our declarative computational implementation of this position is to treat phenomena such as "deletion" as resulting from particular parametric timings of the same phonological representation. *Happily* is shown here with two different timings (compressions) for the parameters of the second syllable. Though these two words were generated from the same phonological representation, the auditory impression gained in listening to these synthetic versions is that the vocalic portion of the middle syllable has been deleted. In fact it is not; the [p] has the correct (i.e. front spread) resonance affiliations in both cases, and the [l] does not show the devoicing or spectral characteristics which it displays in a word such as *plea* (Figure 7), where the consonantal portion is exclusively in the onset.

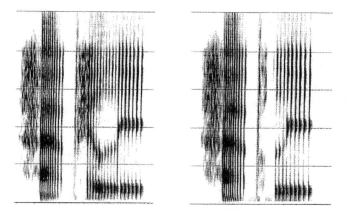

Figure 6. YorkTalk synthesis of *happily* with two different timings for the middle syllable.

The spectral differences between the release of the labiality and plosion in the most compressed synthetic version of *happily* (where the labiality and laterality belong to two different syllable constituents) and that in the synthetic version of *plea* (where the labiality and laterality are exponents of the onset) can be seen in the two LPC spectra shown in Figure 8.

The first of these shows a spectral slice taken at the release of the closure in the compressed *happily*. The second shows a spectral slice taken at the release of the closure in *plea*. While there are similarities, as would be expected, the spectra also reveal noticeable appropriate differences in the relative peak amplitudes, as would be expected under a hypothesis of preserving the "underlying" phonological structure.

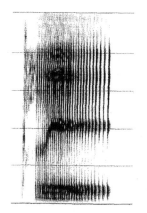

Figure 7. YorkTalk synthesis of *plea*.

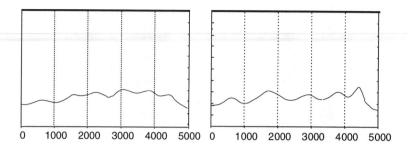

Figure 8. LPC spectral slices taken around the release of plosion in synthetic versions of *happily* (left) and *plea* (right).

Conclusion

I have given a brief description of an approach to the analysis and representation of sound structure which is simpler than the established synthesis-by-rule method. Phonological theory has changed greatly since the normal synthesis-by-rule method was first developed, especially theories of the representation of phonological information. By making use of this knowledge, and by incorporating it explicitly into the York synthesis system, we have been able to overcome many of the problems encountered by extant speech synthesis systems. In particular, not only have we overcome a number of theoretical problems (such as rule-ordering), we have also been able to improve, with comparatively little effort, the naturalness of synthetic speech.

References

Abramson, H. & Dahl, V. (1989). *Logic grammars*. Springer Symbolic Computation — Artificial Intelligence series. Berlin: Springer: Verlag.

Allen, J., Hunnicutt, M. S., & Klatt, D. (1987). *From text to speech: The MITalk system*. Cambridge, England: Cambridge University Press.

Browman, C.P., & Goldstein, L. (1985). Dynamic modeling of phonetic structure. In V.A. Fromkin (Ed.) *Phonetic linguistics: essays in honor of Peter Ladefoged* (pp. 35-53). Orlando, Florida: Academic Press.

Carnochan, J. (1957). Gemination in Hausa. In *Studies in linguistic analysis*. Special Volume of the Philological Society (pp. 149-181). Oxford: Basil Blackwell.

Chomsky, N. (1957). *Syntactic structures*. The Hague: Mouton.

Church, K. (1985). Stress assignment in letter to sound rules for speech synthesis. In *Proceedings of the 23rd annual meeting of the association for computational linguistics.* 246-253.

Coker, C. H. (1976). A model of articulatory dynamics and control. *Proceedings of the I. E. E. E. 64,* 452-460.

Coleman, J.S. (1990). Unification phonology: Another look at "synthesis-by-rule". In *Proceedings of the thirteenth international conference on computational linguistics. COLING 90, 3,* 75-84.

Coleman, J.S. (1992). The phonetic interpretation of headed phonological structures containing overlapping constituents. *Phonology, 9,* 1-44.

Coleman, J.S. (in press). Polysyllabic words in the YorkTalk synthesis system. In P. Keating (Ed.) *Papers from LabPhon III.* Cambridge, England: Cambridge University Press.

Duffy, S.A., & Pisoni, D.B. (1992). Comprehension of synthetic speech produced by rule: A review and theoretical interpretation. *Language and Speech, 35,* 351-389.

Firth, J.R. (1948). Sounds and prosodies. *Transactions of the Philological Society,* 129-152.

Fourakis, M., & Port, R. (1986). *Journal of Phonetics, 14,* 197-221.

Fowler, C.A. (1980). Coarticulation and theories of extrinsic timing. *Journal of Phonetics, 8,* 113-133.

Fudge, E. (1969). Syllables. *Journal of Linguistics, 5,* 253-286.

Hertz, S.R. (1982). From text to speech with SRS. *Journal of the Acoustical Society of America, 72,* 1155-1170.

Johnson, C.D. (1972). *Formal aspects of phonological description.* The Hague: Mouton.

Kelly, J., & Local, J.K. (1989). *Doing phonology.* Manchester: Manchester University Press.

Kewley-Port, D. (1982). Measurement of formant transitions in naturally produced stop consonant-vowel syllables. *Journal of the Acoustical Society of America, 72,* 379-389.

Klatt, D.H. (1980). Software for a cascade/parallel formant synthesizer. *Journal of the Acoustical Society of America, 67,* 971-995.

Ladefoged, P. (1980). What are linguistic sounds made of? *Language, 56,* 485-502.

Lass, R. (1988). *The shape of English.* London: Dent.

Local, J.K. (1990). Some rhythm, resonance and quality variations in urban Tyneside Speech. In S Ramsaran (Ed.) *Studies in the pronunciation of English: A commemorative volume in honour of A.C.Gimson* (pp. 286-292). Routledge: London.

Local, J.K. (1992a). Modelling assimilation in a non-segmental, rule-free phonology. In Docherty, G.J. & Ladd, D.R. (Eds.) *Papers in laboratory phonology II* (pp. 190-223). Cambridge, England: Cambridge University Press.

Local, J.K. (1992b). On the phonetic interpretation of rhythm in non-segmental synthesis. *Proceedings of the Institute of Acoustics, 14,* 473-480.

Local, J.K. (1993). 'Segmental' Intelligibility of the YorkTalk non-segmental speech synthesis system. *York Research Papers in Linguistics, YLLS-RP 1993-2.*

Local, J.K. (in press). Testing a Firthian non-segmental phonology: Rhythm and syllabification and ambisyllabicity. *York Research Papers in Linguistics.*

Manuel, S., Shattuck-Huffnagel, S., Huffman, M., Stevens, K.N., Carlsson, R., & Hunnicutt, S. (1992). *Proceedings of ICSLP-1992, International Conference on Spoken Language Processing, Banff, Vol. 2,* 943-946.

Ogden, R. (1992). Parametric Interpretation in YorkTalk. *York Papers in Linguistics, 16,* 81-99.

Partee, B.H. (1984). Compositionality. In F. Landman & F. Veltman (Eds.),*Varieties of formal semantics* (pp. 281-312). Dordrecht: Foris.

Pereira, F.C.N., & Shieber, S.M. (1987). *Prolog and natural-language analysis*. Stanford: C.S L.I.

Shieber, S.M. (1986). *An introduction to unification-based approaches to grammar*. Stanford: C.S.L.I.

Sondhi, M.M., & Schroeter, J. (1987). A hybrid time-frequency domain articulatory speech synthesizer. *I. E. E. E. Transactions on acoustics, speech, and signal processing. ASSP-35,* 955-967.

Sprigg, R.K. (1957). Junction in Spoken Burmese. In *Studies in linguistic analysis*. Special Volume of the Philological Society. (pp. 104-138). Oxford: Basil Blackwell.

Wells, J C. (1990). Syllabification and allophony. In Ramsaran, S. (Ed.), *Studies in the pronunciation of English: A commemorative volume in honour of A. C. Gimson.* (pp. 76-86). London: Routledge

Whitley, E. (1955-1969). Unpublished lecture notes on English Phonology. York Prosodic Archive, Department of Language and Linguistic Science, University of York.

Semantic and Pragmatic Prediction of Prosodic Structures 13

Geneviève Caelen-Haumont

Institut de la Communication Parlée, CNRS URA 368,
INPG and Université Stendhal, 46 avenue F. Viallet
F-38031 GRENOBLE CEDEX 1, France

Relations between prosody and other levels of linguistic analysis have traditionally focused on syntax (especially the description of the constituents: Their nature, length, functions, levels of hierarchy, etc.) and semantics (restricted to theme/rheme structure in relation to focus). These two lines of inquiry are reviewed here. In addition we report on a large-scale study that assessed interactions between syntax, semantics, pragmatics and prosodic parameters, within the specific context of French. Syntactic and semantic functions were shown to be interlaced. While duration and energy deep organisation were clearly related to syntax (demarcation function), Fo organisation in conjunction with known linguistic models could be seen to provide fundamental information relating to semantics at different levels. Speakers did have recourse to syntactic models, but that appeared to be less frequent. This interaction with syntax occurred especially in places where speech was initiated, or where semantic instantiation was less crucial. Finally on the prosodic level, the information was structured in terms of Fo range. The more the meaning was new, unexpected or difficult to understand, the greater was the difference between minimum and maximum Fo measured in the word.

In the history of relations between prosody and linguistics, two main trends have emerged. Whatever the language, prosody is either taken to be determined by syntactic organisation, or it is considered as essentially determined by semantic and pragmatic factors.

This debate is not simply relevant to our understanding of prosodic theory, psycholinguistics or linguistic analysis, but also has some important consequences for speech recognition and synthesis, as they are concerned with the choice of strategy and methods for speech processing. As prosody is implicated at all levels of linguistic organisation, any failure to comprehend prosody and its nature is likely to complicate computation, increase the rate of errors in speech recognition, and in the case of synthesis, yield somewhat artificial and monotonous prosodic patterns. The issue of adequate predictors of prosodic parameters is therefore of crucial importance.

This chapter first places the problem of syntax or semantic prevalence into its historic context. After that, the various linguistic models emerging from the different approaches are presented, and are discussed with particular emphasis on their predictions for prosody. The discussion of the results of our own experimentation allows us to deduce speaker strategies, and to better specify the respective roles of syntax and semantics in relation to prosody.

Relations between Syntax, Semantics and Prosody in Previous Research

Before 1970, the status of prosody was not clearly established, particularly in relation to linguistics. For instance, its aesthetic and affective functions were generally admitted, but in the linguistic domain, only the differentiation of sentence modalities (assertion, question, order, etc.) was acknowledged by most specialists. With the emergence of computing sciences and the development of generative grammar which put an emphasis on syntax, many new studies were undertaken, and investigations into the status of prosody began to be conducted more thoroughly. It was generally hoped that a close relationship between syntax and prosody could be established.

In generative and transformational grammar, any sentence can be rewritten as immediate constituents of successively lower rank, until the level of the word in the sentence is reached. Sentence organisation is conceived in terms of hierarchic levels. Likewise, fundamental frequency (Fo) organisation is routinely thought of as a structure involving hierarchic levels. Given this, it was natural to treat intonation and syntax as being amenable to a similar, inter-relatable treatment.

Moreover, the idea that Fo structures can provide reliable cues of syntactic organisation was wide-spread in North America and in Europe, and this linguistic position found acceptance in the fields of speech recognition and synthesis. For Chomsky (1970) and Jackendoff (1972) for instance, intonation is independent on and parallel to syntax, and its function consists of the reorganisation of syntactic structure. Though this approach to the relationship between syntax and Fo did not prove particularly fruitful, four schools of thought have extended this approach, the first in direct descent from Chomsky and Halle (1955, 1968) to Dell (1973) for instance, then categorial phonology theory (Kahn, 1976; Selkirk, 1978, 1980), autosegmental phonology theory (Goldsmith, 1976; Clements, 1976; Halle and Vergnaud, 1978), and metrical phonology (Liberman, 1975; Liberman and Prince, 1977; Dell, 1984; Selkirk, 1984).

Di Cristo (1975) and Martin (1975) undertook empirically-oriented work on French in this direction, and developed a set of "intono-syntactic" rules. Nowadays research in this domain has been somewhat usurped by formal phonological endeavours — especially metrical phonology (Hirst, 1981, 1986; Ladd, 1991; Ladd and Campbell, 1991). Focusing on surface representations, Hirst and Di Cristo (in preparation) propose a system of tonal characterisations which seems to be relevant for languages as different as French (Di Cristo, in press), Swedish (Bruce, 1988), and Japanese (Pierrehumbert and Beckman, 1988).

Functional Syntax and the Semantic Approach

In the tradition of functional syntax, the situation has been similar, and strong correlations have been seen between syntactic phrases and prosodic cues (especially Fo and duration). In most languages for example, the prosodic group is considered to map straightforwardly onto the syntactic phrase. The final "accent", characterised by pitch and intensity variations, and by a lengthening of the last syllable in the group capable of bearing stress, is taken as signalling the syntactic function of group demarcation. Consequently, many studies have been undertaken in order to find relevant cues to syntactic structure.

In the United States, for instance, Gaitenby (1965), Oller (1973), Klatt (1975) examined lengthening effects in the final syllable of the group. Cooper (1975) and Martin (1970) studied relations between phonetic segment lengthening and the nature of the constituents and phrases, and Goldhor (1976) examined these relations in terms of type of constituent unit. In speech recognition, Lea *et al.* (1975) proposed the use of prosodic information at all levels of the system, i.e. acoustical, lexical, syntactical, pragmatic and semantic levels. In Sweden, Lindblom (1975), House *et al.* (1987), Garding (1989), Fant *et al.* (1991), employing large corpora, have revealed the behaviour of prosodic correlates in relation to linguistic units, words, phrases, sentences. In France, Vaissière (1982), Carbonnel *et al.* (1988), and Nasri *et al.* (1989, 1990), have found relevant cues for the segmentation of linguistic units. This tradition of work is well established. The semantic approach to prosody originates in the work of the Prague School (Karcevskij, 1931; Mathesius, 1939; Danes, 1968; Firbas, 1974). A central problem which Prague school linguistics tackled, was that of syntactic and semantic relations associated with the concept of *theme* and *rheme*. More precisely, they endeavoured to provide a clear separation of subject/predicate structures (inherited from the Aristotelian distinction), and given/new information. Confusion on this matter had existed in previous work (for instance Karcevskij, 1931) and continued later (Danes, 1960). The central problem was to understand that "saying *something about something*" could be analysed in terms of syntactic relations (subject/predicate) or in terms of semantic relations (support/supply) expressed by different syntactic functions.

In prosody, Halliday (1967) clarified the problem by distinguishing a number of different levels of linguistic stratification and by proposing a particular kind of prosodic interpretation. This yielded an actual correlate for new information. According to Halliday, prosodic cue matches with the notion of *focus: "what is focal is 'new' information"*. This seminal work opened the way to a strong line of research (Bolinger, 1972, 1978; Caelen-Haumont, 1978, 1981, 1991; Gussenhoven, 1983; Kruyt, 1985; Terken, 1985; Rossi, 1985; Horne, 1988; Fowler and Housum, 1987; etc.), where the problem of definition of focus is analysed in relation to the processes of accentuation and deaccentuation, as well as from the psycholinguistic perspective of speech comprehension.

The Two Positions

It can be seen that prosodic prominence can be explained by two different factors, each in line with its own tradition, and that the two schools are in opposition. The approach adopted here does not seek to deny the existence of either syntactic or semantic relations, but rather attempts to assess the importance of one domain or the other in the prediction of prosodic parameters.

An example of this debate grew out of the analysis of English and of a number of other languages characterised as "stress-timed" (Pike, 1945; Abercrombie, 1967). The two schools agree on the fact that phrasal accent conveys information, but disagree on the role of syntax and semantics. In one view, syntax is prevalent in the sense that it governs all factors, particularly semantic and accentual ones. In the other view, prevalence is given to semantics which determines the accentual factors. In other words, is it syntax or semantics that determines the position of the accent?

The 10th ICPhS[1] in Utrecht provided an occasion to explore this disagreement around the same data set, i.e. slips of the tongue. Fromkin (1983) claimed: "The semantic function of accents does not exclude a dependence on syntax and morphology. There is no new evidence to counter the claim made by Fromkin (1971, 1977, 1980) and Garrett (1975)

---

[1] International Congress of the Phonetic Sciences.

that phrasal stress (which can coincide with accent) is determined by syntactic structure. [...] primary stress or accent [...] must be assigned after the syntax is determined". By contrast, Cutler (1983) put forward that "Performance evidence [...] suggests that in producing, comprehending and acquiring language, language users behave as if sentence accent placement were concerned with semantic and pragmatic structure of utterances, rather than with their syntax".

For Cutler (idem), things were clear. Speaker intention and speech contents have priority: "In producing accent patterns, speakers have in mind the meaning of their message rather than its form." But for Fromkin (1991), reinvoking Denes and Pinson's statements (1963), linguistic form was first: "The aphasic data [...] show us something about how a speaker puts what he wants to say into linguistic form', even if the 'wrong' words or wrong inflections are selected, or if the right words are distorted".

A recent research project of ours was defined in the framework of these questions. On the basis of a computerised database of French, an assessment was made of the interactions between syntax, semantics, pragmatics and fundamental frequency parameters. In reviewing this evidence, emphasis will be placed on results for Fo. For results for energy and duration, please refer to Caelen-Haumont (1991, 1993).

Which Kind of Predictive Model?

In order to evaluate different models, it is of fundamental importance to establish a set of valid criteria. To be valid, a model has to be representative of speakers' information processing mechanism, that is, the assessment must take into account human psycholinguistic processes.

The first parameter is the *generality* of the analysis. Since each word is prosodically determined, the model must make a prediction for each word. Linguistic processing may result in a minimal or null effect, but it cannot be undetermined. In elaborating models for this study, one of the conditions was therefore that they focus on representative, recurrent linguistic phenomena which are, hopefully, also fundamental ones.

Another aspect of linguistic modelling concerns the problem of *quantification*. More precisely, the problem consists of transforming symbolic (linguistic) categories into a numeric scale (prosodic levels), i.e. obtaining quantified results from a qualitative analysis. Three linguistic criteria were thus incorporated into the models, as they were judged to be amenable to producing a numeric scale: 1° the concept of hierarchy, 2° the concept of distance, and 3° the concept of complexity.

And finally, a fundamental parameter relates to *analysis* and *generalisation*. These are two important human cognitive skills in speech production and speech comprehension. At the same time, they represent fundamental aspects of any type of information processing. Three models of the six models were thus devoted to global linguistic characterisations (CSI, EN, ER), and three others to analytic characterisations (DP, CM, CP).

Hypotheses and Experimental Method

The experiment was based on a range of constrained reading tasks[2] (1° natural and intelligible reading, 2° very intelligible reading, 3° extremely intelligible reading, appropriate to man-machine interaction), performed by 12 speakers. The goal was to examine what strategies speakers use, not with respect to their text comprehension, but in speech production. Thus before recordings were made, the text was read and reread and all the words were explained if necessary. A database was then constructed from these utterances, in which the signal and other speech representations were manually annotated with about 40,000 labels relating to the various linguistic domains (acoustics, phonetics, Fo, accentuation, morphology, syntax, and semantics).

The fundamental hypothesis underlying this research was that in oral communication, the processing of an utterance's contents and prosodic processing are not independent. Consequently, there must exist some deep structures that provide the source for well-formed utterances. Such structures should be numerically verifiable. Within such a methodology, models must be defined that govern the abstract organisation of the indices of prosodic coding, particularly those relating to fundamental frequency (Fo), and possibly those that relate to duration and energy.

From the methodological point of view, this approach resulted in two constraints. First, models must be able to predict a given quantity, particularly the height of fundamental frequency. Such measures were expected to reflect speakers' melodic targets, used during the encoding process. Second, strictly phonetic information had to be discounted in the search for underlying linguistic structures, that is, micro-prosodic effects and intra- and inter-subject variations of sociolinguistic or other origin had to be eliminated. To this effect, all numeric information issuing from the prosodic indices was converted into a four-tiered space. This space of distinctions has been considered appropriate by a large number of papers on French as well as on other languages. Furthermore, this method permitted interesting comparisons of the prosodic space used by each of

---

[2] The text is as follows : "D'éminents biologistes et d'éminents zoologistes américains ont créé pour des vers géants un nouveau phylum dans l'actuelle classification des nombreuses espèces vivantes. Ces longs vers prospèrent sur le plancher marin des zones sous-marines profondes. Des sources thermales chaudes y maintiennent une température moyenne élevée."

the speakers. Finally, since this experimentation was oriented towards the analysis of lexical words and their constituent units, it was appropriate to both linguistic and prosodic experimentation. Lexical words constitute the primary framework for linguistic models, and prosodic variations are more contrastive for lexical than for grammatical words.

In this perspective, six linguistic models were defined in such a way that they predicted Fo levels for the key parts of the utterance, i.e. the lexical words. In this manner, numerical coincidences ("matching coefficients") between prosodic indices and the six predictive models (2 syntactic, 3 semantic, 1 pragmatic) were examined. Other than durational and energy parameters, the following melodic indices were examined: The "classic" indices of maximum Fo ("FoM") and mean Fo ("Fom"), plus an original Fo index that proved to be very efficient, i.e. the absolute difference (" $|\Delta Fo|$ ") between a lexeme's maximum and minimum Fo, as calculated over 10 ms-samples. All models, as well as all indices of the same parameter, were considered to enter into competition with each other.

Initially, nothing could be assumed about the relation between information and its Fo correlates. If FoM or Fom are prevalent, lexical information is probably a matter of Fo organisation at the sentence level, therefore a matter of intonation, since FoM or Fom are more directly related to other word Fo values in the sentence than to their own lexical density scale. If $|\Delta Fo|$ is the most recurrent cue in speaker utterances, then it is obvious that Fo organisation of lexical information, given in absolute values by Fo range in the word, is a dominant factor. Relations to other lexical information is given by FoM, which is one of the two targets of ΔFo, but within the lexical word, FoM height is modulated by the Fo range which conveys the importance that the speaker gives to the local meaning in the sentence.

Linguistic Models and Prediction

Three of the models attempted to evaluate linguistic organisation according to a holistic perspective, the other three evaluated it according to an analytic perspective. In this chapter, the presentation of the models will be kept to a minimum, and discussion will focus on the nature of the predictions arising from the study.

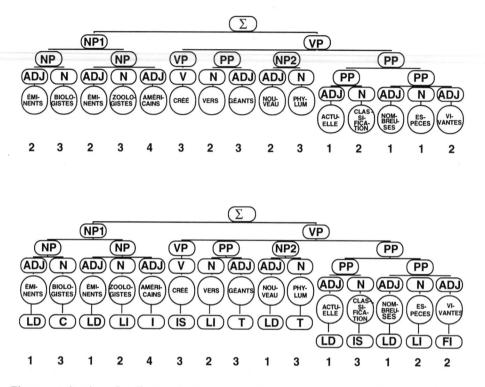

Figures 1 (top) and 2 (bottom). Top: Syntactic structure in immediate constituents, sentence 1 (CSI model). Bottom: Syntactic dependence model of lexical units, sentence 1 (DP model). The numbers below the lexical units indicate their level in the hierarchy (left) or the weight of their syntactic dependence (right). The sentence is as follows: "D'éminents biologistes et d'éminents zoologistes américains ont créé pour des vers géants un nouveau phylum dans l'actuelle classification des nombreuses espèces vivantes." As it happens, this CSI model presents four hierarchical levels, and thus was not subjected to value reduction. As to the DP model, its values have been reduced according to a four-level scale.

The Holistic Models

The CSI, EN and ER models were "holistic" in the sense that, in contrast to the analytical models, they required a consideration of the entire sentence for the processing of a given lexical word. This was true, whether the processing was syntactic or semantic in nature. All of these models proposed an analysis in terms of hierarchic levels, and reproduced the tree structure proposed by the American structuralists. It was not considered crucial if this structure was not entirely consonant with those proposed in recent grammatical theories, because the real problem consisted in assessing whether hierarchical linguistic representation indeed matched hierarchical melodic organisation.

The *first model, CSI*, was derived from the "classical" American tradition[3]. According to this tradition, any sentence can be decomposed into the immediate syntactic constituents of the next lower level. This recursive operation allowed us to differentiate various levels in the hierarchy of phrases to which a different metric could be associated, from the so-called deep structures (the largest expansion phrase) to the surface structure (the word level). Figure 1 illustrates its quantification scheme.

This model instantiated the hypothesis that Fo levels and the Fo range within the word were of proportional value to the syntactic level in the hierarchy. The higher the phrase in the tree structure, the stronger the Fo prominence and the higher the level of Fo values. In other words, the Fo level at the end of the phrase should be higher than the level of any lexical word inside the same phrase, and at the surface, two words had different levels according to their place in the hierarchy.

The *EN and ER models*, which are not considered separately here, explored the same idea of a hierarchical structure as did the CSI model. The difference lay in the fact that these constituents were not syntactic, but semantic. These models were restatements of the theme-rheme opposition developed first by Functional Sentence Theory (see above), but introduced in another perspective, that of the hierarchical constituents analysis. "Rheme", as was said before, supports the expressive act, and "theme" provides the necessary support for this process. Figure 3, below, presents the model as it is applied to sentence 1.

In the EN model, the hypothesis which underlies Fo prediction was the same as for the CSI model: The higher the (semantic) constituents, the higher the Fo level and/or the greater the Fo range in the lexical word. A higher Fo level was predicted at the end of the phrase than for any lexical word inside the same phrase, and at the surface, two words could have different levels according to their place in the hierarchy. The ER model entertained a supplementary hypothesis by attributing a major weight to the rheme constituent. This conveyed the idea that rheme is the part of the utterance that expresses the most information, and that a focus may be placed on this information by significant Fo variations.

---

[3] It derives from the classical tradition except in one respect: The last word of the sentence (for instance "vivantes" in sentence 1, Figure 1) received a weighting corresponding to the first group to which it is attached (level 2), and not to the group to which it belongs in the traditional model (the end of the constituent sentence). As the Fo level in the last word in a declarative sentence is usually low, and Fo declination in the word not extremely steep, this correction was made in order not to exclude too easily and artificially a model based on this linguistic representation (CSI and EN, ER as well).

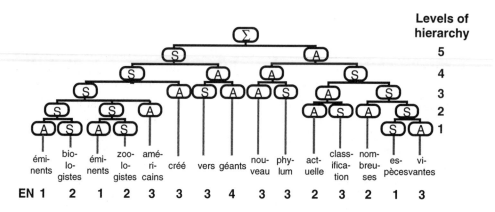

Figure 3. The enunciative hierarchical structure in immediate constituents, sentence 1 ("EN" model). The symbol "S" indicates the notion of "support" (or theme in the standard theory), the symbol "A" corresponds to the notion of "apport" (or rheme).

The question of how rhemes are identified in a sentence and which criteria govern their hierarchisation is an important issue. In the absence of an automatic procedure for the extraction of theme and rheme units, a set of intuitive rules was employed. The analysis steps were as follows: first, the "apport" of the expressive act (the major rheme) was identified with respect to its support (the major theme). Rheme identification requires the distinction of the semantic structure (the rheme) from the syntactic structure (the predicate), since the two do not necessarily overlap. This step is delicate, because there could be an opposition between the verb — which represents a rheme unit — and another phrase following the verb that could constitute a second rheme unit. At the same time, any *syntactic subordination* between such a subsequent unit and the verb could hamper the identification of the true major rheme. It was thus particularly important to clearly distinguish semantic and syntactic structures in a given sentence.

Once this problem of linguistic stratification was taken care of, the method evaluated which of the two competing units provided the most information, and identified which theme corresponded to which unit. Its very existence, as well as its position in the utterance hierarchy, provided important indices for the identification of the rheme situated at the same level. At this stage of hierarchisation, the two competing rhemes were thus identified, as well as the precise demarcations of major theme and major rheme. This set of operations was applied iteratively for each constituent unit until the surface level was reached, i.e. the chain of lexical words.

The Analytic Models

With the aid of three models (DP, CM and CP), analytic processing was used to appraise lexical relations at the phrase, sentence or text levels. The *DP model* was a syntactic appraisal of relations between two successive lexical words. This model fit into the tradition initiated by Tesnière (1959), but was in large part original. This model took into account left-right syntactic relations, and thus reflected the order within the utterance.

The most important hypotheses on which the model was constructed were:

1° the stronger the syntactic or the dependency relation, the weaker the Fo amplitude and/or the lowest Fo maximum in the word,

2° relations inside the phrase are more dependent than those at boundaries,

3° inside the phrase, there are more dependent local relations (e.g. symbol LD, e.g. the adjective-noun relationship, weight +1), and more independent ones (e.g. symbol LI, e.g. the noun-adjective relationship, weight +2),

4° at the phrase boundary, increasing weights were given to relations ranging from: Direct subordination of the verb (DS, +2), any form of indirect subordination (IS, +3), the juxtaposition of two phrases which entertain no direct relation, but are two successive verbal complements (verbal trans-subordination, T, +3), the coordination and juxtaposition (C, +4), and finally, total independence which occurs for lexical words in absolutely final position in the highest-level phrase, except sentence-final position (I, +5),

5° sentence-final position was considered to be a special place, as no specific lexical word is expected in this position. For this reason, Fo demarcation is not useful. Its level of syntactic independence was thus evaluated at the minimum (FI, +2).

Figure 3, above, shows the quantification method as it was applied to sentence 1.

The *CM model* dealt with any source of lexical complexity in the text, intrinsic or contextual. It attempted to provide an overall view of the principal factors contributing to the structure of meaning, by classing them in order of increasing complexity and by quantifying them accordingly. The fundamental hypothesis for this model rested upon the idea that the more complex the meaning, the more prominent are likely to be Fo variations in the word.

The principal factors contributing to meaning increasing at each level were the following.

1° The nature of the register. It is well-known that a given word may relate to a fundamental vocabulary, may be specialised, or may be specialised but common. Dictionaries may be used for this classification.

In this model, increasing degree of specialisation corresponded to greater weights.

2° The referent designated by the lexical item could be *concrete* or *abstract*, or somehow concrete and abstract at the same time, which was often the case when an "object" (taken in the wide sense of the word) is considered in terms of its function (for instance a "biologist" which is an abstract characterisation of a concrete individual).

3° Another distinction differentiated the notions of *substance* and *attributes*. The notion of "substance" was applied to the "object", while the notion of "attribute" was applied to the qualities of this object. Substance is a general characterisation, as it includes dynamic process (e.g. running), or state (e.g. peace), or either (e.g. a miscalculation). The degree of complexity of the notion "attribute" may be understood differently, according to whether the attribute expresses a complementary meaning in respect of the meaning of this object, or an "extrinsic" meaning. These notions of "substance" and "attribute" were evaluated, no matter of the morphosyntactic units they referred to.

4° *Figurativeness* in its various forms (ranging from "zero figurativeness" for clichés, lexicalised figurativeness, and original figurativeness) legitimately participated in this assessment of complexity.

5° The last category was that of *lexical field*. A change or an initialisation of lexical field (but not its continuation) was considered to increase the amount of complexity to be handled by the speaker (and as well by the listener).

From the semantic and pragmatic perspectives, the CP model was a reformulation and an amplification of Prince's model (1983). Though Prince presented her model as one of shared knowledge, the definition of the CP model covered more exactly the domain of expected and unexpected knowledge. This model attempted to account for the different operations that speakers or listeners use during the semantic processing of a text. Also, it attempted to evaluate the degree of complexity required to understand the text and to transmit its meaning. Figure 4 presents Prince's model (grey boxes) and its extension (CP model). The model's major hypothesis was that the more a piece of information is unexpected, the higher are Fo values and the wider are the Fo ranges measured within a lexical word.

In the CP model, the central notion was the *"seme"*, or the "minimal meaning unit in the word". Generally, lexical words display at least a few semes. These minimal semantic units making up the word correspond to its extra-contextual meaning, i.e. that which can be found in a dictionary. However in context, they entertain between them, by the interplay of word associations in the text or in the context of the situation in speech, different types of relationships based on the activation (and sometimes on the addition) or the neutralisation of certain lexical semes. Such an analysis is based on the concept of a differential seme.

The oppositions that the CP model highlights, are fundamental to the notions of *extension* and *comprehension*. For example, the categories of "new knowledge" and of "evoked knowledge" belong to the notion of comprehension, because these categories deal with the different semes which form the concept of the lexical word. As for the category of "inferable knowledge", it belongs mostly to the notion of extension, since the analysis evaluated the semes of two words at a time, as they entered into the same semantic field.

Without entering too deeply into the details of this analysis, some characteristics can be specified. In terms of "new knowledge", the major distinction bore upon the difference between what is completely new and what is partially new. By contrast, "evoked knowledge" referred to the use of the same semes in the words, no matter whether or not it was a repetition of the same word. The model focused on the intention of the writer (or speaker) by distinguishing an insistence repetition from a non-relevant repetition.

The inferable information implicates two domains of processing. The first one is related to the development of a complex semantic structure (or *isotopy*) with its subordinated lexical (abstract or figurative) fields interlaced, feeding the semantic structure with new semes that display the true information content. A supplementary meaning (second word) brings a seme or more to a previous one, which does not enter into the semantic range of this previous word at the level of its definition or its use in a particular situation. A complementary meaning supplies one or more semes which is non-redundant and totally compatible with the semes of the previous word, providing, for instance, a more concrete specification of meaning.

The second domain of processing arises from what is called "logical operations" with two subordinate categories, "notional deduction" and "inclusion". The processing of "notional deduction" operates when a listener or reader extracts from a previous lexical item the semantic cues (i.e. the semes) in order to understand some others in the current context belonging to the same semantic field. For instance, when one reads (or hears) the word "glass", a semantic field is activated in the comprehender who might legitimately expect words designating drinks (fruit juice, wine or so on...). From a general point of view, the processing of "inclusion" is operative when the reader or the listener considers the semantic content of a lexical word as a part (or a whole) of another content (for instance "drink/fruit juice").

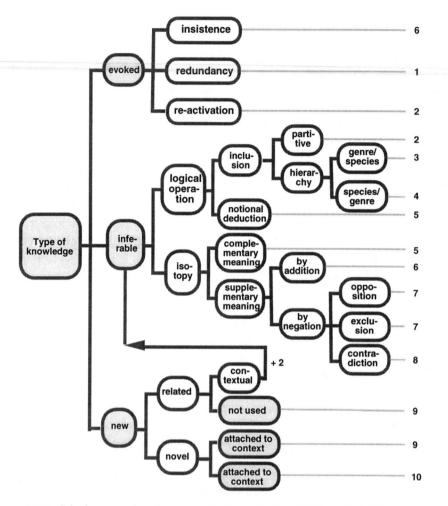

Figure 4. Model of expected and unexpected knowledge ("CP" model). The grey boxes represent the first version of this model proposed in Prince (1983).

Analysis Method and Results

The method used to match linguistic indices (deriving from the application of the models to the text of the experiment) and Fo indices consisted, first, in establishing the numeric values in a four-tiered scale, and secondly, in selecting the best linguistic prediction of the Fo values. Once the lists of numeric values had been derived from the linguistic and the frequency domains, the purpose was *not* to establish a correlation between the two lists of values. Rather, the intent was to determine to what extent the linguistic models can directly predict Fo indices (measure used: "matching coefficient"). Also, it was specified which models and indices are the most frequent when such a method is applied. This approach permits to evaluate speaker strategies.

This operation is subordinate to the condition that this search of the strongest linguistic predictions fulfil the principle of *speaker strategy coherence*. This means that if a first solution allows a slight increase in prediction for a given text segment by changing the model, and a second solution uses the same model, but with only a minimally lower prediction rate, the second solution is chosen for coherence in communication intent.

The search for the best prediction model was always initiated at the minimal syntactic group (or two of them, when there were too few syllables, i.e. fewer than five). Once predictions in the first group were appraised, the evaluation was extended to the next group. Once the whole utterance was evaluated, a prediction map was created for the utterance. Melodic discourse modulations could thus be seen in terms of an underlying linguistic organisation, which in turn illuminated the preponderance of a given model.

Text Chunks and their Interpretation by the Speaker-Hearer

According to numerous psycholinguistic comprehension studies (Kintsch and Van Dijk, 1978; Le Ny *et al.*, 1982, etc.), read discourse is constituted by the *production* of successive portions of text ("text chunks"), whereby the realisation depends on a principal organising model of melodic structure. This constitutes in our view the speaker-specific *interpretation of the text* which is then conveyed to the listener. This is in agreement with our studies on production. Le Ny *et al.* write (passage translated from French): "Comprehension is essentially transitory, because it concerns primarily the speech segment which is being processed. [...] one could prefer the idea that the syntactic boundaries represent only one of the possible determinants of segmentation in comprehension, and that in fact, discourse is essentially processed by semantic chunks (Kintsch and Van Dijk, 1978)." Since it relies on the principle of the economic use of resources, the idea that the processes of comprehension obey the same constraints as those of production is satisfying, because it relies on the concept of the identity of processes.

In terms of the size of these text chunks, in our study the mean average over the three reading tasks was 6.8 lexical words, and they varied on the average from 8 to 6.2 lexical words over tasks 1 to 3.

Speech Rate and Matching Coefficients

Over the three reading tasks, speech rates (including pauses) differed considerably. In effect, the average rate of the 12 speakers was 2.23 words/second for task 1, 1.82 words/second for task 2 and 1.05 words/second for task 3. The speech rate for task 3 was thus rather reduced, with numerous pauses that interrupted the flow of discourse. For many speakers, pauses surrounded every lexical word. Thus, for 12 speakers, the median (a more reliable distribution measure than the mean) was 22 pauses for 30 lexical words. This reveals a rather severe constraint on working memory.

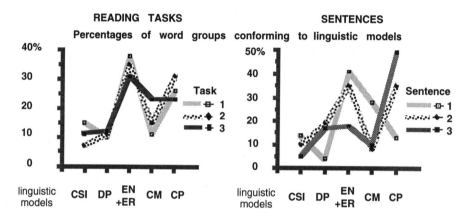

Figures 5 (left) and 6 (right). Distribution of the use of different models across speakers and sentences: left, as a function of task; right, as a function of sentences. The names of the models are given as in the text (CSI syntactic hierarchy, DP syntactic dependence, EN enunciative hierarchy, ER enunciative hierarchy and rhematisation, CM semantic complexity, CP expected/unexpected knowledge).

The matching coefficients (i.e. the percentage of exact matches between the four-tiered prediction and the corresponding Fo measure) were also evaluated over all 6 models using the median. For task 1, the median corresponded to 87% (standard deviation 5.316), for task 2, it was 86.5% (s.d. 6.524), and for task 3, 80% (s.d. 7.299). The total score for all 3 tasks was 84.5% (s.d. 6.427). For the third task, the median score of 80% remained high with respect to the other two scores, in spite of its reduced value. This may well reflect some speakers' difficulty in maintaining conceptual and melodic coherence in very slow discourse, i.e. keeping in working memory all conceptual and Fo references while processing speech. Some speakers showed rates lower than others (the lowest rate was 70%), which indicates that the models employed may have been somehow inadequate, or that speakers produced some deviant targets with respect of the linguistic model being used. Both the hypothesis for the linguistic organisation underlying melodic organisation, and the methodology employed in this experiment were considered to have received ample support from this data set.

Utterance Content, Tasks and Distribution of the Models

It is now appropriate to consider the relative importance of syntactic and semantic factors (Figures 5 and 6). In the detailed analysis of the utterances, it turned out that the holistic models (CSI, EN and ER), were used most often by subjects at points of difficulty, especially at the beginning of a text. These were places where the conceptual and prosodic references of the discourse were created *ex nihilo*. Sometimes certain speakers of task 3 also had recourse to these models when an extremely reduced speech rate imposed a substantial extra load on working memory. To explain this distribution, a consistent hypothesis would be that these models are in fact simple cognitive schemes that must be processed before speaking, and then are likely to require a reduced effort during actual speech production.

The holistic models gave progressively way to the analytic models over the course of the text. It was remarkable that an increase of semantic or pragmatic salience was paralleled by an increase in the frequency of models designed to analyse exactly this type of salience.

Thus, sentence 1 was the longest of the three and contained the most specialised vocabulary ("biologiste", "zoologiste", "phylum", "classification", "espèces" [species]...). Sentence 2 was short, but contained rather unexpected knowledge (the thriving of giant worms in an environment of a particularly inhospitable reputation, the bottom of oceans). Sentence 3 is equally short, but provided information about unexpected facts in the common sense (1. the existence of thermal sources at the bottom of oceans, 2. hot temperature). Taking all tasks together (i.e. 36 utterances), the following observations can be made (see Figure 6 above).

The CM model was used the most in sentence 1. It ranked second (28% of minimal groups) behind the utterance models (EN + ER, 42%) and its proportions decrease over the following two sentences, where the words were simpler. Inversely, the model of expected/unexpected knowledge, CP, was very little in evidence in sentence 1, presumably because the expressed facts were expected after the elements at the beginning of the sentence («zoologistes» and «biologistes»). The CP model ranked first in sentence 2, on same level as the EN+ER models (35% of uses). It accounted for the highest proportion of uses in sentence 3 (approx. 50%).

Thus, a succession of strategies that can be qualified as "intelligent" was established for one type of text and in a situation of precise reading. A first strategy appeared to be used for psychological reasons when production was more difficult: In this case, the vast majority of speakers resorted to models that organise the distribution of linguistic entities according to a simple schematic principle (the holistic models CSI, EN, ER). Inversely, when speakers had control over their conceptual and prosodic means, a different strategy emerged — even during a period of difficulty at the beginning of the reading, as e.g. in sentence 1 with the lexical complexity model CM (see Figure 6). Under these circumstances, speakers could more precisely evaluate the textual content according to their specificity, whether the context became lexically more complex or more unexpected.

Fo Indices and the Cost of Verbal Expression

As shown in Figure 7 above, Fo indices are related to the "cost" of verbal expression. They have in charge the precision of the discourse but at the same time they support the load of the whole system of communication.

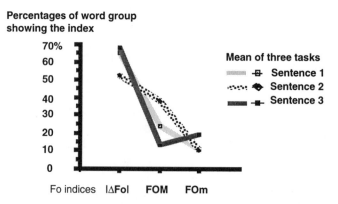

Figure 7. Distribution of different Fo indices across speakers and tasks sentences as a function of sentences. |ΔFo| is the absolute difference between a lexeme's maximum and minimum Fo, FoM is the maximum Fo, and Fom is mean Fo.

This figure displays the clear superiority of a new index, |ΔFo|, defined for this study. Maximum Fo (FoM) was also used frequently, particularly in sentence 2 which comes after the long and lexically specialised sentence 1. But when the conditions of verbal expression become easier, for instance after the short and simple sentence 2, |ΔFo|

increases its distribution rate even more than in sentence 1, and precisely at the expense of FoM.

However, it should be observed that for some speakers, the end of the text may represent an extra load, which apparently led to the use of mean Fo and which is probably easy to use and less specific. On the whole, this behaviour leads us to think of FoM and Fom not as distinct indices, but as progressively deteriorated forms of |ΔFo| that are used when utterance and/or production conditions impose too great an effort.

Duration and Energy Indices

The fundamental organisation of duration and energy indices were found to be similar to each other (Caelen-Haumont, 1991). Both types of organisation apparently parse utterances in terms of syntactic minimal groups, so duration and energy also operate on the basis of syntactic or pseudo-syntactic processes (in the case where the syntactic group is too short to form a prosodic unit).

Prosodic cues actualise an internal and an external structure. The internal structure consists of a progressive increase in syllable duration, at the same time as energy is decreased: All values are obviously oriented in one direction. The external structure breaks this scheme and re-initiates it at the beginning of the next syntactic group. With this recurrent and simple syntactic organisation of duration and energy parameters, Fo can modulate its output base more easily.

Importance for Synthesis and Recognition

From this study, it appears that the speaker's semantic and pragmatic organisation is related to the discourse melody of an utterance. Specifically, intonation appears to be controlled differently in passages with great semantic and pragmatic salience than in those that carry less such salience. Moments of great salience are reflected by direct melodic modifications, while other passages tend to contain melodic structures that are more directly related to the underlying syntactic structure.

In the context of a speech synthesis system, such a differentiation would probably have a direct incidence on its intelligibility, since it can be argued that lack of semantico-pragmatic prominence constitutes one of the prime deficiencies of current synthesis systems. Places in the sentence which human speakers mark by melodic prominence are generally handled by the usual synthesis rule systems, as if there were no semantico-pragmatic emphasis at all. It is understood that semantico-pragmatic emphasis can be motivated by a series of circumstances such as the presence of new or unexpected information, semantic complexity, clarification of unclear terms, and the like. In French, we have seen that these parameters are expressed by a scale of maximum Fo values and Fo ranges within a single word. Concretely, it thus seems possible to replace or modulate the "default rules" for generating "normal" Fo contours with "emphasis and de-emphasising rules" for generating special contours in selected speech segments.

Similarly, these results could have a direct incidence on prosodic processing in automatic speech recognition (ASR). Although concretely speaking, few current ASR systems make active use of prosodic information, it is reasonable to suppose that the above-mentioned Fo parameters could be recognised and could be used as indicators of semantic or pragmatic salience.

Conclusion

The results presented here are in agreement with psycholinguistic studies mentioned above. When speakers read, they gather minimal syntactic groups into chunks of more or less similar size that are semantically organised. Fo range within the lexical word has to convey this information in the most precise manner.

When there is no particular focus on the speaker's intention, when the semantic or pragmatic salience is of less importance, or when the speaker reads without an appropriate listener response, then a syntactic model may come to the fore. By contrast, when speakers make genuine efforts to be well understood by their listeners, they make primary use of the semantic and semantic-pragmatic models, as demonstrated above.

These findings are relevant for automatic speech processing. In the domain of synthesis, the utterance models (EN, ER) are particularly relevant, since they also benefit from structural simplicity. In subsequent research we hope to develop an automatic extraction procedure for the theme/rheme structure.

Acknowledgements

Warm thanks to John Local, from the University of York, and to Eric Keller, University of Lausanne, for their help with the English expression.

References

Abercrombie, D. (1967). *Elements of general phonetics*. Edinburgh University Press.
Bolinger, D.L. (1972). Accent is predictable (if you're a mind reader). *Language, 48,* 633-644.

Bolinger, D.L. (1978). Intonation accross language. In J. H. Greenberg (Ed.), *Universals of Human Language* (pp. 471-524). Stanford, CA: Stanford University Press.

Bruce, G. (1988). How floating is focal accent? *Nordic Prosody, 4,* 41-49.

Caelen-Haumont, G. (1978). *Structures prosodiques de la phrase énonciative simple et étendue..* These de doctorat de 3ème cycle, Toulouse.

Caelen-Haumont, G. (1981). *Structures prosodiques de la phrase énonciative simple et étendue.* Hamburger Phonetische Beiträge. Band 34, Hamburg: Buske.

Caelen-Haumont, G. (1991). *Stratégies des locuteurs et consignes de lecture d'un texte: analyse des interactions entre modèles syntaxiques, sémantiques, pragmatique et paramètres prosodiques.* Thèse d'Etat, Aix-en-Provence.

Caelen-Haumont, G. (1993). Cognitive processes and prosodic encoding: Speakers' adaptation to discourse conditions. *Communication and Cognition - Artificial Intelligence.* Special Issue on Cognition by 5 European Reviews, *10,* 4.

Carbonnel, N., & Bonin, J.J. (1988). Détection de frontières syntagmatiques en parole continue: utilisation de la fréquence fondamentale. *Actes des 17èmes Journées d'Etudes sur la Parole, SFA,* Nancy, 163-167.

Chomsky, N. (1970). Deep structures, surface structures and semantic interpretation. In R. Jakobson (Ed.), *Studies in General and Oriental Linguistics* (pp. 52-91). Tokyo: TEC.

Chomsky, N., & Halle, M. (1968). *The sound pattern of English.* New-York: Harper and Row.

Clements, G. N. (1976). *Vowel harmony in non-linear generative phonology.* IULC, Bloomington, Indiana.

Coleman, J.S., & Local, J. K. (1991). The no crossing constraint in autosegmental phonology. *Linguistics and Philosophy, 14,* 295-338.

Cooper, W.E. (1975). *Syntactic control of speech timing.* Unpublished doctoral dissertation, MIT.

Cutler, A. (1983). Semantics, syntax and sentence accent. *Proc. Xth ICPhS II A* (pp. 85-91). Utrecht: Foris Publications.

Danes, F. (1968). Some thoughts on the semantic structure of the sentence. *Lingua, 21,* 55-69.

Danes, F. (1960). Sentence intonation from a functional point of view. *Word, 16,* 34-54.

Dell, F. (1973). *Les Règles et les sons.* Hermann, Paris.

Dell, F. (1984). L'accentuation dans les phrases en français. In F. Dell, D. Hirst, J.-R. Vergnaud (Eds.), *Forme sonore du langage* (pp. 65-122). Paris: Hermann.

Denes, P. B., & Pinson, E. N. (1963). *The speech chain.* Bell Telephone.

Di Cristo, A. (1975). Recherches sur la structuration prosodique de la phrase française. *Actes des 6èmes JEP* (pp. 95-116). Toulouse: GALF-CNRS.

Fant, G., Kruckenberg, A., & Nord, L. (1991). Durational correlates of stress in Swedish, French and English. *Journal of Phonetics, 19,* 351-365.

Firbas, J. (1974). Some aspects of the Czechoslovak approach to problems of functional sentence perspective. In F. Danes (Ed.), *Papers on Functional Sentence Perspective.* (pp. 11-37). The Hague: Mouton.

Fowler, C. A., & Housum, J. (1987). Talker's signalling of 'new' and 'old' words in speech, and 'listeners' perception and use of the 'distinction'. *The Journal of Memory and Language, 26,* 489-504.

Fromkin, V. (1971). The non-anamalous nature of anomalous utterances. *Language, 47,* 27-52.

Fromkin, V. (1977). Putting the emphasis on the wrong syLLABle. In L. Hyman (Ed.), *Studies in Stress and Accent* (pp. 15-26). Los Angeles: USC.

Fromkin, V. (Ed.) (1980). *Errors in linguistic performance slips of the tongue, ear, pen and hand*. New York Academic Press.

Fromkin, V. (1983). The independence and dependence of syntax, semantics and prosody. *PROC. Xth ICPHS II a* (pp. 93-97). Utrecht: Foris Publications.

Fromkin, V. (1991). What pathology tell us about lexical access in speech production. *Actes du 12ème ICPhS, Aix-en-Provence, 1*, 136-140.

Gaitenby, J. (1965). The elastic word. *Status Report on Speech Research, SR-2* (pp. 3.1-3.12). New York: Haskins Laboratories (unpublished).

Garding, E. (1989). Intonation in Swedish. *Working Papers, 35*, 63-88. Lund University (Sweden), Department of Linguistics.

Garrett, M. F. (1975). The analysis of sentence production. In G. Bower (Ed.), *Psychology of Learning and Motivation, 9* (pp. 133-177). New York: Academic Press.

Goldhor, R. (1976). *Sentential determinates of duration in speech*. Unpublished doctoral dissertation, Massachusetts Institute of Technology.

Goldsmith, J. (1976). *Autosegmental phonology*. Indiana University Linguistics Club.

Gussenhoven, C. (1983). Focus, mode and nucleus, *Journal of Linguistics, 19*, 377-417.

Halle, M., & Vergnaud, J-R. (1978). *Metrical structures in phonology*. M.I.T. and L.A.D.L., CNRS Paris (unpublished).

Halliday, M.A.K. (1967). Notes on transitivity and theme, II, *Journal of Linguistics, 3*, 199-244.

Hirst D., & Di Cristo, A. (in press). Intonation in French in *Intonation systems: A survey of 20 languages*. Cambridge University Press.

Hirst, D. (1981). Phonological implications of a production model of English intonation. In W.U. Dressler, O. Pfeiffer & J. Rennison (Eds.), *Phonologica*, 195-202.

Hirst, D. (1985-6). Représentations phonologique et phonétique de l'intonation des langues naturelles: présentation d'un projet, *Travaux de l'Institut de Phonétique d'Aix-en-Provence, 10*, 123-149.

Hirst, D., & Di Cristo, A. (in press). *Intonation systems: A survey of 20 languages*, Cambridge University Press.

Horne M. (1988). Towards a quantified, focus-based model for synthesizing English sentence intonation. *Lingua, 75*, 25-54.

House, D., Bruce, G., Lacerda, F., & Lindblom, B. (1987). Automatic prosodic analysis for swedish speech recognition. *Proceedings of European Conference on Speech Technology*, Edinburgh, 215-218.

Jackendoff, R. (1972). *Semantic interpretation in generative grammar*. Cambridge, MA: MIT Press.

Kahn, D. (1976). *Syllable-based generalizations in phonology*, Doctoral dissertation, Massachusetts Institute of Technology. Published by IULC, Bloomington, Indiana.

Karcevskij, S. (1931). Sur la phonologie de la phrase. *TCLP, 4*, 188-227.

Kintsch, W., & Van Dijk, T.A. (1978). Toward a model of discourse comprehension and production, *Psychological Review, 85*, 363-394.

Klatt, D. H. (1975). Vowel lengthening is syntactically determined in a connected discourse. *Journal of Phonetics, 3*, 129 -140.

Kruyt, J. G. (1985). *Accents from speakers to listeners. an experimental study of the production and perception of accents patterns in Dutch*. Doctoral dissertation, Leyden.

Ladd, D. R. (1991). Integrating syntagmatic and paradigmatic aspects of stress. *Proceedings of the 12th ICPhS*, Aix-en-Provence, Vol. 1, 283-287.

Ladd, D. R., & Campbell, W. N. (1991). Theories of prosodic structure: Evidence from syllable duration. *Proceedings of the 12th ICPhS*, Aix-en-Provence, Vol. 2, 290-293.

Le Ny J.-F., Carfatan, M., & Verstiggel, J.-C. (1982). Accessibilité en mémoire de travail et rôle d'un retraitement lors de la compréhension de phrases, *Bulletin de Psychologie, 356*, XXXV, 627-34.

Lea, W.A., Medress, M.F., & Skinner, T.E. (1974). A prosodically guided speech understanding strategy, *IEEE Transactions on Acoustics, Speech and Signal Processing, AASP-23, 1*, 30-37.

Liberman, M. (1975). *The intonational system of English*. Doctoral dissertation, Massachusetts Institute of Technology. Published by IULC, Bloomington, Indiana.

Liberman, M., & Prince A. (1977). On stress and linguistic rhythm. *Linguistic Inquiry, 8*, 249-336.

Lindblom, B. (1975). Some temporal regularities in spoken Swedish. In G. Fant and M. Tatham (Eds.), *Auditory analysis and perception of speech* (pp. 387-396), Academic Press.

Martin P. (1975). Intonation et reconnaissance automatique de la structure syntaxique. *6èmes JEP, Galf-CNRS*, Toulouse, 52-62.

Martin, G. J. (1970). On judging pauses in spontaneous speech. *Journal of Verbal Learning and Verbal Behavior, 9*, 75-78

Mathesius, V. (1939). O tak zvaném aktualnim cleneni vetrem. *Slovo a Slovesnost, 5*, 171-174.

Nasri, M.K., Caelen-Haumont, G., & Caelen, J. (1989). Using prosodic rules in speech recognition expert system. *ICASSP Proceedings, IEEE*, Glasgow, Scotland, Vol. 1, Speech Processing 1, 671-674.

Nasri, M.K., Caelen-Haumont, G., & Caelen, J. (1990). Comparative study between uniform and variable coding used for inferring prosodic rules in automatic speech recognition expert systems. *Eurospeech Proceedings, European Conference on Speech Communication*, Paris, Vol. 1, 518-521.

Oller, D. K. (1973). The effect of position in utterance on speech segment duration in English. *The Journal of the Acoustical Society of America, 54*, 1235-1247.

Pierrehumbert, J., & Beckman, M. (1988). *Japanese tone structure*. Cambridge, MA: MIT Press.

Pike, K.L. (1945). *The Intonation of American English*. University of Michigan Publications, Linguistics I. Ann Arbor, MI: University of Michigan Press.

Prince, E.F. (1983). Toward a taxonomy of given-new information. In P. Cole (Ed.), *Radical Pragmatics* (pp. 223-255). Academic Press.

Rossi, M. (1985). L'intonation et l'organisation de l'énoncé. *Phonetica, 42*, 135-153.

Selkirk, E. (1978). *On prosodic structure and its relation to syntactic structure*. Conference on the Mental Representation of Phonology, IULC, Bloomington, Indiana.

Selkirk, E.O. (1980). The role of prosodic categories in English word stress. *Linguistic Inquiry, 11*, 563-605.

Selkirk, E. (1984). *Phonology and syntax: The relations between sounds and structure*. Cambridge, MA: MIT Press.

Terken, J. M. B. (1985). *Use and function of accentuation: Some experiments*. Doctoral dissertation, University of Leiden, The Netherlands.

Tesnière, L. (1959, 1965). *Eléments de syntaxe structurale*. Paris: Editions Klincksieck.

Vaissière, J. (1982), Utilisation des paramètres suprasegmentaux en reconnaissance automatique comme aide à la segmentation en phonèmes. Actes du Séminaire "Prosodie et Reconnaissance Automatique de la Parole", GRECO-PRC, Aix-en-Provence, 123-140.

Separating Simultaneous Sound Sources: Issues, Challenges and Models

14

Martin Cooke and *Guy J. Brown*

Department of Computer Science
University of Sheffield, SHEFFIELD S1 4DP, United Kingdom

Speech is often perceived against a background of other acoustic sources, yet listeners use strategies that enable them to follow a conversation even at unfavourable signal-to-noise ratios. Building these strategies into an early acoustic analysis for automatic speech recognition is essential if speech technology is to be successfully exploited in noisy environments. This chapter describes the main challenges involved in the development of computational systems for source separation, and reviews the representations and search strategies which have been deployed in existing systems.

A problem that often faces computer scientists such as ourselves is following a conversation in a drinking establishment. In such situations, there are many acoustic distractions — music from the jukebox, other conversations, clinking glasses, guffaws of laughter and so on. Each sound is distinct and recognisable, and competes for our attention. Nevertheless, even at low signal-to-noise ratios, it is usually possible to hold a conversation, a feat which appears to require selection of particular acoustic sources from the mêlée.

This realistic scenario raises some important points about hearing. These points may appear rather obvious, but it is worth stating them in a straightforward manner in order to expose the simplifying assumptions which are made in current automatic speech recognition (ASR) systems.

A Mixture of Sounds Usually Reaches our Ears

In most listening situations, a number of acoustic sources will be active at the same time. Hence, a mixture of sound usually reaches our ears, and this mixture contains some energy from each of the active sources (this account is simplified, ignoring factors such as reverberation, for which the auditory system has to compensate).

This fact has a number of ramifications. First, in attempting to recognise the nature and content of any one of the acoustic sources present in the mixture, it would be inappropriate to assign all of the energy in all time intervals to a single sound source. Indeed, there is evidence that the auditory system is quite sensitive to small amounts of extra energy added to sources such as speech (Darwin, 1984). Equally, it would be wrong to assume a *fixed* number of sources, since the number of sources (and their prominence) usually varies over time. Secondly, the fact that a mixture of sounds reaches the ears suggests that one role of early auditory processing must be to tease apart the sources present in the mixture. When we listen, we are able to attend selectively to one source, so that the remaining sounds form an acoustic "background".

Listeners are Able to Attend Selectively to Specific Acoustic Sources

This observation implies an active function for auditory processing. Whatever algorithms underlie hearing, they do not constrain listeners' attention to any specific source. On the other hand, attention has to allow new sources (e.g. a knock at the door) to intrude where necessary. One implication is that pre-processing algorithms which operate in a passive manner do not appear to leave enough room for choice, unfairly promoting one source at the expense of others. This suggests that early processes in hearing do not aim to remove the "background", but rather to parcel up the acoustic material into separate centres of description, which some active selection mechanism is able to process further.

The Definition of "Noise" is Subjective

The speech enhancement literature (e.g. Boll, 1979) often conveys the impression that speech communication takes place against a background of "noise", with the implication that the noise is itself unstructured.

However, the term "noise" is a subjective one. In a group of people where several conversations are taking place, a listener's attention may shift between them, so that conversations that are currently not of interest become the background "noise". Most strategies for automatic speech recognition *accommodate* the variation due to factors such as the presence of "background noise" or inter-speaker differences. A better strategy, as pointed out by Huckvale (1986) and Carlson (1992), is to *model* variability, producing an explanatory account of the sources present in a mixture.

The Results of Segregation May Not Be Perfect

For a variety of reasons, it may not be possible to perform perfect segregation of a mixture into its constituents. If we are to assume that recognition of sources such as speech operates after some source segregation has taken place, then this recognition process may be forced to handle impoverished, partial representations. A strong conclusion would be that a communication process requiring invariant, fine distinctions would not survive in a noisy acoustic environment. This suggests that effort spent on producing highly-detailed signal representations might be better directed at adapting recognition systems to deal with partially-specified input data.

There is More to Hearing than Speech Understanding

The auditory system is not merely a speech processor. Whatever representations and strategies are used in the early stages of speech recognition are likely to be used in the perception of music too, for example. Awareness of the structure of other acoustic sources is likely to enrich our understanding of those processes which act in a source-independent manner in early audition.

In summary, the problem posed by hearing is quite different than the task which most systems for automatic speech recognition set out to solve. A different perspective is obtained by casting the goal of early processes in hearing in the following functional way: The listener understands the acoustic environment by determining which parts of the mixture belong together, and which should be kept separate, for the purpose of identifying the sources present. In the following section, we review a theoretical and experimental account of how listeners might make sense of their acoustic environment.

Gestalt Principles of Perceptual Organisation and Auditory Scene Analysis

More than two decades of psychoacoustic investigation (e.g. Bregman and Campbell, 1971; Darwin, 1981, 1984; Scheffers, 1983) has supported the notion that principles of perceptual organisation similar to those proposed by the gestalt psychologists in the early part of this century (e.g. Koffka, 1936) underlie early auditory processing. Bregman's *Auditory Scene Analysis* (1990) is a comprehensive account of this work.

The German word "Gestalt" means "pattern" or "figure" (as in "figure and ground"), and the gestalt psychologists proposed a number of principles governing the manner in which the brain could form mental patterns from elements of its sensory input. Three of these principles are *common fate, similarity* and *continuity. Common fate* describes the tendency to group sensory elements which covary in time. This is a useful principle in audition, since components of a single acoustic source tend to start and stop at the same time, and to covary in frequency, and — to some extent — in amplitude. *Similarity* and *continuity* can be considered to operate together in binding together sound components across time. Perceptual representations of sound may possess low-level similarity in pitch, timbre, loudness or spatial location, or higher-level similarity in, for example, speaker identity. These properties tend to change smoothly most of the time, and a smooth flow indicates a continuation of the same sound source. In contrast, an abrupt change usually announces the presence of a new source.

Bregman differentiates between supposedly pre-attentive, "primitive" grouping principles which are deemed to operate in source-independent fashion, and "schema-driven" organisation which invokes previously-formed "templates" or "schemas" for particular sources. Thus, grouping by onset synchrony is viewed as an example of a *primitive process*, whilst interpreting elements of an auditory scene as vowel formants exemplifies a *schema-driven process*.

Computational systems for auditory scene analysis (e.g. Weintraub, 1985; Mellinger, 1991; Brown, 1992; Cooke, 1993) employ similar principles in an attempt to segregate acoustic mixtures automatically. In the remainder of this paper, we describe the issues which such systems must address, and treat computational auditory scene analysis as a problem of artificial intelligence, focusing on the two concerns which are central to that field — *representation* and *search*.

Representations for Computational Auditory Scene Analysis

What is the *representational substrate* upon which auditory scene analysis takes place? A low-level answer might invoke detailed neural mechanisms. For example, neural models of pitch perception (Licklider, 1951; Langner, 1981), binaural localisation (Jeffress, 1948) and stream segregation (von der Malsburg and Schneider, 1986; Beauvois and Meddis, 1991) have been proposed. Such modelling provides an explanation which is likely to be computable by our auditory system, but is somewhat constrained by our limited knowledge of actual neural mechanisms.

An alternative way to progress is to ask the functional question: What aspects of the incoming signal need to be made explicit to facilitate auditory scene analysis? This is essentially the approach popularised by Marr (1982) for computational vision. Marr identified three levels at which work in computational vision should be understood — *function, process* and *mechanism* — corresponding to *abstract task description, algorithm* and *neural implementation*, respectively. The issue of representation is thus closely linked to the role of early audition.

Consideration of the principles of auditory perceptual organisation suggests some aspects of the signal which a model of auditory scene analysis should represent. These include onsets, offsets, amplitude, amplitude modulation, frequency modulation, periodicity and spatial location. These properties have to be attached to some time-frequency representation. One common approach is to compute properties at each location in a time-frequency grid. We'll refer to this as a *sub-symbolic* representation. An alternative is to compute a number of components (*symbols*) to which these properties may be attached. Such components are usually derived by tracking spectral dominances through time (e.g. Heinbach, 1988; Riley, 1989; Cooke, 1992; Brown, 1992).

Symbolic and sub-symbolic forms of representation can be contrasted with respect to criteria such as functional utility, robustness and invertibility. These and other factors are shown in Table 1. Some of these criteria find echoes in Marr's principles, as noted in the table. Advantages of one form of description tend to become drawbacks in the other representation. However, it is possible to exploit both representational forms in the same system by maintaining links between explicit descriptions and the data on which they were based.

Table 1. Comparing sub-symbolic and symbolic auditory representations.

Criterion	Sub-symbolic	Symbolic
Plausibility: How likely is it that the auditory system computes this representation, or something similar to it?	Often inspired by auditory physiology. For example, Brown's auditory maps (Figure 1) are motivated by descriptions of topographical organisation in higher auditory centres.	The existence of symbols amongst the neurones is a matter of some interest in philosophical, psychological, neurophysiological and computational circles. See, e.g. Silvers (1989) for some views on this debate.
Functionality (*principle of explicit naming*): How useful is it for auditory scene analysis? Does it make any aspect of the data explicit?	Useful for posing questions such as "what is the likelihood of an onset at this point in time-frequency?". Requires further processing to answer a question like "what pitches are present?".	Purpose is usually to represent some aspect of the data explicitly, although further processing may be required to derive properties from the representation.
Atomicity (*principle of least commitment*): Is the representation monolithic, or is it likely to be sub-divided at some later stage?	Provides a fine-grained analysis, though it may still be necessary to partition activity (for example, within a single time-frequency cell) to two or more sources.	Quite likely to require subdivision e.g. symbolic descriptions computed on the basis of good continuation in time may need to be split if some competing organisation manages to capture part of the structure (e.g. Darwin and Sutherland, 1984)
Invertibility: Is it possible to resynthesise from the representation?	Information is available quasi-continuously in time and frequency, so it may be possible to reconstruct a signal from one or more such representations.	Sometimes, though with loss of information. Symbolic representations are an abstraction, where essentials are maintained at the expense of detail. Any inversion is therefore approximate.
Robustness (*principle of graceful degradation*): Do small perturbations in the data lead to large changes in the representation?	Nonlinear transformations can create large effects from small causes. However it may be possible to ensure that sub-symbolic representations vary continuously with their input.	Symbolic representations can suffer from such "brittleness". Consider peak-picking, for instance, where small quantitative changes in the input can lead to large qualitative changes in the description.
Efficiency: Does the representation lead to rapid auditory scene exploration?	Maintains large amount of data in a form which makes for inefficient search, in, e.g. across-frequency comparisons	Usually accompanied by data reduction. Permits rapid search of auditory scene. For example, across frequency comparisons are usually feasible.

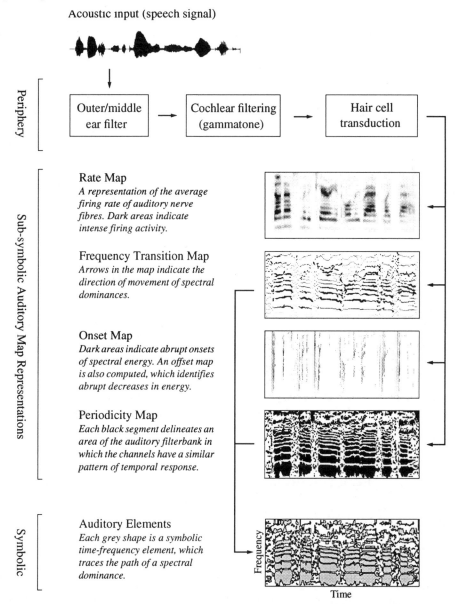

Figure 1. Processing scheme in a computational model of auditory scene analysis (Brown, 1992). Initially, the acoustic input (in this example, speech) is passed through a bank of gammatone filters and a model of hair cell transduction in order to simulate processing in the auditory periphery. Subsequently, a number of auditory map representations are computed, each of which makes a feature of the acoustic input explicit. Information from the frequency transition and periodicity maps is combined to form a symbolic representation of the auditory scene, which can be searched efficiently in order to group components that are likely to have originated from the same acoustic source. Other maps (such as the onset map) provide information for this grouping process.

Our own work (Cooke, 1993; Brown, 1992) has used a combination of sub-symbolic and symbolic representations, some of which are depicted in Figure 1. The sub-symbolic descriptions in Brown's work were motivated by recent physiological studies of the higher auditory system, which suggest that functionally important parameters of the acoustic input appear to be place-coded within neural arrays called *auditory maps*. Maps are two-dimensional, with frequency represented on one axis and the value of the parameter represented on an orthogonal axis. The value of the parameter at a particular frequency is coded by the firing rate of the neurone in the appropriate position of the neural array. Such maps have been used to code information about onsets, offset, frequency transition and periodicities, as shown in the figure.

Challenges for Models of Auditory Grouping

Having constructed the auditory scene by decomposing the signal in some fashion, it is necessary to regroup those elements of the scene which are likely to have arisen from the same acoustic source. Some of the factors which appear to determine "belongingness" of elements to groups have already been mentioned. In this section, we show that computational grouping is far from straightforward by identifying some of the challenges faced by any model. We consider various strategies which have been proposed to facilitate the *searching of the auditory scene*.

Interactions Between Grouping Principles

Most systems for automatically grouping sound components have used a single cue based on differences in fundamental frequency[1]. Any attempt to employ two or more grouping principles runs into the issue of interactions, which potentially leads to contradictory explanations of the sensory evidence.

A simple example is provided by the work of Bregman and Pinker (1978), whose three-tone stimulus configuration is shown in the left panel of Figure 2. Factors such as the frequency of A in relation to that of B (frequency proximity) or the location of C in time relative to B (onset/offset synchrony) give rise to alternative vertical (A and BC in separate groups) or horizontal (AB and C) organisations of this stimulus.

---

[1] An exception is the system of Kashino and Tanaka (1992) which uses the Dempster-Shafer rule of evidence combination to calculate interactions between grouping by onset synchrony and frequency proximity.

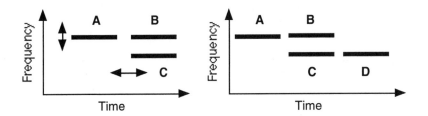

Figure 2. Left: Three-tone stimulus configuration used by Bregman and Pinker (1978) to investigate the interaction between frequency proximity and onset/offset synchrony. Right: The addition of tone D can be used to illustrate retroactive propagation of grouping effects (redrawn from Bregman and Tougas, 1989).

Other examples of interactions abound: The scale illusion (Deutsch, 1975) sets frequency proximity cues against those indicating spatial location, whilst Bregman and Levitan (reported in Bregman, 1990) explored the interaction between timbre and pitch. Explicit modelling of these effects is frustrated by the paucity of quantitative experimental data on all but the simplest interactions.

Retroactive Effects

At what point can decisions about grouping be made? Can events at some later time modify groupings formed at some earlier time? Using a repeated pattern of four tones depicted in the right panel of Figure 2, Bregman and Tougas (1989) illustrated backwards propagation of effects across time and frequency. They showed that manipulation of tone D could affect the AB grouping in the following way.

If D is brought into frequency proximity with C, it is more likely to capture C from a competing BC grouping. Capture of C leaves B more likely to fuse with A by frequency proximity. Another demonstration of a retroactive decision was provided by Warren (1982), using the stimulus configuration depicted in Figure 3 (see caption for details).

Darwin and Sutherland (1984) showed that a harmonic which starts at the same time as a short vowel, but which continues after the remainder of the vowel has ended, contributes less to the vowel's phonetic quality than if it had ended synchronously with the rest of the vowel. This illustrates that to some extent, the auditory system adopts a "wait-and-see" attitude to vowel recognition.

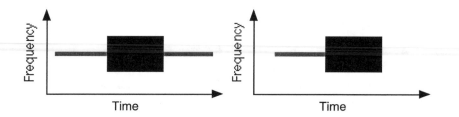

Figure 3. Left: Stimulus used by Warren (1982) to show illusory continuity of a tone. The tone (grey line) stops as a more intense noise burst (black patch) starts, and a further tone is switched on as the noise burst ends. Under appropriate spectro-temporal-intensity conditions for the noise burst, the tone is heard to continue through the occluding noise. Right: the second tone is absent, and the tone is heard to stop as the noise burst starts. The grouping decision appears to be made at the offset of the noise burst, or later.

Further examples of possible undoing of grouping decisions are reported in Mellinger (1991). One such is the demonstration by Pierce (1983) that harmonics with onsets staggered by one second are initially perceived as distinct entities, but later merge with the rest of the complex. The reverse is true for McAdams' oboe (Reynolds, 1983), an illusion in which the odd and even harmonics of a synthetic oboe sound are given different rates of frequency modulation (FM). They initially merge, presumably due to common onset, but later separate, probably due to inharmonicity caused by the differential rates of FM.

The Default Condition of Perceptual Organisation

A high-level consideration for any model of grouping is the *mode* of perceptual organisation. That is, are auditory scene elements assumed to belong together unless there is some reason to segregate them, or is the reverse true, are they organised into groups only if some grouping principle can be applied to fuse them?

Bregman (1990) uses the example of white noise, which is usually perceived as a coherent sound, to argue that the default is *fusion*. There are other examples where the auditory system appears to fuse elements in the absence of cues for grouping them. For example, Remez *et al.* (1981) created stimuli consisting of three time-varying sinusoids of constant amplitude and with frequencies taken from the formant frequencies of naturally-spoken sentences. Such "sine-wave speech" exemplars contain no obvious cues for primitive grouping, yet listeners typically identify up to 60% of the words in such sentences[2].

---

[2] However, cues for primitive grouping added to such sentences greatly improve identification performance. Carrell (1988) shows that amplitude co-modulation at 100 Hz increased phonetic intelligibility from 69% to 97%.

Computational Complexity

Searching the auditory scene involves much computation. For example, the number of across-frequency comparisons necessary to detect correlated changes in amplitude might vary as the square of the number of objects which exist at each time frame. For sub-symbolic representations which maintain the abstraction of the frequency-specific channel, this can amount to tens of thousands of comparisons. Symbolic representations are more efficient in this regard, since they generally result in smaller numbers of abstractions (see Cooke, 1993). Similarly, representations in which the temporal evolution of auditory scene elements has been made explicit, generally help to reduce the search space, since grouping decisions made at some moment will constrain possible groupings at earlier and later times. The AI maxim "more representation, less search" applies here to auditory scene exploration.

Strategies for Auditory Scene Exploration

In an attempt to meet some of the challenges outlined in the previous section, various search strategies have been adopted by systems for computational auditory scene analysis. This section categorises some of these recent models[3].

Simultaneous-then-Sequential

A common strategy is to perform a grouping of components which occur at the same time (*simultaneous organisation*), independently in each time frame. Continuity of properties computed from such groups can then be used to group across time (*sequential integration*). These strategies are conceptually simple, and have the additional attraction of being supported by experimental data from studies on listeners' ability to segregate simultaneous vowel sounds (Scheffers, 1983), as well as from physiological studies (Palmer, 1990). Several computational models of double vowel segregation based on factors such as differences in fundamental frequency between the vowels have been evaluated (e.g.

---

[3] Models could be categorised with respect to alternative criteria such as the degree to which they embody "auditory knowledge", or whether they use predominantly primitive grouping principles (a classification which would include most of those mentioned here), or top-down schema (*e.g.*, Kopec and Bush, 1989; Moore *et al.*, 1991).

Assmann and Summerfield, 1990; Meddis and Hewitt, 1992), and have been shown to correspond well to listeners' performance. A recent review of these and other models for the segregation of concurrent harmonic sounds is presented in de Cheveigné (1993).

The main drawback of the simultaneous-then-sequential strategy is its rather narrow temporal focus. It may be rather difficult to estimate the number of sources present, for example, in each time frame. Sources with crossing pitch contours can also present problems due to this local perspective (Weintraub, 1985). A deeper issue involves the question of whether properties such as pitch are computed locally at all. Darwin and Ciocca (1992) have shown that the pitch of a complex sound depends on the time at which its components start. Whilst many models use pitch to *effect* simultaneous organisation, these results suggest that pitch is a *result* of grouping.

Old-Plus-New

Bregman (1990) notes that "if part of a sound can be interpreted as part of an earlier sound, then it should be". This "old-plus-new" heuristic suggests a predominantly left-to-right search strategy in which later representations are interpreted either as continuations of existing organisation, or as an indication to start a new group. The computational models of Mellinger (1991) and Denbigh and Zhao (1992) make use of such a strategy. Mellinger's system makes use of computational maps of onsets and frequency variation. Onset synchrony is used to bind components together, whilst differences in frequency variation are used both to segregate existing groups and to bind them. Sounds that have not started synchronously can subsequently be grouped by common frequency variation. Denbigh and Zhao's model, though not inspired by considerations of auditory processing, looks for sudden increases in the number of spectral peaks. Such peaks are subtracted from a weighted combination of previous spectra, and a pitch detection scheme then operates on this difference spectrum.

Strategies operating in this fashion have the potential to be used predictively. As the point at which the "old-plus-new" heuristic is applied sweeps forward in time, it leaves in its wake grouped structures from which more complex properties might be calculated. For example, the repetitive structure of the ring of a modern telephone might result in the creation of a "dynamic schema", which could then be applied to interpret later parts of the sound.

Left-to-right strategies clearly have problems in modelling retroactive effects, since grouping decisions take place as soon as new information arrives. However, it would be possible to cater for these through the use of some temporal buffer, whose length would be chosen to account for the tardiest retroaction.

Time-Frequency Grouping

One way to handle retroactive effects is to allow grouping to operate upon a representation in which temporal relations between components are already explicit. Our own grouping systems have employed this strategy (Cooke, 1993; Brown, 1992) using, as their representational basis, the sorts of time-frequency descriptions depicted in the lower panel of Figure 1. Rather than grouping representations in each time frame separately, these schemes make use of temporal continuity constraints. Groups are formed solely from constituents which are sufficiently similar across their whole temporal extent, not just in individual time frames. This leads to a more robust system than is possible in schemes which make decisions locally in time. For example, we have shown that time-frequency grouping can correctly handle crossing pitch contours (Cooke, 1993).

In contrast with most other approaches, our models search for organisation in the auditory scene, and make no *a priori* decisions about the number of sources present. An efficient search for organisation is made possible largely as a result of exploiting low-level temporal continuity constraints at an early stage in processing.

One problem with this approach is the hard-and-fast nature of these early tracking decisions. To see why this might present difficulties, consider Darwin and Sutherland's (1984) demonstration that a harmonic of a vowel which starts before and stops after the others makes a reduced contribution to the phonetic quality of the vowel. However, this effect can be reduced (that is, the leading harmonic can make a greater contribution to vowel quality), if it is accompanied by an additional tone which starts at the same time as the leading tone, and ends as the vowel starts (thus providing sensory material for the leading tone to group with). The harmonic is almost certainly denoted as a single entity in most time-frequency representations, yet it is split into two for grouping purposes. This can be viewed as violating Marr's "principle of least commitment", since it requires that earlier decisions — in this case concerning the temporal continuity of the harmonic — be undone.

Autonomous Agents

Virtually all systems for computational auditory scene analysis developed to date have utilised a small number of grouping principles, operating independently. It is easy to see why: modelling larger numbers of principles requires a consideration of their interactions. Competitions between groups have to be fought and resolved, yet there is very little quantitative data available on how to mediate this fight.

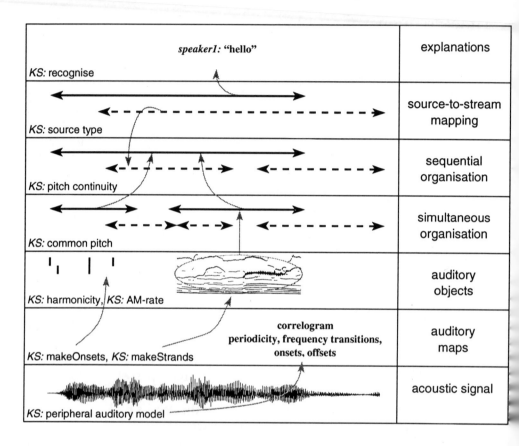

Figure 4. An illustration of a blackboard for auditory scene analysis. Independent programs — knowledge sources (KS) — operate by adding and modifying entries on appropriate levels of the blackboard.

A further consideration is the role of stored knowledge, or "schemas", in influencing grouping decisions. Whilst pre-attentive "primitive" grouping processes appear to parcel up the incoming data into coherent bundles, top-down, or "schema-driven" mechanisms attempt to make sense of it all. Primitive grouping decisions are not sacrosanct[4]; the auditory system appears ready to re-partition its perceptual representations, if necessary, to explain the acoustic environment. An example occurs in the "duplex"

---

[4] Furthermore, primitive grouping appears not to be a *necessary* condition for schema-driven interpretation, as illustrated by the sine-wave speech demonstration of Remez *et al.* (1981).

perception of speech described by Rand (1974) and Liberman *et al.* (1981). Liberman presented — to one ear — a synthetic three-formant syllable from which the third formant transition was removed, and played the missing transition simultaneously to the other ear. The transition contributed to the percept of the syllable, but was also heard as an isolated "chirp". Grouping by making "schema-sense" in this case overrides grouping by ear of presentation.

To address these issues, we are exploring a different computational metaphor for grouping (Crawford *et al.*, 1993) — that of *autonomous agents* communicating via a global data structure called a *blackboard* (Erman and Lesser, 1975). In essence, each agent encapsulates a specific area of expertise (for example, sequential grouping) which, on its own, is insufficient to solve a complex problem such as auditory scene analysis. The blackboard exists to allow these experts to communicate, given that each knows nothing about the others' domain. Each agent is alerted when something of interest to them is placed on the blackboard (for example, the onset synchrony expert would be invoked when new onsets appear). Agents can modify, add and delete entries. The blackboard represents a record of the solution process, including failed attempts. Figure 4 depicts some structures and knowledge sources which may be necessary in the auditory scene analysis domain.

It ought to be possible to implement approximations to all of the search regimes described in this section using the blackboard framework. However, the main goal is to investigate how the more flexible control strategy afforded by the blackboard system permits (and resolves) competitions between interpretations, and how both schema-driven and primitive grouping processes can cooperate in explaining the auditory scene.

New Directions

Virtually all work to date in automatic sound source segregation operates in a purely bottom-up fashion, and primarily uses cues related to differences in the fundamental frequency of sources which make up the mixture. Most schemes make gross assumptions about the number and types of sources present, and are usually restricted to the processing of voiced speech. Binaural processing is not widely modelled[5].

Perhaps the least well-understood aspect of auditory grouping is the appropriate way to treat *time*. Extensive efforts have gone into segregating simultaneous vowels using representations computed in separate time

---

[5] But see Denbigh and Zhao (1992) and Chapter 15, this volume.

frames, yet little work has been done on temporal integration[6]. We have shown that the inherent continuity of acoustic source components provides a valuable constraint which acts to disambiguate local interpretations and helps to make a more widespread search of the auditory scene possible (Cooke, 1991). However, many such schemes proposed to date involve information loss. An alternative which may provide a more gradual transition from the sub-symbolic to the symbolic is the auditory wavelet representation of d'Alessandro (1993).

One issue which arose out of the introductory discussion is the nature of *representations* used for the identification of sources such as speech. Since segregation in both humans and machines is likely to be imperfect, it appears necessary to develop recognition architectures which can deal with partially-specified inputs. *Grouping* provides an important piece of extra information for such recognition processes: In principle, it allows identification of those regions (in time-frequency) of the signal which are likely to belong to the speech source. The recognition system is thus able to conclude that the other regions may be occluded by other sources, and hence should be configured to generate a set of matches which account for the partially-specified material, plus the assumption of occlusion. We are currently exploring recognition algorithms which can employ this extra information; our initial studies have exploited principles of perceptual continuity (Cooke and Brown, in press).

In addition to widening the range of environments in which automatic speech recognition systems can operate (e.g. to include in-vehicle use), we see a role for computational auditory scene analysis in *synthesis applications*. Whenever sound is used to communicate an idea — from synthetic speech through to auditory visualisation of complex data and virtual reality — it will be necessary to check that the synthesised artefact is likely to be perceived in the intended fashion. So, for example, the quality of a speech synthesis system might be judged partly on the basis of the coherence of the auditory images it forms. This "synthesis-by-auditory scene analysis" promises to improve the clarity of the auditory image by ensuring that the generated signal contains compelling cues for grouping together those components which the listener is intended to perceive holistically.

References

Assmann, P.F., & Summerfield, Q. (1990). Modelling the perception of concurrent vowels: Vowels with different fundamental frequencies. *Journal of the Acoustical Society of America, 88,* 680-697.

Beauvois, M.W., & Meddis, R. (1991). A computer model of auditory stream segregation. *Quarterly Journal of Experimental Psychology, 43A,* 517-541.

---

[6] Patterson's stabilised auditory image (Patterson *et al.*, 1992) and the work of von der Malsburg and Schneider (1986) have attempted to address this issue.

Boll, S.F. (1979). Suppression of acoustic noise in speech using spectral subtraction. *IEEE Transactions on Acoustics, Speech and Signal Processing, ASSP-27*, 113-120.

Bregman, A.S. (1990). *Auditory scene analysis*. London: MIT Press.

Bregman, A.S., & Campbell, J. (1971). Primary auditory stream segregation and perception of order in rapid sequences of tones. *Journal of Experimental Psychology, 89*, 244-249.

Bregman, A.S., & Pinker, S. (1978). Auditory streaming and the building of timbre. *Canadian Journal of Psychology, 32*, 19-31.

Bregman, A.S., & Tougas, Y. (1989). Propagation of constraints in auditory organisation. *Perception and Psychophysics, 46*, 395-396.

Brown, G.J. (1992). *Computational auditory scene analysis: A representational approach*. Unpublished Ph. D. Thesis, University of Sheffield.

Carlson, R. (1992). Synthesis: Modelling variability and constraints. *Speech Communication, 11*, 159-166.

Carrell, T.D. (1988). Naturalness and intelligibility of amplitude modulated time-varying sinusoidal speech. *Journal of the Acoustical Society of America, 88*, S174.

Cooke, M.P. (1992). An explicit time-frequency characterisation of synchrony in an auditory model. *Computer Speech and Language, 6*, 153-173.

Cooke, M.P. (1993). *Modelling auditory processing and organisation*. Cambridge: Cambridge University Press.

Cooke, M.P., & Brown, G.J. (in press). Computational auditory scene analysis: Exploiting principles of perceived continuity. *Speech Communication*.

Crawford, M.D., Cooke, M.P., Brown, G.J., & Green, P.D. (1993). Interactive computational auditory scene analysis: An environment for exploring auditory representations and groups. *Journal of the Acoustical Society of America, 94*, 2454.

D'Alessandro, C. (1993). Auditory-based wavelet representation. In M.P. Cooke, S.W. Beet, & M.D. Crawford (Eds.) *Visual representations of speech signals*. (pp. 131-138). Chichester: John Wiley & Sons.

Darwin, C.J. (1981). Perceptual grouping of speech components differing in fundamental frequency and onset time. *The Quarterly Journal of Experimental Psychology, 33A*, 185-207.

Darwin, C.J. (1984). Perceiving vowels in the presence of another sound: Constraints on formant perception. *Journal of the Acoustical Society of America, 76*, 1636-1647.

Darwin, C.J., & Ciocca, V. (1992). Grouping in pitch perception: Effects of onset asynchrony and ear of presentation of a mistuned component. *Journal of the Acoustical Society of America, 91*, 3381-3390.

Darwin, C.J., & Sutherland, N.S. (1984). Grouping frequency components of vowels: When is a harmonic not a harmonic? *The Quarterly Journal of Experimental Psychology, 36A*, 193-208.

de Cheveigné, A. (1993). Separation of concurrent harmonic sounds: Fundamental frequency estimation and a time-domain cancellation model of auditory processing. *Journal of the Acoustical Society of America, 93*, 3271-3290.

Denbigh, P.N., & Zhao, J. (1992). Pitch extraction and separation of overlapping speech. *Speech Communication, 11*, 119-125.

Deutsch, D. (1975). Two-channel listening to musical scales. *Journal of the Acoustical Society of America, 57*, 1156-1160.

Erman, L.D., & Lesser, V.R. (1975). A multi-level organisation for problem solving using many diverse cooperating sources of knowledge. *Proceedings of the International Joint Conference on Artificial Intelligence*, 483-490.

Heinbach, W. (1988). Aurally adequate signal representation: The part-tone-time-pattern. *Acoustica, 67*, 113-121.

Huckvale, M.A. (1986). Modelling acoustic and phonetic variability of speech. *Proceedings of the International Conference on Speech Input/Output: Techniques and Applications*, 54-58.

Jeffress, L. A. (1948). A place theory of sound localisation. *Journal of Comparative Physiology and Psychophysics, 41*, 35-39.

Kashino, K., & Tanaka, H. (1992). A sound source separation system using spectral features integrated by the Dempster's law of combination. *Annual Report of the Engineering Research Institute, University of Tokyo, 51*, 67-72.

Koffka, K. (1936). *Principles of Gestalt psychology*. London: Harcourt and Brace.

Kopec, G.E., & Bush, M.A. (1989). An LPC-based spectral similarity measure for speech recognition in the presence of co-channel speech interference. *Proceedings of ICASSP, 270-273*.

Langner (1981). Neuronal mechanisms for pitch analysis in the time domain. *Experimental Brain Research, 44*, 450-454.

Liberman, A.M., Isenberg, D., & Rackerd, B. (1981). Duplex perception of cues for stop consonants: Evidence for a phonetic mode. *Perception & Psychophysics, 30*, 133-143.

Licklider, J.C.R. (1951). A duplex theory of pitch perception. *Experientia, 7*, 128-134.

Marr, D. (1982). *Vision*. New York: Freeman.

Meddis, R., & Hewitt, M.J. (1992). Modelling the identification of concurrent vowels with different fundamental frequencies. *Journal of the Acoustical Society of America, 91*, 233-245.

Mellinger, D. (1991). *Event formation and separation in musical sound*. Unpublished Ph.D. Thesis, Stanford University.

Moore, R.K., Varga, A.P., & Kadirkamanatha, M. (1991). Automatic separation of speech and other complex sounds using hidden Markov model decomposition. *Institute of Acoustics Speech Group Meeting*, Sussex University, 27th February.

Palmer, A.R. (1990). The representation of the spectra and fundamental frequencies of steady-state single- and double-vowel sounds in the temporal discharge patterns of guinea pig cochlear-nerve fibres. *Journal of the Acoustical Society of America, 88*, 1412-1426.

Patterson, R.D., Robinson, K., Holdsworth, J., McKeown, D., Zhang, C., & Allerhand, M. (1992). Complex sounds and auditory images. In Y. Cazals, L. Demany, & K. Horner (Eds.), *Auditory physiology and perception* (pp. 429-453). Oxford: Pergamon Press.

Pierce, J.R. (1983). *The science of musical sound*. New York: Freeman.

Rand, T.C. (1974). Dichotic release from masking for speech. *Journal of the Acoustical Society of America, 55*, 678-680.

Remez, R.E., Rubin, P.E., Pisoni, D.B., & Carrell, T.D. (1981). Speech perception without traditional speech cues. *Science, 212*, 947-950.

Reynolds, R. (1983). *Archipelago*. C.F. Peters.

Riley, M.R. (1989). *Speech time-frequency representations*. Boston: Kluwer.

Scheffers, M.T.M. (1983). *Sifting vowels: Auditory pitch analysis and sound segregation*. Unpublished Ph.D. Thesis, University of Gröningen.

Silvers, S. (1989). *Rerepresentation: Readings in the Philosophy of Mental Representation*. Boston: Kluwer.

Von Der Malsburg, C., & Schneider, W. (1986). A neural cocktail-party processor. *Biological Cybernetics, 54*, 29-40.

Warren, R.M. (1982). *Auditory perception: A new synthesis*. New York: Pergamon.

Weintraub, M. (1985). *A theory and computational model of monaural auditory sound separation*. Unpublished Ph.D. Thesis, Stanford University.

Auditory Computations that Separate Speech from Competing Sounds: **15**
A Comparison of Monaural and Binaural Processes

Quentin Summerfield and *John F. Culling*

MRC Institute of Hearing Research, University of Nottingham,
NOTTINGHAM NG7 2RD, United Kingdom

Human listeners can understand speech despite the presence of competing sounds. Building such robustness into automatic speech recognisers has proved difficult. There is interest, therefore, in establishing how speech is separated from competing sounds during auditory analysis. This chapter illustrates two such processes using perceptual data and computational models.

As listeners, we possess remarkable powers of auditory selective attention. Some of us can follow the tune played by a single instrument in an orchestra. Others can hear out the song of one bird in the dawn chorus. Most of us can listen to individual talkers in a cocktail party. We can understand their words with little difficulty, provided the power in their voice is greater than a quarter of the power in the competing voices; i.e. so long as the signal to noise ratio (SNR) is better than -6 dB. In comparison, at this SNR, many listeners with impaired hearing and all systems for automatic speech recognition perform poorly. Hence, there is interest in establishing how listeners with normal hearing segregate speech from other sounds. Results are of fundamental interest, but might also contribute to better hearing aids and to more robust speech recognisers.

The pattern of sounds produced by a source is rarely arbitrary. Rather, most sources produce systematic patterns whose structure reflects constraints in the processes that generated the sounds. Listeners exploit their knowledge of these constraints in order to group the elements of sound produced by one source, and thereby separate them from sounds produced by competing sources. The production of speech is governed by many such constraints which listeners can exploit in order to separate competing voices. For example, they use the lexical and syntactic rules that govern the legitimate ordering of speech sounds in their language. As a result, words in sentences can be reported with 90% accuracy at an SNR about 10 dB lower than that required to identify nonsense syllables (Kryter, 1985). Similarly, listeners know about the legitimate acoustical forms that individual speech sounds can possess. For example, if one harmonic of a vowel is increased step-wise in intensity over repeated presentations, the boosted harmonic initially is incorporated into the percept of the vowel and the vowel colour changes. Ultimately, it is implausible that the combined spectral envelope could be that of a vowel, and two separate sources are heard: a vowel and a sinusoid.

These are examples of the type of constraint that Bregman (1990) has described as "schema-based". They reflect the listener's knowledge of a particular type of source, speech in this instance. They contrast with "primitive" constraints which reflect basic physical properties which may be shared by many types of source. For example, many sources generate sounds that are strongly periodic; i.e. they repeat regularly in time. These sources include machines, musical instruments, and talkers producing voiced speech. The sounds which they generate are composed of harmonics whose frequencies are integer multiples of the fundamental frequency (F_O, the reciprocal of the repetition period). Correspondingly, listeners generally perceive frequency components that obey this integer relationship as originating from the same source and perceive components that are mistuned from the integer relationship as originating from different sources. A second example follows from the fact that different sources generally occupy different locations in space and so generate different patterns of inter-aural cues of intensity and timing. Correspondingly, when a stimulus generates more than one pattern of interaural level and timing cues, listeners may perceive more than one source.

In this chapter, we are concerned with the auditory mechanisms which separate competing voices by exploiting these two types of primitive constraint: differences in F_O and in inter-aural timing. We shall explore the possibility that the two types of constraint are exploited by similar computations during auditory analysis. The chapter complements Chapter 14 by Cooke and Brown which considers the computational strategies required to exploit a wider range of constraints.

Use of Differences in Fundamental Frequency to Separate the Voiced Speech of Concurrent Talkers

Brokx and Nooteboom (1982) presented test sentences against a background of continuous speech, spoken by the same talker, to listeners who were required to identify the words in the test sentences. When the stimuli had monotone F_0 contours, listeners performed more accurately when the F_0s were different rather than the same. When the stimuli contained natural time-varying F_0 contours, listeners performed more accurately when the F_0 ranges were separate rather than overlapping. Brokx and Nooteboom concluded that differences in F_0 between talkers (ΔF_0s) assist selective attention in two ways. First, when the F_0s are the same, the voices fuse to give the impression of a single source, and it is difficult to attend selectively to either one of them. Thus, one role played by a ΔF_0 is to allow concurrent segregation of simultaneous voices. Second, the fact that the F_0 changes continuously during the voiced speech of a single talker provides a means of grouping the elements of that voice sequentially. Thus, when two voices are present, sequential grouping can link together segments that have been segregated following processes of simultaneous grouping. Sequential grouping is easier when F_0 contours do not intersect or overlap, than when they do.

Perception of "Double Vowels"

We shall concentrate on the role of ΔF_0s in simultaneous grouping. To study their effects, it has been useful to reduce the rich linguistic and acoustical interplay of the cocktail party to a situation that is more tractable experimentally: a pair of synthetic steady-state vowels presented simultaneously. The technique was introduced by Scheffers (1983) and the stimuli are often referred to as "double vowels". The task for listeners is to identify both members of the pair of vowels presented on each trial. The open circles in Figure 1 show the results of one such experiment (Assmann and Summerfield, 1990). The single vowels that made up the stimuli were 200-ms segments of the five long British-English vowels: /i/, /a/, /u/, /ɔ/, and /ɛ/. All possible pairs were presented. In each pair, one vowel had an F_O of 100 Hz while the other had a higher F_O. The graph shows the percentage of trials on which listeners identified both vowels correctly, as a function of the size of the difference in F_O between them. Performance was above the chance level of 6.7% when the two F_Os were the same, improved abruptly as the ΔF_O was increased to 1 semitone, and remained approximately constant for larger ΔF_Os.

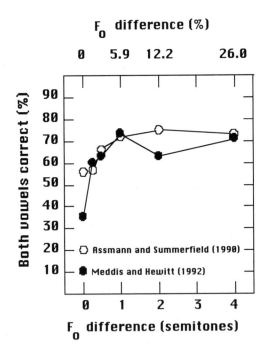

Figure 1. (Open circles) Accuracy achieved by listeners in identifying both constituents of double vowels as a function of the size of the difference in F_O between them (Assmann and Summerfield, 1990). One vowel had an F_O of 100 Hz. The other vowel had an F_O that was greater than 100 Hz by the amount shown (in semitones on the lower horizontal axis and in percent on the upper horizontal axis). (Filled circles) Accuracy of identification predicted by the model of Meddis and Hewitt (1992).

When competing vowels have the same F_O, listeners hear a single talker producing a "dominant" vowel whose phonetic quality is coloured by the impression of a second vowel. They identify the dominant vowel accurately, but make errors in identifying the second vowel. When the F_Os differ by about 2 semitones or more, listeners generally hear two talkers producing vowels on different pitches. These impressions are compatible with the idea that the introduction of the difference in F_O allows listeners to partition the stimulus into two streams, and that accuracy of identification improves because attention can be directed selectively to each stream in turn. In fact, a more complex set of processes underlie the pattern of identification shown in Figure 1. Some of these complications are examined later in this chapter. First, we consider how auditory analysis might compute the two pitches in a double vowel, and might then use their values to guide a process of segregation that recovers evidence of the individual constituents.

Computing the Pitches in Double Vowels

The starting point for most models of auditory processes is a simulation of the frequency analysis performed in the cochlea. The analysis can be simulated by a bank of linear overlapping band-pass filters (e.g. Patterson *et al.*, 1988). Panel (a) of Figure 2 shows the waveforms that emerge from 16 of the channels of such a filter-bank when the stimulus is the single vowel /i(100)/ (an exemplar of /i/ with an F_O of 100 Hz). The waveforms provide a first-order approximation to the pattern of vibration of the basilar membrane at different places along its length.

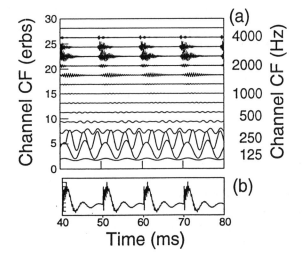

Figure 2. (a) Outputs of 16 channels of an auditory filter bank excited by the synthetic vowel /i/ (F_O = 100 Hz) whose waveform is shown in (b). The channels have been spaced evenly on a scale of their equivalent rectangular bandwidths (erbs). Equal increments along this scale correspond to equal distances of about 0.85 mm/erb along the cochlear partition in the inner ear. The scale is approximately logarithmic in Hz, as can bee seen from the frequency scale on the right-hand axis of panel (a).

At low frequencies, the bandwidths of the filters are narrow in relation to the spacing between harmonics with the result that different harmonics largely excite different filters and the outputs of the filters are more-or-less sinusoidal. Such harmonics are said to be "resolved". The bandwidths of auditory filters increase with their centre frequency so that at higher frequencies several harmonics excite each filter and the output is an amplitude-modulated waveform. However, despite this difference, all of the filtered waveforms share the common property of repeating themselves with a period of 10 ms. This outcome follows inevitably from the fact that every filtered waveform is composed of one or more of the harmonics of the original vowel, each of which contains the period of 10 ms among other periods. If auditory analysis could detect the common periodicity, it would have a means of establishing that every channel was being excited by the same source, and thus that the energy in each of the channels should be interpreted together. Conversely, if a different periodicity was detected in one or more channels from the rest, it would be appropriate to assign those channels to a different source.

A useful technique for making explicit the common periodicity in different channels is to compute the autocorrelation function (ACF) of each filtered waveform (Licklider, 1951; Meddis and Hewitt, 1991). In brief, the analysis is as follows. A copy is taken of a segment of the waveform. The copy is aligned with the original. Corresponding samples in the copy and the original are multiplied together and the products are summed. These steps generate the first point in the ACF. The copy is then delayed by one sample with respect to the original and the process of multiplication and summation is repeated, and so on for a range of delays, to generate the sequence of values that form the ACF. When the copy is delayed by one period with respect to the original, high amplitude samples in the copy align with high amplitude samples in original and sum of cross-products is large. Therefore a peak occurs in the ACF when the delay equals the period of the original waveform. Conversely, the delays at which peaks are found in the ACF provide evidence of the different periodicities contained in a waveform.

Figure 3 shows the result of applying this analysis to the vowel /a(100)/. The ACFs of 64 channels have been plotted as a waterfall display, referred to as an "autocorrelogram" (ACG). The presence of the vertical spine of peaks at 10-ms delay reflects the fact that all channels contain this periodicity. If the ACFs are summed across frequency, the peaks at 10 ms reinforce one another while peaks at other delays are diffused, resulting in a single clear peak at a delay of 10 ms in the pooled ACF. Meddis and Hewitt (1991) have shown that the positions and relative amplitudes of peaks in pooled ACFs give good predictions of the pitches which listeners hear in complex sounds. Thus, the analysis shown in Figure 3 is a model of pitch perception, not merely a clever piece of signal processing for recovering the period of a vowel. Note that evidence of pitch is distributed across frequency; in accordance with everyday experience and psychoacoustical experiments, masking a subset of the channels, or removing energy from them by filtering, would have no effect on the frequency of the pitch predicted by the model.

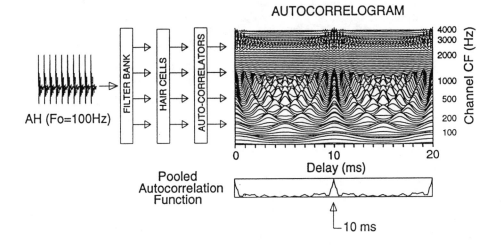

Figure 3. The steps taken to compute the autocorrelogram and the pooled autocorrelation function of a synthetic exemplar of the vowel /a/ (F_0 = 100 Hz). The hair-cell model (Meddis *et al.*, 1990) simulates the process of mechanical to neural transduction at an inner hair cell. Its chief effects here are to half-wave rectify each filtered waveform and to compress its amplitude.

Modelling the Segregation of Double Vowels

We can now consider the ACG of a double vowel. Panel (a) of Figure 4 shows the ACG and pooled ACF of the double vowel /a(100), i(112)/. The ACG contains evidence of two periodicities: 10 ms across the middle range of frequencies and 8.9 ms in the low and high frequencies. The pooled ACF contains a major peak at 10 ms and a second peak at 8.9 ms. The presence of two peaks is compatible with the experience of hearing two pitches in the stimulus.

The next step in the analysis is to use the evidence of pitch in the pooled ACF to guide a process that partitions the ACG in order to recover separate evidence of the two constituents of the double vowel. A general instance of the problem was discussed by Weintraub (1985) who outlined two solutions. One was subsequently applied to double vowels by Assmann and Summerfield (1990). The other, which generates more accurate predictions of the identification responses made by listeners, was implemented by Meddis and Hewitt (1992). They argued that the non-dominant pitch in many double vowels is estimated unreliably. Therefore, the dominant pitch should be used to guide the process of segregation.

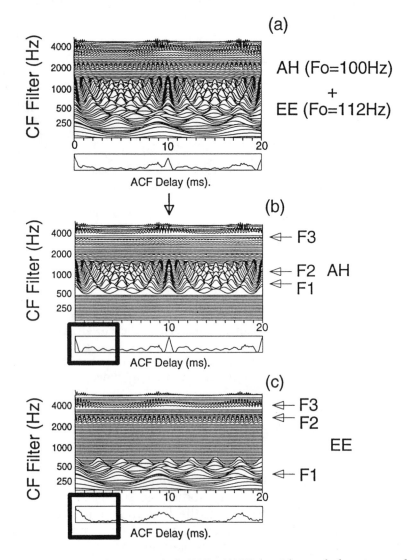

Figure 4. (a) Autocorrelogram of /a(100), i(112)/ with pooled autocorrelation function beneath; (b) Channels displaying the dominant periodicity (10 ms); arrows on the right show that these channels are excited by harmonics which define the first and second formants of the /a/; (c) Remaining channels; these channels are excited by harmonic defining the first and higher formants of the /i/. The heavy frames identify the "short-time" portions of the pooled autocorrelation functions (see Figure 5).

The procedure implemented in their model involves two stages. First, those channels that individually display the dominant periodicity are grouped together. They are used to provide evidence of the dominant vowel. Second, the remaining channels are used to provide evidence of the non-dominant vowel. These steps are illustrated in the lower two panels of Figure 4. Panel (b) shows the channels whose ACFs individually contain a peak at the delay of the largest peak in the pooled ACF. Most of these channels are clustered around the frequencies of the first two formants of the /a/ constituent. Panel (c) shows the remaining channels. They form three groups clustered close to the three formants of the /i/ constituent. Thus, by segregating channels displaying one periodicity from those displaying different periodicities, the analysis has segregated the channels dominated by the formants of one vowel from those dominated by the formants of the other vowel.

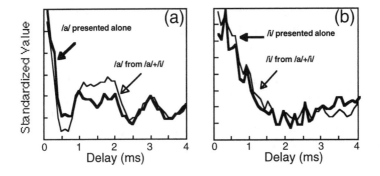

Figure 5. "Low-time" regions of pooled autocorrelation functions derived from single vowels (thicker lines) or by segregation from the double vowel /a(100),i(112)/ (thinner lines). The thin functions are those ringed by the heavy frames in Figure 4.

The final step in Meddis and Hewitt's (1992) model is to predict the identification responses that listeners make to the stimuli. The best match was sought between the low-time part of the pooled ACFs of each segregated pattern (framed in black in Figure 4) and low-time templates representing the five single vowels. Figure 5 shows that a close match is found in the case of the example stimulus, /a(100), i(112)/, used in Figure 4. In general, the match is not a close as this, because the formants of the constituents of many double vowels are not as widely separated in frequency as is the case with /a/ and /i/. The accuracy of identification predicted by the model is plotted as the filled circles in Figure 1, where it can be compared with listeners' performance plotted as the open circles.

Although, the model under-predicts listeners' performance when there is no difference in F_0, the match is impressively accurate overall.

Implications of the Model

Meddis and Hewitt's model embodies three claims about the segregation of competing sources. The first claim is that the process which computes the pitches that are present in a mixture of sources precedes source segregation and takes evidence from all channels indiscriminately. Evidence to support this idea has been provided by Darwin *et al.* (1991). They presented pairs of harmonic series with different F_0s simultaneously to listeners. One "harmonic" was shared between the two series. It was placed at a harmonic frequency of one series, but was mistuned slightly from a harmonic frequency of the other series. Listeners were required to adjust the repetition rate of a pulse train until its pitch matched that of each series in turn. Potentially, the shared harmonic might have been captured by the series of which it was a true member, and might not have contributed to the pitch of the competing series. In fact, this was not the outcome that was found. The shared harmonic influenced the pitch of the series from which it was mistuned. Therefore, the outcome is compatible with the idea that the pitches provided by a mixture of sounds are established *before* the mixture is segregated into its constituents.

The second claim made by the model is that segregation can be guided by the dominant pitch heard in a mixture of sounds. Evidence of a non-dominant source may be recovered by removing those channels that contain evidence of the dominant source. It is not necessary for the non-dominant source to assert its pitch explicitly. This is a good strategy for auditory analysis to have adopted, since it allows some evidence of a non-dominant source to be recovered at disadvantageous SNRs.

The third claim made by the version of the model described above is that the process of segregation involves assigning whole channels to one source or another. In Bregman's (1990) terms, the strategy is one of "disjoint" rather than "conjoint" allocation. A channel contributes to one source or the other, but not to both. However, the model does not assert this claim strongly. Meddis and Hewitt (1992) acknowledged that categorical assignment of channels to sources was not essential. They demonstrated that the model produced a broadly similar pattern of predictions, if the contribution of a channel to a source was reduced by attenuating the energy in the channel without eliminating it.

Limitations of the Model

Meddis and Hewitt's model of the perception of double vowels makes remarkably accurate predictions, given the great difficulty of predicting performance in speech identification tasks. However, autocorrelation-based models of pitch perception and source segregation have limitations. We shall discuss them first by considering the subjective quality of double vowels in two ranges of ΔF_0s, and then by considering the plausibility of implementing autocorrelation analysis physiologically.

Effects Found with Small ΔF_0s: $0 < \Delta F_0 < 1$ semitone

Double vowels which contain small ΔF_0s have a "gritty" timbre. Many do not give the impression of containing two voices with different pitches. If listeners are required to indicate the pitches that they hear (by adjusting the F_0 of a series of equal-amplitude harmonics until its pitch matches each of the pitches heard in the double vowel in turn), they tend to match to the mean of the F_0s in the stimulus (Assmann and Paschall, 1993). This outcome suggests that pitch-guided segregation is unlikely to underpin the abrupt improvement in accuracy of identification shown in Figure 1 between ΔF_0s of 0 and 1 semitone.

Instead, Culling and Darwin (1993a) argued that the improvement arises because of "beating" between corresponding harmonics from the two vowels. When the vowels have the same F_0, they are composed of harmonics with the same frequencies, but different phases. When the waveforms of the vowels are summed to create a double vowel, corresponding harmonics may either reinforce or partly cancel each other. As a result, each vowel distorts the spectrum envelope of the other. When the vowels have different F_0s, on the other hand, corresponding harmonics have different frequencies. Over the duration of the double vowel, they alternately come into phase and reinforce each other, and then out of phase and partly cancel each other. Thus, the amplitudes of low-frequency harmonics fluctuate over the duration of the double vowel. As a result, the first formants (F1s) of the constituents may be defined more clearly at one point in the stimulus than another. Moreover, at these points they may be defined more clearly than at *any* point in a double vowel whose constituents have the same F_0. Culling and Darwin argued that listeners can listen to the stimulus through a relatively narrow "temporal window", which enables them to base their identification responses on the segments of the stimulus where the constituents are defined best.

To test some of these ideas, Culling and Darwin created pairs of single vowels, one of which was composed of the odd harmonics of F_{O1} and the even harmonics of F_{O2}, while for the other, the assignment of harmonics was reversed. Thus, when paired to form a double vowel, the spectral envelopes of both vowels were defined by harmonics of both F_Os, so a process of pitch-guided segregation would not recover the constituents. Nonetheless, the accuracy with which listeners identified the constituent vowels improved as the difference between F_{O1} and F_{O2} was increased from 0 to 0.5 semitones. Performance was significantly below that obtained with the normal assignment of harmonics to constituents only for differences of 2 semitones or more. The outcome is compatible with the idea that consequences of "beating", rather than pitch-guided segregation, underlie the abrupt improvement in performance as the ΔF_O increases from 0 to 1 semitone.

Effects Found with Larger ΔF_Os: $\Delta F_O > 1$ semitone

When a double vowel contains a ΔF_O of about 2 semitones or more, listeners often hear two pitches, and the distribution of their pitch matches correlates quite highly with the shape of the pooled autocorrelation function (Assmann and Paschall, 1993). These outcomes suggest that, in this range of ΔF_Os, the model of Meddis and Hewitt provides a good functional description of the processes of pitch estimation and pitch-guided segregation.

However, the model requires modification in detail. In particular, it is unlikely that listeners segregate high-frequency channels excited by unresolved components to the extent implied in Figure 4. Certainly, listeners can judge whether the pitch defined by a group of resolved harmonics is the same as the pitch defined by a simultaneous group of unresolved harmonics (Carlyon *et al.*, 1992), provided the phase relationships among the unresolved harmonics produce a filtered waveform with a high peak factor.

However, it is less clear whether listeners can group a formant defined by unresolved harmonics when identifying speech. Again, evidence comes from an experiment of Culling and Darwin (1993b). They created double vowels in which the ΔF_O was carried either on only the F1s of the constituent vowels (the "same F2-5" condition where the same harmonic frequencies defined the higher formants of both vowels), or on all five formants (the "normal" condition). Listeners identified the constituent vowels equally accurately in both conditions for ΔF_Os in the range from 0-2 semitones. Only for ΔF_Os greater than 2 semitones was performance significantly more accurate in the normal condition. This result suggests that listeners can use pitch differences to segregate formants above F1 only when the ΔF_0 is large. Thus, the model illustrated in Figures 3 and 4 either overestimates the availability of periodicity in higher frequency regions, or overestimates the ability of subsequent analyses to use the information.

Physiological Feasibility

Palmer (1992) measured the patterns of neural discharges evoked by double vowels in auditory nerve fibres in anaesthetised guinea pigs. He computed neural autocorrelograms from the patterns of discharge and showed that they could provide accurate estimates of the fundamental periodicities in the stimuli. Palmer then applied Meddis and Hewitt's strategy for segregation to the neural data and showed that it yielded segregated patterns whose low-time pooled ACFs matched closely the low-time pooled ACFs of the isolated constituent vowels. Thus, the temporal patterns of neural discharges found in the mammalian auditory nerve contain adequate information to drive Meddis and Hewitt's strategy for segregation.

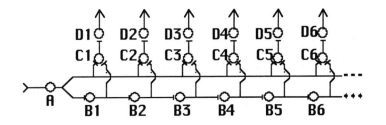

Figure 6. Hypothetical neural autocorrelator (redrawn from Licklider, 1951). A is the input neurone; B1, B2, etc., are delay units; C1, C2, etc., are coincidence detectors; the excitatory states of D1, D2, etc., display the autocorrelation function. If the input repeats with a period equal to (say) 4 delays, excitation is maximal at D4.

The question then arises of whether the auditory nervous system contains the neural machinery required to implement an autocorrelation analysis. Figure 6 shows part of the circuitry that would be required. It is a neural delay line and set of coincidence detectors proposed by Licklider (1951) for computing a neural autocorrelation function. A network like the one shown in Figure 6 would be required in each frequency channel, along with a mechanism for pooling coincidences at the same delay across different channels. A substantial limitation on the plausibility of autocorrelation-based models of pitch estimation is that the neural circuitry is elaborate and has not been found in the mammalian auditory system. A current issue in auditory modelling is to transform autocorrelation models into a physiologically plausible form without losing their conceptual simplicity or their power to predict the pitches that listeners hear in complex sounds.

Interim Summary

Notwithstanding these limitations, it seems likely that the major principles embodied in Meddis and Hewitt's model are those adopted in auditory analysis for segregating the low-frequency components of competing sounds that have different F_Os, provided the F_Os differ by at least 1-2 semitones. Those principles are (i) that the pitches of complex signals are estimated by an across-frequency analysis of the temporal periodicities contained in signals, and (ii) that sources whose F_Os differ are segregated by grouping energy that displays the same periodicity and segregating it from energy that displays other periodicities.

We now consider whether analogous processes are involved in the ability of listeners to segregate sources that occupy different positions in space.

Use of Inter-aural Timing Cues to Separate Speech from Noise

Consider a source of sound that is directly ahead of a listener in an open space (so that there are no echoes). The sounds that reach the listener's ears are more or less identical. Now imagine that the source is displaced 90° to the right. In this situation, sounds reach the left ear about 700 μs after they reach the right ear (because they have to travel further). They are more intense at the right ear (because sound intensity attenuates with the square of distance and because the head is an acoustic baffle and acts as a low-pass filter). Furthermore, the spectra of the sounds at the two ears differ at high frequencies because the detailed pattern of cancellation and reinforcement brought about by reflections among the surfaces of the pinnae depend on the direction from which sounds reach the ear. These inter-aural differences in time and spectral intensity provide cues to the location of the source. However, for relatively distant (>~1m) broadband signals, inter-aural differences in timing (ITDs) are the dominant cue; inter-aural differences in level (ILDs) and pinna cues play a role only when the direction indicated by ITDs is ambiguous (Wightman and Kistler, 1992).

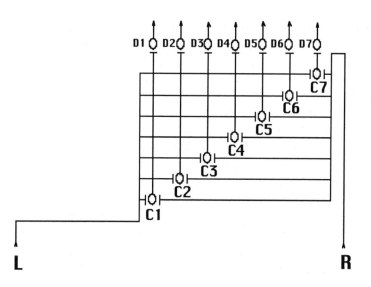

Figure 7. Hypothetical neural cross-correlator (redrawn from Jeffress, 1948). Inputs from the two cochleae (L, R) converge through delay lines onto coincidence detectors (C1, C2, etc.). The excitatory states of D1, D2, etc. display the cross-correlation function. If a signal reaches the left ear before the right, one of units C5, C6, or C7 is most active. If a signal reaches the right ear before the left, one of units C3, C2, or C1 is most active.

Now consider the situation where a talker and a source of noise are straight ahead of the listener. We measure the speech-reception threshold (SRT: the minimal SNR at which the speech can be reported correctly). We then move the noise source 90° to the right and repeat the measurement. We find that listeners can tolerate an addition 10 dB of noise (Bronkhorst and Plomp, 1988). The advantage occurs for two reasons. First, displacing the noise improves the SNR at the ear further from the noise because of the effect of head-shadow. Second, the speech produces a different ITD (0 µs) from the noise (700 µs). Individually, the ILD improves the SRT by 8 dB and the ITD improves it by 5 dB. Thus, the monaural effect (the 8-dB improvement in SNR at the ear further from the noise) makes a major contribution, but the binaural effect (the 5-dB improvement brought about by the introduction of different ITDs) is also material. In what follows, we shall be concerned with the way in which auditory analysis exploits a difference in ITDs between competing sources to segregate those sources. One reason for our interest is the possible similarity between the form of temporal analysis used binaurally and the one described in the first part of this chapter for segregating sources on the basis of differences in pitch.

The similarity can be seen by considering the neural circuitry needed to exploit ITDs for localising sounds. The circuit was sketched by Jeffress

(1948). Part of one of his diagrams has been redrawn in Figure 7. It consists of a set of delay lines and coincidence detectors and converts a particular difference in time of arrival at the two ears into activity in a particular member of an ordered array of nerve fibres. The network is similar to the one shown in Figure 6 which might underlie the use of pitch differences. Mathematically, the function computed by Jeffress' network is a cross-correlation. It is similar to the autocorrelation used in computing pitch except that the correlation is computed between signals originating in each ear, rather than between a monaural signal and a copy of itself. There is good evidence for the existence of such circuitry. It has been traced anatomically in birds (Konishi *et al.*, 1988) and physiological evidence for the existence of delay lines and coincidence detectors has been demonstrated in a mammal, the cat (e.g. Yin and Chan, 1988).

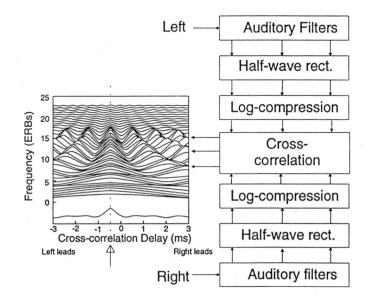

Figure 8. Steps taken to compute a cross-correlogram. The stimulus was a synthetic exemplar of the /a/ ($F_0 = 100$ Hz) simulated to originate from a source displaced 60° to the left of the midline, giving maxima in the cross-correlogram at -450 ms. The maxima are emphasised in the pooled cross-correlation function (isolated line at the bottom of the cross-correlogram).

The parallel between pitch analysis and binaural analysis is reinforced in Figure 8. The boxes on the right show the steps in the computational implementation of Jeffress' model that we use. The waterfall display on the left is the "cross-correlogram" that results from the analysis. The stimulus was the vowel /a/ simulated to originate from a source displaced 60° to the left of the midline. The cross-correlogram contains a prominent column of peaks at a delay of -450 μs, which is the ITD generated by the stimulus. The isolated line at the bottom of the cross-correlogram is the "pooled cross-correlation function", by analogy with the pooled autocorrelation functions displayed in Figures 3 and 4. It contains a clear peak at -450 μs. Such summation across frequency may be the process by which the lateralisation of broad-band signals is computed (Shackleton *et al.*, 1992). However, the issue is the subject of debate and more elaborate analyses of the patterns of peaks in cross-correlograms may be involved (Stern *et al.*, 1988).

We sought to answer the question: Do listeners segregate signals that give rise to different ITDs in the same way that they segregate signals that contain different F_Os? Putting the issue in more specific terms, we wanted to know whether cross-correlograms and autocorrelograms provide similar computational bases for the process of source segregation.

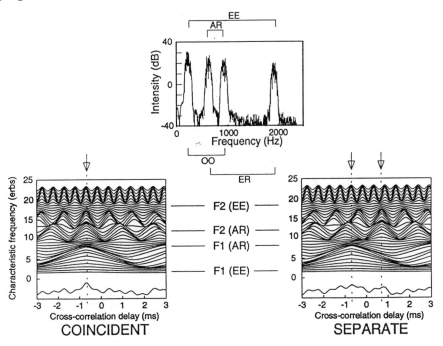

Figure 9. (Upper panel) Fourier spectra and (lower panel) cross-correlograms of the stimuli used in Experiment 1.

Experiment 1

The stimuli are shown in Figure 9. They consisted of four 150-Hz wide bands filtered from a pink noise. The bands can be grouped in different ways to give percepts of four whispered vowels. We compared two ways of encouraging listeners to hear particular vowels. One way was to increase the intensity of the two bands which define the "formants" of the vowel, relative to the other two bands. So, for example, to increase the prominence of the /i/ vowel we raised the level of the outer two bands.

The second manipulation is shown by the cross-correlograms in Figure 9. In the "coincident" condition, all four bands were given the same ITD of -700 µs. In the "separate" condition, the first and fourth bands were given an ITD of -700 µs while the second and third bands were given an ITD of +700 µs. The task for the listeners was to report the most prominent vowel that they heard on the left. If listeners group frequency bands that display the same ITD and segregate them from bands that display a different ITD, then they should be more accurate in reporting /i/ in the separate condition than in the coincident condition.

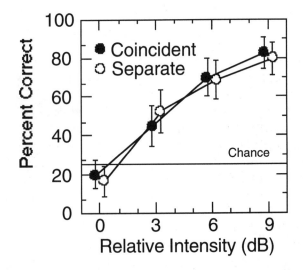

Figure 10. Results of Experiment 1 averaged over two listeners and four target vowels. Error bars show 95% confidence intervals. Accuracy of identification increases as the relative intensity of the target vowel is increased. However, there is no difference in performance between the coincident and separate conditions. Thus, giving the competing bands different ITDs did not help the listeners to separate them perceptually.

On each trial of the experiment any of the four pairs of bands could be boosted (by either 0, +3, +6, or +9 dB) and be either coincident with, or separate from, the other two bands. Average results from two experienced listeners are shown in Figure 10. The accuracy with which the "target" vowel was identified increased as the relative intensity of its pair of bands was increased. However, there was no difference in performance between the coincident and separate conditions. The result is clear-cut, therefore: Listeners did not group channels that displayed the same ITD, and separate them from channels that displayed a different ITD.

Experiment 2

The question therefore arises of what binaural computation is performed to exploit a difference in inter-aural timing between competing sounds. Some light is thrown upon the issue by the experiment whose stimuli are illustrated in Figure 11.

We presented a pink noise to each ear. The noises were identical, except that the phase of the frequency components in a mid-frequency band is shifted by π radians. The cross-correlogram of the stimulus contains a vertical ridge in the low and high frequencies at a delay of 0 μs, and a vertical valley in the mid-frequency region. What might one expect to hear when listening to this stimulus? The results of the previous experiment rule out the possibility that one would hear an /a/ (from the mid-frequency band) and an /i/ (from the low- and high-frequency bands).

In fact, listeners hear a vowel, plus a broad-band noise. The identity of the vowel depends on the frequencies at the edges of the inverted band of noise. Here, with the edges at 450 Hz and 1250 Hz, the vowel is /ɛ/. Figure 12 is the confusion matrix from an experiment in which the edges of the band were set to frequencies appropriate for the first two formants of five vowels. Data have been pooled from two listeners. The entries in the larger font show that the majority of responses to each stimulus were correct.

What auditory computation gives rise to this type of effect? Several explanations have been offered (Frijns *et al.*, 1986). A plausible explanation which we favour was provided by the results of the extensive series of experiments which have explored the phenomenon of the "Binaural Masking Level Difference" (BMLD). (See Durlach and Colburn, 1978, for a review.)

In the simplest of the many conditions used to explore the phenomenon, a broad-band noise is presented identically to the two ears. A signal, typically a pure tone, is also presented. In one condition (N_0S_0)

the tone is in phase at the two ears. In the other (N_0S_π), its waveform is inverted (i.e. it is given a phase shift of π radians which, in the case of a pure tone, corresponds to a time shift of half its period). The threshold for detecting the tone is lower in the N_0S_π condition by up to 15 dB depending on its frequency.

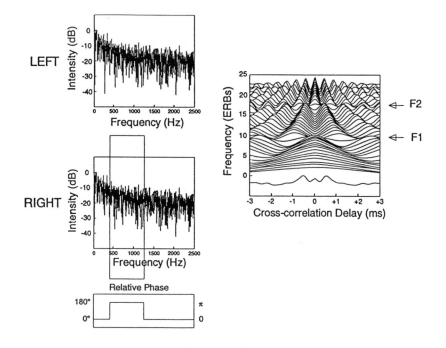

Figure 11. (Left top and middle) Fourier spectra, (left bottom) inter-aural phase spectrum, and (right) cross-correlogram of one of the stimuli used in Experiment 2. The sound presented to each ear is a pink noise. Inter-aural phase transitions of 180° have been placed at 450 Hz and 1250 Hz. The stimulus sounds like a pink noise accompanied by the vowel /ɛ/.

A model which explains this result, and a wide range of related phenomena, is the "equalisation-cancellation" account of Durlach. This account proposes that binaural analysis performs two operations to recover a signal that generates a different ITD and ILD from an interfering noise. The signals from each ear are "equalised" by shifting one in time and level with respect to the other. They are then subtracted one from the other. The equalisation step is necessary, because the condition $N_\pi S_0$ also results in lower thresholds than N_0S_0. The time shift chosen for the equalisation stage is the one that minimises the residual following the cancellation stage. It is easy to see that the procedure cancels both the signal and the noise in the N_0S_0 condition, but cancels only the noise, leaving the signal, in the N_oS_π condition. Thus, the threshold for detecting the signal is lower in the N_oS_π condition than in N_oS_o.

Figure 13 illustrates the results of applying equalisation and cancellation to the stimulus shown in Figure 11. The two steps were applied *independently* in each channel. The figure shows the size of the residual after cancellation plotted as a function of the centre frequency of the channel. The plot shows a crude spectrum containing two peaks that are aligned with the borders of the band of frequencies that received the inter-aural phase inversion in the stimulus. Thus, the peaks coincide with the first two formants of the vowel /ɛ/. If listeners had access to this "residual spectrum", they would identify the vowel as /ɛ/.

Responses

S1	AR	EE	ER	OO	OR
ar	69		11		
ee		48	10	19	3
er	2	2	73	1	2
oo		1	7	62	10
or	1		5	20	54

Stimuli

Figure 12. Confusion matrix showing the results of Experiment 2 with data pooled from two listeners. Stimuli were sounds like the one shown in Figure 11, but with inter-aural phase transitions at the frequencies of the first two formants of five different vowels. Correct responses (out of a total of 80) are shown in the larger font. Listeners identified each of the five "vowels" with an accuracy significantly greater than chance.

Reference to the cross-correlogram in Figure 11 shows that the residual spectrum is shaped in the way that it is for the following reasons. In the low and high frequencies, almost perfect cancellation of the noise is possible, with no time shift required in the equalisation stage. In the middle band, a time shift in each channel of half the period of the CF of that channel cancels most of the noise. Cancellation is not perfect because auditory filters have bandwidths that are greater than zero, so each channel contains a small spread of frequencies, and there is no one value of the time shift that cancels all of them perfectly. However, the problem of optimising the time shift is serious only in those channels that span the borders between the bands of noise. Consider a channel that is centred on the border at 450 Hz. The energy in this channel at frequencies below 450 Hz is in-phase and requires no time shift for cancellation, while the energy above 450 Hz is half a period out of phase and requires a time shift of 2.2 µs for cancellation. Thus there is no time shift that fully cancels the interaural difference in the channel, and a large residue remains and appears as a peak in the residual spectrum. The same problem arises in channels close to the upper edge of the inverted band of noise.

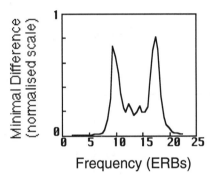

Figure 13. The "residual spectrum" that remains after applying equalisation and cancellation to each channel of the stimulus shown in Figure 11. Peaks are found in the residual spectrum at the frequencies of the two inter-aural phase transitions. It is argued that these peaks are interpreted as the first two formants of a vowel (/ɛ/ in this example).

Discussion

The results of the two experiments are clear. Experiment 1 shows that listeners cannot segregate spatially separate sources by grouping channels that contain a common pattern of inter-aural timing and by separating them from channels that display a different pattern. The results of Experiment 2, in contrast, show that listeners can carry out within-channel cancellation. In Experiment 2, the process generated the percept of a vowel from an artificial stimulus. More usually, the process recovers the weaker of two signals within each channel. The reason why the process could not help segregate the vowels in Experiment 1 is that there was no overlap of energy from the two vowels within any channel.

Comparison of Monaural and Binaural Segregation

We have reviewed evidence that monaural processes of pitch perception and binaural processes of localisation entail similar types of computation in auditory analysis. Both use temporal patterning in the outputs of auditory filters. Both may involve the pooling of temporal information across frequency: the one to estimate the pitches of sources; the other to estimate their locations.

However, the experiments described in this chapter demonstrate that qualitatively different computations are used to *separate* sources which give rise to different F_Os, compared to sources which give rise to different ITDs. In segregating sources with different F_Os, listeners group energy from different frequency regions that display the same periodicity; the model of Meddis and Hewitt (1992) proposes that they assign channels to one source or the other. In comparison, in segregating sources with different ITDs, listeners are not able to group energy in different frequency regions that display the same pattern of interaural timing; instead, they perform within-channel subtraction, removing evidence of the more intense source to reveal evidence of the less intense source.

The point is worth stressing: The residual spectrum in Figure 13 was generated by independent processes of equalisation and cancellation working within each channel. No across-channel mechanism was involved. Thus, despite the potential similarities of the demands of the two tasks, and the potential similarities of the bases of the solutions (autocorrelation and cross-correlation), auditory analysis has adopted different strategies.

It is not clear why this should be, but the reasons may be related to a body of observations which suggest that auditory analyses which partition the acoustic array into different sources are performed *before* processes which work out *where* sources are positioned. For example, Shackleton and Meddis (1992) have shown that a difference in ITDs between the constituents of a double vowel does not help listeners to segregate the constituents, but observations of our own have shown that a difference in F_O helps listeners to lateralise the constituents. It may be that auditory analysis uses robust evidence that more than one source is present, such as a difference in periodicity or onset time between different frequency regions, to partition frequency channels into separate groups. Only then do binaural processes work out the spatial position specified by each group. At this stage in the sequence of analyses, it would be undesirable to partition the groups of channels again. Accordingly, binaural processes of segregation operate within channels, rather than across channels.

Our uncertainty about why auditory analysis is organised in this way should not be allowed to distract attention from the major point illustrated in this chapter, which is that auditory analysis achieves robustness in the face of noise by using a variety of signal-processing strategies: (i) filtering the signal into many parallel channels with different centre frequencies, so that noise or hearing impairment in one frequency region need not affect analyses in other frequency regions; (ii) exploiting redundancy by pooling evidence across frequency channels to estimate important parameters, such as the pitches and positions (specifically, the lateralisations) of the sources that are present; (iii) partitioning the array of channels into different groups so that central analyses which perform pattern-recognising operations, such as determining the shapes of the spectral envelopes of speech sounds, obtain their evidence from channels providing a clear display of important properties such as formant peaks; and (iv) exploiting the fact that we have two ears to sample the signal at different points in space, so as to be able to subtract evidence of a more intense source to reveal evidence of a weaker source.

Acknowledgements

Our understanding of the issues raised in this chapter has benefited greatly from discussions with Alan Palmer, Peter Assmann, Ray Meddis, and Trevor Shackleton.

References

Assmann, P.F. & Paschall, D.D. (1993). Perception of concurrent vowels: Pitch judgements. *Abstracts of the XVIth Midwinter Meeting of the Association for Research in Otolaryngology* (p. 65).

Assmann, P.F. & Summerfield, A.Q. (1990). Modelling the perception of concurrent vowels: Vowels with different fundamental frequencies. *Journal of the Acoustical Society of America, 88*, 680-697.

Bregman, A.S. (1990). *Auditory scene analysis.* Cambridge, MA: MIT Press.

Brokx, J.P.L. & Nooteboom, S.G. (1982). Intonation and the perceptual separation of simultaneous voices. *Journal of Phonetics, 10*, 23-36.

Bronkhorst, A.W. & Plomp, R. (1988). The effect of head-induced interaural time and level differences on speech intelligibility in noise. *Journal of the Acoustical Society of America, 83*, 1508-1516.

Carlyon, R.P, Demany, L., & Semal, C. (1992). Detection of across-frequency differences in fundamental frequency. *Journal of the Acoustical Society of America, 91*, 279-292.

Culling, J.F. & Darwin, C.J. (1993a). Perceptual and computational separation of simultaneous vowels: Cues from low-frequency beating. Submitted to the *Journal of the Acoustical Society of America* (in press).

Culling, J.F. & Darwin, C.J. (1993b). Perceptual separation of simultaneous vowels: Within- and across-formant grouping. *Journal of the Acoustical Society of America* (in press).

Darwin, C.J., Buffa, A., Williams, D., & Ciocca, V. (1991). Pitch of dichotic complex tones with a mistuned frequency component. In Y. Cazals, L. Demany, & K. Horner (Eds.), *Auditory physiology and perception* (pp. 223-229). Oxford: Pergamon.

Durlach, N.I. & Colburn, H.S. (1978). Binaural phenomena. In E.C. Carterette & M.P. Friedman (Eds.), *Handbook of perception Vol. IV: Hearing* (pp. 365-466). New York, Academic.

Frijns, J.H.M., Raatgever, J, & Bilsen, F.A. (1986). A central spectrum theory of binaural processing: The binaural edge pitch revisited. *Journal of the Acoustical Society of America, 80*, 442-451.

Jeffress, L.A. (1948). A place theory of sound localization. *Journal of Comparative Physiology and Psychology, 41*, 35-39.

Konishi, M., Takahashi, T.T., Wagner, H., Sullivan, W.E., & Carr, C.E. (1988). Neurophysiological and anatomical substrates of sound localization in the owl. In G.M. Edelman, W.E. Gall, & W.M. Cowan (Eds.), *Auditory function* (pp. 721-746). New York: Wiley.

Kryter, K.D. (1985). *The effects of noise on man* (2nd ed.). London: Academic.

Licklider, J.C.R. (1951). A duplex theory of pitch perception. *Experientia, 7*, 128-133.

Meddis, R. & Hewitt, M.J. (1991). Virtual pitch and phase sensitivity of a computer model of the auditory periphery: I. Pitch identification. *Journal of the Acoustical Society of America, 89*, 2866-2882.

Meddis, R. & Hewitt, M.J. (1992). Modeling the identification of concurrent vowels with different fundamental frequencies. *Journal of the Acoustical Society of America, 91*, 233-245.

Meddis, R., Hewitt, M.J., & Shackleton, T.M. (1990). Implementation details of a computational model of the inner hair-cell/auditory-nerve synapse. *Journal of the Acoustical Society of America, 87*, 1813-1818.

Palmer, A.R. (1992). Segregation of the responses to paired vowels in the auditory nerve of the guinea-pig using autocorrelation. In M.E.H. Schouten (Ed.), *The auditory processing of speech* (pp. 115-124). Berlin: Mouton de Gruyter.

Patterson, R.D., Holdsworth, J., Nimmo-Smith, I., & Rice, P. (1988). *SVOS Final Report: The auditory filterbank.* (APU Report 2341). Cambridge: Applied Psychology Unit.

Scheffers, M.T.M. (1983). *Sifting vowels: Auditory pitch analysis and sound segregation.* Unpublished doctoral dissertation, University of Groningen, Groningen.

Shackleton, T.M. & Meddis, R. (1992). The role of interaural time differences in the improvement in identification of concurrent vowel pairs. *Journal of the Acoustical Society of America, 91*, 3579-3581.

Shackleton, T.M., Meddis, R., & Hewitt, M.J. (1992). Across frequency integration in a model of lateralization. *Journal of the Acoustical Society of America, 91*, 2276-2279(L).

Stern, R.M., Zeiberg, A.S. & Trahiotis, C. (1988). Lateralization of complex binaural stimuli: A weighted-image model. *Journal of the Acoustical Society of America, 84*, 156-165.

Weintraub, M. (1985). *A theory and computational model of monaural auditory sound segregation.* Unpublished doctoral dissertation, Stanford University, Stanford, CA.

Wightman, F.L. & Kistler, D.J. (1992). The dominant role of low-frequency interaural time differences in sound localization. *Journal of the Acoustical Society of America, 91,* 1648-1661.

Yin, T.C.T. & Chan, J.C.K. (1988), Neural mechanisms underlying interaural time sensitivity to tones and noise. In G.M. Edelman, W.E. Gall, & W.M. Cowan (Eds.), *Auditory function* (pp. 385-430). New York: Wiley.

Multimodal Human-Computer Interface 16

Jean Caelen

Institut de la Communication Parlée, CNRS URA 368,
INPG and Université Stendhal, 46 avenue F. Viallet
F-38031 GRENOBLE Cédex 1, France

This paper presents problems, concepts and principles concerning the design of multimodal human-machine interfaces that implement speech recognition and speech synthesis in real contexts: Modality relevance in the human factors area, context of interaction (exclusive, concurrent, alternative, and synergistic), event management with respect to coherence, chronology, the redundancy of events, the interpretation of the cross-information (co-reference phenomena), and adequacy in meaning representation. Taxonomies for interfaces and applications are proposed in order to discuss some of these issues, and we provide a possible solution for solving the co-reference problem between modes. Concepts are illustrated by an example: *ICPdraw* is a drawing application which has a multimodal interface (voice + gesture). The ICPdraw architecture is described in detail, especially with respect to event management and the interpretation of multimodal information. Its multilayered organisation is structured as follows: Dedicated hardware for speech recognition and synthesis, as well as for gestures (if any), low-level event servers (speech, mouse and keyboard), an event manager for mixing multimodal information, a dialogue controller, and a high level communication interface with the application.

There are several situations where a computer assists in human tasks or human "communication" (the latter term should be used with caution):
1. The machine acts as a *mediator* — it enables long-distance communication between people working together or collaborating on an objective (via "groupware", Pankoke and Babatz, 1989, or by teleconferencing, Stefik *et al.*, 1989). In this situation, the documents which are exchanged or manipulated should be multimedia to be fully informative.

2. The machine animates a *virtual reality* by extending human creative or expressive capabilities. The user is immersed in a world with which he or she interacts. Currently, this interaction is mainly gestural. However, in the near future, language may be used as well (Brooks, 1988).

3. The machine acts as a partner — it *collaborates* with the user on a given task using dialogue to understand user objectives or even user intentions. This may increase the efficiency of the work session (Vernant, 1992).

In all these cases, the interaction between humans and machines can be conceived to be multi-sensory (Coutaz and Caelen, 1990). Such interactions can be said to be multimodal, if they meet two conditions. First, the interaction should draw on several human sensory and motor modalities (or *modes*), such as vision, speech (spoken and heard) and gesture (movement, pointing, writing, drawing) in a simultaneous and cooperative way. Second, the machine must understand and interpret the information carried by several input-output devices (called *medias*) (Collectif, 1991, 1992).

Please note that the mere presence of several independent modes does not yield an efficient interaction. The software architecture must be designed to allow cooperation among these modes. Functionally, this means that the software must be able to accept a typical multimodal message such as "put that there", where *speech* is used to give the command and *mouse gestures* are used to designate an object ("that") and a location ("there"). This type of message, multi-sensory in essence, can be interpreted only by merging the spoken and gestural information. This *"fusion"* thus gives rise to the problem of intermodal temporal and intermodal spatial references. This problem may be resolved through a complex interpretation of multimodal events.

For the human-computer interface (HCI) designer, situations 1, 2 and 3 (above) show common characteristics, and the corresponding systems should therefore use common modules. For example, the multimedia level which involves the *transmission of information* is the lowest level and is common to all three situations. Above the transmission level however, situations differ in their management and interpretation of input and output information.

In situation 1 (mediation), the information management may be synchronous (e.g. for word processing groupware) or asynchronous (e.g. for a mail-box application) (Bastide and Palenque, 1992). Here, the second level concerns human-computer dialogue, which can be more or less sophisticated. The third level concerns the management of the participant's roles, which in turn determine the rights and privileges attached to the shared objects of the application.

In situation 2 (virtual reality), the user's behaviour is favoured over the dialogue itself, which is then reduced to a basic action-reaction scheme.

In situation 3 (task collaboration), the opposite occurs. Here the user-system relationship (or more precisely, the operator-task relationship) is favoured, since the user is alone in interacting with the machine. The machine's communication capabilities should therefore be modelled on human communication in order to increase the efficiency and reliability of task execution.

We see that the refinement in the interpretation of multimodal information depends on the situation at hand. However, despite the variability in both these situations and the system's level of sophistication, a multimodal interface will involve three processes: *Mode management*, *fusion* (or merging) of the input information, and *fission* (or splitting) of the output information.

This paper focuses on these three aspects for multimodality (see also Caelen and Coutaz, 1992). For simplicity, the modes are restricted to voice and gesture. Multimodality is approached from two perspectives: That of the user and that of the machine (or more precisely, of the technology). Indeed, HCI is the meeting point of the two, and its design is a compromise between ergonomic requirements and technological constraints.

Elements of Ergonomics

Multimodal HCI gives rise to some new ergonomic problems concerning the available communication modes, *i.e.*, speech, gesture, vision, etc. In particular, it raises a question concerning the *adequacy* between a given mode and the user objectives and reasoning (Scapin, 1986; Barthet, 1988), a question which is added to the traditional interface questions of adequacy of representation and of processing. Specifically, the question of the adequacy of the modes concerns the sensory and motor modalities by themselves, as well as their optimum use with respect to a given task, the cognitive load it imposes, the mental representation it employs, the user type that it attempts to accommodate, and the like.

In terms of an overall and generalised schema, these interface requirements may be represented as follows:

H	<->	W	+	m
sensory modalities				modes
representations		scripts, frames		
reasoning				processing

H represents the human user (or operator), **m** the machine of which the user has only an abstract representation and **W** the world he or she perceives (metaphorical, real or virtual), which gives meaning to his/her representations. The essential requirement is that the sensory and motor modalities of **H** must match the modes of **m,** and that his/her reasoning must match **m**'s processes.

This means that a plan for *multimodal human-computer interaction —* as it derives from human multi-sensory capacity — must take into account the following factors:
- The use of modes and mode adequacy to the task,
- Interaction strategies adapted to user competence and performance,
- Management of low-level events (such as coherence, chronology, redundancy, etc.), given the limits of human perceptive and motor capacities,
- Common levels of abstraction and representation,
- Multimodal presentation and points of view,
- And more generally, a user-based (not machine-based) cognitive model.

Within such a multimodal interface, the user should be able to perceive (at the interface level) a reflection of the machine's data and task structures. In the past, these structures were imposed by technological constraints. Today however, *the focus is on the user,* and ergonomic constraints tend to replace technological constraints. We are now at the other end of the spectrum, and the current question concerns the degree to which the structure of the HCI should model user behaviour. As applied to the question of speech synthesis and speech recognition, the essential question is *how much speech is optimal for human-computer interaction in a given task situation.*

Some elements of an answer to this question derive from the fact that the user has an intention, an objective and that his/her activity is planned to some degree (depending on training, experience with the task, practice or know-how), and that it can be re-organised according to the constraints imposed by the machine. The user also has preferences, habits and idiosyncrasies. Current observations show that new "gestural habits" emerge for mouse users. These habits are often far from optimal, and in some cases, language may well be a more appropriate communication medium than gesture. Let us now turn to these issues, and analyse them in terms of two types of operating mode: Language-based modes and non-language-based modes.

Language-based Modes

Global studies of mode usage that evaluate multimodal HCIs in terms of their efficiency, reliability and flexibility are not available, since such interfaces do not yet exist outside a few laboratory situations. However, partial experiments show that speech is desirable in certain situations. Here are some conclusions regarding HCIs that use speech as input (Brandetti *et al.*, 1988; Falzon, 1990):

- User satisfaction depends on socio-professional category.
- The learning of the interface is usually faster.
- Error-repair is usually more efficient. But —
- The context may be restrictive (noise, confidentiality, etc.).
- The machine's linguistic level (that is, the level of language understood by the machine) requires an adaptation from the user.

The design of a "dialect" derived from natural language may thus be an appropriate HCI solution (as opposed to a sub-language, a formal or an artificial language), in order to facilitate user learning of entities and operations. Such a "dialect" would also be appropriate for activating the machine, since it can be so constructed that its lexicon is well-defined and that its syntax remains limited.

Such "dialects" have the same characteristics as human *"operative languages"*[1], which, in extreme cases, have almost no syntax and a very limited and specialised lexicon (Falzon, 1990). Operative languages are very much linked to the nature of the application. Conversely, public applications for vocal database queries involve great linguistic variety and elliptic phenomena[2]. Users adapt to the machine by simplifying their utterances. This leads to fewer ellipses or anaphoras, and to correct syntax (even if it is not required) (Morel, 1988, 1989). The same phenomenon occurs with respect to prosody (speech intonation and rhythm) in situations where subjects read texts out loud under intelligibility constraints (Caelen-Haumont, 1991). In such situations, it is observed that subjects accentuate the gaps between words, and even between syllables. On the other hand, verbal production is degraded with an increase in either work load or in cases where there is intense concentration on objectives.

These studies show that such restrictions in the use of speech are not only due to poor performance of speech recognition systems (Siroux *et al.*, 1989), since the languages recognised by the machine correspond to categories of operative languages. In fact, these limits seem to be linked to

---

[1] Language used in interactions that assist in accomplishing a given task.

[2] Ellipsis: The omission of one or several words that can be understood from the context.

the very characteristics of the spoken mode itself. Let us also note that the spoken mode is superior to the written mode in that the keyboard limits input speed and mobilises user sensori-motor resources — though it is possible that the introduction of the numeric pad for input may still modify this situation (Faure, 1993).

Non-language-based Modes

Gesture

Human *communication* almost always involves a language, that is, an exchange of symbols (or relevant cues) via a code shared by the participants. *Interaction*, on the other hand, is a form of non-symbolic communication. To interact is to emit commands, or to take actions and to receive stimulations. Gesture is clearly a form of interaction (to push a button, for example), but it is not necessarily a form of communication in the strict sense of the term.

The fact that gesture was not introduced earlier as a mode of human-computer interaction may be attributed to two factors. First, the acknowledgement that it may interact well with other modes is only recent. In fact, human gesture control is transmodal, involving vision, hearing or proprioception (Hécaen and Jeannerod, 1975). Second, its capture requires a rather cumbersome apparatus (Rubine, 1991).

In gesture, action and perception are heavily intertwined. Any gestural action is also a perceptual event concerning the gesture and its effects. Hence, gesture is difficult to model. Humans have some 700 muscles, 110 articulations, and about a hundred degrees of freedom. Analogous to vision, there is a type of "gestural fovea", located at the finger tips, through which energy is exchanged with the environment. In order to make sense out of this complex human function, we can begin by distinguishing three main functions for gestures (Cadoz, 1992):

1. The *"ergotic"* function, which is a transformation of either energy or matter in the environment. Here, gesture is seen as an energy or a force.
2. The *epistemic* (or cognitive) function, which allows the acquisition of knowledge about the environment (notably through touch). This function has three parameters (T, P, K) where T = tactile, P = proprioceptive and K = kinaesthetic. These three terms are inseparable, since in order to explore an object's shape for example, one must emit an action on this shape involving all three parameters, *i.e.*, pressure, movement, etc.
3. The *semiotic* (communicative) function, which can be communicative in itself (sign language of the deaf), or which can

complement other languages (e.g. speech) to designate, to indicate rhythm, etc. This function may be found in several domains, such as in ideographs, drawing, writing, as language support, as an instrumental gesture, or in the form of linguistic communication (for example signed languages or totally artificial languages such as those used in direct-manipulation HCIs).

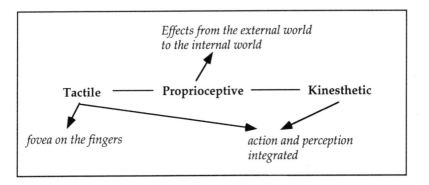

Figure 1. Epistemic function of the gesture.

Note that some gestures accomplish several functions simultaneously. For example, the gestures of an orchestra director mark rhythm (emphasis), indicate a musical expression (language), and tell the musicians when to start playing (command).

From this point of view, writing and scribbling are not classified as gestures, because only the results count, and not the manner in which they were produced. This raises the question of which has a semiotic function — the gesture itself or its trace on the input device? Similarly, should actions on a keyboard or a mouse (where the "how" and the "when" are disregarded) be considered as gestures?

To conclude, a HCI may use gesture in very different and even paradoxical ways. The user may go from an instrumental-type interface (e.g. a keyboard or a mouse), where gesture is both action and perception, to an interface where gesture is no longer significant by itself, but is *seen* (in the proper sense) and *recognised* merely as the trace of another meaning.

Vision

Vision via cameras allows the capture of gestures, and more notably, of facial expressions (Turk and Pentland, 1991). These expressions are identified using pattern recognition techniques. Vision of lip movement can also be used to support speech recognition. In general, vision used for the capture of gesture is only a technical issue, and does not fundamentally modify the role of gesture. However, vision in robotics is different if the robot is seen as a mechanical interface with the environment. In this case, vision becomes a perceiver of spatial movement and location in space, and is used for the control of gestures (movement or grasping) (Brooks, 1988).

Mode Adequacy

The paradigm of direct manipulation in graphical interfaces seems to have reached its limits (Buxton, 1993). Only visible objects can be designated, and the sequence of commands (that is, *selection* followed by *operation*) is counter-intuitive (i.e. opposite to the order found in natural language) and often inadequate. A multimodal HCI thus appears useful. Despite the fact that very few ergonomic studies have been carried out on these HCIs (since they are not yet available), a few general observations may be made about the adequacy and applicability of each mode:

- Spoken mode:
  — Input as: commands, macro-commands (isolated words, continuous speech)
  — Output as: help, examples, requests, explanation, suggestion (synthesis, pre-recorded sentences)
- Written mode:
  — Input as: identifiers, digits (keyboard, graphic pad)
  — Output as: Detailed explanation (screen)
- Gestural mode:
  — Input as: 2D or 3D designation (mouse, numeric glove, touch-screen), sign language (camera), ergotic action (interactive keyboard)
- Visual mode:
  — Input as: user orientation, user facial expression
  — Output as: graphics, images, animation (computer graphics and animation)

No one mode predominates systematically: The predominance of one mode or another in a given HCI situation depends on user competence and performance (motor, perceptual and cognitive), task, cognitive load, interaction context, communicational context, etc.

The Problems of Multimodal HCI

The problems specific to multimodal HCI, as compared to traditional HCI, stem from the diversity of input and output modes. The information on the various modes is interdependent and must be cross-analysed, cross-interpreted and cross-generated.

These problems concern three main areas. At the level of *mode management* (Bourguet and Caelen, 1992), questions arise concerning event chronology and event synchrony, the units or acts which constitute the information to be exchanged, and the context in which the interaction occurs. At the level where the *fusion and fission of information* occurs, questions arise concerning the morphosyntax of language-based interactions, as well as the semantics and pragmatics (e.g. co-reference problems) of all types of interaction. Finally, problems must be addressed concerning how *information is exchanged* between the various HCI modules, as well as between the HCI and the functional core of the application.

To each mode is associated a representational model of the information it carries. For example, the model for *gesture* may be vectors of space co-ordinates in time, while the model for *speech* consists of character strings corresponding to recognised words, sentences or even unprocessed signals. The sampling frequency may also vary from one media to the other.

Regarding only the input (the problem is symmetrical for output), a functionalist view shows different "layers" in HCIs, proceeding from the concrete level of signals to the more abstract level of action triggers. These layers are signal acquisition, automatic signal recognition, comprehension of the signs they carry, interpretation of the signs in a co-referential manner, and construction of an action-oriented multimodal message.

Through these different phases, information is first formatted, then converted to an abstract representation (which may differ not only among modes but also for one mode, among the different layers). It is finally transmitted to the highest-level, the dialogue "layer" (Taylor *et al.*, 1989). In the following sections, we shall examine in some detail each of these layers of information processing.

Mode Management

To begin with, it seems important to establish a clear distinction between events (the various events reflecting the physical organisation of actions) and information (or between their composing units).

Events and Information

Definition of an *event*: An event is the beginning or the end of a signal external to the machine. An event flags a perceivable (perceptible) change in one media. This definition is centred on the machine, or more precisely, on the input-output channels, which we call media, and not on the user.

Examples:
— Mouse events: click = k, press = P, release = R; move = 2-D trajectory = (sT, eT) (for start-Trajectory, end-Trajectory)
— Speech events: start-speech = sS, end-speech = eS, start-word = sW, end-word = eW

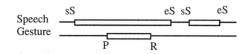

Speech and gesture can overlap along the time line.

Definition of an *information-bearing unit*: An information-bearing unit is a meaningful unit, but its meaning is different for the user and for the machine. From the user's point of view, the information-bearing unit is a semiotic unit (one that conveys meaning or distinctiveness), while from the "machine's point of view", this unit is a referential unit, i.e. one that refers to an event or an action.

Definition of an *act* **and of an** *action*: An *act* is a sequence of semiotic units emitted or received by the user. This sequence is carried by a signal (speech or gesture), which is delimited by flags specific to each mode (pauses for speech, button pressing and releasing for the mouse, etc.). The temporal organisation of this sequence is defined by a syntax. For speech, an act is a notion corresponding to that of a speech act (Austin, 1962; Searle, 1969). An *action* is an operation carried out by the machine, and manifested by a change of state which may (or may not) be perceivable by the user.

Examples:
— gestural information: Act = k(square).P(location).Trajectory.R (means "draw square, here, with this size"); Units = k(square), P(location), Trajectory.R; R = meta-gesture (flag)
— linguistic information: Act = speech act as defined originally by Searle; Units = lexical, syntactic, semantic, prosodic, meta-discursive.

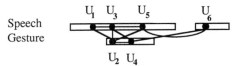

There exist semantic and temporal relationships amongst units. This is the general problem of *multimodal co-reference*.

The Interaction Context

Definition of the *interaction context*: The interaction context is defined by the triplet:

{*use of modes, information dependence, animation*}

where *use of modes* indicates if mode interpretation is sequential or parallel, *information dependence* indicates whether or not the information carried by the different medias depend on one another, and *animation* indicates world dynamics, that is, if the actions are continuous or punctual.

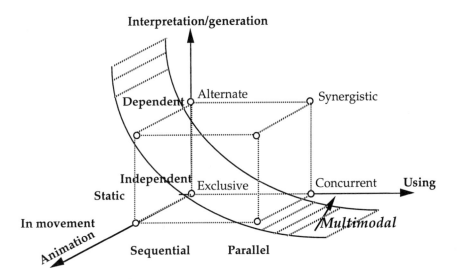

Figure 2. The field of multimodal systems: Alternate, concurrent and synergistic contexts.

For the purposes of this discussion, only the first two terms will be considered. Their combined values define four types of interaction contexts which we call exclusive, concurrent, alternate and synergistic (Caelen, 1991; Coutaz, 1992) (see Figure 2). The exclusive context characterises any system with at least two input or output medias which are used independently. This case is not truly multimodal and therefore lies outside the scope of this paper. The other three types of contexts are described in the following sections.

A. The Concurrent Context

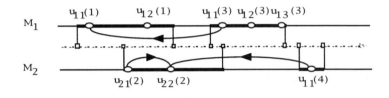

This context is defined, in terms of the *use of modes,* by the absence of temporal constraints, and in terms of *information dependence,* by the absence of cross-reference between units on different medias. The properties of this type of context are illustrated by the example below, which shows a resolution of anaphors and deictics[3]. The user's acts are given in **a1** to **a3**, and the machine's answers are shown in graphical terms. Anaphoric resolution is incorrect when the reference is expressed through another mode, and/or the deictics cannot be resolved.

Example of a false anaphor resolution:
a1: "Draw a circle" + k(green)   speech+gesture
a2: k(square).P(location).Trajectory.R   gesture
a3: "erase it" ("it" is an anaphoric pronoun)   speech

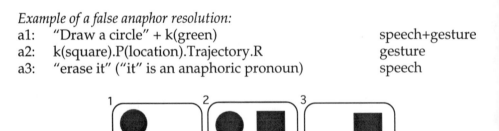

pink circle   green square   it = circle

B. The Alternate Context

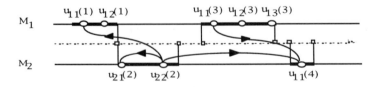

---

[3] Deictics: The showing or pointing out of something.

This context is defined, in terms of the *use of modes*, by $\text{Startu}_i(k) \geq \text{Endu}_{i'}(k\text{-}1)$ with media Mi $\neq$ Mi', and in terms of *information dependence*, by the absence of co-referential constraints between units. The properties of the alternate context concerning the resolution of anaphoras and deictics are illustrated by the example below (where **a1** to **a5** denote the user's acts, and the graphics represent the machine's answers). Here, anaphoric resolution is correct, when the reference is expressed through another mode and the deictics can be resolved. However, the alternate context, being rather cumbersome, may reduce the user's perceptual and motor co-ordination.

Example of anaphor and deictic resolutions:

a1:	"Draw a circle here"	speech
a2:	k(location)	gesture
a3:	k(green)	gesture
a4:	k(square).P(location).Trajectory R	gesture
a5:	"erase it"	speech

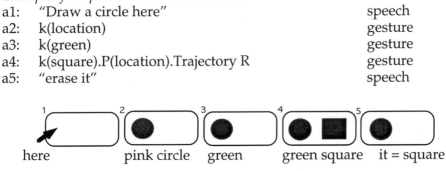

here   pink circle   green   green square   it = square

C. The Syngergistic Context

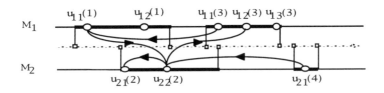

This context is defined, in terms of the *use of modes*, by the absence of constraints, and in terms of *information dependence*, by co-referential constraints between units. The properties of the synergistic context concerning the resolution of anaphors and deictics are illustrated by the example below (where **a1** to **a3** denote the user's acts, and the graphics represent the machine's answers). Here, both anaphoric and deictic resolutions are correct, when the reference is expressed through another mode and the deictics can be resolved. The synergistic context is also the most economical in terms of user perceptual and motor co-ordination. Although the synergistic context seems to be the best solution, it is problematic with regard to the processing of anticipated or delayed acts (as shall be discussed below).

Examples of anaphoric and deictic resolutions:

a1:   "Draw a circle here" + k(location)   speech+gesture
        co-referential acts are denoted by "+"
a2:   "green" - k(square).A(location).Trajectory R   speech+gesture
        acts that do not necessarily co-refer are denoted by "-"
a3:   "erase it"   speech

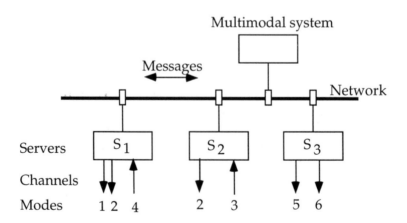

circle here   green + square   it = square

Formalisation

In the most general case, a multimedia system is not necessarily centralised. We assume that it uses distributed resources (Decouchant *et al.*, 1989), called media servers (see Figure 3). These servers may include voice recognition or voice synthesis hardware. There may also exist software for gesture recognition, and no specialised hardware may be in place, other than a mouse.

In this case, the multimodal system itself becomes a server with no media. This server may, in turn, be distributed. In this case, its functions are to manage modes, events and services, and to merge the information into some common level, in order to be able to transmit it to the application itself (the dialogue module or the shareware module, etc.).

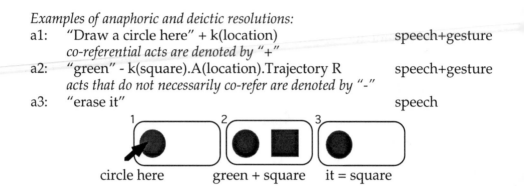

Figure 3. A multimodal system organised around media servers. (By definition, a media is a physical channel. A media differs from a mode).

Formally, the distinction between an event and an information-bearing unit is maintained. Let us define:

Event Structures

1. Let $a_i(k)$ be the ith act in mode k received (or emitted) by the multimodal system from (or towards) a set of servers {S}.
   We have:

       event-from-act: attached-to $a_i(k)$
               type: $e_i(k)$ = {Start $a_i(k)$, End $a_i(k)$}
               mode: k
               date: $t(e_i(k))$
               rank: i
               source / destination: {S}
       end-event

2. Let $u_{ij}(k)$ be the jth unit contained in $a_i(k)$
   We have:

       event-from-unit: attached-to $u_{ij}(k)$
               type: $e_{ij}(k)$ = {Start u_{ij} j(k), End $u_{ij}(k)$}
               act: a_i i(k)
               date: $t(e_{ij}(k))$
               rank: j
       end-event

Relationships between Events

1. *Chronological (noted $\leq$), monomodal*
   $e_{ij-p}(k) \leq e_{ij}(k)$ iff ® p≥1, $t(e_{ij-p}(k)) \leq t(e_{ij}(k))$

2. *Synchronised (noted $\approx$), multimodal*
   ®k≠k', $e_{ij}(k) \approx e_{i'j'}(k')$ iff $e_{ij}(k) \in$ [Startu$_{i'j'}$(k'), Endu$_{i'j'}$(k')] or $e_{i'j'}(k') \in$ [Startu$_{ij}$(k), Endu$_{ij}$(k)]

   with

   $e_{ij}(k) \in$ [Startu$_{i'j'}$(k'), Endu$_{i'j'}$(k')] iff $t($Startu$_{i'j'}$(k')) $\leq t(e_{ij}(k)) \leq t($Endu$_{i'j'}$(k'))

   where   ($\leq$) indicates partial order and
            ($\approx$) indicates equivalence relationships
   These relationships may also be applied to events of acts.

3. *Synchronous units (acts)*
   Two units (acts) are synchronous if they contain two synchronous events.
   ®k≠k', $u_{ij}(k) \approx u_{i'j'}(k')$ iff ∃ $e_{ij}(k) \approx e_{i'j'}(k')$ -same- for the acts a_i

The duration of two synchronous units (acts) is:

$$d(u_{ij}(k) \approx u_{i'j'}(k')) = \max[t(e_{ij}(k)),t(e_{i'j'}(k'))] - \min[t(e_{ij}(k)),t(e_{i'j'}(k'))] \text{ -same for the acts } a_i$$

Two Definitions of Present-time

1. *Instantaneous present-time:* The duration of the smallest unit at a given instant.

2. *"Density"of present-time:* The time interval defined by the duration of every synchronous act at a given instant. The density of present-time varies with time.

Particular cases:
- In alternate-type systems there is no synchronous act or unit.
- In concurrent-type systems, mode management is the same as in synergistic-type systems, except for the level of the merging of the information which does not exist.

Interaction Context in a Dynamic System

A system is said to be dynamic, if it can manage several interaction contexts. Each type of interaction context has been described above as a triplet:

{use of modes, information dependence, animation}.

1. Use of modes is determined by the action-perception loop and by the mechanical constraints of the system.

Example: put (object, location)
"put that here" < gd(that) < gd(here) => alternate
("put that here" ≈ gd(that)) < gd(here) => synergistic(s+)
("put that" ≈ gd(that)) < ("here" ≈ gd(here)) => synergistic
("put" < ("that" ≈ gd(that)) < ("here" ≈ gd(here)) => synergistic(g+)

   where
       " " = speech act
       gd = gestural designation act
       p+ = predominance of speech mode
       g+ = predominance of gestural mode

In this last case, gesture punctuates speech and determines temporal granularity. Here, events are synchronous and the information is dependent. We conclude therefore that the interaction context is *synergistic* with *gestural predominance.*

2. Information dependence is determined by the semantic / pragmatic relationships among units.

Example:

dg(triangle) ≈ "move the circle" => *concurrent* context

Here, both acts are synchronous and independent, since the designated triangle does not co-refer with the circle from the speech act. We therefore conclude that the interaction context is "concurrent".

These few examples show that the interaction context may be inferred from the organisation and the contents of the acts. This means that it can only be determined indirectly.

Management Functions

To summarise, mode management consists of:

- The capture of events from the media servers (inversely to the media servers for output).
- The building of event structures and information structures.
- The management of the interaction context, as a function of information type and of knowledge transmitted by adjacent levels (fusion module or dialogue module, for example).
- The updating of a history of this context.
- The use of knowledge on the user's sensory-motor characteristics (reaction-time, modal preferences, etc.).

The Fusion and the Fission of Information

The core problem in multimodal HCIs concerns the fusion (for input) and the fission (for output) of the intermodal information. The module dealing with fusion (or, respectively, fission) links the module for mode management (which is lower) to the module dealing with dialogue (which is higher). The latter has well-defined functions in multimodal HCIs.

These functions are to:

- Build a semiotic world of communication (metaphors, languages, etc.).
- Structure and organise communication.
- Manage and dynamically control the cooperative interaction.
- Repair communicational errors.
- Provide help in learning, guidance in the task, etc.

The necessity for a distinct fusion module has been questioned (Gaiffe *et al.*, 1991). Indeed, every one of its functions could be placed in the dialogue module instead, in which case the dialogue module would encompass the analysis of low-level information and its fusion. What are the arguments in favour of a distinct fusion module for multimodal HCIs? This is a very broad question. We propose to restrict it to the following points.

Fusion strategy. *When* is the fusion to occur? As soon as possible (in terms of a bottom-up strategy)? As late as possible (i.e. time-delayed)? In stages? *How* is the fusion performed? Around a common meaning representation structure and a predominant mode? This would involve a "unifying grammar", i.e. a grammar insuring well-formedness and linguistic adequacy of the combined input. Or without predominant mode? This would imply the use of a multimodal grammar, using a general action theory with no common structure. *Where* (i.e. in which module) is the fusion performed? Is it centralised in the dialogue module or is it performed in a distributed and progressive manner throughout the different modules?

Fusion criteria. Another question concerns the criteria for fusing information events. Should they be fused with regard to temporal proximity (e.g. according to sensory-motor rules)? Should the determining criterion be structural consistency and or semantic completeness? Should it be semantic isotopy (similarity/identity)? Or should one proceed by action logic or by intentional logic (Cohen, 1978, 1979), (Searle, 1983)? Should fusion emerge as a function of the interaction context or as a function of user performance (Valot and Amalberti, 1991)?

The scope of this paper does not allow a detailed review of each of these points. Only a few of the most relevant issues are examined below, mostly for illustrative purposes. To exemplify reference resolution, and in order to open the discussion, let us examine a few typical cases of simple multimodal commands.

Types of Reference

1. Reference to a Set of Objets

Let the speech act *"erase the triangles"* be synchronous with the gestural act of selecting (by surrounding) several graphical objects on the screen (as illustrated below).

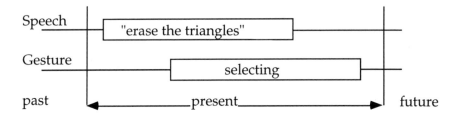

Using the above definition of density of present-time, a correct interpretation of these two acts depends on the user's intentions and on the context in which the acts were produced. This context may, in turn, be subdivided into the interaction context, the linguistic context, the discursive or dialogue context, and the action or task context.

These contexts all depend on one another. This is illustrated by the following example.

— If interaction context = *synergistic*, the message must be interpreted as a meaningful entity (erase "all the" triangles among those selected). The article "the" is then interpreted as a deictic and must be merged with the gestural information. Conversely, if the speech act had been "erase *these* triangles", the linguistic context would have imposed a synergistic context through the deictic "these" (at the risk of waiting for a future piece of gestural information).

— If the interaction context = *concurrent*, the interpretation yields two messages: On the one hand, the command to erase "the" triangles that were referred to in the past, and on the other hand, a selection of objects for some future action. The article "the" is then interpreted as an anaphora[4], and must not be merged with the gestural information.

— If there is an inter-modal conflict concerning the current interaction context, then this context may be questioned, and other contexts may be tried for interpretation. This would be the case if, for example, the set of objects designated by the gestural act did not include a triangle.

As this example shows, the ambiguity of the linguistic context and the indeterminate interaction context can give rise to considerable interpretation problems.

2. Reference to a Sequence of Objects

In the second of the two cases that were just discussed, the speech act "erase these triangles" was not interpreted as ambiguous with regard to gesture. Note, however, that the concurrent interpretation of the designating gesture results in a very repetitive mode of operation, since to

---

[4] Anaphora: Repeating, reinforcing element.

designate a sequence of objects, each object must be pointed to one after the other, e.g. using mouse-clicks.

The alternative is to bind information to present time (as defined above) in a synergistic context:

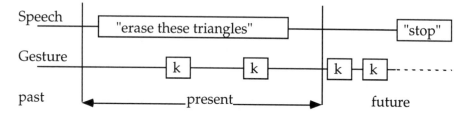

Here, a "end-of-present marker" or "end-of-act marker", such as a double-click or the verbal command "stop", sets the bounds of "present-time". This example illustrates that an ambiguity created by the task context can be resolved by the dialogue context.

3. Reference to a Moving Object

In the next case, the speech act "put it on the green square" refers to a moving object, which is virtually designated, since it is being grabbed using the mouse. Here the question is the following: Is the object referred to by the speech act really the same as the grabbed object?

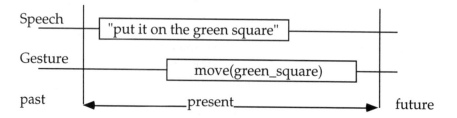

Another similar case has been observed in real situations, when the user wanted to optimise his/her actions by taking advantage of the available mode parallelism. For example, the user would say "put it on the green triangle", while at the same time changing the colour of the triangle, thereby destroying the reference. Here, both the task context and the interaction context create the ambiguity.

4. Direct Reference

In this case, the user may, for example, draw a curve using the mouse, and simultaneously change the colour of segments of the curve using speech. The reference of "colour" is only valid during the gesture and takes indirectly the value of the object instantiated through gesture.

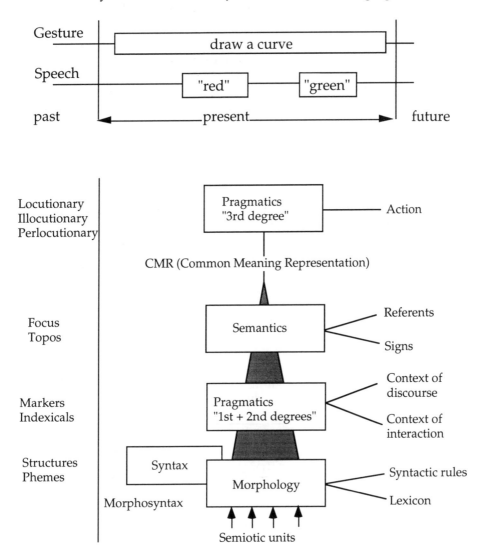

Figure 4. The levels of fusion in a multimodal system.

Levels of Fusion

The following examples illustrate the role of the fusion module, which is two-fold. First, it must make the interpretation as independent as possible of the contexts, and then it must allow a gradual resolution of references in cases of ambiguity. Furthermore, the fusion module as defined here can allow for new modes with no major modification of the dialogue module. This double role leads us to propose a gradual fusion of the information, starting at the morpho-syntactic level and ending at the semantic level. This is illustrated in Figure 4.

In this figure, fusion is performed on units collected from the density of present-time. It yields abstract representational structures that no longer include a modal component (CMR stands for common meaning representation). These structures are then transmitted to the dialogue controller. Here is a detailed review of each stage of the fusion process.

Morpho-syntactic Modal Analysis

This type of analysis is performed for each act detected in present-time. It yields a representation adapted to each mode, which describes both the structure of the components and the functional structure. For example, in the case of the command: ("erase the triangles" + gestural selection of objects), this analysis yields the following representation:

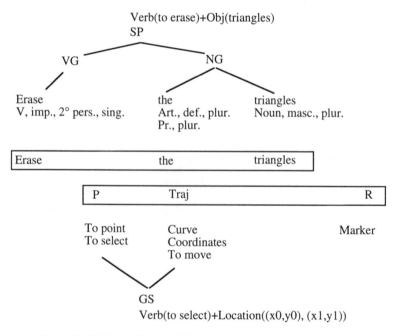

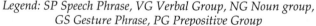

Legend: SP Speech Phrase, VG Verbal Group, NG Noun group,
GS Gesture Phrase, PG Prepositive Group

Pragmatic Analysis of the First and Second Degrees

This stage involves the intermodal binding of indices and pragmatic markers. This analysis results in the creation of links between free referential elements from one mode, and referential elements from other modes. The analysis also allows the creation links between acts.

Returning to the same example, assume that the following values are transmitted to neighbouring modules: interaction context = synergistic, dialogue context = directive, task context = current action.

Analysis of the index "the": The binding of the word "the" to the objects which are gesturally designated, whether as a deictic or as an anaphora, uses the following logical rules:

® (objects): object ∈ Domain

® (objects): object ∈ History of visible objects

Domain = Interior (Trajectory).

The resolution yields a list of objects, regardless of their semantic category (that is, regardless of the fact that they are triangles or not).

Analysis of the pragmatic markers: Prosody, "R" act. Prosodic analysis (which is outside the scope of this paper) helps to categorise a speech act. In the case of the example, a continuously descending melodic curve could indicate an assertive speech act. "R" is analysed as a marker indicating the end of a gestural act. These two information-bearing units indicate that the act is complete. It is therefore reasonable to assume that it forms an entity. Assuming a synergistic interaction context, we continue with spatio-temporal semantic analysis.

Spatio-temporal Semantic Analysis

Here, action and object schemas are instantiated, yielding a CMR (Common Meaning Representation). Complex mechanisms for semantic interpretation of natural language are involved at this stage (Sabah, 1988). These mechanisms use knowledge bases of actions and objects (see table, next page), as well as inference rules, in order to instantiate the schemas on the current situation. These various mechanisms are more or less linked to the application domain, depending on their degree of generality. The formalism for knowledge representation (see table) uses case-based (Fillmore, 1968) multimodal grammar. $ indicates a prototype or a class (adding the suffix S for semantic and C for syntactical). "Link" is an attribute used for linking two multimodal information. (For example, the lexeme "here" is linked to another mode designating a $Location.)

The Knowledge Base of Actions

Action: To erase
    Activation = double-click($SObj) | Verb($SErase)
    OBJ = NG($Dominant = $SObj) | click($SObj)
    Time = PG(prep($CTime).GN) | Adv($CTime)

Action: To put
    Activation = mvt-click($SObj) | Verb($SMove
    OBJ = NG($Dominant = $SObj) | click($SObj)
    Location = PG(prep($CLocation).NG) | Adv($CLocation) | click($SLocation)
    Time = PG(prep($CTime).NG) | Adv($CTime)
etc.

The Knowledge Base of Objects

Triangle: Kind-of geometric-object
    Size: AG($Dominant = $SObj) | mvt-click($SObj)
    Colour: NC($Dominant = $SObj) | click($SPalette)
    Coordinates: (x,y)
    Actions: {To erase, To put}
    Referential-World: artificial
    Semantic-Link = Synonym($Pyramid)
etc.

Lexicon for "Grammatical Words" and "Indexicals"

these:
    demonstrative = simple-click($Obj) | Demonstrative($These)
    Pragmatic-Link = Deictic($Obj)
it:
    personal-pronoun, plural = P-P($It)
    Pragmatic-Link = Anaphor($Obj
the:
    article-def., plural = Art-def($The)
    Pragmatic-Link = Deictic($Obj)
here:
    adverb of location = Adv-Loc($here)
    Pragmatic-Link = Deictic($Loc)
etc.

Rules: Rules instantiate action and object schemas from previously interrelated multimodal acts. Several types of rules may be distinguished:

•   Rules for the activation of actions using a search for the predicate (taken in a wide sense, that is, either a linguistic word or a defined gestural unit). In cases where two predicates are found, other rules are used to process either redundancy (whereby two schemas are instantiated) or conflict (whereby only one schema is kept).

•   Rules for the activation of objects using specialisation operations on the list of objects from the previous step.

•   Rules to refine object attributes and world activation.

•   Rules to instantiate the time and location attributes of actions, using a search through the lexicon and the syntax structure.

Solutions: The (many) hypotheses are transmitted to the dialogue controller, which acts as a link to the superior levels. These hypotheses are represented by a chained list of instantiated schemas.

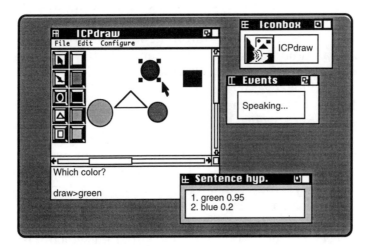

Figure 5. Example of an ICPDraw screen. It consists of four windows. The first window (called ICPDraw) is itself divided into a work-zone, a writing-zone (for written commands), and menus. The second window (called Iconbox) shows a logo. The third window (called Events) shows the status of the communication channels. (For example, this windows indicates when the user can use speech input.) The fourth window (called Sentence hyp.) shows the results of speech recognition. (The four best hypothesis are kept and shown in decreasing order of score.)

ICPdraw: An Example of a Multimodal HCI

ICPDraw is a MacDraw™-type application using multimodality (Caelen *et al.*, 1992). ICPDraw is object-driven. It offers a graphical tool-box and function menus, which can be activated using speech, writing or gesture (via the mouse). ICPDraw includes the usual drawing functions: Selection of (several) objects by either pointing, surrounding or oral designation, moving an object using either speech or mouse-dragging, changing the colour of an object, etc. Objects may be grouped and hidden. Their shape may be changed using "handles". The interaction context is synergistic.

Software Architecture

The system includes:
   a.   The functional core of the ICPDraw application.
   b.   The fusion levels.
   c.   Mode management.
   d.   Multimedia servers.

These modules are treated as UNIX™ processes, which run in parallel and communicate using a protocol (icp). Indeed, the fact that gestural and speech commands may be simultaneous requires a distributed architecture, based on the notion of independent "services". A secondary motivation for this architecture is hardware cost: Here, only one speech server is required for several machines.

The HCI is based on the X-Windows standard, which can manage keyboard and mouse events, but not speech events. In order to do this, a speech service was developed. It includes a signal server (the signal is made available on the entire network) and two client-processes, namely speech recognition and speech synthesis. Clients and servers both share a common memory and exchange data in synchronous fashion (management is controlled by semaphores). As is shown in Figure 6, the entire environment may be distributed on several machines.

The speech server is a background program which has two main functions. The first is to pick up the speech signal. This is done either when the signal is pending or through a reflex triggered when sound level is high enough. The speech server's second function is to send the signal on the network. (These processes are symmetrical for speech output.)

The client processes — recognition and synthesis — are generally "asleep". The speech server "wakes up" the recognition process as soon as a signal is available and ready for analysis. The application "wakes-up" the synthesis process as soon as an output message is ready. When their work is done, clients immediately send out their results, and return control to the server. The server then inserts these results (in incoming order) as external events in the X server's queue of events. The X client is then ready to receive the set of multimodal events which are available for the dialogue module.

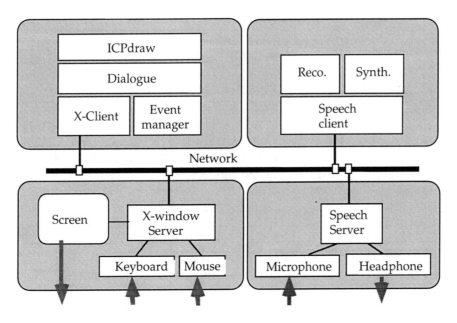

Figure 6. Components of the entire ICPDraw system in a distributed architecture under UNIX™.

Manipulation Languages

ICPDraw's abstract language for object manipulation is defined by the command syntax "Action($<arg_1><arg_2>...<arg_n>$)", to which a gestural or spoken component is attached. Here,

— Action represents an elementary task. It is denoted by the "predicate" (denoted by the verb) in the sentence.

— arg_i are the arguments of the action, of either type NG (nominal group) or PG (prepositive group). NG is usually an application object. In the case of speech, the adjectives are attributes of the object (such as colour, size, etc.), while in the case of gesture, the adjectives are designation or trajectories.

1. Oral Language

Every element of this language is optional. For example, the commands "draw green circle" and "no... green" are accepted forms. The grammar is defined as follows:

Action	->	V.NG1.Location2
Action	->	V.Pr
Réit	->	NG1.Location2
Rectif	->	no.NG1.Location2
Rectif	->	more.AdjT
NG1	->	Det2.AdjT.N.AdjC
Pr	->	{the}
V	->	{draw, move, erase, change, undo, select, duplicate, quit, etc.}
Det	->	{the, one, two, three, four, this, these, etc.}
AdjT	->	{large, small}
N	->	Obj
Obj	->	{square, circle, triangle, etc.}
AdjC	->	{white, black, blue, yellow, red, green}
Location	->	NG2 | LocP2 | LocA
NG2	->	LocP1.N.AdjC
LocP1	->	{under the, under this, on the, on this, besides the, besides this, etc.}
LocP2	->	{to the right, to the left, above, under, in the center, etc.}
LocA	->	{here, there, over there, towards here, towards there, around here, etc.}

2. Gestural Language

An artificial gestural language is added to the usual gestural commands found in direct-manipulation HCIs. This artificial language is formalised as follows:

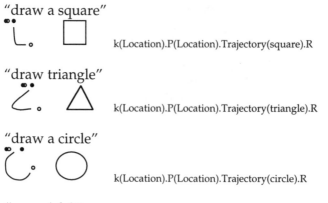

"draw a square"

k(Location).P(Location).Trajectory(square).R

"draw triangle"

k(Location).P(Location).Trajectory(triangle).R

"draw a circle"

k(Location).P(Location).Trajectory(circle).R

"erase (obj)"

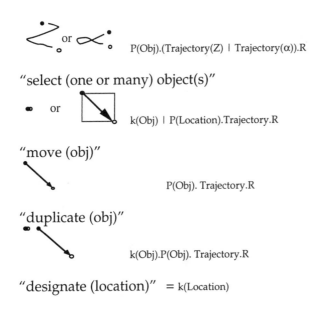

P(Obj).(Trajectory(Z) | Trajectory(α)).R

"select (one or many) object(s)"

k(Obj) | P(Location).Trajectory.R

"move (obj)"

P(Obj). Trajectory.R

"duplicate (obj)"

k(Obj).P(Obj). Trajectory.R

"designate (location)" = k(Location)

The commands may be typed, spoken or gestural (using the mouse). The module which processes natural-language input (whether types or spoken) uses sub-modules for the linguistic analysis of a command. These analysers yield the structure of the command's components (c-structure) and the command's functional structure (f-structure). They provide the four best solutions (as character strings). The analysers use a lexical functional grammar (LFG) and the speech recognition system developed as part of the Esprit Multiworks project (ESPRIT II project no. 2105). The speech recognition system uses Markov models for chained words (Virterby-Ney algorithm). The analysers are described in detail in (Reynier, 1990).

Operating ICPDraw

ICPDraw implements the methods described in the previous sections. Fusion is much simplified however, since the problems linked to reference resolution are limited. Event management is done through a blackboard which stores the events, units, acts and CMRs. A waiting loop is used for observation and blackboard management. Mouse events require two types of management. On the one hand, feedback on some actions must be immediate (example: selection changes an object's presentation to reverse video), and on the other hand, specialised recognition procedures require complete commands. The sampling granularity must also be adjusted in order to process cases such as "move this triangle", where the utterance of the word "this" is synchronised with a mouse-click.

Multimodal events are managed through a blackboard used by the manager. The manager has access to knowledge about the application (in particular, an image of application objects). It maintains a history of events, a history of instantiated objects (as a chained data structure), and it warns the application as soon as a command is ready.

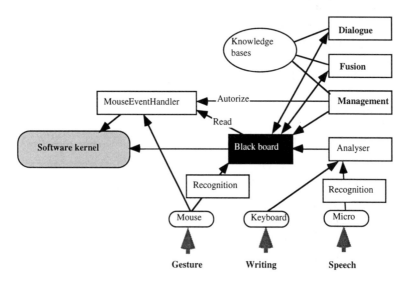

Figure 7. Operating ICPDraw.

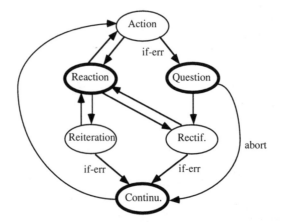

Figure 8. The dialogue model.

ICPDraw's dialogue strategy is entirely reactive (see Figure 8):

— If the interpretation of an act is correct, and if the action is executable, then the system's state is "reaction" (the system executes the user's command). The system then waits for a new command, which may be of the types "action", "reiteration" or "correction".

— If the act leads to an inconsistent situation, the system asks a question and switches to a "waiting" state (waiting for a correction command). The system does not allow for two consecutive errors, and switches to a "continuation" state (waiting for a new action). Deviations in the dialogue are purposely avoided, and are treated as an implicit abandon (and therefore as a return to a new action).

This leads to the following algorithm:

```
Dialogue
|     Introduction (choice(d))
|     Interpretation(Act, Action)
|     While Act "Quit" DO
|     |       If Act = error then Question(d)
|     |       |       Interpretation(Act, Correction)
|     |       |       |       If error then Continuation
|     |       |       |       Else Reaction
|     |       else Reaction
|     Reaction: Interpretation(Act, (Action OR Correction OR Reiteration))
|     |       |       If error then Continuation
|     |       |       else Reaction
|     Continuation: Interpretation(Act, Action)
|     End-While
End-Dialogue
```

where:
Interpretation(X, Y): procedure for building script X in context Y.
Question: Sub-dialogue for request.
Reaction: Execution of an act and waiting for a new act.
Continuation: Waiting for a new action.

Interpretation is done by instantiating action and object schemas. The command is executed if it is complete (and the result is visible right away). If not, then the system does not react.

Results and Discussion

ICPDraw is a platform application, implemented on a workstation (running at 25 MIPS). It offers chained-word speech recognition (which was developed as part of the Multiworks project — Esprit II no. 2105). The lexicon includes around fifty words, and syntax is limited. The station is powerful enough to allow for real-time dialogue (despite the fact that it also runs the speech recognition system).

ICPDraw can be used to test and validate concepts pertaining to both multimodal dialogue and distributed architecture. Regarding the latter, ICPDraw was instrumental in the design of signal distribution and processing on several work stations (client-server notion) which have no special hardware for signal capture or for speech recognition. Regarding multimodal dialogue, using ICPDraw helped uncover problems linked to simultaneous mouse and voice designation, especially in cases of animated objects (for example, lost reference, which happens when a vocal command describes an object, while a mouse command simultaneously changes that object's description).

Furthermore, ICPDraw will enable the study of use of various modalities. Such studies are necessary in order to identify if particular situations favour the use of one mode over another, and if users change their habits to really take advantage of multimodality. A somewhat restricted study (on about ten students) appears to show that multimodality improves the user's efficiency, since several commands can be executed in parallel. In particular, this parallelism is used to anticipate and to prepare drawing objects in advance. This means that planning strategies are optimised as a result of the new possibilities offered by multimodality. For example, a common strategy consists of creating several objects anywhere on screen using vocal commands ("draw a black circle", "a red one", "a green one", etc.), while simultaneously positioning them using the mouse. The user develops such an expertise in a short time. Furthermore, vocal commands are often very short and elliptic.

The use of this parallelism may produce unexpected side effects however, because commands may overlap and hence become ambiguous. Phenomena of desynchronised voice and gesture, repetition, etc., increase with cognitive load or imposed execution speed. The natural tendency is *not* to use a single mode, as might be expected. On the contrary, users tend to specialise the use of the different modes, where speech is used, for example, for repetition or for commands which do not require looking at the screen or precise positioning, and gesture is used for elementary and very reactive-type actions and also to get immediate feedback. This indicates that the two modalities co-exist and complement each other.

The path is ready for other, more systematic validations that already seem to justify further exploration of the multimodal "paradigm" (Bisson and Nogier, 1992) using HCIs that are more and more realistic (Gourdol, 1990; Bourguet, 1992; Condom, 1992).

Conclusion

A HCI is a link between two sets of structures. On the one hand, there are the various levels of knowledge about a world of reference (signs), and on the other hand, there are the various levels of abstraction of the software architecture. Changing levels (between representation, concepts and symbols for example) can be modelled as a two-axis process: The syntagmatic axis (the horizontal axis defined as the combination of signs as a function of time) which uses " dialogue", and the paradigmatic axis (the combinations of signs on the vertical axis) which uses "control". "Interaction" is manifested by a more direct relationship on the material system. This means that in interaction, both the number of syntagmatic combinations as well as the depth of the worlds are restricted, when compared to dialogue. Also note that an HCI is a link between the human environment, the machine environment and their common environment. This means that an HCI acts a captor, effector, transductor, (multimodal) mirror of the machine, (transmodal) mirror of the user and (meta-modal) meeting point of two.

The HCI designer must take into account the user's cognitive, sensory and motor characteristics, and must do so as early as at the stage of mode management. The fusion and the fission of information gives rise to problems typical of multimodal HCI.

Several aspects of multimodality have not been discussed in this paper. One of these concerns evaluation issues, which are as fundamental as design issues for real applications (Coutaz, 1990). These issues highlight the importance of the identification of various types of comprehension errors (Siroux *et al.*, 1989). These errors are due not only to the low performance of voice recognition systems, but to more fundamental phenomena concerning motor anticipation/concurrency *vs.* delay/hesitation, intermodal conflict and unexpected acts. Further studies concerning these issues are required.

Acknowledgements

Warm thanks to Nadine Ozkan, from the Institute of Speech Communication for her help with English expression, and to my Multimodal Interface colleagues from the French PRC "Man-Machine Communication" organisation for their help with discussion.

References

Austin, J.L. (1962). *How to do things with words*. Oxford University Press.
Barthet, M.F. (1988). *Logiciels interactifs et ergonomie. Modèles et méthodes de conception*. Paris: Dunod-Informatique, Bordas.
Bastide, R., & Palanque, P., (1991). *Modélisation de l'interface d'un logiciel de groupe par Objets Coopératifs*. Document de travail IHM'91, 1-10.
Bisson, P., & Nogier, J.F. (1992). Interaction homme-machine multimodale: le système MELODIA. *Actes ERGO IA'92*, Biarritz, 69-90.

Bourguet, M.L. & Caelen, J. (1992). Interfaces homme-machine multimodales: gestion des événements et représentation des informations. *ERGO-IA'92 proceedings*, EC2 (Eds.), Biarritz.

Bourguet, M.L. (1992). *Conception et réalisation d'une interface de dialogue personne-machine multimodale*. Thèse INPG (doctoral dissertation), Grenoble.

Brandetti, M., D'Orta, P., Ferretti, M., Scarsi, S. (1988). Experiments on the usage of a voice activated text editor. *Proceedings Euro-Speech'88*, ESCA (Eds.), 1305-1310.

Brooks, F.P. (1988). Grasping reality through illusion: Interactive graphics serving science. *5th Conference on Computer and Human Interaction, CHI'88*.

Buxton, B. (1993). HCI and the inadequacies of direct manipulation systems. *SIGCHI Bulletin, Vol. 25, n°1*, 21-22.

Cadoz, Cl. (1992). Le geste canal de communication homme-machine. La communication instrumentale. *Actes des Entretiens de Lyon*, CNRS ed.

Caelen, J. (1991). *Interaction multimodale dans ICPdraw: expérience et perspectives*. Ecole de printemps PRC "communication homme-machine", Ecole Centrale de Lyon (Eds.).

Caelen, J., & Coutaz J. (1992). Interaction homme-machine multimodale: quelques problèmes. *Bulletin de la communication parlée n°2*, 125-140.

Caelen, J., Garcin P., Wretö, J., & Reynier, E. (1992). Interaction multimodale autour de l'application ICPdraw. *Bulletin de la Communication Parlée n°2*, 141-151.

Caelen-Haumont, G. (1991). *Stratégie des locuteurs en réponse à des consignes de lecture d'un texte: analyse des interactions entre modèles syntaxiques, sémantiques, pragmatiques et paramètres prosodiques*. Thèse de doctorat d'état, vols. I and II, Aix-en-Provence.

Cohen, Ph.R. (1978). *On knowing what to say: Planning speech acts*. Ph.D. Thesis, Technical Report n°118, Department of Computer Science, University of Toronto.

Collectif IHM'91 (1991). *Groupe de travail interfaces multimodales*. Dourdan.

Collectif IHM'92 (1992). *Groupe de travail interfaces multimodales*. Paris.

Condom, J.M. (1992). *Un système de dialogue multimodal pour la communication avec un robot manipulateur*. Thèse Université P. Sabatier, Toulouse.

Coutaz, J. (1990). *Interface homme-ordinateur: conception et réalisation*. Paris: Dunod.

Coutaz, J. (1992). *Multimedia and Multimodal User Interfaces: A Taxonomy for Software Engineering Research Issues*. St. Petersburg HCI Workshop, August.

Coutaz, J., & Caelen, J. (1990). Opération de Recherche Concertée interface homme-machine multimodale. *In PRC communication homme-machine*, EC2 (Eds.), Paris.

Decouchant, D., Duda, A., & Freyssinet, A. *et al.* (1988). GUIDE: an implementation of the Comandos object-oriented architecture on Unix. *Proceedings of EUUG Autumn Conference*, Lisbon (pp. 181-193). October, 1988.

Falzon, P. (1990). *Ergonomie Cognitive du Dialogue*. Grenoble: PUG.

Faure, C. (1993). *Communication écrite, concepts et perspectives*. Journée du GDR-PRC "Communication Homme-Machine", Montpellier, EC2 (Eds.).

Fillmore, C.J. (1968). The Case For Case. In E. Bach & R. Harms (Eds.), *Universals in Linguistic Theory* (pp 1-90). New York: Holt, Rinehart & Winston.

Gaiffe, B., Pierrel, J.M., & Romary, L. (1991). *Reference in a multimodal dialogue: Towards a unified processing*. Proceedings EUROSPEECH'91, 2nd Euopean Conference on Speech Communication and Technology, Genova, Italy.

Gourdol, A. (1991). *Voice Paint*. Rapport de DEA, UJF Grenoble.

Grice, H.P. (1975). Logic and conversation. In P. Cole & J. L. Morgan (Eds.), *Syntax and Semantics, 3:Speech Acts* (pp. 41-58). New York: Academic Press.

Hécaen, H., & Jeannerod, M. (1975). *Du contrôle moteur à l'organisation du geste*. Paris: Masson.

Morel, M.A. (1988). *Analyse linguistique d'un corpus de dialogues homme-machine.* Paris: Publications de la Sorbonne Nouvelle, Tomes I et II.

Morel, M.A. (1989). Analyse linguistique d'un corpus, Deuxième corpus: Centre d'Information et d'orientation de l'université de Paris V. Paris: *Publications de la Sorbonne Nouvelle,* Paris.

Pankoke, E., & Babatz, U. (1989). *Computer based Group Communication, the AMIGO Activity Model.* Ellis Horwood.

Reynier, E. (1990). *Analyseurs linguistiques pour la compréhension de la parole.* Thèse de doctorat INPG, Grenoble.

Rubine, D. (1991). *The automatic recognition of gesture.* PhD thesis, School of Computer Science, Carnegie Mellon University, CMU-CS-91-202.

Sabah, G. (1989). *L'intelligence artificielle et le langage.* 2 volumes. Paris: Hermès.

Scapin, D.L. (1986). Guide ergonomique de conception des interfaces homme-machine. *Rapport Technique INRIA no. 77,* Octobre 1986

Searle, J.R. (1969). *Speech Acts.* Cambridge University Press.

Searle, J.R. (1983). *Intentionality.* Cambridge University Press.

Siroux, J., Gilloux, M., Guyomard, M., & Sorin, C. (1989). Le dialogue homme-machine en langue naturelle: un défi? *Annales des télécommunications, 44, n°1-2.*

Stefik, M., Bobrow, D., Foster, S., & Tatar, D. (1987). WYSIWIS: Early experiences with multi-user interfaces. *ACM transactions on office information system, Vol.5, n°2,* 147-167.

Taylor, M.M., Neel, F., & Bouwhuis, D.G. (1989). *The Structure of Multimodal Dialogue.* Elsevier Science Publishers B.V., North-Holland.

Turk, M., & Pentland, A. (1991). Eigenfaces for recognition, *Journal of Cognitive Neuroscience, 3,* 71-86.

Valot, C., & Amalberti, R. (1991). *Description et analyse de l'activité de l'opérateur.* Ecole IHM-M. Lyon: Ecole Centrale.

Vernant, D. (1992). Modèles projectifs et structure actionnelle du dialogue. In *Recherches sur la philosophie et le langage du dialogue.* Paris: Vrin.

Index